Nothing but Honour

Nothing but Honour

The Story of the Warsaw Uprising, 1944

J. K. ŻAWODNY

Avery Professor of International Relations
Claremont Graduate School
and
Pomona College

HOOVER INSTITUTION PRESS • 1978
STANFORD UNIVERSITY   STANFORD, CALIFORNIA

HOOVER INSTITUTION PRESS 1978
STANFORD CALIFORNIA

© *J. K. Zawodny 1978*

First published 1978 by
MACMILLAN LONDON LIMITED
4 Little Essex Street London WC2R 3LF
and Basingstoke
Associated companies in New York Dublin
Melbourne Johannesburg and Delhi

Hoover Institution Publication 183

The Hoover Institution on War, Revolution and Peace, founded at Stanford
University in 1919 by the late President Herbert Hoover, is an interdisciplinary
research center on domestic and international public affairs in the twentieth
century. The views expressed in its publications are entirely those of the authors
and do not necessarily reflect the views of the staff, officers, or Board of Overseers
of the Hoover Institution.

Library of Congress Catalog card No: 76-51880

ISBN: 0-8179-6831-8

TO MY SON ROMAN JANUSZ

All that is necessary for the triumph of evil
is that good men do nothing.

EDMUND BURKE

Contents

List of Illustrations

Acknowledgements for permission to reproduce illustrations are due to
the following: The Polish Underground Movement Study Trust, 2,
3(a), 3(b), 4, 5(b), 6(a), 6(b), 8; Eugeniusz Lokajski, 7. The picture of
the devastation of Warsaw, 1, is taken from *Dni Powstania (Days of the
Uprising)*, Pax, Warsaw, 1957.
   The map of Warsaw on pages 18–19 is reproduced from George
Bruce, *The Warsaw Uprising* (Pan, 1974).

Preface

THIS is the story of the desperate rising against German occupational forces in Warsaw, the capital of Poland, during the Second World War. The Uprising was initiated by the Polish Underground Army, Armia Krajowa (Ar-mee-a Cra-yova) or AK, and carried out with the assistance of civilians. For sixty-three days, from 1 August to 2 October 1944, Warsaw was ablaze as its citizens fought the enemy from house to house, from floor to floor, in the basements and in the sewers.

A comprehensive discussion of two related matters – the origin and development of the AK organization and the complex factors leading to the decision by the Poles to stage an uprising in Warsaw – is not within the scope of this study. The latter would involve the analysis of cultural and political catalysts as well as the interactions of personalities; that is another story and a complex research project in itself.

This book considers the *results* of that decision – the actual fighting in the city and its diplomatic repercussions – and the natural place to begin is 1 August 1944, the day the insurgents took to the streets. Only when it is necessary for an understanding of events do I refer to occurrences before this date.

Because I was born in Poland, and participated in the Uprising, there may be a propensity on the part of some readers to ascribe to me, as a person, all the views representing the Polish side of the story. This would not be a valid assumption. This book is not a special plea for Poles.

The research for this study took eleven years, necessitated travel in seven countries, and resulted in the accumulation of more than 200 pounds of military and diplomatic documents in five languages. I was helped by the release in 1972 and 1973 of the diplomatic papers of the British Government dealing with the Second World War and by the declassification of some of Roosevelt's Presidential Papers at the Franklin D. Roosevelt Library in Hyde Park, New York, in 1972.

Reliability of data was a problem. Many who were connected with the Uprising – Poles, Russians, British, Americans, and Germans – have had the same 'passion for truth, but different senses of evidence.' Whenever possible, I supplemented printed sources with observations and experiences obtained from interviews with seventy-six persons. These included eight Polish generals, regimental commanders, battalion commanders, company commanders, platoon commanders, privates, nurses, cooks and messengers; I also interviewed the Prime Minister of Poland at the time, Stanislaw Mikolajczyk; several members of the underground Polish Parliament and two Ministers of the Polish Government-in-Exile.

Foreign names are used throughout the book only when absolutely necessary for clarity of substance. The underground pseudonyms of insurgents have been translated into English whenever possible in order to convey their intrinsic nuances and the self-images of the insurgents (who selected the pseudonyms themselves).

Finally, the purpose of this book is not to accuse the Allies or the Poles, but to unravel the story, strand by strand, of one beleaguered city in one small nation in the final months of the Second World War. There are and always have been ordinary people going about their daily lives until the fateful moment when they are caught in a net of circumstances, usually not of their own making, and become part of history. In the Uprising of Warsaw in the sultry autumn days of 1944, more than two million people – Poles, Germans, and others – struggled for possession of the city. This is their story.

Without the co-operation of many organizations and the unselfish assistance of many men and women of good will, I could not have collected such highly diversified data in the eleven years of research.

George F. Kennan, Professor at the Institute for Advanced Study, Princeton, New Jersey, and Minister-Counsellor of the United States Embassy in Moscow, 1944–6, gave me the benefit of his knowledge, experience, and encouragement in an often frustrating and difficult search for data concerning the American position with respect to the Uprising. He was also kind enough to read part of the draft typescript and to suggest improvements in it and to give his permission to include an interview with him, and his letter to me, in this book. Colonel St Koszutski has thoughtfully provided some support.

The following organizations assisted financially and/or by providing facilities for my research and writing: American Council of Learned Societies, jointly with Social Science Research Council, New York; American Philosophical Society, Philadelphia; Claremont Graduate School, Claremont, California; Earhart Foundation, Ann Arbor; the Ford Foundation, New York; Foreign Policy Research Institute, Philadelphia; Harvard University Center for International Affairs, Cambridge; the Hoover Institution on War, Revolution and Peace, Stanford; the Institute for Advanced Study, Princeton; St Antony's College, Oxford; Pomona College, Claremont, California; University of Pennsylvania, Philadelphia.

Mrs Janina Pierre-Skrzynska, a member of my platoon during the Uprising, came to the United States from her home in Belgium to assist me in the collation of all the documents.

Mrs Wieslawa B. Szmajdowicz spent many evenings typing Polish correspondence and thousands of bibliographical cards. To her and her husband I owe special thanks.

My deep appreciation goes to Professors Harry V. Jaffa, Darcy G. O'Brien, Vernon Van Dyke and Piotr Wandycz for reading the draft manuscript, and also to Mr Richard A. Ware, Professor Loren Eiseley and Mrs Jadwiga Deren for their assistance and support.

Mr Jan Weiss of the Harvard University Library willingly devoted many days and nights to bibliographical research and translations.

A special expression of appreciation is due to the late General Karol Ziemski (pseudonym 'Wachnowski'), Deputy Commander of the Uprising of Warsaw and of Warsaw's AK Corps in 1944, and commander of the defence of Old Town. During our conversations about the Uprising, he was able to shed light on many relatively unknown aspects of the battle.

The following persons have co-operated in providing data, or were helpful: the late General Tadeusz Bor-Komorowski, Commander-in-Chief of the Armia Krajowa (Polish Home Army), 1943–4; the late Stanislaw Mikolajczyk, Prime Minister of the Polish Government-in-Exile at the time of the Uprising; Mr Andrzej Pomian, an envoy on special mission from the Headquarters of Armia Krajowa in Warsaw to the Polish authorities in London, April 1944.

Many people were kind enough to be concerned or help with research, collation of data, translations and typing. For their efforts, I express appreciation. Over 200 people assisted me by granting interviews or by exchanging correspondence.

However, the conclusions, opinions and other statements in this publication are my own, and are not necessarily those of any person or institution mentioned here.

The following institutions co-operated by making available their unique collections of documents dealing with the Uprising of Warsaw: the Archives of the Polish Underground Movement (1939–1945) Study Trust, London; the Chancery of the President of the Polish Republic, London; the Pilsudski Institute of America for Research in the Modern History of Poland Inc., New York; the Polish Institute and Sikorski Museum, London.

Neither the Government of the Polish Republic (in-exile) in London, nor the Government of the Polish People's Republic in Warsaw, nor their subordinate institutions were asked for financial or any other kind of assistance beyond access to sources. Neither did they offer encouragement or inducement in any form to undertake this study.

To my LaRae, a gentle flower of a woman, heart-felt gratitude for her working side by side with me. Both of us are grateful to Lorraine. Her editorial assistance was indispensable.

J. K. ZAWODNY

Introduction: Warsaw Erupts

July 31, 1944: Warsaw, the capital of Poland, under German occupation since 1939. At 6 p.m. General Tadeusz Bor-Komorowski, Commander of the Polish Underground Home Army (Armia Krajowa, AK), ordered an armed insurrection, shooting to begin 1 August at 5 p.m.

The German armies were in full retreat from their Eastern Front, pursued by the Russians. Warsaw lay in their path. One purpose of the insurrection was to prevent the retreating Germans from destroying the population and city of Warsaw. Another powerful incentive was the desire of the Poles to overcome the Germans in order to reassert Polish independence and the political authority of the legal Polish Government before the Soviet Army entered Warsaw. Soviet tanks were reported to the east of Warsaw, between six and seven miles away. General Bor expected that 'the Russians, under their own impetus . . . would be forced to take Warsaw'.[1]

Stanislaw Jankowski, Delegate and Vice-Prime Minister of the legal Polish government, subsequently enumerated these reasons in a broadcast over the insurgents' radio:

> There were several reasons for our uprising. We wanted to repel by force of arms the last blow that the Germans were preparing to deal at the moment of their departure to all that was still living Poland; we wanted to thwart them in their declared aim of revenge on insurgent Warsaw. We wanted to show the world that although we wanted to have an independent Poland, we were not prepared to accept this gift of freedom from anyone [if it meant accepting] conditions contrary to the interests, traditions and dignity of our nation. Finally, we wanted to free Poland from the nightmare of Gestapo punishment, murder and prisons.
>
> We wanted to be free and to owe this freedom to nobody but ourselves.[2]

The pressures on the Polish leaders in Warsaw were considerable. The sound of Soviet artillery was already heard in the city. A Soviet radio station was calling on Poles to start the uprising immediately. German authorities had ordered 100,000 Polish men in Warsaw to report for compulsory labour–to build fortifications against Soviet forces. The Armia Krajowa's 40,000 insurgents were waiting, ready to strike the Germans in Warsaw's streets. These volunteers had been trained underground, risking their lives, during the five years of

15

German occupation.

The first shots of the Uprising of Warsaw were fired on 1 August 1944 at 1.50 p.m., in Zoliborz Sector. The insurgents poured into the streets. The longest and bloodiest urban insurgency of the Second World War had begun.

The battleground encompassed 140 square kilometres (or 54 square miles). Its shape roughly resembled a watermelon cut in half lengthwise. Through this area the Vistula river ran lengthwise from south to north, a grey ribbon slightly off-centre. To the east of the Vistula was the smaller arc of the suburb Praga. The Soviet Army was approaching from this side. West of the Vistula lay Warsaw proper. Eight major roads and seven railway lines converged on the city. Five bridges – two for railway, three for auto and pedestrian traffic – spanned the river. The Vistula ranged in width from 400 to 600 metres, but it was so shallow throughout the summer of 1944 that in some places it was possible to wade across on sandbars.[3]

German quarters, magazines, and office buildings were dispersed throughout the city. Pillboxes and barbed wire fortified their positions. The two lower floors of buildings they occupied were usually packed with sandbags for additional protection.

Within Warsaw was a population of between one million and one and a half million. (The precise number cannot be established because of the constant flux of inhabitants during the German occupation.)

Who were the insurgents? They were the people of Warsaw. They came from all social strata: the richest and poorest, university professors, students, former governmental officials, artists, priests, unskilled labourers, and some known criminals. The youngest soldier I encountered was eight years old; the oldest was a gentleman nearly ninety years old who stood guard duty regularly. All political viewpoints were represented – right-wing, liberal and Communist.

The Polish strategy was relatively simple. The primary objective of the commander, General Monter, according to his Chief of Staff, Colonel Weber, was 'literally to sit down across the main arteries of Warsaw. The Germans would then be disorganized and disarmed and we would take the city.'[4] It was expected by the AK command that 'the Uprising would last no longer than two or three days, at maximum a week, but never two months.'[5] The AK had assumed that the surprise and fury of the initial attacks would give the necessary impetus to overrun German positions and liberate Warsaw.

In Combat Report Number One, issued on 2 August, General Monter honestly faced the results of the first day of fighting: 'The most important objectives [were] . . . not seized. . . . I have no hope to seize the objectives that by this time have not been won.'[6] He repeats this gloomy observation in Combat Report Number Two: 'In [none of] the streets [were] the important objectives seized.'[7] Already, on the second day of combat, General Monter shared his misgivings with others: 'He was anxious because of the heavy and protracted fighting.'[8] General Bor, Commander-in-Chief of Armia Krajowa, was also aware that the primary objectives of the Uprising had not been attained. As early as 5 a.m. on the third day, he summarized the insurgents' plight to a Polish official as follows: 'Our attack has not been successful, we do not have ammunition for its continuation. Now we have to assume a defensive position. The behaviour of the Soviet Army may clarify our situation.'[9]

The truth was that the Poles had never been equipped to take German positions. One objective, 'Pawiak' (the infamous German prison in which thousands of Poles were murdered), was fortified by several concrete-and-steel pillboxes. It was armed with heavy machine guns that were protected by partially armoured visors, and twelve machine guns located on tall towers, which had been constructed by Germans to give a commanding view over the surrounding area, previously cleared of any natural protection or camouflage. It was defended by one battalion of German police and SS. The insurgent unit assigned to take this position had one small mortar – not even a machine gun.[10] Strategic aims had to yield to deficiencies in tactics and equipment.

For the first two days waves of insurgents attacked isolated German positions, but were not sufficiently well armed to take them. After that AK action was concentrated in a number of sectors, where the Poles tried to consolidate their defences against what had become a systematic German counter-attack. Although in some places a German position was still surrounded by insurgents, tactically the roles had been reversed. By the fourth day German forces controlled and firmly held 194 blocks.[11]

By the fifth day of the Uprising, however, the Germans had ceased improvising and launched into systematic suppression.[12] Though the initiative was taken from the Poles on the second day, German counteraction was unco-ordinated until 5 August. Thereafter they proceeded methodically, block by block, destroying the buildings and annihilating insurgents and civilians alike.

The Poles now found themselves trapped in isolated sectors.[13] Both sides intensified their efforts to secure their lines of communication. The German forces sought to maintain several thoroughfares across the Vistula for communication with their units still on the eastern bank, while in Combat Report Number Thirteen, General Monter stated: 'I am aiming to fight for and to widen corridors through the enemy's territory . . . to secure communication.'[14] At the same time he seemed to believe that the insurgents should initiate other action only for protection and defence of the population.[15]

The Poles fought for sixty-three days.

To understand the story it is necessary first to describe those who for five years were preparing the city for the Uprising – the leaders of the Polish Home Army (AK) – and to review their resources.

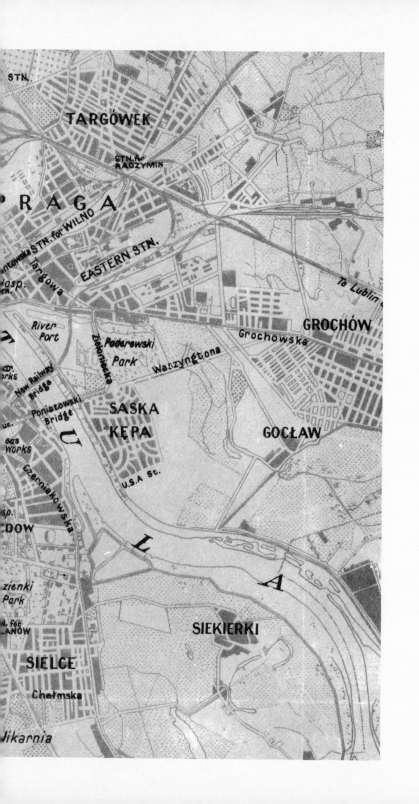

STN.

TARGÓWEK

STN. for
RADZYMIN

RAGA

STN. for WILNO

Targowa

Hosp.

EASTERN STN.

To Lublin

GROCHÓW

Grochowska

River
Port

Paderewski
Park

Zieleniecka

Warszyngtona

New Railway
Bridge

Poniatowski
Bridge

SASKA
KĘPA

GOCŁAW

Gas
Works

Czerniakowska

U.S.A St.

DOW

L

A

zienki
Park

for
LANÓW

SIEKIERKI

SIELCE

Chałmska

likarnia

CHAPTER ONE

AK: Leadership and Resources

AK COMMANDERS were concentrated in two headquarters. In the first was the Armia Krajowa's Commander-in-Chief, General Tadeusz Komorowski, whose pseudonym was Bor, and his Chief of Staff, General Tadeusz Pelczynski, whose pseudonym was Grzegorz. In the second was the Commander of the District of Warsaw, General Antoni Chrusciel (pseudonym Monter), who was subordinate to General Bor. The city itself, the District Warsaw, was Monter's responsibility. General Monter's Deputy Commander was Colonel Wachnowski, who commanded Group North, co-ordinating the Zoliborz, Old Town and Kampinos Forest Sectors from Old Town, where he was cut off. Their Chief of Staff was Lieutenant Colonel Stanislaw Weber (pseudonyms Surgeon and Popiel). The locations of both headquarters were shifted more than once during the Uprising.[1]

Although General Bor was present in Warsaw, and it had been he who, as AK Commander-in-Chief for all Poland, had issued the order that the Uprising was to begin, *he did not command the Uprising*. The commanding officer was General Monter. General Monter consulted General Bor and his staff on major decisions, but he alone was responsible for initiating and implementing orders during the Uprising. He was in charge of all the insurgents' administrative affairs, including logistics and personnel: efforts to establish liaison with the approaching Red Army; organization of military intelligence; co-ordination of co-operation among individual combat zones; organization of the delivery and distribution of war materials arriving by air; inspection of combat zones and giving of orders on the spot; final approval or rejection of sentences passed by field courts; co-operation with civilian authorities over civilian living conditions; and contacts with distinguished civic leaders and attention to problems submitted by them.[2]

According to those who knew him personally, General Monter was not an easy man to associate with or to serve under. He tended to be suspicious of his subordinates, jealous in guarding his prerogatives, and impetuous in his judgments. On the other hand, no one could deny his personal courage, self-sacrifice, and patriotism. His tenacity and hardness were manifested in unexpected ways. Once, when he was informed that a particular combat zone had fallen to the Germans, he responded, 'I do not accept this information.'[3] His order to the commanders of the Mokotow Sector, beleaguered and bleeding to death, on the fifty-sixth day of the Uprising was: 'You are forbidden to withdraw.'[4]

General Bor's headquarters,[5] too, carried an awesome responsibility. Bor communicated by radio with the Polish Government-in-Exile in London, with the command of the Soviet Army across the Vistula, and with the AK territorial units outside Warsaw. It was suggested to General Bor that he move his headquarters outside Warsaw to facilitate his command of the AK for all of Poland and the better to secure assistance to the city. Influenced by his Chief of Staff, Bor rejected the idea and remained with the insurgents in besieged Warsaw,[6] where he received reports from General Monter twice a day and was consulted on major decisions about the management of the Uprising. He was also responsible for maintaining contact with the Government Delegate in Poland, Stanislaw Jankowski, to whom he was subordinate. Finally, Bor was the ultimate recipient of all the frustration and despair of the suffering population.

As the Uprising went on, there were ominous signs of restlessness among civilian authorities and within the numerous political parties. Warsaw citizens, although still supporting and co-operating with the insurgents, were becoming resentful and downhearted over the daily loss of life and the destruction. There was, for example, an independent attempt on the part of the Peasants' Party to get in touch with the Polish Communist Party and the Polish Committee of National Liberation, set up by the Soviet Union in Lublin.[7] Of course, General Bor was aware of the shift in morale. As already mentioned, his activities were also directed outside Warsaw. Analysis of messages sent out of Warsaw reveals that the most numerous messages and those radioed with the greatest emotional intensity were those directed by Bor to his superiors in London. They were written, edited, coded, and dispatched despite daily bombardment and the psychological pressures of combat raging sometimes only a few hundred yards from the central command post.

The wires sent to London pleaded for ammunition, pointing out Soviet passivity: 'From the Soviet side – silence.'[8] Bor informed London that the AK units still carrying out Operation Tempest (fighting German troops in eastern Poland) were being arrested by the Soviet Army. The messages were in terse military style, but the language became progressively more demanding. On the fourth day of the Uprising, General Bor wired to his government: 'I categorically demand assistance, ammunition, and anti-tank weapons immediately, and also during the forthcoming days. This battle is going to continue for at least several days, and we must have supplies during this time. We have put everything at stake to hold the capital – you should make an effort.[9] Two days later his tone was even more forceful. 'We do not ask for material assistance; we demand that it be sent to us immediately.'[10]

General Monter issued combat reports daily, and sometimes more frequently – 91 during the 63 days. These reports, cited as 'Monter's Reports', provide reliable insights into his difficulties and feelings. They were distributed to a carefully selected audience, including General Bor, the commanders of large insurgent units or sectors in which there was fighting, and the commanding officers of the insurgents' special services. But General Monter and the high-ranking officers in both headquarters communicated on two levels: first, among themselves (an analysis of these reports reveals an honest evaluation of the struggle) and, second, with the insurgents and civilians, to whom they reported with undue optimism.

In headquarters the living conditions of the leaders and their staffs did not differ from those of the insurgents. They were subject to the same deprivations, the same meagre rations. There was none of the comfort of being 'in the rear', and the traditional Polish style of officers' behaviour was such that even staff officers had close contacts with soldiers and with combat. The Chief of Staff, General Pelczynski, once personally led an attack in which he was wounded. General Monter inspected the front lines daily, thereby giving rise to criticism for leaving his command post so often. Whether or not it was proper, their presence among the soldiers created a sense of cohesion and developed respect for and appreciation of their leaders among the soldiers.

These visits created some amusing situations. In one instance General Monter approached a house held by Poles. Like the majority of Polish soldiers in the battle, he was dressed in civilian clothing, his only mark of distinction being the AK armband and a little field cap. Trying to enter, he was stopped by a young boy guarding the building. The boy was a stutterer and it took him some time to ask the General who he was and what he wanted. The General answered, 'I am Monter.' (The Polish word *monter* means 'repairman'.) Again with great difficulty, the guard explained to the General, 'We don't need you now, because our light is working all right.'[11]

General Bor also visited insurgents' positions. The soldiers' response was again uniformly enthusiastic and respectful. In one instance, in order to show their admiration for General Bor, the insurgents asked permission to entertain him by singing. Bor, who was an extremely gentle, shy, and cultured man, agreed to listen. The song chosen for the General was bawdy in the extreme. It was delivered with a background noise of machine-gun and artillery fire; and what was lacking in musical quality was compensated for by the enthusiasm of the singers. After some indications of uneasiness and embarrassment, the General thanked the soldiers and left.[12]

Other nationalities and ethnic groups besides Poles fought against the German forces in the Uprising. Some came to the insurgents from the German side. Among them were several Italians who, according to reports, always went to their positions accompanied by their Polish girls, but 'they were very good soldiers'.[13] There were also several Hungarians,[14] one Frenchman, and a platoon of Slovaks commanded by Lieutenant Stanko.[15] One unit, commanded by a former captain in the Soviet Army, was composed entirely of inhabitants of the Caucasian mountains. They were post-Revolution exiles from a colony in Warsaw, Red Army deserters, and men of the Caucasus who escaped from German prisoner-of-war camps.[16]

At least a dozen former soldiers of the Red Army who had escaped from German camps were admitted to the service of the AK and fought side by side with the insurgents.

Another group deserves particular attention because not much has been said about their participation in the Uprising. They were Jews. Some were Polish citizens, some had been arrested by Germans in foreign countries, and kept in a prison in Warsaw, and used as workers of various kinds. They had been liberated by insurgents.

On the third day of the Uprising, their leader, Isaac Cukierman (Antek), issued a proclamation on behalf of the Jewish Fighters' Organization: 'We summon all surviving fighters of the ZOB [Jewish Fighters' Organization] and all able-bodied Jewish young people to continue their resistance and fight; nobody should be allowed to stand aside. Join the ranks of insurgents! Through battle to victory, to a free, independent, strong, and just Poland!'[17]

The Jews did join. According to one Jewish source they numbered approximately 1,000.[18] The precise number cannot be ascertained, because many used false names and documents in order to survive persecution during the German occupation. Most were known only by pseudonyms, as were the rest of the insurgents. Because of the mutual distrust between them and the Poles, it is even more to their credit that they took up weapons and risked their lives for the common cause.

One AK battalion liberated 324 men and 24 women from a German camp for Jews in the Old Town Sector. Eighty-nine were Polish citizens; the rest were victims of German persecution in Romania, Holland and Hungary.[19]

About 150 of them joined a unit of Armia Ludowa (the Communist underground army), where they built barricades and, after securing enough weapons took combat positions. On 23 August, German forces violently attacked and destroyed this unit.[20] In another sector, AK insurgents liberated 10 Jews. Most of these joined the insurgents. In Colonel Radoslaws' unit alone 50 Jews were attached to the quartermaster.[21] At least 20 members of the Jewish Fighters' Organization formed a platoon (commanded by Isaac Cukierman) in the Third Battalion of Armia Ludowa.[22] This does not mean that members of the Jewish Fighters' Organization fought only in Communist units. They joined AK and AL combat platoons throughout Warsaw.

In Mokotow Sector eighteen soldiers identified themselves as Jews.

Two who belonged to a unit of Armia Ludowa at the end of the Uprising came to the AK unit commander and asked him to give them AK identity cards. They believed that these cards would ensure more safety than similar identification given by the Communists. Major Szternal gave an order to give them AK identity cards for their protection.[23]

There was also a platoon of forty Jews commanded by Samuel Kenigswein which fought in Wigry Battalion of the AK.[24]

Whether they fought in the AK or in Communist units, some Jews experienced anti-Semitism, and some the warm camaraderie and unity of purpose that only people about to die together for a cause can share.

Some Jewish heroes of the Uprising were given official recognition. General Bor Personally decorated two lieutenants of Jewish origin who fought in Armia Ludowa. The Order of Virtuti Militari was bestowed upon a Jew (whose name could not be established) for his successful action against a German tank.[25] Many Polish Crosses of Valour were given to Jews, both men and women. One woman, Szoszona (Emilka) Kosower, a messenger of the Jewish National Committee, received this distinction and the rank of second lieutenant in the AK for her assistance in leading insurgents' units through the sewers.[26] It was a member of the Jewish Fighters' Organization who led the Commander-in-Chief General Bor and his staff through the sewers from one part of the city to another.[27]

On 25 October 1944, nearly three weeks after the surrender of Warsaw, the Central Committee of the Jewish Organization Bund sent a message from Poland by underground radio to Polish authorities in London with these proud words: 'We took part in the Uprising.'[28] Even after the surrender, some Jews left Warsaw with the civilians and rejoined the underground guerrilla forces to continue fighting the Germans. A small group near Suchedniow contacted a guerrilla unit of the Polish Socialist Party led by Michael Borwicz, also a Jew.[29]

Rank promotions and military distinctions were distributed according to Polish Army regulations and provided some incentive for insurgents. The former were given in a democratic fashion, by European standards, on the basis of leadership and aptitudes. A shoemaker who displayed leadership qualities was promoted from corporal to second lieutenant during combat, despite his lack of education and military training suited to an officer.[30]

Both AK and the Polish Forces-in-Exile had a very small number of distinctions for bravery in comparison with other Allied powers. There were two: Virtuti Militari, the highest, given for the most heroic display of courage in the face of the enemy; and the Cross of Valour. Both were rarely awarded in the AK. They were so coveted and brought such prestige that there were a few cases of wearing them unlawfully.[31]

How well were the insurgents equipped?

During the clandestine meetings of the Council of National Unity in

Warsaw five months before the Uprising, one of the members, Mr Baginski, asked General Bor a crucial question: 'What is the state of AK arms equipment?'

General Bor replied, 'Ten per cent of the membership.'

Baginski said, 'Under those conditions a general uprising is an impossibility.'[32]

Other Polish sources from which one would expect reliable data about the arms preparedness of the insurgents are either clearly exaggerated or too vague to be reliable. For example, General Monter maintained that 'seventy-nine per cent of the insurgents [there were, in total, about 40,000] were initially equipped with weapons'.[33] This was an overstatement.

The most reliable source is a Polish general, a member of AK Headquarters, whose dispassionate and well-supported evaluation appeared in Poland in 1964. He stated that on 1 August 1944, the insurgents' equipment consisted of these weapons:

> 1,000 carbines
> 300 pistols
> 60 light machine guns
> 7 heavy machine guns
> 35 special carbines and bazookas
> 1,700 revolvers
> 25,000 hand-grenades

The number of insurgents was estimated to be between, 36,500 and 40,000.[34] Therefore it is reasonable to assume that at the outbreak of the Uprising only about 1,500 (or at best 2,500), or four to six per cent of the insurgents, were armed. In view of these statistics, the General's judgment was that the state of armament for the insurgents was 'desperate'.[35]

With regard to ammunition the situation was no better:

> 35 bullets to a pistol
> 300 bullets for a machine pistol
> 50 shells for anti-armour cannon (but not even one cannon)
> 190 pieces of ammunition per carbine
> 500 rounds of ammunition for a light machine gun
> 2,300 rounds for the heavy machine guns[36]

As a professional soldier who participated in the Uprising and spent several years afterwards studying it, he said that the weapons and ammunition at the moment of the alarm were sufficient for about two days of fighting, so that ninety per cent of the mobilized soldiers had to be treated as reserves.[37]

How did the commanding officers responsible for large units of insurgents feel about the allotment of weapons? What were they told by AK Headquarters prior to the outbreak of insurgency? A colonel reports: 'I was told that weapons would be available. As a soldier I didn't question or interpret this. I was preparing my soldiers to use these [expected] weapons.'[38] Another officer responsible for the valiant defence of the Zoliborz Sector reports that among about 1,500 insurgents under his command he had 2 heavy machine guns, about 100 rifles, 2 sacks of hand-grenades, 30 machine pistols and 100 revolvers. When he reported to General Monter that his subordinates were complaining about arms deficiencies, Monter responded, 'You have to win arms from Germans, even if it means fighting with sticks and clubs. Those dissatisfied will be court-martialled.'[39] This attitude was shared by Jankowski, the Delegate of the Government-in-Exile. Several days before the Uprising, when asked about weapons by Mr Jerzy Braun, a member of the Council of National Unity, Jankowski responded, 'They [the insurgents] will get them from Germans.'[40]

The commanding officer of the AK Engineers in Warsaw had about 120 pounds of explosives at his disposal. That amount was pitifully insufficient when one considers that the hundreds of German positions in Warsaw were fortified with pillboxes, specially strengthened walls, and concrete reinforced machine-gun pits.

Strength of motivation and commitment were expected to compensate for deficiencies in equipment, but it is on the level of individuals within platoons and sections that one sees the full meaning of the tragic lack of weapons. According to one AK soldier, 'On the day of the Uprising there were sixty of us. . . . We had seven revolvers, [and] to one of them, only five pieces of ammunition would fit. Another one was of such a small calibre that [it was] not for fighting. The remaining five revolvers were all right, and we had about 200 rounds of ammunition for them.'[41] Another insurgent tells his story: 'For my squad, which was then [on the first day of the Uprising] eleven people, I received one light machine pistol with three magazines, two revolvers with a handful of ammunition, and one rusted rifle. . . . It was obvious that this rifle could shoot only once. Besides that, each of us received two handmade hand-grenades.'[42] Numbers of insurgents who were actually sent into direct combat against the enemy reported weaponry such as the following:

'For twelve people we had four rifles.'[43]

'Among sixty people we had one rifle and nine pistols.'[44]

'Among ninety soldiers we had seven carbines and twenty pistols.'[45]

When attacking German fortified positions, some entire units were equipped with as little as one carbine, two revolvers, and several hand-grenades.[46] But, for the rank and file of the insurgents, once the Uprising had begun and the meagre stock of resources had been revealed there was no recourse but to continue fighting. During the first weeks of the Uprising the Germans did not take prisoners.

In the post-war years, while interviewing former participants of the Uprising, I asked about their most tragic and their most exhilarating experiences during the Uprising. One response was: 'Yes, this was the most tragic moment for me. On 21 August a sergeant of AK and a German fought so closely that they were fighting hand-to-hand. The stronger German overturned the Pole, and sat on him, choking him to death. (This was during our attack on the German Police Headquarters.) There were four other Germans involved, but they surrendered; so we gathered around these two fighting men. Everybody was shouting, "Use a bayonet on the German," but we didn't have bayonets. Finally, I killed the German with the butt of my machine gun. It took about two or three minutes for the sergeant to get enough air into his lungs. He was bent under the wall gasping for air. Then he straightened up with relief, and at that very moment a German sniper shot him in the head.'[47]

From attics, basements and elsewhere an unusual variety of antique armaments appeared. Once I noticed a young insurgent carrying a blunderbuss, probably from some museum. Bottles with petrol and improvised flame-throwers, as well as home-made catapults for casting petrol bottles against German tanks, were used. During the second week of fighting, one platoon was ordered to protect a house where 'a very important person [would] arrive for a conference'. The only man in the platoon available for dispatch at this moment was a slightly wounded sixteen-year-old insurgent. He stood guard in front of the building armed with a *scythe*. It was the only weapon he had, and it was the only weapon with which he served till he was killed.[48]

The weapons most commonly made by insurgents themselves were hand-grenades. They were produced in shops in areas held by insurgents. The first to be made weighed 800 grams and were too heavy to throw; the next batch weighed only 500 grams each. One shop alone produced 20,000 hand-grenades;[49] another produced 400 grenades of several varieties. Explosives were salvaged from unexploded German artillery shells and bombs. The identities of the courageous men who disarmed these live shells and bombs could not be established.[50]

The ingenuity of the insurgents was boundless. Old socks stuffed with a mixture of metal (nuts, bolts, scraps of iron) and explosives were plugged with corks and used as hand-grenades.[51] Even the function of fire-brigade equipment paradoxically was reversed. Motor-pumps were adapted to spout gasoline or other flammable materials and, in at least one instance, a building defended by Germans was sprayed and partially burned by this means.[52] In Old Town, when ammunition ran out, bricks were used against the Germans who were overrunning insurgent positions.[53]

After a few days of fighting, some priorities in the assignment of weapons emerged. Commanders of larger units arranged that the most dangerously exposed platoons would get, when possible, more ammunition and better weapons.

The rank and file developed their own habits. First, there was a propensity to give weapons to the younger insurgents. In one instance, an officer with the rank of general, volunteering to fight as a member of an insurgent squad, begged for a rifle. It was refused on the basis of his age.[54] Usual standards of conduct were modified. Unarmed insurgents would sometimes desert a unit that was poorly equipped in the hope of acquiring even one hand-grenade by joining another. They often 'deserted' toward the sound of firing with the hope of obtaining a weapon from a dead enemy or friend.[55]

Some units tried rotation. Those soldiers who were actually defending barricades or a building would collect weapons and ammunition from the rest of the unit: 'While on duty we had about fifteen ammunition pieces for one rifle, about twenty for a machine pistol, and always several hand-grenades.'[56]

This procedure led to resentments and quarrels, since under these circumstances it was easier to part with a girl than with a rifle. Wounded insurgents being taken to field hospitals would struggle to keep their weapons and ammunition with them. The most emotionally distressing alternative was waiting for another member of the unit to be wounded or killed in order to get his weapon. In some cases, there were mutual agreements 'in the event of death' for such courtesies as a piece of bread, clean underwear, or the promise to contact one another's families.

Orders from Headquarters were to save ammunition. Posters on walls in the areas occupied by insurgents called for 'One bullet, one German!'[57]

Ammunition was treated like precious jewellery. If a single piece of ammunition was damaged, it was restored with a hammer or a file.[58]

On the eighth day of the Uprising the AK command sent the following telegram to the Polish General Staff in London: 'Possibility of offensive action practically out of question because we are using remnants of ammunition.'[59]

A force of approximately 400 men of Armia Ludowa, a military arm of the Polish Communists at least technically fighting under AK command, was equally ill-equipped. A sympathetic source using official Communist documents of May 1944 reports that these units in Warsaw had at their disposal 1 heavy machine gun, 3 machine pistols, 6 rifles, 40 revolvers, 51 hand-grenades, and 13 bottles of petrol. This modest supply was augmented before the Uprising by several pistols and some explosives.[60]

According to Colonel Weber, Chief of Staff to General Monter, 'On 25 or 26 July in the presence of Generals Bor, Okulicki, Pelczynski, and Colonel Iranek, I reported the state of weapons and ammunition. We had [at that time] ammunition for only three days of fighting. It was a miracle that we lasted two months.[61]

It is difficult to reconcile the initiation of the Uprising by the leaders of the AK in Warsaw with their awareness of the grave state of their own forces' fighting power. However, it is possible that AK Headquarters counted on several factors: the quick entry of Soviet forces into Warsaw, which would relieve the insurgents; the defeat of the Germans in Warsaw within two or three days; capturing armament and ammunition from the Germans; at least some support from Allied planes; and, above all, a more effective distribution of the weapons and ammunition gathered in the Underground magazines than actually took place.

Documents concerning the AK's preparations for armed action reveal that they were organizationally well-designed. For example, responsibility for underground production of weapons in 1943–4 was divided among four interrelated departments. Three departments were under military supervision and one under civilian (the Delegate of the Polish Government-in-Exile). These were further subdivided into fifty-five highly specialized offices marshalling resources, producing arms, co-ordinating production, delivering the weapons, and storing them in magazines.[62]

In 1944, in only one of these departments (the Department of War Industry of AK Headquarters), 150 engineers, 300 draughtsmen and technicians, and about 3,000 labourers were employed.[63] This was 'a society within a society' – a clandestine industry working in an occupied country to arm its own soldiers. In fact, one-third of all AK armament in occupied Poland came from its own clandestine factories.[64]

When the Uprising began on 1 August many small ammunition dumps were found to be in German-held areas where they could not be reached. Only forty per cent of the weapons' stores were accessible.[65] Prior to the Uprising there were four main AK store-houses of weapons in Warsaw, of which two were in the Praga Sector, across the Vistula. The Uprising in this sector collapsed in a few days, leaving two main sources of weapons inaccessible to insurgents fighting the major battle on the western side of the river.

Some ammunition dumps were so well hidden that if those directly responsible for them died, or if communication with AK Headquarters was broken, their existence was simply forgotten. This is best illustrated by the fact that in 1947, long after the Uprising, one AK weapons' store with 678 machine pistols and 60,000 rounds of ammunition was found under one of the ruins on Leszno Street. In another instance, paradoxically enough, General Bor and his whole staff were literally sitting over one of the largest underground accumulations of weapons in Warsaw, of which they had no knowledge, and which was not discovered until 1957. The quantity of weapons was so large that it took two weeks to remove it in trucks.

Other stores of weapons were lost in an event that was a tragedy for the AK. A few months before the Uprising, in the spring of 1944, German officials uncovered two large secret stores of weapons in basements. One contained 70,000 hand-grenades (of the total 320,000 that were actually stored in Warsaw at the time); the other included 450 flame-throwers adapted for infantry use (about half of the flame-throwers that had been prepared for the insurgents). Expecting that the staff would defend themselves with tenacity the Germans flooded the basements, and all the personnel were drowned.[66]

An event related to this discovery may give insight into some AK members' sense of responsibility. According to General Bor, the Germans were shocked to discover such a large amount of hand-grenades. All production and transport had carried on in spite of nearly five years of German surveillance. This alerted the Germans to the possibility that there might be many more AK ammunition dumps and that there probably were underground factories still producing weapons; so the Germans intensified their efforts to destroy the factories' personnel and technicians.

Of the many men arrested, one, named Jurek, was a technician in heavy-machine-gun production. Instead of 'normal processing' – torture – the Gestapo made him a proposition. They did not want to know the names and addresses of his collaborators. Instead, they wanted the details of production, transport and camouflage for such a large-scale operation. If he collaborated, he would be sent to Switzerland, given a private villa, and protected from any sort of revenge on the part of the Polish Underground. He was promised a Swiss bank account and a secure future. Jurek was one of the AK's best technicians. He not only refused to give information, but also managed to send a message to AK Headquarters about the German propositions and his refusal. He knew the alternative. The Gestapo shot him.[67]

But, however well planned the efforts of the AK command to secure weapons for the Uprising had been, the insurgents were insufficiently equipped. Several months after the Uprising General Okulicki told his liaison-secretary that he had been 'cheated'. He was referring to the state of equipment and weapons in the Uprising.[68] Perhaps his statement was related to the fact that AK Headquarters, some months before the Uprising, had been sending weapons and ammunition *out of the city*. On 7 July 1944 General Bor allocated 900 machine pistols with ammunition to the eastern part of Poland.[69]

All revolutions, underground movements, and *coups d'état*, particularly those that are systematically prepared in advance, need money. It has been impossible to establish with precision how much money the Headquarters of the AK and the District of Warsaw had at their disposal when the Uprising began. It is evident, however, that millions of Polish zloty had been spent preparing food, equipment, and supplies for the Uprising. The Chief Quartermaster of the Uprising, Colonel Dolega, records that on the first day of the Uprising, at 2.00 p.m., he went to collect five million Polish zlotys allocated 'for the first expenditures of the Quartermaster'.[70] It cannot be established how this money was spent. Indeed, the Armia Krajowa's fiscal policy and its mechanism are beyond the scope of this study. However, its sources of money should be noted.

Four basic types of finance were available to the Fiscal Department of the AK. First, money that belonged to the Polish state before 1939 and that was returned by private persons and organizations to the local underground authorities; second, private donations from citizens, including contributions from individual soldiers (during our four years of service, all members of my unit paid small, voluntary, monthly dues that were collected by our immediate superiors); third, money that was taken from the Germans in several daring actions; and fourth, and most important, money from the Polish Government-in-Exile in London.[71]

Money was sent from England in a variety of currencies. Initially, delivery was arranged through citizens of neutral countries and foreign banks, but after 1942 it was confined to airdrops, via either supply containers or emissaries.

According to official documents the planned budget for the AK for 1944 was approximately $12,480,000. The Polish Government-in-Exile also planned that civilian authorities in Poland should receive $3,326,000 for the same period.[72] Money actually delivered for both of these branches was as follows: $11,000,000 in paper money, $200,000 in gold, 45,000,000 Polish zlotys printed by Germans in occupied Poland, and 11,500,000 in German marks.[73]

An American reader might be surprised that such large sums of American currency were involved. Prime Minister Mikolajczyk stated that he received $10 million from President Roosevelt for the activities of the Polish Underground. His predecessor, General Sikorski, received (also from President Roosevelt's special fund) $90 million for the same purpose.[74]

In total, about ten per cent of the money sent by the Government-in-Exile never reached Poles in occupied Poland.[75] Sometimes an emissary was lost in a parachute drop during the night, or the aircraft delivering money was shot down. Dishonesty also accounted from some losses. Money was inadvertently burned during the Uprising, too, although such sums are not included in this calculation.

Mystery surrounds the disappearance of a large sum of money at one of the Polish bases in Italy. The base commander, Colonel Hancza, was found dead in suspicious circumstances, and $7 million was missing.[76]

The Chief Quartermaster reported that in the year preceding the Uprising of Warsaw there existed 'a great disorder in fiscal management of the District [of Warsaw] and a lack of balance between deposits and expenditures'.[77] This mismanagement was subsequently remedied.

Once during the Uprising one insurgent unit received soldier's pay. No other instance of insurgents receiving payment during the Uprising has been discovered. However, when the units were marching out of

Warsaw into German captivity after surrender, each soldier, regardless of rank, received about five dollars in American money.

Diversity of dress among the insurgents was the obvious indication that they were a volunteer army of voluntary soldiers. Some wore uniforms saved, at the risk of their owners' lives, from the Polish Army of 1939. If, before the Uprising, German police found such a uniform, they would invariably either shoot the owner or send him to a concentration camp. The uniforms worn by the British were rare and eagerly sought. Some Poles in England and/or Italy had decided to wrap weapons in them; they were packed into supply containers and dropped from planes.

Intelligence headquarters of the commander of the AK District of Warsaw assembled a list of German warehouses in Warsaw that stocked uniforms. About 3,000 German uniforms, with some alterations, as well as German underwear, were used by the insurgents.[78]

Units fighting in the Old Town seized German stores and dressed themselves in the camouflage shirts usually worn by SS troops. Of course, all German insignia were torn off, but these distinctive shirts were worn through the Uprising by men and women from Old Town units, giving this group an identification of its own.

The custom of wearing German uniforms created great confusion during the fighting. In the furious tempo of street combat, instantaneous distinction between the enemy and fellow-insurgents was literally a matter of life or death. There were instances of mistaken identity.

A platoon of insurgents dressed in German camouflage shirts was charging over the ruins directly toward a German position. The second lieutenant who led the platoon ran past an insurgent with his machine pistol pointed in the direction from which the lieutenant had come. The implication struck him one or two seconds later. He whirled – to find the 'insurgent' already facing him. They shot at each other from a distance of 12–15 feet. The second lieutenant survived. He had momentarily assumed that the German was one of his men who was advancing ahead of him; the German had evidently mistaken the Pole for a withdrawing German. There were several instances when men shot their fellow-soldiers. One man shot his brother, mistaking him for a German.

The insurgents were a motley crowd with one visible bond – their red and white armbands. The band, white over red, was usually stamped with either the name or number of the unit, and usually with the letters 'AK'. The armband indicated that after five years of occupation the wearers were free men.

A surprisingly effective network of communication, which strove to maintain contact between units within Warsaw and to establish contact with the outside world, was developed during the Uprising. There were ten separate sources of radio activity affecting insurgents, each with one or more stations at its disposal.

1. Ten underground radio-telegraph stations belonging to the AK were located just outside Warsaw.[79] Since these were cut off from the city after fighting erupted, the responsibility for communication fell on thirteen radio-telegraph stations, plus one voice-broadcasting station called Lightning, that were in the city.[80]

2. Four radio-telegraph stations in Warsaw were operated by civilian authorities of the Polish Government. One was Polish Radio; one linked the Delegate in Warsaw of the Polish Government-in-Exile with London; another was organized and directed by the Department of Civil Resistance; the fourth was operated by the Peasants' Party, a political organization.[81]

3. There was also active in Warsaw a radio-telegraph station operated by the Communist Polish People's Army.

4. Transmitting in the Polish language, another 'Lightning' gave the impression that it was operating from Warsaw. It was actually a German army station that attempted to confuse Poles by purporting to be the AK station of that name, which was known for the outstanding regularity of its performance.

5. A Soviet radio under the control of the official Soviet Information Agency, TASS, was in England, of all places.[82] This station affected the insurgents in a curious way, to be described later.

6. The voice-broadcasting radio station, Dawn, was operated by the Polish Government-in-Exile. By a technical trick it gave the impression of being in Warsaw, although it was actually transmitting from England.[83] (An additional station that was especially geared to the interests of women was organized by the same sources as Dawn, but it has not been possible to establish any details of its activities.)

7. A Soviet voice-broadcasting station introduced its programmes under the name Tadeusz Kosciuszko (a Polish national hero). Poles believed it to be just outside Warsaw with the Soviet forces, but its microphones were actually in the Soviet Union (Tashkent).[84]

8. Radio-telegraph station Seagull, belonging to the Polish Armed Forces-in-Exile, was located in Italy.

9. For several days in September a field combat radio, Hawk, served soldiers of General Berling's 1st Polish Army who reached insurgents' positions.[85]

10. Two Soviet liaison officers with a field combat radio parachuted into the area held by insurgents.

The air above Warsaw obviously was pulsating with radio waves. AK radio communication was efficient despite the efforts of the enemy. The German Army, by using wave-length measuring devices, could locate radio stations to direct artillery fire and bombing raids on them. As a result, they had to move frequently from place to place.[86] Countless lives and immense effort were spent before and during the Uprising in establishing the AK's network of radio stations. Between the spring of 1943 and the fall of 1944, equipment for 877 radio stations was dropped from planes to occupied Poland.[87] Although much of this equipment was destroyed or immediately fell into German hands, some reached its destination. The stations in operation during the Uprising were equipped from these drops. To provide specialists for liaison and communication (including the recovery, transportation and operation of radio stations) AK assigned 2,084 soldiers, including 783 women, to Warsaw on 31 July 1944.[88]

AK Headquarters stations in Warsaw transmitted on three levels: 'upward' to the Polish radio centre in Stanmore, England, and through it to the Polish Supreme Commander-in-Chief in London or to the special Polish liaison base near Bari in Italy; 'horizontally' to cut-off units of insurgents fighting within Warsaw (for example, Group North); 'downward' to Polish territory outside Warsaw, where subordinate units of the AK were organized and operating. These units had fifty-seven stations, spread throughout occupied Poland.[89]

The first radio-telegraph message out of Warsaw stated, 'We are fighting.'[90] It was 1 August 1944.

AK station Lightning[91] in Warsaw had the greatest impact on listeners outside the city. On the seventh day of the Uprising it began broadcasting by voice three times daily. The speakers described what was happening in Warsaw and asked for assistance; they also broadcast the AK Headquarters' combat communiqués. After ten days the BBC acknowledged that they were receiving Lightning. The Poles were overjoyed that someone could hear them.[92]

Radio station personnel were always in peril. The antenna on the roof of Lightning was frequently damaged by artillery fire. Many technicians and personnel were wounded while attempting to repair it under fire. They found some consolation at one point, however, from learning they were heard, not only in England, but even in New York.

The Germans concentrated their heaviest mortar on the station the day after this encouraging news. One shell hit the six-storey building, fell through six floors, and landed in the basement but did not explode.[93] The station continued its broadcasts in Polish, English and German.[94]

The sound of German planes approaching could be heard very soon after broadcasting began again. Their purpose was to locate with precision the building in which the station was located. Observers stood on what was left of the roof to give the alarm to stop broadcasting when the planes came near and report when they had departed.[95]

'The place in which the station was operating consisted of two rooms. In the first were several technicians responsible for care of the station and several broadcasters waiting to make their evening transmissions; in the second was a makeshift studio. This created an unforgettable impression. The windows were missing, and sandbags filled the gaps. The walls and floor were covered with carpets and blankets to create the proper acoustical conditions. In the middle of the room was a little table with a microphone, and in front of it was a chair. This was the complete equipment of the place from which we could speak openly to the free world.'[96]

The radio station providing direct contact with London ceased to be operational soon after the Uprising began, so its activities were shifted to share the facilities of another station, which continued to broadcast throughout the Uprising. The latter station had been established and directed by Stefan Korbonski, head of the Department of Civil Resistance (a civilian administrative body subordinate to the Polish Government-in-Exile).

Even before the Uprising, the Peasant Party had its own radio station. This party was distinguished by its insistence on democratic principles and its opposition to the Polish régime prior to 1939. The party leadership in Warsaw was in direct contact with their counterparts in England. However, because of a technical breakdown, they too were compelled to utilize Mr Korbonski's station. In the democratic tradition, Mr Korbonski allowed other parties to use it for contacting their party people in England as the need arose.[97]

A Soviet-made station broadcasting from Warsaw belonged to the Communist Polish People's Army. The station commander was Captain Karol Wieckowski.[98] Although during research I scrutinized about 6000 messages exchanged between all military and civilian branches of the Government-in-Exile in London and the insurgents' stations, I found no record of any exchange of messages between that station and England.

The Germans operated their 'Polish' radio station on the same frequency as the insurgents' Lightning. 'They were supplying [the insurgents with] false information and false orders from General Bor and General Monter.'[99]

The Polish monitors in England who listened most intently to the insurgents' station reported an interesting phenomenon: Lightning's broadcasts from Warsaw were purposely interfered with by a Soviet station belonging to the Soviet press agency TASS. (This station, as previously mentioned, was in England, near London.)[100] But the Soviet station did not interfere while the Germans' counterfeit Lightning was operating.[101]

In London the Polish Government-in-Exile had at its disposal Dawn. Although the content of its broadcasts was under British control, this station actively disputed and engaged in political discussion with the Soviet radio station Kosciuszko, which beamed its broadcasts specifically to Poland. It was Kosciuszko that in the last days of July

1944 called the people of Warsaw to begin the Uprising. During the Uprising the activities of Dawn were sporadic and often suspended by British authorities.[102] (There were 30,000 radio stations operating in England at that time.)[103]

In Mesagne, Italy, about six miles south-west of Brindisi, there was a communication centre code-named Seagull, which belonged to Polish Forces-in-Exile: Base Number 11.[104] The chief purpose of the centre was to maintain contact with Warsaw and the Polish Government in England in order to organize air drops and landings if and when possible.

Radio stations operating under combat conditions in Warsaw encountered enormous difficulties. In a memo on this subject, the Polish Army Chief of Staff in London, General Kopanski, said:

> Although the communication centre of the Special Section of the Supreme Polish Headquarters near London was always ready for contact with occupied Poland . . . the radio stations in Poland, in order to avoid discovery by the Germans, quite often had to limit their transmissions to twenty, and sometimes only ten, minutes. . . . Often they were under such a direct threat that they could not receive [the radio messages sent to them from London].
>
> Of course, delivery of messages from the radio stations to AK Headquarters or from Headquarters to the radio stations also presented great difficulties. . . . There were cases when radio messages, especially longer ones, were received in London in parts, or when the sequence of parts of messages was transposed.
>
> Obviously, the coding and decoding of messages in underground combat conditions could not always be done without . . . interference.[105]

The entire spectrum of human tragedy is reflected in the messages from Warsaw: the anxious demands for assistance; the succinct reporting of desperate combat conditions.

On 12 August 1944 a communiqué said: 'Broadcast several times through BBC that on Skorupki Street, number 12, in apartment number 6, there are lost children: Szczygiel, Janusz, three years old. . . .'[106] The names of other children followed. The sender apparently hoped that among listeners in Warsaw, perhaps in sectors that had been cut off by Germans, the children's parents might be found.

Some messages were desperate and blunt. One sent 31 August 1944 to Prime Minister Mikolajczyk said: 'We are afraid, that as in the case of the outbreak of the Uprising (which could not be a surprise to the Government) the Government was not prepared either . . . militarily or in terms of international politics. . . .'[107]

Despair was also evident in London. The President of the Council of Ministers of the Polish Government-in-Exile wept in his radio speech to the insurgents via the BBC: 'What else can I tell you, my beloved, than to pay homage. . . .'[108]

One communiqué from London said, 'I wanted to talk to you on Sunday. Unfortunately, because of conflict with censorship, to which I did not want to subject myself, I had to decline. I wanted to give you something concrete. . . .'[109] These remarks were made by the Deputy Prime Minister in London to the Council of National Unity, the highest Polish legislative body in Warsaw. Whether the 'censorship' was Polish or British it was impossible to ascertain.

The flow of radio messages was intense. 'During the two months of battle 6,600 messages were received or transmitted. . . .'[110] (About 104 messages per day.) In many, insurgents demanded air assistance from the Allies.

CHAPTER TWO

Insurgents in and outside Warsaw

THERE was also a group of Polish Communists involved in the Uprising – those who had remained in Poland throughout the German occupation. They were not represented in the Polish Government-in-Exile, nor were they accepted by the Presidium of the Council of National Unity, although this body (the legal parliament of underground Poland) encompassed a broad spectrum of political parties.[1] On 20 July 1944, Jankowski in Poland sent a radiogram to the Government in London informing it that the Communists would not be accepted by the other political parties.[2] Thus, as one writer in contemporary Poland has pointed out, co-operation on the basis of compromise was impossible for the Communists.[3] Several weeks earlier, the combined leadership of the Polish Communist organizations (PPR, KRN and PAL) in Poland had decided that some of them should meet the 'Polish Committee' of the incoming Red Army in order to participate in policy formulation; the rest were to remain in territories still under German occupation. This plan was carried out.[4]

About a week before the outbreak of the Uprising, on 25 July 1944, a political agreement of co-operation was signed. It united all splinter Communist and pro-Communist factions under one command, with a direct link to the Polish Committee of National Liberation in Lublin.

This was the opportunity for Polish Communists to strengthen and unify their leadership in preparation for the power struggle with the AK in Warsaw, and with the nucleus of the Polish Committee for National Liberation that was to arrive from the east.

On 28 July, Communist General Franciszek Jozwiak (pseudonym Witold) conferred with the Warsaw command of the Communist Armia Ludowa (People's Army). According to a Communist source, it was decided as a result of that conference ' . . . to mobilize within the nearest days our forces of AL (Armia Ludowa) in Warsaw and to put them in a state of alarm'.[5] These units in Warsaw were supposed to co-operate with the Red Army and the Polish forces [General Berling's First Army] in liberating the capital. However, their identity was to be revealed only after the fighting for Warsaw had actually started. The chief objective of the AL units was to prevent the Germans from blowing up the bridges on the Vistula and to secure the main administrative and utilities buildings (post office, telegraph, railway stations) against destruction. The purpose of such action was to make possible the seizure of power by the Communist National Council and the Polish Committee of National Liberation (KRN and PKWN).[6] According to this source, the strength of the Armia Ludowa in Warsaw was 'about 2,000' people.[7]

Without doubt, the local Communists expected the Soviet – German fighting to reach Warsaw at any moment. Although their sources of information and contacts with the Soviet command were more intimate than those of General Bor and his staff, they too anticipated the Red Army's entry into Warsaw. On the basis of this assessment, the Communist leadership also put its units in a state of alarm during the night of 31 July–1 August.[8] But the command of the People's Army assumed that Bor-Komorowski would not start his action without informing them.[9] So the Communist leadership with its 2,000 troops was biding its time, waiting for the Red Army and General Berling while submerged in a sea of 40,000 AK members who were loyal to the legal Polish Government-in-Exile.

It is difficult to assess to what degree the following incident affected General Bor and the AK Headquarters. Bor knew through AK intelligence that all Communist units expected to align themselves with the Red Army for the purpose of seizing power in Warsaw. He also knew from radio messages that the Communists and the Red Army were arresting AK members in the eastern territories. Then, on 29 July, just two days before the outbreak of the Uprising, there appeared on the walls of Warsaw public proclamations signed by 'General' J. S. Skokowski (he was, in fact, a colonel), commander of the Communist organization PAL. The proclamations declared that General Bor and his staff had escaped from the city, that Skokowski was taking over the leadership of *all underground organizations and units in Warsaw*, and that Skokowski was announcing mobilization for fighting Germans.[10] Not only was this untrue (General Bor-Komorowski and the AK Headquarters were in Warsaw and had no intention of leaving), but the false 'General' further alerted Germans to the probability of an uprising in Warsaw, and AK leaders considered this proclamation a provocation and an act of subversion directed against the AK.[11] The proclamation also alerted AK leaders to danger. They realized that, if the Communists were to start an uprising before AK acted, a number of the consequences affecting the AK and the outcome of the struggle for freedom in Poland would follow. They saw, for example, that the proclamation could have resulted in an immediate uprising from which the Communists could have withdrawn their units by merging with the population, leaving the AK vulnerable to German repression and destruction. Thus the largest concentration of armed underground forces loyal to the legal parliament (Krajowa Rada Narodowa) in

Warsaw would be wiped out, and into this vacuum the 'Lublin Government' would move. (In any event, this is what ultimately happened.)

If, at any time during the forty-eight hours preceding the Uprising, several determined Communists had opened fire with automatic weapons in various parts of the city, AK youth would have poured into the streets shooting. The insurgents were, in those last days of July, like gunpowder – anything could spark an explosion into armed rebellion. This author has no explanation as to why the Communists did not act. In any case, on the second day of the Uprising, the command of Armia Ludowa in Warsaw decided to fight shoulder to shoulder with the AK. From a survey of Communist documents that are available for that period, it is evident that General Bor-Komorowski did not inform them about the outbreak of the Uprising as the Polish Communists claim. But, from the perspective of time, a distinction should be made between what the AK leaders told the Communists and what the Communists in Warsaw knew from their own sources.

The AK Chief of Intelligence, Section Eastern Front, who was interviewed, stated that he actually had contacts (with the knowledge of the AK command) with the leaders of the Communist Party in Warsaw until May 1944, when the AK command ordered the contact terminated.[12] But the mobilization of 40,000 insurgents in Warsaw (each of whom had, on the average, two members in his family, making a total of more than 120,000 people who knew) could not have escaped the attention of the local pro-Communist population, which, although numerically insignificant, was dispersed throughout Warsaw. Moreover, according to Prime Minister Mikolajczyk, the mistress of one of the Communist Party leaders, Wladyslaw Gomulka, had access to radio messages of the AK command in Warsaw.[13]

So the Soviet Union's claim that it was not informed about the Uprising in advance officially is probably true, but it is misleading. That the Polish Communists knew, through their contacts, of the first AK mobilization on 29 July, two days before the Uprising, is shown by their own subsequent mobilization of 31 July. It is a valid assumption that they expected an uprising at any moment.[14]

The Polish Communist leaders in Warsaw who knew about the decision of 28 July to mobilize the AL reached Lublin before the Uprising. Therefore, the Polish Committee of National Liberation in Lublin must also have been aware of the mobilization. If the Polish Communists in Lublin knew the AK was preparing for an uprising, then Red Army liaison officers and political advisers among them in Lublin also knew, as of course did the Soviet Government.

The contribution of the Polish Socialist Party to the Uprising merits special mention. This party, known for its support of democratic principles and social justice, identified itself with the Uprising and sealed its traditional bond with the city by active participation, support and efforts to obtain assistance from socialists and Allied governments abroad.

Even the handicapped fought. An armed platoon of deaf-mutes, one of whom was a woman, defended their own building, assisted by an elderly priest who served as their chaplain and interpreter. General Bor personally awarded the Cross of Valour to the priest.[15]

What were the mutual attitudes of insurgents belonging to different political groups? The 1,500–2,000 insurgents who belonged to Communist organizations, although technically subordinated to the orders of General Bor, preserved the identity of their own units, and had their own press and a separate chain of command. Their position was unusual. They were Poles who, by virtue of the fact that they had volunteered to join the Uprising, apparently shared the AK soldiers' commitment to free Warsaw from German control. However, their political aim was to seize power for their own political leaders. The rank and file of the AK were aware of this, but their distrust of the Polish Communists appears to have been temporarily overcome during battle by common suffering and combat experience. With the progress of the Uprising this distrust returned because of the seeming inactivity on the part of the Soviet Army.

It was commonly assumed by AK and Communist insurgents alike that the Soviet forces were unwilling to come to the aid of Warsaw. This was dramatically underscored when, very early one morning in the fourth week of Uprising, five soldiers – four men and a girl – emerged from the smoke of burning houses in Old Town, carrying the body of a dead soldier. Their white and red armbands with the letters AL identified them as members of the Armia Ludowa. They were looking for a piece of ground free from rubble, and that was not easy to find.

They dug the grave. After a little while the girl reached into her blouse and brought into the daylight a beautiful white carnation. With great delicacy and composure she kissed the flower and put it beside the dead man's face. And then the composure broke. She turned to the eastern shore of the Vistula, toward the Soviet forces, and exploded with an eerie high-pitched scream of an intensity unexpected from such a small body, 'You sons of bitches – you haven't come!'

On the whole, relations between the AK and the AL were friendly, but not cordial. There were exceptions, of course. A messenger girl from the AL was frantically looking for a pistol that had been dropped by a wounded soldier from her unit. She encountered an AK platoon, a member of which took pity on her and gave her his own pistol, with the words, 'Please take it, if you need it so badly. I will get along somehow without it.'[16] This incident was certainly unusual. To give away one's weapon was to put one's own life on the line. A more common collaboration was the exchange of weapons and foodstuffs on the basis of mutual advantage.[17]

As fighting progressed, an additional avenue was explored in the hope of bringing assistance to Warsaw. On the fourteenth day of the Uprising, General Bor radioed London, 'Please repeat and broadcast through BBC the following order:

> Commander-in-Chief of Armia Krajowa, 14 August 1944. (Headquarters of the Armia Krajowa L6 – III, 14 August 1944, at 10.30 a.m.) Fighting for Warsaw is being extended. It is being continued against overwhelming enemy power. Our situation demands an immediate march to the assistance of the capital. I am immediately ordering all available well armed units to fight the enemy in the outskirts and suburbs of Warsaw, and to enter the city in order to participate in the fighting within. Signed: Commander-in-Chief of Armia Krajowa, Bor.'[18]

On the same day he also issued an order by radio calling for a 'strong blow' in the area of Cracow.[19] It is not clear what he meant by this order. Cracow, the ancient capital of Poland, was the site of priceless buildings – among them the Castle, the national treasury of art objects and archives going back to medieval times. Was this an order for another uprising veiled in ambiguity? If so, it was not implemented, and Cracow survived.

It was not only a desperate concern for the fate of Warsaw that compelled General Bor to appeal to all AK units outside it. He was responsible for their survival, which was already threatened. German troops were hunting them down; so was the Soviet Army. In both instances, depending on the mood of the local army commanders, the possibility of a massacre of units in the countryside was very real. General's Bor concern led him to send an order on the twenty-second day of the Uprising informing AK units outside the city that 'in case Warsaw is taken by the Soviet Army [and he was] unable to give orders to the units still fighting . . . [they should be] directly subordinated to the orders of the Polish Government-in-Exile from London'.[20]

From areas as distant as two or three hundred miles, evading both German and Soviet forces, AK units tried to join Bor. Armed AK volunteers gathered: in one district there were 5,600; in another 4,500; in still another 1,200.[21] But they faced an impossible situation: their spirit and numbers guaranteed sufficient strength to break through the steel ring surrounding Warsaw, but the same strength in numbers made their detection inevitable.

AK units in Polish territory already seized by the Soviet Army had an extremely difficult task. They had been ordered by Polish civilian authorities and General Bor to co-operate with the Red Army in combating German forces. Yet, while trying to come to the assistance of Warsaw, they were arrested and disarmed by the Russians. And, even if these AK units survived the Soviet gauntlet, there remained the German-occupied territory outside Warsaw to negotiate. Poorly armed and supplied, they made the attempt, but few survived the double hazard of Russian allies and German enemies.

Still, remnants of some AK units were able to reach Warsaw. About 200 people reached Mokotow Sector.[22] One unit fought more than a hundred engagements on its way to Warsaw, coming within sight of the smoke pall over the city, but it could not get through. On the twentieth day of the Uprising, 750 AK men commanded by Major Okon reached Zoliborz Sector. Then the Major returned to nearby Kampinos forest to organize and lead another group of 2,368 soldiers. It never reached Warsaw. After losing about forty-five per cent of its men in combat with German army units, it was completely destroyed while making a desperate attempt to flee and hide in the mountains.[23]

It is not an overstatement to say that without women the AK could not have existed. In occupied Poland between 35,000 and 40,000 women took the Polish Soldiers' oath to protect the Constitution.[24] A special decree by the President of Poland of 27 October 1943 proclaimed that women soldiers had the same rights and obligations as men. This decree was amended by an order of the Commander-in-Chief of the AK on 23 September 1944, allocating to women military ranks, including those of both noncommissioned and commissioned officers. From the outset, even before the decree that formalized their status, Polish women participated in underground activities.[25]

They undertook many functions of high responsibility. A woman was the chief of liaison and communication in the staff and headquarters of AK. A woman reorganized liaison and communication with the eastern territory. For some time a woman was responsible for liaison and communication with the West. A woman was deputy commander of the Women's Sabotage Officers' School, which had 120 women instructors. The supervisor of the couriers' exchange points was a woman, as was the chief of all insurgents' magazines and storage points during the Uprising.

On the women rested the responsibility for operational liaison, coding and decoding, contacts with Polish prisoner-of-war camps, and the medical department. [They were responsible for] watching places possibly endangered [by German surveillance], guarding the clandestine meetings and radio stations, [and for the] transport of money, weapons, and printed material. Women also [arranged] contacts with concentration camps, intelligence parties and units [and planned] diversion and sabotage. . . . Within the AK alone 35,000 women underwent military training; [of this number there were] 5,000 in para-medical training, 700 in liaison and communication, 550 in military administration, and 500 in military escort and guard.[26]

In the Underground, Girl Scouts of sixteen years and older numbered more than 4,000. They were dispersed among 250 locations, working in communications, and also as medics.[27]

The bravery of women was boundless, as this interview with Mr Boleslaw Szmajdowicz, the commander of a Polish air-supply receiving-post in occupied Poland, shows. He describes the recovery of an agent from England:

> We were showing the direction of the wind by forming a cross on the ground. There were either eleven or thirteen people involved. At the central point of the cross, I stood with a white-and-red spotlight. It was night. The rest of the men had white spotlights. There was a prearranged Morse signal, and the airplane responded with its blinker when we turned on our lights. On our signal the plane made several passes; first they dropped supplies and then the people jumped. My ambition was always to be first to reach the people. They came down near the building. I ran, shouting the password. They shouted the countersign. The first parachutist takes off his helmet – and what do I see? Long hair! A woman![28]

In fact, two women parachuted into occupied Poland: 'One was a courier-soldier in the AK; another . . . a member of the British Mission, was on liaison with the AK.'[29]

Of course, to parachute into enemy-held territory during the night is an act requiring considerable personal courage; but there were thousands of women, particularly in the liaison department, whose lives were in constant danger, although the circumstances were much less spectacular:

> The private apartment of a [messenger] woman was frequently placed at the disposal of the Underground. She could never be allowed out of sight, had to live where she could be found easily, and was not allowed to change her name or address without permission. As long as she was active she could not be permitted to go into hiding or to lose contact with us. To do this meant breaking the contacts between members and branches of the Underground. . . . She was, therefore, in constant danger. All the details of her life were known to many people; this itself is undesirable in underground work. She constantly carried incriminating documents. Her movements were of a kind that aroused suspicion, and her presence was necessary at many [dangerous] places. The average 'life' of a . . . [messenger] woman did not exceed a few months.
>
> They were invariably caught by the Gestapo in incriminating circumstances and were treated with bestial cruelty in the Nazi jails. Most of them carried poison and were under orders to use it without hesitation when the need arose. It was almost impossible to get them out of prison and the AK could not take the risk of their succumbing to torture. It can be said that of all the workers in the Underground their lot was the most severe, their sacrifices the greatest, and their contribution the least rewarded. They were overworked and doomed. They received neither high rank nor honours for their heroism.[30]

Before the outbreak of fighting there were 8,000 women in Warsaw who had taken the AK soldier's oath.[31] On 18 August 1944, the Department of Internal Affairs in Free Warsaw ordered compulsory labour for the State for men and women aged from seventeen to sixty.[32] As far as women were concerned, such an order was not necessary. There were more volunteers than the fighting units could absorb, and many of the women who had not been assigned to units followed the ebb and flow of the insurgents' needs, now helping the units, now searching for their own families. These women were not included in official statistics but were active in the fighting. It is very difficult to establish exactly how many women were in combat. A telegram from Warsaw to the Polish Government in London on the eighteenth day of the Uprising said that women constituted 'one-seventh of AK forces'.[33] Ninety-eight per cent of AK nurses reported to their units during the Uprising.[34]

There were some Lysistratas in reverse among the women. In one instance, a gentle-faced blonde poked her head from the window of a partly bombed apartment and shouted down to her husband, 'I will not let you into my bed unless you [shoot] me a German!'

In many instances women demanded to be in 'the first line' of action (and the demand was often accompanied by the ultimate in feminine weaponry – tears). Of course, in the street fighting there could be no such thing as a 'front line'.[35] All areas seized by insurgents were under constant German artillery and air bombardment, but the feeling of being directly useful to the fighting unit was psychologically of overriding importance.

To have a weapon, either a rifle or a revolver, was the usual aspiration of the women in combat. Those with such weapons who were attached to units as volunteers were expected to fight. They did. A fourteen-year-old girl singlehandedly attacked and burned two German tanks, and a girl of eighteen blew up the door of a German police stronghold, enabling her unit to get inside the building.[36]

Women produced a variety of tensions within the Underground. First of all, there was inevitably conscious or unconscious competition for them (never admitted) in the units in which they served. These tensions were suppressed to the point of self-consciously playing down the problem. The tensions affected relationships among the men.

Women's ability to manipulate the membership of the organization on an informal level was another problem. The following story may serve as an example. The officer who was responsible for the logistics of the AK in Warsaw designated one of the women's underground organizations to be responsible for feeding the soldiers from the moment when street fighting was to commence. This selection infuriated the other women's auxiliary organizations who wanted to do that very thing. Ultimately the ladies started to lobby on an informal level – their husbands, sons, brothers, and acquaintances in the Underground were properly informed (or misinformed) about the rejection and apparent injustice. The high command was bombarded with informal reports, inquiries, accusations and counter-accusations. Before the problem was unravelled and settled to the satisfaction of all concerned, the officer's activities were partially paralysed for four months![37]

Many acts of courage were performed without witnesses and without weapons. Colonel Wachnowski, the stoic defender of Old Town Sector, said:

> I must mention the girl who was my own messenger during the conspiracy stage and also during the fighting for Old Town. I am referring to Black Barbara. . . . In fact, she was not only a messenger, but also an adjutant in the full meaning of the word. She was tremendously courageous, ready to sacrifice herself. She had under her command all the other messenger girls, of whom I had several on my staff. . . . In addition, there were many messenger girls from the units which defended particular sectors. We know how these women sacrificed themselves! . . . Only the people who were actually in Old Town can understand.[38]

Air bombardment and collapsing houses were indeed changing the configuration of the city. It was necessary for messengers to find their way through the basements. These had been connected by breaking through the foundation walls under the apartment houses, but often a passage through a basement was blocked by fire or rubble. Messengers also moved in the open, through the ruins of the streets. The mortality rate was very high, in Pine battalion over fifty per cent of the women messengers were killed while performing their duties. But there was never a lack of volunteers to replace them. One colonel observed, 'We had to put brakes on the women – they didn't know how to camouflage and protect themselves, but they were most eager to run and to accomplish the task.'[39]

One of the former girl-messengers recalls: 'I was only fifteen years old. Two of us were told to deliver a message, and we had to cross Napoleon's Square. We were caught by crossfire on the streets. At that I was so terribly frightened that I just couldn't move. I froze – I was so frightened. There were two of us, because if one should be killed the other one was supposed to take the message and deliver it. . . .'[40] (She did deliver it.)

Another girl ran through the burning streets with a slip of paper in her hands, screaming at the top of her voice, 'I am still a child, and I am so frightened.'[41] But she held on to the message. One lieutenant described the messengers' devotion succinctly: 'Either they were killed, or they brought the message.'[42] Generally, their coolness and self-control was superb, particularly since they did not carry weapons, and therefore lacked the feeling of reassurance that a weapon gives a human being under stress.

A special group of these girls were messengers in the dark, threatening sewers, linking groups of insurgents isolated by Germans. Small girls were preferred, since it was often necessary for them to crawl through very narrow passages. 'Messenger Marysia went six times back and forth from Mokotow Sector to the Centre City; she had to crawl through the sewers.'[43]

Some girls carried ammunition and supplies. The trips could take up to six hours. In at least one case after emerging the girl collapsed. Others never emerged. One of these was a nineteen-year-old Girl Scout who was a path-finder in the sewers. Her name was not known.[44]

The women had courage. AK Colonel Niedzielski, who had tenaciously defended every yard of Zoliborz Sector, recalled, 'When one platoon refused to go back to Old Town through the sewer, I went to see them personally. I met them just at the manhole and asked, "Cadets, are you going, or not?" Then a little girl of about sixteen, her hair in long braids, stepped out of formation and said, "I will go." I kissed her, and the whole unit descended into the sewers.'[45]

The majority of women were occupied in tending the wounded. Some women were attached directly to fighting units; some were on duty in 'field hospitals' hastily arranged in buildings and basements. A small group of 15–30 insurgents accompanied by 3–5 women carrying stretchers or knapsacks with medications and bandages was a common sight. They assisted the wounded with tenacity, determinaton and tenderness.

They gave their lives in this service, too. On 3 September 1944, in Warecka Street, three girl medics, one after another, tried to recover the body of an AK soldier who was lying in front of a German position. The first was shot, the second was shot, and the third was able to recover him. In another district Medical Officer 'Tuleja' reported a similar incident, but all three women who tried to remove a wounded soldier died in the attempt.[46]

A woman messenger reported, 'While attacking the university building we had several wounded who were left on the street under direct German fire. Five Catholic sisters . . . ran into the open . . . and approached the wounded. They were dressed in their habits, they had Red Cross bands, and they carried stretchers. The Germans opened fire on them. They could, of course, have withdrawn. Instead, they started to give assistance to the wounded. All of them were shot, one after another. During the night we went after them, and were able to bring back one of them. She had many machine-gun bullets in her body. Her name was Pulaska; I don't know whether she survived.'[47] Statistics and interviews indicate that the acts described above were an everyday occurrence.

Other women helped the wounded by assisting doctors. Doctor Morwa reports: 'Once, I was performing an opening of the abdominal cavity (we had to remove a bullet). At that very moment we heard German diving planes above us and the sound of bombing approaching our area. All our doors and windows were blown out, but none of the nurses and medics left the operating-room.' Only some survived.[48]

Whether' fighting or not, the people of Warsaw had to eat. The women of the AK organized approximately 200 field kitchens in the city. Even when performing such chores as cooking, women revealed the same spirit of self-sacrifice and insistence on 'doing their part'.

The insurgents' meals were haphazardly timed, but they were fed. There were many statements like this one: 'There appeared a blonde with a fruit soup and *pierogi* [similar to ravioli]. She said that her mother sent it to us. . . .' [49] Very often the women had to bring the food from faraway streets, exposing themselves to death along the way. I must add that, judging by the description of the food (pork chops are also mentioned), the references are to the first two or three days of the Uprising. There were no pork chops or fruit soup after that. By the end all the horses, dogs and cats had been eaten.

Although some AK women had predetermined functions, their sense of duty and desire to contribute compelled them to seek other outlets. Marianna (Professor Maria Ludwika Bernhard), then Deputy Chief of the liaison service for women in one sector, volunteered to organize a laundry to wash used bandages for one hospital. Such measures were necessary because there were no fresh supplies of any sort. Marianna, with the assistance of other female volunteers, was able to bring a big basket of clean bandages to the hospital approximately every three hours. One day, while they were carrying the basket, bombs from aircraft fell so near that the women were blown over a street barricade. On regaining consciousness they realized that 'their hospital' had been destroyed. A few days later the same fate befell their laundry.

Women from outside Warsaw tried to help. 'Throughout August two peasant women from the country regularly brought to the barricades two containers of milk for wounded soldiers. We just could not believe them, because they had to pass through German territory, so we didn't let them inside the barricades. They left the milk on the German side of the barricade. This happened day after day until Ukrainian units [part of the German Army], took a position opposite us. . . . The women did not come anymore'.[50]

Women who fought in the Uprising consistently report that the men showed special concern for them. 'Five of us medics were given quarters in an apartment in which several elderly bachelors were living. Every day they crossed from their bedroom through our room [the only access to the bathroom] holding a beautiful vase for flowers. They carried it with the greatest delicacy and dignity. We ultimately discovered that they were using it instead of the chamber pot that was under their bed.'[51]

Of course, there were a variety of 'romances' and sexual relationships. Mutual attraction was not necessarily the basis for an attachment. As one woman-soldier reports: 'One man fell in love with me, but what he really wanted was my Walther pistol.'[52] In a beleaguered town where more than a million people were subjected to intense stress it would be too much to expect that everyone behaved at all times with virtue and gallantry.

Women soldiers, products of the same culture as the men, had an equal capacity for grand gestures and symbolic behaviour. A woman messenger crawled, under German fire, to a garden to pick flowers for the wounded because they were 'national heroes, and I wanted to do something for them, and that was all I could do'.[53]

The women had some impediments peculiar to their sex. One woman said, 'I was aware of the fact that I was one among so many boys. When they were afraid, it was normal, but I just couldn't show my fear because they could laugh at me.' [54] They also had a variety of feminine concerns. 'In spite of the fact that I was taking care of wounded I had to carry wheat from the [stores]. I didn't have trousers, and I was concerned not with the fact that I could be killed, but whether, when I was climbing up the walls, the men would be seeing what they shouldn't.'[55] Some women reported that their menstrual periods stopped during the fighting.

As one survivor remembered, they not only sacrificed their lives: 'Above us the ceiling was in embers; the walls were warm, like stoves. Smoke and the smell of burning . . . were trickling into the basement where a German soldier pushed three of us. We didn't want to be separated. The basement was full of bedding. Perspiration was trickling down our dirty faces. . . . One came . . . then another. I held the girl's mother in my arms so she wouldn't see it. I wanted to pray to the Mother of God, but the words were all mixed up. One came at me; I pulled my handkerchief off my head. He saw my silver hair and left me alone, and then we were by ourselves.[56]

Large numbers of children participated in the Uprising. How many, it is impossible to ascertain with any degree of reliability; neither is it possible to say how many were killed while on duty. But it is estimated that at the outbreak of the Uprising there were 200,000 children and teenagers in the city, of whom about 30,000 were members of the underground Girl Scouts and Boy Scouts. A broad survey of unrelated sources indicates that between 1939 and 1945 more than two million children and teenagers died in Poland as a result of the German occupation. Five hundred and fifty children actually belonged to units and after capitulation decided to go with them into German prisoner-of-war camps.[57] These were boys from ten to eighteen years old.

There are several reasons why it is impossible to ascertain the number of children who fought as insurgents. First, they were not in any sense drafted. In fact, commanders of small units were very hesitant to permit children to take part in action. They entered units only with the permission of one or both of the parents. In other cases the mother or father joined and asked that their child also be accepted by the unit. Sometimes the child had been separated from his family by the street fighting, or, in the saddest cases, both parents of a child had been killed.

What did they do in the units? There were young girls [and boys] . . . all volunteers, many of whom fell – shot by German snipers or in direct fighting. Only yesterday they had been playing 'policemen and insurgents' on the streets, spanked by their parents who were anxious about their exuberance; then all at once they had become real, very real, soldiers. They stood at their posts with real devotion, very often undertaking jobs far beyond their strength. They were responsible for the delivery of insurgents' mail, distribution of the press, and served as messengers. They cleaned weapons . . . and, when necessary, they would attack.[58]

The children who actually wore the red and white bands of the AK gained a tremendous feeling of their own identity and worth. In one of the districts they even had their own handwritten and hand-illustrated paper (*Dzieci Mokotowa*), which came out twice a week. Here is an excerpt from a poem written by a child, printed in paper No. 2, dated 9 September 1944.

> When will the help
> Which is so badly needed – weapons, ammunition –
> Come down from the sky?
> All that remains is a circle of blood
> And a ring of fire
> Around Warsaw.

Some pre-teenage boys were promoted to the rank of lance-corporal or corporal; some actually carried pistols or hand-grenades. However, there was no conscious attempt by the command of the AK to indoctrinate or train the children to kill. (There are several photographs available in which such training is shown as taking place during the Uprising. In all probability these photographs were spontaneously arranged by some overzealous soldier.)

Mr Zeev Ben-Shlomo, from the Institute of Contemporary History and Wiener Library, London, informed this author in a letter dated 8 May 1969 that, during the Uprising in Warsaw, Mr Jozef Ziemian maintained contact with a group of homeless Jewish children who passed as Gentile children earning their living as cigarette vendors. These children participated in the Warsaw Uprising, rendering various services to the Home Army.

In human conflict losses are usually measured by the number of maimed, dead or imprisoned. It is not possible to ascertain the psychological effect upon participants. The impact on Warsaw children was terrible. How many psychotic children were the direct result of the Uprising will never be known.

Why did women and children participate in this insurrection in such numbers? Partly because of Polish cultural style, and partly because they, too, literally were fighting for their own homes, and partly because many felt they had no other option.

CHAPTER THREE
The German Army

THAT the Germans perceived the mounting tension in the city and
expected the Poles to make an armed rising is clear from the war log of
the 9th German Army. An entry dated 25 July 1944 states, 'It is known
that preparations for the Uprising in Warsaw are being made; details
are not available as to the degree of preparation and the day of the
outbreak.' Three days later the topic appears again: 'Definite expectation that the Uprising will break out on 28 July at 11 p.m.' It is said
that a Polish mistress of a German flyer, in loyalty to her lover rather
than to her compatriots, told him that an uprising was planned, which
information he duly reported to his superiors. The story is plausible. In
a city of 1,200,000 people, of whom about 40,000 were preparing
physically and psychologically for mortal combat, townspeople would
have known, and it undoubtedly was discussed. In this tension-ridden
situation, any Polish woman would have had no difficulty in assessing
that there would be rebellion at any moment.

About a week before the outbreak, in a well-known Warsaw brewery
there was a party, organized by its German administration, at which
some Poles were present. After some drinks, one of the Germans made a
passionate plea for Poles not to make an uprising in Warsaw.[1]

The Germans were jumpy. The night curfew was enforced, and
anyone appearing on the streets without a pass during the hours it was
in effect was shot. Mass hunts for young men on the streets of Warsaw
were intensified. (Throughout the occupation, it was a common
practice for German police to appear unexpectedly and round up all
the men in a certain street or area; these were used as hostages, shot, or
sent to concentration camps.) German patrols were doubled or tripled
in strength. A member of the Gestapo from another Polish city arrived
in Warsaw and went, dressed in civilian clothes, into the streets with a
machine pistol in his possession. He was shot on sight, in front of the
Church of the Holy Cross by a German patrol.[2] Nerves were strained on
both sides.

In September 1951, seven years after the Uprising, the Polish
Communist Government was detaining two men in a prison cell in
Warsaw. One was General Geibel, formerly of the SS, and deputy

commander of German police in Warsaw during the Uprising. The other was a hero of the Uprising, Father Tomasz, whose real name was Rostworowski. General Geibel said to Father Tomasz, whom I interviewed in Rome in 1965: 'We [Germans in Warsaw] were expecting the Uprising at the end of July when the Soviet battle line approached the Vistula. For that reason, we evacuated German civilians from Warsaw in July and waited for our front units to approach us. But the front units had not arrived yet. Nevertheless, we had a red alert while evacuating the city. I reported to the commander of the police that in the morning hours of 1 August the decision was made [for] an Uprising, but he did not believe me.'[3]

Why were Germans in Warsaw in the first place? Poland after her defeat in 1939 was divided into two spheres of interest, of which Germany claimed almost 73,000 square miles and the Soviet Union about 77,000.

Less than two years later these partners were locked in deadly combat, and by 1944 the Soviet armies were rolling German forces back through the very territory Russia had divided with Germany. The Germans occupying Warsaw saw the Soviet armies approaching from the east; and, unconcerned as they were for Poland and for the welfare of its people, their feelings for their own plight, when they were suddenly caught in the battle of Warsaw, are very understandable. It was the fifth year of the war, and they were being forced to give up territory they had conquered and ruthlessly occupied at the outset of the war. They were aware that the pincers of approaching Soviet armies would converge on their homeland, which was already reeling under persistent Allied bombing attacks. What they saw on their short leaves back in Germany confirmed that the end was approaching; and then, as they were preparing a last-minute desperate defence of Warsaw, which lay in the line of Soviet advance, the Poles rose in armed rebellion. Before German strength could reassert itself, the insurgents had disrupted the German transport system and forced German troops to expend in Warsaw forces that they had been keeping to fight the Russians. Although their fighting strength was divided on two fronts, the German armies in the late summer of 1944 still represented a considerable force, amounting to 327 divisions and brigades, including 31 armoured divisions and 13 armoured brigades. Of these, 252 divisions and 15–20 brigades were actually engaged in combat in several theatres. Their losses by the late summer of 1944 had approached three million, and yet their fighting strength still was estimated at more than ten million.[4] On the two million men in combat on the Soviet front, however, the daily losses inflicted by the Russian offensive were telling: as the German Army Group Centre and forces defending the Ukraine pulled back through Polish territory – with Warsaw in the line of their retreat – they reported at least 916,860 dead, wounded or missing during the months of June, July and August 1944.[5]

Between 22 and 24 July the German 9th Army was ordered to stabilize the front in the area of Warsaw, to defend a line along the rivers Bug and Dęblin, and to hold Warsaw 'under all circumstances'. All Warsaw bridges were mined on 29 July. Flanking the 9th Army to the south was the North Ukrainian Army (German), to the north the 2nd German Army.

The city of Warsaw came within the area controlled by the 9th Army and according to German military sources, was 'under suspicion of rising'.[6] Nor was the city itself the only threat to the German command, for the Polish territories west of Warsaw, between the capital and the German border, were in such a ferment of anti-German activities initiated by AK and Armia Ludowa (Polish Communist) units that a German general, Eric von dem Bach-Zelewski was appointed Commander-in-Chief of special anti-partisan forces. He was directly responsible to SS Reichsführer Himmler, Chief of German Security and Police. (General von dem Bach-Zelewski, whose nickname among Germans was 'Reichsführer, I report!' had joined the Nazi Party in 1930 and had become a member of the SS. He played a major rele in the suppression of the Uprising and after the war was charged with a variety of war crimes. During his trial by a German court in 1961 he declared 'I am still an absolute Hitler man', and according to his own testimony it was he who smuggled poison to Hermann Goering during the Nuremberg trials to prevent his being hanged.)

The area outside the actual combat zone of Warsaw came under the jurisdiction of the German civilian authorities. Because the boundaries of these jurisdictional zones were changing constantly with the battle, and because General von dem Bach was not subordinate to the 9th Army in Warsaw's combat zone, but directly responsible to Himmler, the resulting shifts in authority hindered the German effort.[7] The German military commandant of Warsaw was responsible to the German armed forces, and not to Himmler, while air defence of the area was under the command of Luftflotte VI.[8] The Nazi Party and the German Governor of Polish territories, Hans Frank, also had separate networks of administration and were part of different chains of command. Confusion reigned.

On 27 July 1944 the Soviet front approached the towns Garwolin and Siedlce, 11 miles south-east and 25 miles east, respectively, from Warsaw, but German resistance stiffened.

On 1 August, the first day of the Uprising, the German 9th and 2nd Armies linked their positions. On that same day the units of the 1st Polish Army (Soviet) established two bridgeheads on the western shore of the Vistula: near Magnuszew, 11 miles south-east of Warsaw; and in the area between Deblin, 19 miles, and Pulawy, 23 miles south-east of Warsaw. Although some detachments on the eastern bank of the Vistula were now encircled by Soviet forces, they were fighting desperately and with some success. On 3 August in the area east of

Warsaw, they encircled and destroyed one Soviet armoured corps. The next day German fighter planes made 560 sorties.[9]

By the fifth day of Uprising, German command concentrated on the defence of the Vistula *between* Warsaw and the Soviet positions, placing there the following units: 1131 Infantry Brigade, the Hermann Goering Divisions, XXXIX Panzer Corps, IV SS Panzer Corps, 45 Infantry Division, and 19 Panzer Division.[10]

In fact, as early as February 1940, SS General Petrie had sent Himmler a study by the Research Department of the German Armed Forces' General Staff, entitled 'Polish Tactics in the Area of Preparation and Implementation of the Uprising against Russians in 1863: The Methods of Russian Defence', and Himmler had ordered its distribution to all SS and police battalion commanders in Polish territory, and to the Gestapo. The last paragraph of the report reflects the German administration's posture: 'As can be learned from the experience of 1863, the only . . . means [of coping with an uprising] is unmerciful severity applied at the first show of resistance. Any indecisive behaviour of the authorities [must] end in disaster.'[11]

In July 1942, to facilitate defence in case of armed rebellion, the Germans divided Warsaw into sectors on the principle that strong autonomous regions could defend themselves. A commander for all the sectors, who would be responsible for co-ordinating anti-insurgency efforts, was nominated on 31 July 1944. He was Air Force General Reiner Stahel, an officer who had won the personal confidence of Adolf Hitler.

Himmler was notified of the Uprising half an hour after its outbreak. A reliable source reports that he went immediately to Hitler and declared that from the historical perspective the Uprising was really a blessing. Five weeks later he was still saying, 'We shall solve this problem, and afterwards Warsaw as the capital and the pool of intelligentsia of that nation will be destroyed.'[12]

Hitler's reaction was in keeping with his behaviour at that time. He first of all demanded that all German units be withdrawn from Warsaw and the city bombed out of existence by the VI Air Fleet of the Luftwaffe. This was impossible because insurgents were blocking withdrawal, so he then left the solution to Himmler and Guderian with the same over-all directive – that Warsaw was to be completely destroyed.[13] General Guderian consequently had no qualms about ordering the use of heavy artillery in street fighting 'in order to destroy this city completely', while Himmler responded with an order definitely forbidding the taking of prisoners and explicitly ordering that every Warsaw citizen, including women and children, be killed: Warsaw was to be levelled to the ground, thereby creating an example for the rest of Europe.[14] This order was implemented for the first five or six days of fighting – until General von dem Bach-Zelewski arrived and, in spite of Hitler's confidence in him as 'one of the handiest men', modified the edict, officially forbidding the murder of civilians.

Hitler personally indicated on the map of Warsaw which areas should be attacked and directed that special mines be dropped by air to destroy even the gutted ruins of Warsaw houses.[15] He also ordered that all people not in German uniform in the areas around Warsaw were to be hunted down. It is to the credit of some officers of the Wehrmacht that they found these procedures offensive and against their consciences. General von Vormann, for example, gave the order that the manhunts around Warsaw be stopped, but it was rescinded by Hitler within twenty-four hours.[16]

Himmler arrived in Poznan, on Polish territory, on 2 August and dispatched reinforcements to Warsaw: a police unit and a reserve regiment under the command of Lieutenant-General of SS and Police, Heinz Reinefarth, and two additional units that were to become 'famous'. The first of these units was Storm Brigade RONA, composed of former Soviet citizens, and led by SS General Kaminski, Himmler's protégé. Though born in Poland, he had gone to Russia after the First World War and considered himself Russian. In the Soviet Army he had held the rank of captain. The behaviour of Kaminski's men during the Uprising outraged von dem Bach-Zelewski, who brought pressure to bear on a private contact of his in Hitler's entourage, Hitler's brother-in-law Fegelein. Thereafter Himmler renounced his protégé.[17] General von dem Bach-Zelewski withdrew Storm Brigade RONA on 27 August and on 28 August 1944 Kaminski was court-martialled by the German military court and sentenced to death. He and his whole staff were shot by a firing squad on 4 October 1944, though in order to prevent wild reprisals by his men the Germans announced that Kaminski had been shot by AK men.[18]

The other unit was SS Brigade Dirlewanger, named after its commander SS Senior Colonel Dirlewanger.[19] This unit was unusual in several respects: 50 per cent of its soldiers were common criminals (5 per cent had been charged only, not tried or convicted) and 40 per cent of its officers were volunteers from the Soviet Union, former Soviet citizens.[20] Dirlewanger believed that he was personally responsible only to Himmler. He apparently felt ostracized by General von dem Bach-Zelewski and other SS officers, who rejected him and his unit because of its composition and its barbarous fighting methods, and he attempted to terrorize his superior officers. To General von dem Bach-Zelewski, Dirlewanger threatened that he would kill Colonel Golz, the Chief of Staff,[21] while his unit of Soviet collaborators at one time threatened von dem Bach's headquarters with machine guns.[22] In spite of his unpopularity with his immediate superiors, Dirlewanger was rewarded by higher levels of authority: on 30 September 1944 he received the Knight's Cross of the Iron Cross for his action in Warsaw[23] where his unit fought till the end of September.[24]

Both units arrived in Warsaw on 4 August and on the fifth they launched an attack on Wola Sector. They went into battle with *élan* and by 6 August had murdered more than 40,000 civilians, including women, children, hospital staff, priests, and the wounded and sick in the Wola and Ochota Sectors.

At least one German source maintains that, whereas Hitler wanted to destroy Warsaw completely, von dem Bach considered his actions in Warsaw a military operation to put down the Uprising.[25] His task was arduous, given the poor quality of the troops initially at his disposal, but with these he had to make do until real soldiers of the Wehrmacht came to Warsaw with General von Lüttwitz (successor to von Vormann) on 21 September.[26]

According to Polish estimates, German forces in Warsaw proper when the Uprising began numbered approximately 40,000.[27] According to German estimates, which appear to be more reliable, they numbered between 15,000 and 16,000; by 20 August, when reinforcements came to Warsaw, the total was 21,250.[28] Initially, the ratio of SS and police to the Wehrmacht was 50–50. Later, when Dirlewanger's men were withdrawn, the ratio changed to 50–70.[29]

As reported, German soldiers here and there held a position surrounded by insurgents. German men suffered, too, as shown by the pocket diary of a German soldier, one Kurt Heller, from Munich, who was taken prisoner by Polish insurgents when one such stronghold fell to Poles after a hand-to-hand engagement.

1.8. This afternoon beginning of street fighting in Warsaw.
2.8. We are still surrounded.
3.8. Ulrich killed. SS Sergeant killed and many others.
4.8. Still cut off. No help from outside. We expect relief today or tomorrow. No food. Water very short.
5.8. Rudolf killed. Others with him. Can't keep going much longer. Luttewitz killed. Hollweg badly wounded.
6.8. At noon shelled by own artillery; no losses. Attempt at sortie failed; one killed, four badly wounded, of which one died. Fourteen of us now killed. Buried at eight this morning in the courtyard. Bad air from the dead; they smell.
8.8. Our men a hundred yards away, but opposition of bandits [insurgents] too strong.
9.8. Food very scarce.
11.8. All remainders [food] taken by police, even our cigarettes. Situation no good for resistance.
12.8. Hunger acute. Every day only a drop of soup and six cigarettes. Police have taken everything from us. [Evidently German police were among the defenders.] Was not even allowed to keep a bit of jam. When will this suffering stop?
13.8. Heavy fire from tanks on bandits' positions. Our tower often hit, but no losses. Tank brought food for five days. When shall we be freed?
16.8. Terrible hunger. At night we are terrified. When first stars appear, think of home, wife, and my boy who is buried

somewhere near Stettin. Can't take it all in. Now [I] am in same position.

17.8. Poles try to smoke us out by fire, throwing bottles of petrol. More men lost their nerve and committed suicide. Frightful smell from corpses in the street.

18.8. Completely cut off from outside world.

19.8. No hope of relief. Surrounded by Poles. Who will be next for the mass grave down in the courtyard?[30]

To protect themselves from the incursion of German tanks and self-propelled artillery, Poles built barricades across the streets, whenever possible, using any available material – pavement, furniture, abandoned vehicles.

Insurgents actually did not remain behind these barricades, which attracted fire from German tanks. They took positions on either side of the street just before or just beyond the barricades, where they waited to return with light weapons the fire of German infantry or to throw bottles filled with gasoline on to the tanks. Sometimes children volunteered to approach tanks with these bottles, and they had to be restrained from running into the open and throwing them from directly in front of the tanks.[31]

While the weapons most dreaded by the insurgents were mortars, which fell unannounced by sound, giving no opportunity for taking cover, air raids also ranked among the most terrifying experiences. Lieutenant Peaceful reported in his combat diary that German planes flew over his position hourly. On a single flight they dropped seventeen bombs on and near his position.[32]

Whole apartment blocks collapsed under the bombing, which was followed by attacks of German infantry over the ruins. Insurgents frequently were torn between their desire to assist civilians and fellow soldiers buried alive and the immediate necessity of stopping German infantry emerging from the dust, smoke, and heaps of fallen buildings. On one occasion in Old Town, a whole unit was buried alive in a basement. The medic with the unit did not lose his composure. He reported: 'I shouted, "Urinate in your own hankies, and try to breathe through them." There were six girls, and evidently they were too emotionally shocked to wet their hankies. I had some gauze; so I urinated on it and gave them pieces. There were several persons who simply choked to death because of the dust, but these girls and I survived. We were dug up, although we were spitting dirt for several days.'[33]

The Germans admitted that on many occasions the fighting was bitter in spite of their superiority in weapons and equipment. The battle for one apartment house wore on for twenty-four hours in a series of struggles from room to room before the German troops were able to wrest it from the Poles.[34] The battle for St John's Cathedral in Old Town Sector, already half-ruined by bombs, dragged on in see-saw fashion for two weeks. One insurgent remembered, 'The Germans were in the choir, and we were downstairs. We were defending our church! During the night Germans would withdraw from the choir [using ladders and rooftops]. We killed twenty-six of them inside the church, but more than twenty of us had fallen.'[35] The struggle was so intense and quarters so close that fire was exchanged at distances of four to eight feet and even at point-blank range.

On both sides there were examples of extraordinary self-control and endurance. Once, during an attack, several insurgents were caught in the open under heavy German machine-gun fire. They lay frozen, playing dead for several hours in front of the German position. Some of them survived by waiting till dark.[36] In one instance the body of a German soldier that had been lying in no-man's-land, twenty feet from the insurgents' position, for three days, 'came to life' and successfully escaped.

Caught in an open field with German tanks rolling toward him, one medical officer describes his experience: 'I covered myself with earth and potato plants to survive, expecting that a tank would roll over either my head or my legs.'[37] Had he run, he undoubtedly would have been mowed down by machine-gun fire from the tanks. Another insurgent spent three days lying on a tall bookshelf in a room temporarily occupied by Germans. On the fourth day the building changed hands, and the insurgent survived. These instances reflect the capacity of some human beings for self-control when survival is at stake. At the other extreme, one AK soldier shot at his own reflection in a large mirror.[38]

Confusion resulting from the irregular dispersion of Polish and German positions created some unusual situations. Because the insurgents were not uniformly dressed, Germans were able to send snipers dressed in civilian clothing into areas held by Poles. After finding a place that gave them protection as well as a good field of vision, snipers would hole up with food and ammunition and shoot at anyone within range. On one occasion more than ten persons were shot within a day at a single crossing-point (the only one within the sector and, therefore, much used). Soldier, messenger, child, woman – everything that moved was a target. Snipers were hunted constantly, but they were extremely difficult to locate. Two soldiers from my platoon discovered a sniper's nest, but several minutes too late – the sniper had escaped and merged with the population. He left behind several empty cartridges that were still warm and a piece of German-made bread.

The presence of snipers among the population created a mistrust of outsiders that often complicated relationships between insurgent units and the population. There was, for example, the elderly topographer who was making drawings for the AK Headquarters. He was arrested several times by young soldiers who were naturally suspicious of anyone wandering about and making drawings of their positions. The poor man finally accepted as a professional hazard the occasional 'roughing-up' he received by the insurgents before he could explain his identity.[39]

The shooting of small children and poisoning of food by men in the German forces was a brutal style of fighting unused, if not unknown, to a regular army in combat. This was 'irregular warfare' at its worst. On 13 August, the thirteenth day of the Uprising, in the Old Town Germans attacked a barricade with three tanks. Two withdrew promptly, but the third, smaller in size, approached the barricade rather speedily, and under the cover of German fire the crew jumped out and escaped. The insurgents, having discovered that the tank was intact and in good running order, dismantled part of the barricade and drove the tank into the insurgents' position, subsequently mending the barricade.

Taking a German tank intact created a sensation. The civilian population and hundreds of insurgents rushed with eagerness and curiosity to see it. Approximately forty minutes later the tank exploded with tremendous force in the midst of the crowd. How many people were killed is difficult to establish, but a modest estimate is more than 300. A friend of mine, Tadeusz Falba, who went to see the tank (after several unsuccessful attempts to persuade me to go with him) was also killed. A part of his body with personal documents was found on the fifth-storey roof of a nearby building. Afterwards it was established by AK engineers that the tank had been purposely rigged with high explosives.

By 15 August, after two weeks, the Germans had forced the Poles out of the main arteries. In one day alone, 300 German trucks crossed Warsaw from east to west, and 95 tanks moved from the west toward Praga. On 27 August, 87 tanks, 100 trucks and 28 artillery pieces, supported by infantry, rolled east.[40] Railway transport also operated undeterred. Twenty-one trains travelled east across Warsaw and three west on 6 September 1944.[41] The Poles were powerless to stop any of this traffic.

Nowhere during the Second World War was there a battle of such magnitude in which the enemies were so unevenly matched. Against Warsaw the Germans could send planes, self-propelled artillery, railway mortars, tanks, armoured trains, and even armoured light boats whenever the water was deep enough for their use. In addition, the German infantry was much better equipped than the Poles.

No army could sustain indefinitely the blood-letting to which the insurgents were subjected. In many units only twenty per cent of the original number remained by the third week.[42] In some instances, companies of more than a hundred were wiped out by bombing. Of 106 men, only 4–6 from Giewont Company survived one air raid.[43] These were heart-breaking, hour-by-hour occurrences. In Koszta Company there were 140 men and 22 women on 1 August 1944. By the end of the Uprising, at least sixty per cent had been killed or wounded. The number was higher, but it could not be established with precision, because incoming volunteers filled the gaps as they occurred (and company records were not always complete, when they did survive).[44]

German firepower was not solely responsible for these losses. The insurgents' ideological motivation gave them the fervour of Crusaders, and they often exposed themselves unnecessarily to danger – understandable enough after five years of Nazi terror. There are limits to oppression beyond which men will become reckless; judging by the mass participation in the Uprising, these limits had been reached.

After the initial attacks failed and the Germans took the offensive, the Poles were desperately pressed. Life was precious, but not as precious as the defence of one's own home. The physical proximity of those things the insurgents were fighting to protect – their loved ones, friends, and city – is also significant. As mentioned, they fought, literally, for their own homes. Given the superiority of German power and the intense motivation of the Poles, it is not surprising that losses were so high.

The German command and soldiers accurately perceived the situation of the insurgents. They knew from their agents of the lack of water and medications, that all animals, including horses, had been eaten, and that there was no food except barley.[45] The German pressure on the Poles increased daily. Gestapo agents among Poles were ordered to ascertain: (1) the location of AK Headquarters; (2) the state of morale of the population; (3) whether AK was co-operating with the Communists; and (4) whether the units of AK outside Warsaw were also going to rise.[46] It was probably through these agents that German artillery pinpointed AK Headquarters on 25 August.

If any special feature characterized German combat during the Uprising of Warsaw, it was atrocities of a kind and frequency usually associated with the ravages of Genghis Khan's hordes. The legal status of AK soldiers throughout the German occupation of Poland was unclear, and indeed continued to be so not only when the underground movement emerged into open battle with the Germans of Polish territory, but also during the first weeks of the Uprising. In almost all instances, the Germans would shoot on the spot any AK soldiers taken prisoner. Prior to the Uprising, in a dispatch to London on 24 July 1944, General Bor said that if the Germans did not stop the executions Poles would reciprocate by shooting German prisoners. The Polish Government-in-Exile relayed this message to the British Government on 27 July. Three days later the Polish Government Delegate in Warsaw and General Bor jointly informed the Polish Government in London by coded radio message that the Soviets also were arresting members of AK and representatives of the Polish Government-in-Exile.

In order to save AK soldiers taken prisoner from execution by Germans and Russians, General Bor and the Delegate requested that the Allied High Command give formal status to Armia Krajowa by accepting it into the ranks of Allied forces and announcing this to the

Germans, as was done with the French Underground. The British and Americans intended to make such an announcement, but only 'jointly', with the third Ally, the Soviet Union. The Soviet Union refused to agree to such a declaration. Thirty days after the Uprising had begun, Anthony Eden finally declared in the House of Commons that members of AK had the status of allies and were an integral part of the Polish Armed Forces-in-exile. The Americans simultaneously made a similar statement.

It should be noted that when, on 18 August, General von dem Bach-Zelewski approached the Poles with surrender proposals they included the promise of rights of combatants to the insurgents (which position the Germans reaffirmed on 9 September and 11 September). Thus, paradoxically, the enemy granted the Polish insurgents military status, but one of the Allies, the Soviet Union, refused to do so to the end. The acquisition of formal status did not, however, afford the soldiers much protection; at the end of September, for example, when about 150 insurgents emerged by mistake from the sewers into German-held territory in the Mokotow Sector, they were all executed on the spot.[47]

The civilian population was in the most unprotected and frightful position, for throughout the fighting they had no status of any kind in the eyes of the Germans. The atrocities inflicted on these noncombatants by German forces would not be believed, were it not for witnesses, photographs and the unimpeachable evidence of dead and defiled bodies.[48] Moreover, it was a premeditated campaign of brutality, carried out according to plan. To remind his subordinates of their duties, Himmler had sent a special message to General Geibel in Warsaw on 1 August 1944 ending with the words: 'Destroy tens of thousands.'[49] They did:

> In the morning, soldiers of the *Kampfgruppe Reinefarth* surrounded individual houses and blocks, as well as whole streets, shooting at windows and then entrances to houses, throwing hand-grenades, killing and wounding a great number of people. Those who were reluctant to leave their houses or flats – [the] sick, wounded, [and] old people, as well as those attempting to hide in cellars and attics – were killed on the spot. [Those who emerged] were driven into groups and robbed of all valuables, then either killed with hand-grenades or shot. The wounded were shot again. Houses were set on fire. [No mercy was shown;] men, women, and children were killed. . . . A great number of people who were hidden or wounded [and unable to move] were burned alive in their houses. Piles of corpses were everywhere – in the courtyards, in the entrances of houses, and in the streets. . . . They were shot in groups – parents in the presence of their children and children in the presence of their parents. [Bodies that] showed any sign of life [were shot again]. Petrol was poured on the piles of corpses, and they were set on fire.[50]

At one spot eighteen women, all the nurses of a field first-aid station, were shot.[51] A woman who had just delivered a baby in the field station was raped by eight SS men. She died there.[52] One man recalled, 'There was a woman in my group with a little baby no more than one year old. She was shot holding the child. She was asking the Gestapo men to kill it first, then her. They smiled and didn't say anything; then she was shot. The baby was crying for a long time after the execution. I heard it myself, and I have no doubt that Hitler's executioners also heard it.'[53]

In the hospital at number 26 Plocka Street, Germans, Ukrainians, and a group in German uniforms with 'Georgian' lettered on armbands, went to the study of the chief doctor, and shot him and another doctor. The sick were ordered to vacate the building and then were executed.[54] German sources do not deny this.

The following is General von dem Bach-Zelewski's own description of what he saw upon his arrival in Warsaw: 'Already on the main road leading from Warsaw toward the west near a cemetery I realized that unbelievable confusion was reigning. Wild masses of policemen and soldiers were shooting civilians. I saw the heap of dead bodies splashed with gasoline and set afire. Toward that fire a woman with a small child in her arms was being led. I turned her about and asked her, "What is going on here?" [From her escort] I received the answer that Hitler's order, which did not allow for taking prisoners, but called for the total destruction of Warsaw, was being carried out.

'I went alongside the battle-line, and then called all the officers, who authenticated the existence of such an order. On my own responsibility, I nullified it immediately.'[55]

The General arrived on 5 August, but by this time, according to German sources, in one sector alone 15,000 civilians had been murdered (40,000 according to Polish sources). Von dem Bach-Zelewski gave an order to stop executions, at least of women and children, at 5.30 p.m. on 5 August; but males were still being shot without ascertaining whether or not they were insurgents[56] until the end of September.

Scholarly German sources admit that even in areas where fighting had actually stopped [57] civilians were still being murdered *en masse* and at random. One German authority tries to deny that the German Army was responsible for such actions, maintaining that 'the Wehrmacht, with the exception of Hermann Goering's Division and regiment 608, which in some instances executed AK insurgents because of their unclear and controversial status, did not murder [the] civilian population during the Uprising of Warsaw'.[58]

On 2 September however, Father Rostworowski was to be seen walking through the corridors of the insurgents' hospital on Dluga Street with tears in his eyes. He was distributing Holy Communion to wounded insurgents lying on the floors, who had become German prisoners just the day before. Behind the priest walked as SS officer, killing each wounded man with a pistol shot. At the end of the last corridor the officer turned to him and said, 'I would shoot you also, but I have run out of bullets.'[59] An SS officer whose name was Kotchke commanded the unit that took this area. His first question had been 'Why isn't this hospital burned?' The priest explained to him there were wounded in it, and within ten minutes Kotchke had given the order to execute all the remaining wounded. Father Rostworowski tried to carry as many as he could out into the street while the executions were under way inside the building. He afterwards recalled: 'Some wounded started to crawl out in order to avoid execution, and I helped two of them, but Ukrainians in German uniforms grabbed these men from me and shot them. All I could hear were shots all around. They executed these wounded by shooting them in the head, and then they poured gasoline over the bodies and burned them.'[60]

On one of the streets held by Germans lived the former President of Poland, Professor Wojciechowski, and his half-blind wife, both by then elderly. A German major, who knew with whom he was dealing, talked with the former President knowledgeably about antique furniture and the paintings still hanging on the walls of the villa. After an elegant discourse, he politely saluted the 'Herr Professor,' and left the building, locked both of these human beings inside, and ordered that the home be burned.[61] Somehow, both survived.

Poles, too, were guilty of excesses. A German source reports that on 1 August, the first day of the Uprising, a company of former Soviet citizens in German uniforms serving under German command were captured and slaughtered on Koszykowa Street by insurgents. One man escaped.[62] Another reputable German source states that 'in numerous cases' Polish civilians killed men in German uniforms who were priests and doctors.[63] The Germans charged insurgents with: (a) fighting without proper combat insignia; (b) wearing German uniforms with the successful intention of deceiving; (c) shooting and hanging German prisoners; (d) robbing and murdering the German civilian population; and (e) forcing German prisoners to build barricades under crossfire and using them as shields (against bullets).[64]

One German source observed with justice that the bitterness of Polish fighting against all German forces increased sharply after the massacres of Polish civilians in Wola Sector to which the Poles responded with a mass execution of German prisoners. This incident has never been mentioned in any written Polish source. The medical officer of an AK battalion revealed in an interview: 'In the Haberbush brewery we held 30–40 prisoners. We knew that Germans were shooting captured insurgents, and Captain Pine was so keyed up and battle-strained that, on hearing of this, he gave an order that all our German prisoners, including the wounded, be shot in revenge for what had happened in

Wola. One SS officer who had murdered Jews in the Ghetto offered a suitcase full of jewellery for his life. It was not accepted.'[65]

On 5 August, Kaminski's SS men raped nurses and cancer-stricken women in the X-ray Institute of Marie Curie and according to the German sources, after 5 August, 'Poles started to shoot captured SS and police on principle. Only the members of the Wehrmacht [soldiers of the German armed forces] were kept alive in small compounds.'[66] From that time it was a policy of the insurgents to shoot all captured non-wounded German police, military police, SS, SD, SA, railway police, and Ukrainians in German uniform. Even so, when duly condemned SS men were to be executed, it was often difficult to find volunteers to perform the executions. A competent German source charges that there was also indiscriminate killing on the Polish side from 1 August to 3 August.[67] However, with the exception of the shootings at the Haberbush brewery, this author found no instance in which German wounded (even SS) were shot without court proceedings, nor German women raped, nor German children murdered.

General Bor reported that, when Warsaw capitulated, about a thousand German prisoners of war in uniforms and many more German civilians who had been arrested by Poles during the Uprising were freed and returned to the victors.[68] Moreover, while Poles and Germans alike were capable of killing indiscriminately in the heat of battle and its accompanying stresses, the Germans were also killing noncombatants as a matter of policy. At the beginning of the Uprising the Polish civilian authority issued an order explicitly forbidding unauthorized arrests and the mistreatment of prisoners. German policy was the reverse – their soldiers were ordered and encouraged to destroy all Poles and did so with impunity even after this order was rescinded by von dem Bach (5 August).

Polish doctors were impartial in their humanitarian efforts, basing the degree of care and treatment given to the wounded only on gravity of wounds. Occasionally, the doctors' altruistic behaviour led to dissatisfaction among some Poles, who felt that under the circumstances Germans should not be given equal treatment. I described one incident in my battle report. It occurred during the struggle for the Old Town Sector:

> One day, as I was running past the ruins of a house, I heard human groans coming from the cellar. I thought it must be inhabitants of the house buried underneath the rubble – a normal occurrence in the Old Town. It turned out to be a group of uniformed German prisoners. How many of them were in that cellar I cannot remember . . . perhaps thirty. An AK military police corporal armed with a pistol was guarding them. Approximately one-third of the prisoners were wounded; two were unconscious and groaning with pain. The corporal acted with restraint, having told the prisoners that he could not go for a doctor since he had orders to

guard them. He could not help the two groaning men. One of the wounded begged for water. I gave the corporal my canteen and went outside. Within a few minutes I came upon a woman of about forty, who was carrying a haversack [with] a Red Cross sign. I asked her where I could find the nearest doctor. She told me she was a doctor. . . . I described to her the state of the two German prisoners and asked if she could help. She said that she would, gladly. Walking back along the street we met Captain Pine, at that time my commanding officer. I gave him a brief report of what I was doing, and why I was at that particular spot at that particular time.

After hearing me out, Pine turned angrily to the woman doctor and shouted, 'What do you think you're doing, wasting your last bandages and medicine on Germans while my men are dying from lack of these things?'

To which the doctor replied, 'Captain, to me there are no uniforms or national flags. To me there are only wounded men.' And she pushed him aside. I escorted her to the cellar with the German prisoners and . . . rushed back to catch up with Pine. The Captain never mentioned the subject again.[69]

When discussing atrocities committed by German forces in Warsaw during the Uprising, it is both important and difficult to ascertain whether they were actually committed by Germans or by other nationalities serving under their command. The two brigades commanded by SS officers Kaminski and Dirlewanger were responsible for most of the atrocities, and the composition of their troops has already been discussed, but there were other ethnic groups serving in the German armed forces.

Available data reveal that until 14 August (the first two weeks of the Uprising) the SS, police, and non-German units of the German Army predominantly were active in Warsaw. This would suggest that, during that time at least, one-fourth to one-third of soldiers in German uniform who were slaughtering noncombatant Poles were not Germans.

It is not widely acknowledged that hundreds of thousands of men other than Germans fought under German command against the Allies in the Second World War. Many of them proudly wore the uniforms of their own countries: Bulgaria, Italy, Spain, Romania, Hungary, Finland and others. Some fought for their image of a future Europe, and some fought against the possibility of Soviet domination of their countries. In total they provided fifty-five divisions under German command.

By 1944, of the thirty-nine divisions of SS troops in the German Army, seventeen were composed of volunteers who were not German. There were no Polish volunteers in German military uniform, but there were Yugoslavs, Moslems (classified as such by Germans), Italians, Dutch, Hungarians, Flemish-Belgians, Walloon-Belgians, French, Ukrainians, Latvians, Estonians, Albanians and Russians.

The term 'Russian' is, of course, not a precise one, since the Soviet Union includes approximately 100 separate ethnic groups. The total number of Soviet citizens serving with German forces was about 800,000. Even in the fall of 1944, at the end of the war, there were 2,500–3,000 applications *daily* to join *the Russian Liberation Army* under German command.[70]

It is not well known that besides the Russian Army of Liberation (ROA), commanded by former Red Army General Andre A. Vlasov, there was another organization of Soviet citizens who served under German command. This was the 15th Cossack Cavalry Corps of the German armed forces. It numbered upwards of 70,000 men in three divisions. It could not be determined if the Cossack cavalry groups in Warsaw were part of this Corps.

During the Second World War numerous non-German groups from the Soviet Union volunteered to serve in German uniform under German command. Among them, numerically prominent were Armenians, Azerbaijanis, Cossacks, Georgians, Mountain and Northern Caucasians, Tartars, Turkomens, Ukrainians and Byelorussians. Some of these groups served with the German Army in the battle of the Warsaw Uprising.[71]

Poles have bitterly accused the Ukrainians, especially, of murdering civilians and insurgents during the Uprising, but perhaps not all these accusations are well founded. It is true that two companies of Ukrainians engaged Warsaw insurgents near the Vistula, while there were others who were members of the German police already in Warsaw prior to the Uprising. Others arrived in the early days of the fighting with German police from Poznan and from Lublin. It is reported, too, that the execution squads commanded by SS Captain Spilke were 'predominantly Ukrainian'.[72] But it is also true that for years the Poles in Warsaw had regarded Ukrainians as German police henchmen and oppressors, and that in consequence all non-German soldiers in German uniforms were apt to be identified as Ukrainians. It is possible that other nationality groups from the Soviet Union who were not Ukrainian were also committing massacres. Kaminski's brigade and Dirlewanger's brigade, the units that were responsible for most of the atrocities in the initial weeks of Uprising, were *not* composed of Ukrainians.

To prevent the possibility of AK units outside the city coming to the assistance of the insurgents, the command of the 9th German Army placed the 2nd Hungarian Reserve Corps as a wedge between the forests to the south of Warsaw and the city. By 1944, however, having sustained losses of over 600,000, Hungary seemed ready to make a separate peace with the Soviet Union, and unrest and dissatisfaction were evident among Hungarian units on the Soviet front. In this combat report of 23 August, General Monter wrote, 'Hungarian units placed south of Mokotow display great cordiality towards the Polish population; they also warn us about Germans and do not interfere with our actions.'[73] A partisan commander, while marching toward Warsaw with his unit, was accosted by Hungarians. He was not detained, but given coffee and the assurance that no shot would be fired toward Poles.

The 2nd Hungarian Corps commander until 21 August 1944 was General Vattay. General Bela Lengyell succeeded him. Representatives of General Monter negotiated with the latter for assistance, proposing: (1) that a Hungarian regiment join the insurgents; and (2) that artillery equipment be given them. The Poles also proposed the formation of a Polish–Hungarian alliance and that the 2nd Hungarian Reserve Corps become the Hungarian Legion, joining the Polish struggle against the German Army. Mindful of the possible consequences to the men under his command, General Lengyell asked, 'What will happen to us if the Soviets come to Warsaw?'[74] General Monter had instructed his representatives to 'promise and guarantee anything to induce them to fight'.[75]

The Hungarian general was too sensible to accept any 'guarantees', but he was accommodating. He asked his government for instructions and was told not to join the Poles, but at the same time not to fight against them.

The German command was uneasy about Polish–Hungarian relations, but attempted to take advantage of them. The combat log of the 9th German Army for 27 August noted, 'It seems that the insurgents received some assistance from the south. There is well-founded suspicion that Hungarian units . . . holding the front alongside the Vistula south of Warsaw are not preventing such assistance. . . .'[76] On 27 August the 9th German Army command instructed General Lengyell to contact formally the commander of AK and encourage him to stop fighting, reaffirming the insurgents' status as combatants.[77] However, three days earlier, on 24 August, the German command forbade the 2nd Hungarian Corps commander direct contact with Budapest – which order the Hungarians apparently circumvented by sending their own planes back and forth to Hungary.

In the meantime, sector after sector of the insurgent defences were being crushed under the weight of armour and bombs. Not without German losses: in clearing the avenue that led to *one* public square and seizing it 400 Germans were killed or severely wounded.[78] By 21 August, Germany had thrown over 21,000 troops into the fight for Warsaw and in approximately 50 days of fighting had lost 9000 men.[79]

CHAPTER FOUR

The Red Army

RUSSIA and Poland have been locked in a series of clashes for nearly 500 years, but because Russia has been the stronger for the past 300 years, and because during this time mass destruction has developed into a science, Poland has been the victim of the most recent and deepest wounds. The repeated partitions of Poland and the ruthless suppression of past Polish uprisings have been remembered in Polish lore. That the Russian Government was now Communist changed nothing for the Poles: Russia was still imperialist if only under a different flag. Each country used past historical experiences as evidence of the other's ill will.

In the Polish view the 1919–20 Polish–Soviet war was an attempt to regain the eastern territories to which, in their judgement, Poles had historical and ethnic claims. The Soviet leadership, on the other hand, claimed that in collaborating with the Nazis in the dismemberment of Poland in 1939 they had only 'occupied non-Polish territories inhabited by Byelorussians and Ukrainians'.[1] After sixteen days of bitter fighting between Germans and Poles in September 1939, the Soviet Union entered Poland from the east, and Polish forces were crushed between the two greatest military powers of that time. Thereafter, while France, England and the Polish Forces-in-Exile fought the German armies, the Soviet Government continued to assist the Nazis with millions of tons of grain, cotton, petroleum products, timber, manganese and chromium, and with copper bought from the United States, and allowed the German Navy to use Soviet and Baltic ports.

Another bitter experience for Poles was the mass deportation of Polish citizens from eastern Polish territories. Between 1,200,000 and 1,480,000[2] people were forcibly removed from their homes at four hours' notice and transported to the northern and eastern territories of the Soviet Union.[3] Another 200,000 Polish prisoners of war, who had fought against the Germans, were captured and detained by the Soviet Union, and this tragedy culminated in the disappearance of 15,000 of these soldiers, including some forty-two per cent of the Polish Officers' Corps; among them 800 Doctors of Medicine. In 1943 the bodies of approximately 4400 of these men were found in the Katyn forest, where they had been murdered, but no trace has been found of the other 11,000 missing men, whose names are known.[4]

By April 1943, after changing sides under the German attack, the Soviet Government had established in Russia a group of Polish Communists and intellectuals with strong Leftist leanings. It was called the Union of Polish Patriots and was introduced as the body that really represented the Polish people. Its president was a woman called Wanda Wasilewska, whose Polish origins were given as evidence of her loyalty to Poland. Facts not mentioned by the Soviet press were that she held the rank of colonel in the Red Army, was a member of the Presidium of the Soviet Union, and the wife of Soviet Vice-Commissar for Foreign Affairs Korneychuk.

The next step of the Soviet Union was to attack the legality of the Polish Government-in-Exile, and here Soviet propaganda was echoed by the Communist press in England and in the United States, who impugned the legality of the Polish Government by questioning the existence of democratic values among exiled Poles.

Then, after the entry of the Soviet armies into Poland early in 1944, arrests of members of Armia Krajowa by Soviet security agencies became routine procedure, not only on the Polish territories ceded to them by Roosevelt and Churchill in Tehran, but *also on non-disputed Polish territory, where the AK was operating against Germans and to which Soviets could claim no legal, historic, political, ethnic, or moral rights whatsoever.* It is now common knowledge that, on this unquestionably Polish territory, Soviet political agents and partisan groups established contacts with the Polish Communist Party, and together with Polish Communists began penetrating Polish civilian and military circles loyal to the Polish Government-in-Exile, in order to undermine that government by all possible means. They created a pro-Communist 'National Council', which collaborated with the Soviet security agencies and the Union of Polish Patriots and whose name was designed to confuse the public, since the legal Polish underground parliament was called the 'Council of National Unity'. The message reiterated to the Polish community by Soviet and Polish Communist propaganda in the summer of 1944 was that neither the AK nor the Polish Government-in-Exile had any genuine wish to fight the Germans!

To describe the activities of the Red Army in Poland *vis-à-vis* the Warsaw Uprising in 1944, it is only fair to rely on primary Soviet sources, but although I approached both the Archives of the USSR Ministry of National Defence, Moscow, and the Institute of Military History, Ministry of National Defence, Moscow, my letters remained unanswered and it was impossible to secure access to original Soviet Army documents.[5]

According to the official Soviet *History of the Great War of the Soviet Union 1941–45*, the Supreme Headquarters of the Soviet Army issued operational orders for the First Byelorussian Front on 7 July 1944.

Under the command of Marshal Konstantin Rokossovsky it was to move in from the north and south to encircle German forces in the fortress of Brzesc and then to push the attack 'in the direction of Warsaw to reach a broad front to the Vistula River'.[6] (There are some indications that consideration of Warsaw by the Soviet command took place earlier, in May 1944, in the Plan Bagration, but the author was unable to secure proof.)

The objective was the liberation of eastern Poland. Nine Soviet armies and one Polish army formed in the USSR were to co-operate in the operation, in addition to one armoured army, two armoured corps, 'one mechanized corps, three cavalry corps, and two Air Force armies'.[7]

After breaking German defences, the Soviet command intended to introduce a highly mobile cavalry corps and its armoured units to push west toward the Polish towns of Siedlce and Lublin. It was expected that with effective planning and mobility the Soviet forces would achieve a preponderance of power over the Germans.[8] Numerically, Soviet forces had three times more soldiers and five times more artillery and tanks. The 6th Soviet Air Army consisted of 1,465 combat planes. The left wing of the First Byelorussian Front alone (not including supporting services and second echelons) had in its combat line 1,750 tanks and self-propelled artillery, 7,600 artillery and mortars, and 416,000 soldiers.[9] The total strength of the First Byelorussian Front was roughly about one and a half million soldiers.

This plan aimed at German forces in the heart of Poland went into action on 18 July and was successful from the outset. Within two days, the attacking forces of the left wing of the First Byelorussian Front reached and crossed the Bug river at three points; it was then, according to the Soviet Government, that they 'entered Polish frontiers', although the Polish frontiers of 1939 had been crossed several months before, and according to the principles of the Allies' territorial integrity as expressed in the Atlantic Charter the Soviet armies were *already several hundred miles deep into Poland*. It was not known either to Polish society as a whole or to the commanders of Armia Krajowa that the United States and Great Britain had given Polish eastern territories to Stalin during the Tehran Conference, and their ignorance of this arrangement had its consequences (to be discussed later).

The First Byelorussian Front took Lublin on 23 July and reached the Vistula river in the region of Deblin two days later. On 27 July 1944 the First Polish Army, commanded by Major-General Zygmunt Berling, came into this region. While the Soviet 2nd Armoured Army proceeded to move in the direction of Warsaw, on 28 July, two other Soviet armies took the fortress of Brzesc by direct attack. In view of these successes, on 28 July 1944 the Soviet Supreme Headquarters sent Order Number 26162, a new assignment for the First Byelorussian Front, to 'attack in the general direction of Warsaw, and between 5 and 8 August at the latest seize Praga [the part of Warsaw on the east side of the Vistula] and secure the bridgeheads on the western shore of the Narew river in the region of Pultusk-Serock. With the left wing secure a bridgehead on the western shore of the Vistula in the Deblin – Zwolen – Solec region.'[10] Orders with strategic objectives were also dispatched to the three other fronts operating on Polish territories, and 'the forces of all four fronts immediately started to pursue these objectives'.[11]

Soviet writers maintain[12] that Warsaw was not the objective of the Soviet Army. This reasoning implies that the objective of the Soviet Army was to take Praga (the suburb of Warsaw east of the Vistula) only. Since this decision to stop before the eastern defences of Warsaw was made several days *before the Uprising*, it could be argued that Warsaw was not the object of the Soviet push *if it were not for the fact that the official Soviet history cites only part of this order*.

The second part of this order was brought to light five years after publication of the *History*[13] – in 1967, in a scholarly journal published, of all unlikely places, in Communist Poland. Here it is:

> The established bridgeheads [are] to be used *to attack in the direction of the north-west*, to overthrow the enemy defences alongside [the rivers] Narew and Vistula . . . to secure the forcing of the Narew by the left wing of the Second Byelorussian Front and . . . [of the] Vistula with the armies of the central group of your [First Byelorussian] Front. Subsequently, consider attacking in the direction of Torun and Lodz.[14]

The author of the article in the Polish journal, K. Sobczak, comments, 'This directive encompasses the . . . seizure of Warsaw by the . . . First Byelorussian Front.'[15] This is correct, since the order specifically advises the 'central group' of the First Byelorussian Front to force the Vistula river in the region of Warsaw and to proceed toward the cities Torun (fifty-six miles north-west of Warsaw) and Lodz (thirty-one miles south-west of Warsaw). This assertion of Sobczak's, based on the fully cited Soviet document which he uncovered,[16] was confirmed in 1970 by Soviet Marshal Alexander Vasilevski, who during the Soviet Summer Offensive of 1944 was Soviet Chief of Staff and member of the Soviet Supreme Command.[17]

Sobczak adds: 'Although the military specialists of the Supreme Headquarters of AK acted without consulting [the Soviet forces] and [based] their operational appraisals of the situation on what their eyes could register . . . they read Soviet intentions correctly.'[18] The intention of the Soviet armed forces to take Warsaw in the beginning of August was no secret. On 2 August *Pravda* exploded: 'On to Warsaw! In an offensive there is a moment when military operation reaches its culminating-point and, having acquired its necessary pressure and impetus, goes ahead [of its own momentum]. At such a time, when full strength of the offensive comes into motion, it starts advancing at great strides; then no power can stop its victorious forward march.'[19]

A political officer from a Polish division that moved westward through Poland at that time confirmed this when I asked him about instructions from his superiors regarding political attitudes: 'Yes, indeed. We were going to liberate Warsaw. We hadn't the slightest doubt that we were going to Warsaw. . . . Everything in our forces was geared for [liberating] Warsaw. . . . All of us thought that Warsaw was the ultimate goal . . . the immediate target was Warsaw.'[20]

General Zygmunt Berling, who at present resides in Poland, was Commander of the First Polish Army. In response to my letter asking him the same questions, he replied courteously in a letter that he was unable to answer the questions for reasons beyond his own volition. He also stated that 'the time has not come to talk about it in depth'.[21]

It seems reasonably clear that Warsaw was the target of the First Byelorussian Front. However, it is also true that the Soviet units racing directly towards Warsaw were compelled to stop by German forces. For, according to Soviet sources, the Soviet 2nd Tank Army was first stopped by German units in the area of Kolbiel, and then crippled by lack of fuel and ammunition. They made progress towards Warsaw[22] on 29 July, but on the afternoon of 30 July the Germans counter-attacked[23] with 450 tanks. On 1 August at 4.10 a.m. the Soviet commander of the Second Armoured Army issued an order that his units should assume a defensive position outside Praga by 12.00 noon the same day,[24] *an hour before the first shots of the Uprising were exchanged.*

German forces attacked again on 3 August with five divisions. In order to avoid encirclement, the Soviet 3rd Armoured Corps had to withdraw. By 5 August it had again taken up a defensive position.

During the ten days of its offensive the Soviet Second Armoured Army covered approximately 220 miles, lost 500 tanks, and was extremely low on fuel and ammunition. This apparently lowered its combat effectiveness.[25] IVOVSS maintains 'that at the end of July, even before the beginning of the Warsaw Uprising, the tempo of the offensive had greatly slowed. The German Supreme Command had by this time thrown very strong reserves against the main sectors of our advance. German resistance was strong and tenacious.'[26] The artillery was also 'lagging behind';[27] the Soviet Air Force was in the process of moving its fields forward and was not as active as the German Air Force. The Russians admit that at the beginning of August their superiority in the air was temporarily lost. The official Soviet position has been that 'Soviet troops could not proceed with the same high speed of advance, and therefore were unable to give immediate help to the insurgents'.[28]

At the end of August likewise, when the Soviet armies reached the Vistula, the enemy's defences stiffened. This, and the lengthening of the Red Army lines of communication, in addition to tiredness of soldiers [who had been] attacking for the past two months, dictated the need to suspend the offensive. On 29 August all four fronts received orders from Supreme Headquarters to assume defensive positions from Jelgava to Jozefow.[29]

In fact, on 8 August the Soviet commanders of the First and Second Byelorussian Fronts had recovered their offensive spirits; they submitted to the Soviet Supreme Command an operational report with a plan for liberating Warsaw. This document, written in the technical language of staff officers, submits in five points the requirements, time-table, and procedures for 'seizure of Warsaw', setting the date of 25 August 1944 for commencement of the operation.[30] In the light of these objectives, commanders of the Second and First Byelorussian Fronts issued operational orders between 6 and 8 August, regrouping their units on the assumption that the Soviet Supreme command would allow them to proceed with the seizure of Warsaw by 25 August. But permission to proceed was not forthcoming.

Five weeks had elapsed since the beginning of the Uprising when Marshal Konstantin Rokossovsky, Commander of the First Byelorussian Front, decided on 'a local operation' to reach Praga and to push beyond the river the southern part of the German bridgehead still on the eastern side of the Vistula. Two Soviet armies – the 47th and 70th – were to be used. As a result of this operation, some units did reach the AK insurgents on their shore, but they were not Soviet units, they were Poles from the First Polish Army, under the command of General Zygmunt Berling. Their plight will be discussed in Chapter 10.

It is this author's contention that it was during the second week of August 1944 that Stalin decided to delay the seizure of Warsaw. The date on which his intentions toward Warsaw were decisively revealed was 13 August, when the Soviet News Agency TASS issued a communication condemning the Uprising.[31]

It is true that, during the first week of the Uprising, Soviet forces earnestly attempted to reach the suburb Praga; that the ultimate objective was not only Warsaw, but also cities beyond it to the west; and that the German divisions under the command of Field-Marshal Walter Model disrupted these plans. For all that, an expert, Mr Andrzej Pomian, has this answer: 'It is not of paramount importance whether the Russians could take Warsaw or not. What is of paramount importance is that [after 8 August] they did not try.'[32] (General Berling's attempts were made by Poles.)

The insurgents in Warsaw surrendered on 2 October, fifty-five days from the time the commanders of the First and Second Byelorussian Fronts had submitted to the Soviet command their plans to seize Warsaw. Had Stalin wanted the liberation of Warsaw by the Soviet Army in conjunction with the AK Uprising, he could have indicated publicly by 9 or 10 August that his armies would attempt this plan, or he could have given approval to Rokossovsky's and Zhukov's project.

On 26 August 1944 a British (Russian-born) journalist, Alexander

Werth, asked Marshal Rokossovsky about his role in the Uprising of Warsaw, which was still in progress, and in particular about the broadcast from Moscow calling for the AK to rise. Rokossovsky responded, 'That was routine stuff.' It was his judgment that the Uprising of Warsaw was a mistake, because the insurgents started it without consulting the Red Army. He explained that the Uprising in Warsaw should have started at the time when the Red Army was actually entering Warsaw and emphasized that the Poles rose before this had occurred. Then he made this important point: 'I will admit that some Soviet correspondents were much too optimistic on August 1. We were pushed back. We could not have taken Warsaw before the middle of August, even in the best of circumstances.'[33]

It is significant that Marshal Rokossovsky referred only to the impossibility of taking Warsaw before the middle of August. Though he challenged Werth, 'Do you think that we would not have taken Warsaw if we would have been able to?'[34] He undoubtedly had considered it possible after the middle of August, or he would not have offered to do so in his operational plans submitted to the Soviet Supreme Command on 8 August 1944.

In his memoirs the Marshal reverted to his theme 'that Bor-Komorowski had never even tried to establish direct contact with Front HQ, although the General Staff had provided him with the code',[35] or not until the AK leadership had contacted him via London on 17 September (see Tables 1 and 2, Chapter 11); in fact, there had been many direct contacts with Rokossovsky before that date. There was also an interesting new revelation in his story. After 14 September, when the First Polish Army reached the Vistula river and took up a position in Praga on the shore opposite Warsaw, Rokossovsky spoke with Stalin over the telephone and reported the situation: 'Stalin asked whether the Front was able immediately to launch an operation to liberate Warsaw . . . I replied in the negative, and he directed us to give all possible help to the insurgents to ease their plight.'[36]

In 1955 Marshal Rokossovsky reiterated this information to a French correspondent, but with one addition: that he had had to throw his reserves into combat to the north of Warsaw, because it was in that area that the outcome of the battle would be decided. He also stated that the east side of the Vistula was fortified. As in his interview with Werth in 1944 he did not mention his own proposal of 8 August 1944 to take Warsaw, but he now asserted that before the insurrection he had sent a message to Bor-Komorowski that any initiative on Bor's part 'would be untimely, since the concentration of our troops would not be sufficient to engage in a decisive action'. He claimed to know that this telegram had reached Bor, and that he had never received a reply.[37] Yet, although Rokossovsky dismissed as 'routine' the Radio Moscow broadcasts on 29 and 30 July to Warsaw, calling for a general uprising, the Soviet Government must have had a purpose in making them, and it seems unlikely that Rokossovsky would send such a message to Bor, contradicting the policies of his own government.

In 1954 *The New Leader* published an article by Boris Olshansky, a former major in the Soviet Army who had served on the staff of Marshal Rokossovsky's First Byelorussian Front, and who had defected to the West in 1949. Olshansky maintained that Rokossovsky's adjutant had told him Rokossovsky received a radiogram directly from Stalin ordering him to leave the Warsaw people to their own fate and that later a blunt written order came: 'Stop the offensive! Let the Poles feel their dependence on the actions of our Army!' The original of this order was said to have carried a notation by Stalin himself and was in Rokossovsky's personal possession. To the same adjutant Rokossovsky supposedly once made the statement, 'It was not advantageous for us to hurry on to Warsaw.'[38]

Major Olshansky's information is hearsay, of course, and was written ten years after the event. However, it is buttressed by evidence from another source from outside the Soviet Union. A former officer of the Soviet forces, Nikolai Ivanovitch Syerov, was serving near Warsaw in September 1944 as a captain in the Soviet Army and a war correspondent for the soldiers' paper published by the 60th Division. On or about 15 September, in his capacity of war correspondent, he asked the political officer of the division, Colonel Pagaryelov, why they were not moving forward and what was going on in Warsaw; the Colonel responded that, according to instructions given him by his superior, General K. F. Telegin, there was an uprising in Warsaw, but that it was an uprising of nationalists and bourgeoisie under the auspices of the Polish Government-in-Exile, and it was not in the interest of the Soviet Union to support this uprising.[39]

Three high-ranking Soviet officers – Zhukov, Chuikov, and Shtemenko – have also written on the subject of the First Byelorussian Front and the Uprising. While Chuikov charges Rokossovsky with being too slow in exploiting the 8th Guard's activities on the Vistula bridgehead and with assessing German intentions poorly, so that the Soviet forces were dispersed and the seizure of Warsaw delayed by three months,[40] General Shtemenko, Chief of Operational Division of General Staff, maintains that Rokossovsky's plan of 8 August to liberate Warsaw was 'immediately realized' (though it was not scheduled until the twenty-fifth), but that it was unsuccessful because of German defences. He then states (without citing sources) that 'it was necessary to take a defensive position in order to plan preparation for new aggressive operations'.[41] Which plan must have miscarried, since *the Red Army stayed in its positions east of Warsaw for five and a half months*, and did not enter Warsaw until 17 January 1945, when it was occupied only by rather meagre German forces (several hundred).

At the beginning of September, in either the fifth or sixth week of the Uprising, Shtemenko had a briefing with Stalin, at which he and

General A. R. Antonov, another member of the Soviet General Staff, were asked by Stalin whether the uprising of Warsaw was 'helpful' to the Soviet Army, which both men apparently denied. According to Shtemenko, Stalin was 'thinking aloud' as he walked around the room, and reiterated that the Warsaw Uprising was undertaken without the knowledge of the Soviet command, and therefore the responsibility for it lay with the Polish Government-in-Exile. He also wanted to establish an impartial commission to ascertain on whose orders the Uprising in Warsaw started, and whose fault it was that he was not informed in advance. Had the Soviet Supreme Command been asked, they would have strongly advised against it because Soviet forces were not prepared to take Warsaw, whereas German forces in the area had access to their own armoured reserves. Shtemenko continues, 'Looking at us all, the Supreme Commander continued loudly, "Nobody can charge the Soviet Government with not giving enough assistance to the Polish Government and Warsaw. The most effective form of assistance is the Soviet forces' active military operation against the Germans in Poland, and they have made it possible for one-fourth of Poland to be free. All this is due to the efforts of the Soviet forces and to them alone, they are bleeding for the liberation of Poland." '[42]

Stalin went on to criticize the British Government for not informing him about the imminence of the Uprising saying that, had he been informed, the problem of Warsaw would have taken a different turn: 'Why didn't the British Government consider it proper to tell the Soviet Government? Wasn't this another instance of the attitude taken in 1943, when the Polish Government-in-Exile, without any reaction from the British Government, made its hostile and false statement about Katyn?'[43]

General Shtemenko recalls that on 13 September he reported to Stalin concerning the situation of the First Byelorussian Front, after the First Polish Army reached Praga. Stalin gave an immediate order to do whatever possible, especially to airdrop supplies to the insurgents. Then 'Stalin picked up the telephone, and talked directly with Rokossovsky. The Commander of the Front reported that his forces were unable to liberate Warsaw. . . . Stalin considered this response with understanding and did not insist.'[44] '. . . Then he gave an order to Marshal Zhukov, who [had] just [come] from the Ukrainian Front, to go back to the First Byelorussian Front: "You are there [as in] your own home. Go and assess on the spot what is going on in Warsaw, and undertake remedial steps as necessary. Is it possible to undertake a special operation in order to cross the Vistula by using Berling's forces? . . . This would be very important . . . you yourself, with Rokossovsky, must outline this objective to the Poles, and assist them in this operation." '[45]

When reading Shtemenko, one has the impression that Stalin treated the Warsaw Uprising simply as a military operation which he resented not knowing of in advance. But one thing is certain: as Supreme Commander, he alone had the power to order Rokossovsky's First Byelorussian Front forward, or to stop it, and upon collation of all available data it appears that, in the second week of August, Stalin's decisions about Warsaw were dictated not by military but by political considerations.

It is in Moscow that one must look for the facts that lend colour to this assertion, explain the inactivity of Rokossovsky's army, and demonstrate Stalin's treatment of the Uprising of Warsaw as a political issue and an element of Soviet foreign policy.

CHAPTER FIVE

Diplomacy: Tehran

WHEN, in the seventh week of the Uprising, Soviet artillery fire from Praga once more was heard in Warsaw, the insurgents hoped again that the Soviet Army would cross the Vistula. But again the firing ceased. A group of insurgents huddled around a radio in a basement listened intently to a broadcast in Polish from the United States. In their eyes Roosevelt and Churchill were the champions of freedom, but this was the message: 'What is needed in Warsaw now with regard to the Soviet Union is "mutual understanding". . . .' A soldier grabbed the radio and smashed it against the wall.[1] The hoped-for support from the Allies was not forthcoming: only exhortations which contrasted ironically with the wording of the British and French guarantee of Polish independence of 31 March 1939, when British Prime Minister Chamberlain said publicly, 'in the event of any action which clearly threatened Polish independence, and which the Polish Government accordingly considered it vital to resist with their national forces, His Majesty's Government would feel themselves bound at once to lend the Polish Government all support in their power'.[2] (See Appendix D.)

On 14 August 1941, Churchill and Roosevelt signed the Atlantic Charter, a statement of common principles for national policies subsequently approved, subscribed and signed by twenty-six nations. To the small Allies it guaranteed that they were not bleeding in vain, for articles 1, 2, 3 and 4 explicitly affirmed that 'no territorial changes' would take place without the 'freely expressed wishes of the people concerned' and that 'sovereign rights and self-government [be] restored to those who have been forcibly deprived of them'.[3]

These principles were taken seriously by Poles, politicians and common people alike. Churchill and Roosevelt became for them symbols of integrity and guarantors of freedom.

One month after signing the Charter, in a discussion with the Polish Ambassador to the United States, Ciechanowski, and the Ambassador to Great Britain, Raczynski, President Roosevelt reaffirmed that 'there could be no question . . . [of being] at variance with the Atlantic Charter'.[4] A month later, American Under-Secretary of State Sumner Welles again voiced that position in a talk with Prime Minister Sikorski in the presence of these two ambassadors: 'US policy is strictly defined by the Atlantic Charter. Decisions about future inter-State relations and frontier questions must await the end of the war.'[5]

In mid-December 1941, only four months later, Stalin personally told British Foreign Secretary Anthony Eden that he wanted eastern Poland.[6] This apparently was the first time Stalin had articulated his plan, and Eden was taken aback since, as he noted in his memoirs, Stalin's demand necessitated not only a breach of the Atlantic Charter, but also of the British commitment to support Poland. On 10 February 1942, Eden conveyed the problem to Roosevelt and the United States Department of State.[7] Notwithstanding Eden's moral indignation, Churchill wrote to Roosevelt in a letter of 7 March 1942 that 'the principles of the Atlantic Charter ought not to be construed so as to deny Russia the frontiers she occupied when Germany attacked her'.[8] In other words, the Polish–Soviet border-line should follow the frontier that Germany and the Soviet Union established by attacking Poland in 1939. So the Atlantic Charter was not to apply to Poland. Roosevelt took the cue. While dining with Eden and Harry Hopkins in Washington on 15 March 1943, he told Eden, 'In any event Britain and the United States and Russia should decide at the appropriate time what was a just solution, and Poland would have to accept it.'[9] He, Roosevelt, 'did not intend to go to the Peace Conference and bargain with Poland or other small states. . . .'[10]

On 18 April 1941, General Sikorski, Prime Minister of the Polish Government-in-Exile, had talked for one hour with President Roosevelt in the White House. It was reported that '[Sikorski] came back to the [Polish Embassy] in the most elated, if not joyful, state. According to the General, "President Roosevelt showed full sympathy for the Polish affairs and made the statement to the General that without a free and independent Poland there cannot be peace in Europe." He showed great knowledge of Polish territorial problems and testified to the fact that he respected Poland's right to her frontiers as of 1939.'[11]

To the 200,000 Poles in exile fighting with the Allies, as well as to the 300,000 active members of AK in occupied Poland at that time, Roosevelt's statements had constituted irreversible guarantees.

Churchill's and Roosevelt's change of attitude was undoubtedly known to Stalin and Molotov at least as early as 20 May 1942, when the Soviet Government informed the British Government that they would 'agree to leave the Polish frontier unsettled'. According to Foreign Secretary Eden, 'To agree to leave the Polish frontier unsettled was a Russian concession which should be matched by us: the British Government should therefore not maintain their support of the Polish cause.'[12]

The decision to cede half of Poland to the Soviet Government without obtaining the consent of, or even consulting, the Government of Poland was taken by President Roosevelt and Churchill together;[13] and

Churchill at least forewarned the Poles. On 15 April 1943, during a luncheon at number 10 Downing Street, Churchill told Polish Prime Minister Sikorski and Ambassador Raczynski, '. . . while Poland must be strong and independent, her eastern frontier would have to be revised in Russia's favour, while she would receive compensation in the west'.[14]

Eden on the other hand still believed, in August 1943, that the British Government had not given 'any hint' of its views on the Soviet western frontiers and Polish eastern territories. Eden believed that the United States Government took the same position and that it was not prepared to make any separate deals over Poland.[15] He recognized, however, that once the advancing Soviet armies were in Poland 'our negotiating power . . . would amount to very little.'[16] While attending the Moscow Conference, 18 October to 4 November 1943, on two occasions he approached Cordell Hull, the American Secretary of State, and expressed concern over Poland's future. Mr Hull dodged. He 'argued that he had no instructions about Poland'.[17] Eden prodded him again on 29 October 1943. Hull was still noncommittal.[18]

Eden observed, 'President Roosevelt was reserved about Poland to the point of being unhelpful.'[19] On 22 November 1943, Polish Prime Minister Mikolajczyk (Sikorski's successor) learned through his own channels that a conference would take place in Tehran. The same day he saw Eden, who thought that the Americans would postpone 'discussing territorial questions till the end of the war',[20] but hoped, nevertheless, that he would have a chance to discuss Poland with them. But the meeting between President Roosevelt and Stalin at Tehran on 1 December 1943 (3.20 p.m.) took place *in private*; and on that occasion, as we know today, the fate of the Polish eastern frontier was sealed and with it that of tens of thousands of AK soldiers and several million Poles. 'Long afterwards' Eden learned that, at Tehran, Roosevelt had talked to Stalin about Poland in a manner 'hardly calculated to restrain the Russians'.[21] As the Minutes of that meeting showed:

> The President said he had asked Marshal Stalin to come to see him as he wished to discuss a matter briefly and frankly. He said it referred to internal American politics.
>
> He said that we had an election in 1944 and that while personally he did not wish to run again, if the war was still in progress, he might have to.
>
> He added that there were in the United States from six to seven million Americans of Polish extraction, and as a practical man, he did not wish to lose their vote. He said personally he agreed with the views of Marshal Stalin as to the necessity of the restoration of a Polish state but would like to see the Eastern border moved further to the west and the Western border moved even to the River Oder. He hoped, however, that the Marshal would understand that for political reasons outlined above, he could not participate in any decision here in Tehran or even next winter on this subject and

that he could not publicly take part in any such arrangement at the present time.

Marshal Stalin replied that now the President explained, he had understood.

The President went on to say that there were a number of persons of Lithuanian, Latvian, and Estonian origin, in that order, in the United States. He said that he fully realized the three Baltic Republics had in history and again more recently been a part of Russia and added jokingly that when the Soviet armies re-occupied these areas, he did not intend to go to war with the Soviet Union on this point.[22]

(For the document see Appendix D.) This secret Roosevelt–Stalin discussion was not included in the Soviet text of proceedings from the Tehran Conference.[23] Moreover, on 30 November, three days *before* the Roosevelt–Stalin meeting, and in the presence of Charles Bohlen, Churchill had used three matches to illustrate to Stalin how to carve up Poland: 'He moved all three matches from east to west and said that is what should be done. . . .'[24]

The question of Poland was further discussed two and a half hours later at another meeting in which the United Kingdom was represented by Prime Minister Churchill, Foreign Secretary Eden, Sir Archibald Clark Kerr, and Major Birse. There was an addition to the American delegation: Mr Harry Hopkins. According to Edward Stettinius, United States Under-Secretary of State, Harry Hopkins and Alger Hiss together assisted President Roosevelt in the formulation of his views on the Polish eastern frontier.[25]

The Presidential papers and documents of Roosevelt's White House staff at the Franklin Delano Roosevelt Library in Hyde Park, New York, are revealing. Some of Roosevelt's immediate administrative assistants showed a passionately anti-Polish attitude, while others evinced open hostility toward non-Communist Poles. One of these was Dr Isadore Lubin, a labour relations expert and an administrative assistant in the White House, 1942–4. Dr Lubin was Hopkins' 'aide' and White House 'resident statistician' (as well as the Commissioner of Labour Statistics), who was described as a man 'with exceptionally acute and accurate pairs of eyes and ears', and as being 'constantly available and incalculably valuable to Roosevelt and Hopkins'.[26]

Even before the Tehran Conference, in a memo on White House stationery to Harry Hopkins, dated 30 April 1943, Lubin charged that some Poles were carrying on an anti-Soviet campaign in the United States, and that 'apparently they are working hand in hand with American Firsters'.[27] Dr Lubin was bringing this 'to the attention of some folks around here who are really interested in maintaining political peace'.[28]

Lubin's preoccupation with Polish political affairs and his persistent antipathy toward the Polish Government-in-Exile would not matter were it not for his influential position at the White House.[29] On 6 June 1944, just two months before the Uprising and on the eve of a meeting between the President and the Polish Prime Minister, he attacked the Polish American Congress and the Polish Information Center, which was acting on behalf of the Polish Government-in-Exile, calling the President's attention to 'the newly created Polish American Congress [that] is closely tied up with the Polish Government through one of the Congress's principal leaders, who is Dewey's leader among the Poles'.[30] Lubin implied that the Polish Information Center in the United States had been misusing 'funds made available for underground work by the United States Government'.[31] He also attacked another respectable Polish organization in the United States, the National Committee of Citizens of Polish Descent, as 'ultra-nationalistic' and 'anti-Soviet', and suggested, and emphasized by underlining, a course of Presidential action: '*There is enough information available now to indict some of the Polish leaders who have been working with the Polish Information Center (a Polish Government agency) under the Foreign Agents Registration Act.*'[32]

With his own memo Lubin attached a copy of a memo to the President from Jonathan Daniels (also on the White House staff) written four days earlier; in it Daniels had vilified Polish organizations in the United States, the Polish Government-in-Exile, and nearly everyone connected with them; he also imputed the misuse of funds given to Poles by the United States Government and suggested 'this situation can be effectively dealt with under the terms of the Foreign Agents Registration Act'.[33] Dr Lubin mentioned that the information Daniels submitted to the President was 'received from the Office of Strategic Services and the Department of Justice'.[34] His memo suggests how these agencies saw the European Poles: 'Reactionary ultra-Nationalistic colonels and politicians who hope to influence American and Polish foreign policy by propaganda, pressure, and the threat of weaning Polish-American voters from their traditional Democratic voting habits. Obviously these European Poles seek a Poland not only shaped in the terms of old boundaries but also in terms of old economic and social patterns.'[35]

Had Roosevelt and Hopkins been so inclined, they could have heeded other advice on the subject of Poland, for among the Russian specialists and professional foreign service personnel who had seen service in Russia there were widespread misgivings about Roosevelt's policy. Professor George Kennan, who was at that time Minister-Counsellor in the American Embassy in Moscow, has summarized in an interview (see Appendix C) and in his letter to me cited here:

> . . . the outlook of other people in the State Department, and elsewhere, who had never been reconciled to the acceptance, and in effect, legitimizing, by the Western allies of the Soviet gains originally achieved by the deal with the Nazis in 1939. . . .
>
> (a) I recognized that it was impossible to stop the Soviet forces

from overrunning Poland in the course of the final military operations of the war, and impossible, consequently, to prevent the Soviet leaders from imposing whatever political regime suited their book and from drawing the Polish – Soviet border wherever they wanted it. All this flowed logically from the policy of unconditional surrender and no separate peace. It was clear to me, even in the summer of 1944, that the Kremlin had made up its mind to move the whole country of Poland a couple of hundred miles west, and to impose upon the resulting geographical entity a Communist regime of its own choosing.

(b) I saw no reason why we should sanction, or take any responsibility for, either of these moves. The transplantation of the country westward seemed to me to be undesirable, in Poland's long-term interests; and the imposition of a Communist regime inconsistent both with our traditional ideals and with the Atlantic Charter, as well as strategically dangerous.

(c) I thought that our encouragement to the Polish Government-in-Exile, to feel that if they were only willing to go along with the new border settlement they could have a satisfactory future in Poland, was unjustified in the light of observable circumstances and irresponsible, as well as unfair, to the Poles. I viewed Mikolajczyk as a doomed man, politically, and thought it shabby on our part to make sport of him by pressing him to go to Moscow and to try to deal with Stalin.

(d) I thought the behavior of the Kremlin at the time of, and with relation to, the Warsaw Uprising, coming at the time it did and under the given circumstances, was the time at which we should have confessed to ourselves and the world that our purposes in continuing to wage war were not the same as those of the Soviet Union. [We] should have undertaken a basic change of wartime policy, founded on the recognition of the fact that there could be no effective collaboration with the Soviet Union on the problems of postwar Europe. (This would, of course, have precluded anything like the Yalta and Potsdam conferences.)

(e) I had no great hope that anything we could do or say could bring the Soviet Government to desist from its revealed purposes with respect to Poland. This was because I saw the Soviet leadership as the victim of its own earlier excesses with relation to Poland: those of the 1939–40 period. The Soviet leaders, I strongly (and I think rightly) suspected, were determined that there should not be, at any future time, a government in Poland that could investigate these shocking atrocities and make a public issue of them.

(f) If I did not, for these reasons, suppose that a firm stand, or a break, with the Soviet Union at the time of the Uprising would have had the effect of saving the Polish patriots fighting in Warsaw, I saw it only as a means of making the Soviet leaders understand that they were now on their own, that we could not give them further help or comfort in their war effort, and that they could expect from us no sanctioning of the course they were pursuing.[36]

When, in December 1943, Eden told Mikolajczyk about Stalin's demands, several weeks after Tehran, the Polish Prime Minister found himself subjected to pressures from all corners. British and American leaders expected him to yield to Soviet demands and to forget that the Soviet Government broke diplomatic contacts with the Polish Government-in-Exile in 1943 over the Polish demand for an international inquiry into the deaths of 15,000 Polish prisoners of war on Soviet soil.[37] At the same time he had to cope with those pressures that are part of a democratic system – from the opposition within the Government and from diverse parties within Poland.

Mikolajczyk and the Polish Minister for Foreign Affairs, Tadeusz Romer, met with Churchill and Eden at Churchill's residence on 6 February 1944. The Prime Minister assured the two Englishmen that, even though there were no diplomatic relations between Poland and the USSR at that time, Armia Krajowa was 'prepared to come into the open and meet the conditions [for co-operation] of the Soviet commanders without any prior agreement between the two governments'.[38] But, he pointed out, AK was determined 'to maintain Poland's territorial integrity'.[39]

The attitude of AK had been clearly expressed by Mikolajczyk. Nonetheless, on 22 February 1944, just sixteen days after seeing Mikolajczyk, Churchill made the following statement in the British Parliament, 'Here I may remind the House that we ourselves have never in the past guaranteed, on behalf of his Majesty's Government, any particular frontier line to Poland. We did not approve of the Polish occupation of Vilna in 1920. The British view in 1919 stands expressed in the so-called Curzon line which attempted to deal, at any rate partially, with the problem.'[40] This was plain talk and Poles should have taken note of it. General Marian Kukiel, then Polish Minister of Defence, summarized the British advice at that time: the Polish Government should assume such a posture that no one could charge it with irresponsibility. In February 1944, British and American public opinion was impressed with the Soviet victories over Germany. As the British Ambassador to the Polish government said to Kukiel, 'We are not in Europe yet.'[41] But, he said, the situation might change if British and American forces were in Europe. Then the public would recognize that the British and Americans were suffering losses as well as the Soviet Union; therefore, public opinion might be more sympathetic to the Polish cause and more likely to deal realistically with the Soviet Union. The British Ambassador felt that the Polish Government should not take a definite stand but take every opportunity for contacts with the governments of the Soviet Union, England and the United States.[42]

To Prime Minister Mikolajczyk the British Ambassador's advice was blunt: he should state publicly that 'frontiers are not sacrosanct, and should not be considered immutable . . . that the whole trend of modern history has been in the direction of homogeneity of states [and . . . that he was] ready at an appropriate moment and in appropriate circumstances to negotiate an adjustment of [Poland's] Eastern frontier and a transfer of populations.'[43]

On 25 April, Churchill told Mikolajczyk and five members of the Polish Underground that he could 'not guarantee the whole [of Polish] territory'.[44] A month later he advised Mikolajczyk to 'abstain from any form of political blackmail on the eve of the Presidential election'[45] in the United States. By thus warning him not to marshal support among the American Poles, the British leadership gradually eased the Polish Government in London into dependence on the Soviet Union while fencing them off from American support.

It was in this climate of attitudes that, on 21 February 1944, Prime Minister Mikolajczyk sent a secret letter to Prime Minister Churchill requesting that a British mission of observers be sent to Poland. For the Soviet presence in Poland in the spring of 1944 created anxiety among all politically conscious Poles except those who were Communists.

As early as 9 March 1944 the highest underground legislative body in occupied Poland, the Council of National Unity, sent Mikolajczyk a secret position-paper reflecting the stand of the Polish people in Poland. Point number four contends:

> We object firmly to any discussion with the Soviets with regard to the revision of the eastern boundaries. We stand by the inviolability of the frontiers accepted [in] the Treaty of Riga, which was also signed by the representatives of the Ukraine. . . .
> The Soviets do not want frontier readjustments, just as the Danzig corridor was not the real aim of the Germans: [they] want to destroy the sovereignty and integrity of Poland.
> No one in Poland would understand why Poland is to pay the Soviets for the war with her territories and her independence. . . .
> There will be no peace in Europe, if, instead of justice and right, violence and force . . . triumph. The Polish nation will never surrender to violence and still believes in the bonds of alliance. [We] trust, that, in the interest of all peace-loving nations, the principles of the Atlantic Charter will prevail.[46]

Then, in March 1944, a Soviet agent called Sokolin approached a Polish diplomat in Switzerland, Lados, with the suggestion Poles could secure better terms by making a deal with the Soviet Government behind the backs of the British and American governments.[47] Poles did not respond.

Again, in May 1944, the Soviet Government, through its representatives in London, approached Mikolajczyk with a proposal to talk about Polish affairs. There were two conditions: that the British Government was not to know about it, and that Mikolajczyk would delegate someone for the talks who would be acceptable to the Russians. A Soviet official in London, 'Mr Ludwig', would represent the Soviet Union; Mikolajczyk asked Stanislaw Grabski to represent him during these talks. The first meeting between 'Ludwig' and Grabski had all the atmosphere of a spy thriller. Grabski was instructed to walk in Kensington Gardens, where he would be picked up in the main alley and taken by car to a place unknown to him. Grabski undertook several meetings with 'Ludwig' and considered progress to be 'good'. Mikolajczyk talked to 'Ludwig' either once or twice. On 23 May, Polish Minister of Foreign Affairs Romer told Eden about the Russian initiative. The author has examined Professor Grabski's handwritten notes[48] of these meetings. On 23 June 1944, 'Mr Ludwig' (pseudonym for the Soviet Ambassador Lebiediev) demanded that the Polish President be removed from office. The talks were broken off on 23 June 1944, after Mikolajczyk found the Soviet conditions unacceptable.[49]

The cession of eastern Poland by Roosevelt and Churchill to the Soviet Union is relevant to the Uprising of Warsaw in that it made it plain to Stalin that he did not need to take the Polish Government seriously. When Roosevelt and Churchill gave away the eastern territories (an area of 70,000 square miles that encompassed millions of Polish citizens), they also gave away the prestige, credibility and viability of the legal Polish Government. The arrangement at Tehran was so secret that even American Secretary of State Cordell Hull 'had never been told what was in the minutes'.[50] One result was that whole divisions of AK soldiers, at that time engaged in fighting Germans in eastern Poland, continued to fight on the assumption that they were *on sovereign Polish territory* illegally seized by Germans. Moreover, since he was under no pressure from any major power to take into account the will of the Poles residing in the eastern territories or the armed forces of the Government-in-Exile, including the AK, Stalin proceeded unhesitatingly to set up another 'Polish' government. It was composed of a group of obscure Polish Communists and Soviet Security Police trainees of Polish origin, among them the future 'first president' of Poland, Boleslaw Bierut, who had been in service as a Soviet Security Police agent in Poland and other countries for several years. The British and American action also gave the Soviet Government a free hand to destroy the opposition in '*their*' territory. Polish AK soldiers were 'the opposition' and their leadership was in Warsaw!

The Polish Communists proceeded to establish 'The Polish Committee of National Liberation' and issued a 'Manifesto' to the Polish nation, in which they stated the 'country's National Council' (the Communist-inspired and -organized body) was 'the only legal source of authority in Poland'[51] and that the Polish Government-in-Exile with its delegate in Poland was 'illegal'.[52] Stalin's statements to Churchill and Roosevelt about wanting Poland to be democratic and 'friendly' were now clarified. He had the nucleus of a 'Polish Government' of his own that was obviously 'friendly'.

The 'Manifesto' included this appeal: 'To arms! Fight Germans everywhere, wherever they are and whenever you meet them!'[53] (This

was one week before the Uprising.) It also dealt with the question of the
Polish territories by assigning them to the Soviet Union as 'Ukrainian,
Byelorussian, and Lithuanian lands'.[54]

As a result, the Soviet Commissar for Foreign Affairs issued a formal
statement that in the future he would deal with the Polish Committee of
National Liberation to regulate the relationship between the 'Polish
administration' (meaning the same Polish Communist Committee of
National Liberation) and the Red Army.[55] On that same day an official
communiqué was issued by Molotov, representing the Soviet Union,
and Edward B. Osobka-Morawski, on behalf of the Polish Committee of
National Liberation, announcing the resumption of normal relationships between the Soviet Red Army and the Polish 'administration'.[56] Stalin, Vyshinsky, and NKVD General Zhukov among
others, participated in the ceremony. The Polish side was also
represented by the Chairman of the Section on Agriculture, Andrzej
Witos; Chairman of National Defence, General Michal Rola-
Zymierski; and the Chairman of the Labour, Social Welfare, and
Health Department, Dr Boleslaw Drobner. Also an 'amnesty' for Poles
in the USSR was announced.[57]

The first article of this curious document clarifies the degree of self-
determination and integrity of the new 'Polish Government': 'Article 1:
In regard to military activities on Polish territories after the Red Army
enters [Poland], the highest authority in all matters concerning the war
for the period necessary to continue military operations is concentrated
in the hands of the Supreme Commander of the Army of the Soviet
Union [Stalin].'[58]

The Soviet leadership periodically checked on President Roosevelt's
commitment after the Tehran Conference. On 7 June 1944, in Moscow,
Molotov asked American Ambassador Averell Harriman whether the
President's 'attitude was still the same as expressed in Tehran'.
Harriman replied, 'Of course.'[59] Since this conversation was related to
the impending arrival in America of Polish Prime Minister Mikolajczyk, Molotov was pleased and said that he would inform Marshal
Stalin at once and that Marshal Stalin would be gratified'.[60] With that
assurance the Soviet Government proceeded to the next tasks: isolation
of the Polish Government-in-Exile from its allies and the establishment
of a friendly 'Polish Government' tailored to Stalin's needs.

By 12 June 1944, Ambassador Harriman was entertaining the four
delegates from the Polish National Council (established under Communist auspices and not related in any way to the Polish Government-
in-Exile), and commented, 'I am satisfied they are not (repeat not)
Soviet agents. . . .'[61] 'They gave me a mass of interesting information
concerning present conditions in Poland and the objectives of the
National Council.'[62] They stated that the principal aim of the National
Council was to carry on resistance again the Germans; that the AK in
Poland 'numbered about thirty thousand and was losing supporters'[63]

(verified documents show that, in the first half of 1944, AK membership was at its peak with 380,175 underground soldiers); and that 'The Council takes a realistic attitude toward the boundary dispute and believes that in view of the strength of the Soviet Union it can make a better deal by co-operation with the Soviets'. They also assured Harriman that 'at the appropriate time a representative parliament will be elected which will develop a constitution and a permanent government [in Poland]. The Council expects to give leadership during the formative period.'[64] They indicate that 'cordial relations and agreement have been established with the Union of Polish Patriots'. (The Union, sponsored by the Soviet Union, was the nucleus of the Polish puppet government formed in Lublin, Poland, that illegally assumed power in Soviet-controlled Polish territories.) Harriman further wrote that 'The Soviet Government appears to attach considerable weight to the reports brought by the delegates concerning the situation in Poland.'[65] It was his evaluation, 'The Council that these men represent may well play an important role in the future of Poland, either because they do represent the feelings of the majority of Poles or because of future support from the Soviet Government. They want our help now, and I believe that serious consideration should be given to sending in a military observer if the Soviet Government agrees.'[66]

In July the Polish town of Wilno was seized from Germans by the Soviet Army, with the effective collaboration of Polish AK units. Marshal Stalin promptly announced the liberation of Wilno from the Fascist invaders as 'the capital of Lithuanian Soviet Socialist Republics', and ordered a salute of 24 salvos from 324 guns to be fired in honour of the Soviet troops who had captured the 'capital of Soviet Lithuania'.[67] Of the Polish AK units who also fought and bled for this city, some were scattered; the rest were disarmed and arrested, and of these some were executed. The Poles now realized that their eastern territories were being incorporated into the Soviet Union, but when Prime Minister Mikolajczyk pleaded with Churchill to send a British liaison officer to Wilno, 'Churchill . . . exploded . . . "Poles should get Wilno out of their heads . . .!" '[68] Even then, Churchill did not inform Mikolajczyk of the outcome of the Tehran Conference, and in fact nobody told him of the decisions concerning Poland that had been agreed upon there until the meeting in Moscow on 13 October 1944, *ten days after the Uprising collapsed*. According to Lord Moran, Churchill then openly supported Stalin's demands that the Lublin Government have a bigger share in the post-war Polish Government and advocated that Mikolajczyk accept as his eastern frontier the Curzon Line.

Mikolajczyk: 'I cannot accept the Curzon Line. I have no authority to leave half my countrymen to their fate.'

Molotov (abruptly interrupting): 'But all this was settled at Teheran.'

Mikolajczyk looked from Churchill to Harriman. They were

silent. Harriman gazed at his feet, but the P.M. [Churchill] looked
Mikolajczyk in the face.

'I confirm this,' he said quietly.

Mikolajczyk was shocked.

The revelation of what had happened at Teheran, in the
absence of the Poles, only seemed to make the Prime Minister
angry, as if he wanted to persuade himself that he was the
aggrieved person and not Mikolajczyk. He demanded that
Mikolajczyk should agree there and then to the Russian demands.
The Pole would not give way.

P.M.: 'You can at least agree that the Curzon Line is the
temporary frontier.'

At this, Stalin rose in his place. 'I want no arguments. We will
not change our frontiers from time to time. That's all.'

Churchill held out his hands, looked up to the ceiling in despair
and wheezed. They filed out silently.

Lord Moran goes on to report the scene, later that day, between
Churchill and Mikolajczyk:

'If,' the P.M. shouted, 'you think you can conquer Russia, well,
you are crazy, you ought to be in a lunatic asylum. You would
involve us in a war in which twenty-five million lives might be lost.
You would be liquidated. You hate the Russians. I know you hate
them. We are very friendly with them, more friendly than we have
ever been. I mean to keep things like that. I tell you, we'll become
sick and tired if you continue arguing. We shall tell the world how
unreasonable you are. We shall not part friends.'

This was not diplomacy. Nor did it intimidate Mikolajczyk. He
was not going to be shouted down by anyone. He was furious and
made no attempt to hide his feelings.

Winston told me the sequel with tears in his eyes. Mikolajczyk
asked to be dropped into Poland, where he could rejoin the
Underground Army. Winston in one moment forgot the obstinate
peasant who had threatened our relations with Russia in his warm-
hearted admiration for a soldier . . . without fear.[69]

At Churchill's urging, Mikolajczyk flew to Moscow in the last week of
July. At a stopover in Tehran, he received information that the Polish
Committee of National Liberation had been brought to Lublin by the
Red Army and was already acting there as the Polish Government; the
news disheartened him, and he wanted to go back to England, but
telegrams from Roosevelt and Churchill urged him on. On 31 July, the
day after his arrival, he saw Molotov, whose first words were: 'Why did
you come here? What have you got to say?'[70] Mikolajczyk answered
that he wanted to discuss with Stalin problems of common interest: the
fight against the Germans, collaboration between the Red Army and
Armia Krajowa, and Soviet–Polish relations in general. To this
Molotov responded, 'We will take Warsaw soon. They [the Red Army]
are already about six miles from Warsaw.'[71] Then Molotov told

Mikolajczyk that before he saw Stalin he should meet Poles from the Polish Committee of National Liberation. This Mikolajczyk did but, though the discussion lasted five hours, no results were forthcoming.

On 1 August, while in Moscow, Mikolajczyk received news from London through the British Ambassador that the Uprising had begun in Warsaw. His meeting with Stalin was not scheduled until 3 August 1944, at 9.30 p.m.

In Mikolajczyk's private archives I found an outline of the talks with Stalin, written in the former Prime Minister's own hand. Checked against the actual minutes of the conference which lasted from 9.30 p.m. to midnight, the notes show Mikolajczyk was well prepared; the points to be delivered were outlined. He obviously did not intend to extemporize.[72] After an exchange of pleasantries, during which Stalin recalled that he had met Mr Romer before, Stalin invited all present to sit down at the table. Stalin and Molotov sat along one length of the table opposite Mikolajczyk, Grabski, Romer and Mniszek. The interpreter, Mr Pavlov, was at the end of the table. Romer and Mniszek observed that 'Stalin looked in very good physical shape and carried himself in a very cool manner. He [did] not smoke a pipe, as before, but only cigarettes, from time to time. . . . He is meticulous in social graces [in contrast] to Molotov. He has no hesitation in talking about the Polish Government and in referring to Mr Mikolajczyk as Prime Minister. He speaks quietly, rather slowly, in short sentences. He does not give the impression of personal preoccupation with his own role nor does he appear arrogant because of his military successes. In Stalin's presence Molotov looks rather overshadowed, he doesn't talk, or if he does, his comments are less combative than they used to be.'[73]

The discussion did not begin well, for Mikolajczyk brought up the subject of the Uprising in Warsaw rather soon, asking Stalin to make it possible for him to go to the city. Mikolajczyk also averred that 'Warsaw would be free at any time,' to which Stalin responded, 'Pray God!' Mikolajczyk wanted to go to Warsaw to create a new government there. To this Stalin replied, 'Please remember that the Soviet Government does not recognize the Polish Government-in-Exile. We have broken off relations with it. At the same time the Soviet Government maintains relations with the Polish Committee of National Liberation, [has] signed an agreement with it, and is assisting it. You have to remember that.'[74]

With regard to the Armia Krajowa, Stalin said that in the light of modern warfare it represented no power, because it had no tanks, artillery or air force; in fact, it did not even have enough small weapons. Of the Uprising of Warsaw, he said, 'I hear that the Polish Government ordered these units to chase Germans out of Warsaw; I don't understand how they will do that, because they don't have enough strength. Moreover, as a whole, these people do not fight . . . Germans. They just hide in forests; they are unable to do anything else.'[75] There were no further references to the Uprising in Warsaw. But just before midnight, while saying good-bye, Mikolajczyk asked Stalin aside and pleaded for his personal assurance that the leaders and soldiers of Armia Krajowa, whom he had instructed to collaborate with Soviet forces, would not be harmed. Stalin assured Mikolajczyk that they would not be harmed if they didn't do anything 'silly'.[76]

Mikolajczyk waited for six days in Moscow to see Stalin again, and during this period saw the British Ambassador Sir Archibald Clark Kerr as well as Averell Harriman. Mr Harriman reported to President Roosevelt: 'In some detail I explained [to Mikolajczyk] the evidence that satisfied me that the Soviet government had no intention of communising Poland.

'I told him that I believed he could reach an agreement providing he was willing and in a position to eliminate individuals from his government and bring in some of the members of the new Committee of Liberation [Polish Communists] . . . that it was his responsibility, not my government's, to negotiate a settlement but it was of great interest to the United States that all Poles should unite for the defeat of the Germans in collaboration with the Red Army. . . .'[77]

In a message to the American Secretary of the State, Harriman expressed an 'earnest hope that the British Government bring full pressure on Mikolajczyk and his associates to act quickly and realistically, and I recommend that we support this position'.[78] He also evaluated Mikolajczyk's role, representing him as a rather suspicious man who did not have much faith in the Committee (Polish Communists Committee).[79]

The next day, Churchill told Parliament, 'This, in my opinion, is a hopeful moment for Poland, for whose rights and independence we entered the war against Germany. . . . The Russian Armies now stand before the gates of Warsaw. They bring the liberation of Poland in their hands. They offer freedom, sovereignty, and independence to the Poles. . . .'[80] He did not, however, inform the Members of Parliament about Tehran decisions concerning Poland!

Meanwhile, in Moscow, the British Ambassador to the Soviet Union, Sir Archibald Clark Kerr, was warning the Poles to 'expect the Russians to ask for the remodelling of the Polish Government [admitting Communists, among others], the acceptance of the Curzon Line as a basis of negotiations . . . a withdrawal from the suggestion that the killing at Katyn was done by the Russians . . . and some kind of working arrangement with the Polish Committee of National Liberation [Polish Communists] . . . as well as . . . that the 1921 Constitution be re-established without delay. They would also want some rearrangement of the supreme military command, so as to [be acceptable to Communists], and some arrangement about the functions of the official underground movement. [The Russians naturally preferred the Communist Partisans called "The People's Army".]'

In return, Ambassador Clark Kerr wrote, the Poles might expect:

1. The re-establishment of diplomatic relations.
2. The fullest assurances about:
   (a) The territorial and administrative integrity of the new Poland [because] Stalin has said again and again that he wants to see 'a strong, independent and friendly Poland'.
   (b) Territorial compensation . . . in the North and in the West.
   (c) The fullest co-operation of the Soviet Government in the ejection of the German population from the regions you are to take over.
   (d) Soviet support in keeping Germany in her place thereafter.
3. Adherence to the Soviet–Czech Treaty.
4. The homing of all the Polish exiles scattered about the Soviet Union.[81]

(The 'exiles' were 1,200,000 deportees forcibly removed from the Polish eastern territories by the Soviet Government in 1939–40 and placed in Soviet labour camps.)

Apparently the Soviet Government knew of the positions of the American and British ambassadors and of their reluctance to support Mikolajczyk. On 2 August, Stalin proceeded to strengthen his own 'Polish Government' by appointing Nikolai Alexandrovitch Bulganin as representative of the Supreme Soviet of the USSR to the Polish (Communist) Committee of National Liberation.[82]

For Mikolajczyk it was an unhappy situation. Not only were the Allied ambassadors pressuring him to accommodate Stalin's demands, but also the Uprising of Warsaw, instead of providing support for Mikolajczyk in his parley with Stalin, made him additionally dependent on Stalin's good will – in that he would have to ask Stalin to assist the AK in Warsaw.

The Uprising of Warsaw was much in the public eye and, whether for this reason or for other reasons, it will be seen that both Churchill and Roosevelt asked Stalin many times to help Warsaw. Paradoxically, at the same time, the United States cut off concrete assistance to AK. Ten million dollars allocated by President Roosevelt in June 1944[83] for the underground forces in Poland was not now forthcoming, and on 4 August the Joint Chiefs of Staff gave the reason why: 'In view of the Soviet recognition of the Polish Committee of National Liberation, the Joint Chiefs . . . suggest that the allocation of the funds be temporarily deferred.'[84] (In his interview with the author, Mikolajczyk maintained that he received $10 million. Interview: Princeton, 31 March 1957.)

To Churchill's message of 4 August about British assistance,[85] Stalin sent this reply: 'I think the information given to you by the Poles is greatly exaggerated and unreliable. . . . The Home Army consists of a few detachments misnamed divisions. They have neither guns, aircraft, nor tanks. I cannot imagine detachments like those taking Warsaw, which the Germans are defending with four armoured divisions, including the Hermann Goering Division.'[86]

On 6 August, the Polish Ambassador in Washington, Jan Ciechanowski, submitted to the American Chiefs of Staff the Government-in-Exile's formal request for assistance.[87] The American Joint Chiefs of Staff thought the matter should be referred elsewhere: supplies and equipment for the Polish underground forces were a British responsibility, so the Polish request should be referred to the British Chiefs of Staff for such action as they might deem necessary and desirable.[88]

The Polish representative to CCS (Combined Chiefs of Staff) in Washington, Colonel Leon Mitkiewicz, met with a similar rebuff: 'Our demands were transmitted by CCS to London. I was also told that, as Warsaw was within the zone of military operations of Soviet armies, no intervention was possible without knowledge and agreement of the Soviet High Command.'[89]

On all levels of interaction the Allies were saying to Mikolajczyk, 'You have to deal with Stalin.' The Communist Polish Committee of National Liberation began to establish direct communication with the United States Government and, although they had no official standing, the United States apparently was willing to deal with them. On 8 August, while the Prime Minister of the Polish Government-in-Exile was in Moscow, the Polish Communists were telling President Roosevelt, through Harriman, how they saw their role: 'The Polish Committee of National Liberation, which is directing the civil administration in the liberated regions of Poland, is organizing a section for Foreign Affairs from which the Ministry of Foreign Affairs of the future government of Poland will be formed.'[90] This letter went on to say that they had selected Professor Oscar Lange, a United States citizen, to head that section of Foreign Affairs because he was 'a man who enjoys the sympathy of all the United Nations'[91] – whatever that meant.

Harriman's willingness to deal with this self-appointed future government of Poland while the legal Polish Government was still in existence reveals his own predisposition, perhaps, and especially his sensitivity to Roosevelt's political posture. The President was already very much concerned that his exchange of messages with Stalin 'ought to be got in some way to the Polish Committee of National Liberation',[92] but there is no evidence of any similar concern that copies of his correspondence with Stalin reach the legal government of Poland in London.

The second meeting between Stalin and Mikolajczyk took place on 9 August 1944, again at 9.30 p.m. It lasted only one hour,[93] and the participants were the same as at the previous meeting. This time Mikolajczyk specifically asked for assistance to Warsaw, and Stalin replied:

All these activities in Warsaw are not very realistic to me. It would be different if our forces [were] approaching Warsaw, but unfortunately this is not the case. I was counting on the fact that on 6 August we would enter Warsaw, but we were unable to do so, because on 4 August the Germans brought to the Praga region four armoured divisions. . . . So we undertook an encircling manœuvre after crossing the Vistula river in the area of Pilica. Initially this manœuvre was successful. It was 25 kilometres in width and 30 kilometres in depth. However, yesterday the Germans initiated a very strong counter-attack in this sector, using infantry and two tank divisions. . . . I have no doubt that we will overcome this difficulty, but in order to do so we have to regroup our own forces and to bring artillery forward. This will take time. I feel sorry for your men, who initiated fighting too early in Warsaw and now, with the rifles in hand, are facing the German tanks, artillery and air force. I used to visit Warsaw; I know the narrow streets of Old Town, and I am aware of the fact that its capture doesn't have major strategic value. What is the effect of supplies from the air? We can supply you with a certain number of rifles and machine guns. But artillery we are unable to drop. Finally, the question remains whether the weapons dropped will fall into Polish hands? If such drops of supplies were called for in the areas around Radom or Kielce, that would be easy. But in the city, with such concentration of the German forces as it is, this task is extremely difficult. However, it may work. We ought to try. How much assistance do you need, and where should we drop it?[94]

Mikolajczyk started by agreeing with Stalin's misgivings, but also called his attention to the fact that the fight was in progress and that the Poles were holding areas which were protected by barricades: if the drops fell in these areas they would come into Polish hands.

Subsequently, Stalin agreed that dropping supplies would be an easy task as long as good communications were established. Then he said, 'I want to assure you that on our part we shall do everything that is possible to help Warsaw. . . .' There ensued a prophetic exchange:

Mikolajczyk said, 'I wish, Mr Marshal, that in these moments of farewell you could tell us something to gladden Polish hearts in such a difficult hour.'

And Stalin replied: 'Are you not attaching too great value to words? Don't believe words. Actions are much more important than words.'[95]

As the Polish Prime Minister departed from Moscow, although the fates of his government in London and the eastern Polish frontiers were both still unsettled, he believed in his own mind that Stalin would assist Warsaw. He had missed the import of Stalin's comments about the unimportance of 'words'. When this author interviewed him after the war about his experience in Moscow, he was emphatic about Stalin's having promised his assistance to Warsaw and also about how knowledgeable Stalin was on Polish affairs. 'Nine-tenths of my ministers', he commented, 'didn't know as much [about Polish affairs] as Stalin did.'[96]

Stalin's knowledge derived not only from Soviet Intelligence and the Polish Communists, but probably, where the Poles in London are concerned, from Mr Kim Philby, who during the period 1941–51 was a universally trusted member of the British Intelligence Service with contacts and knowledge about European underground movements, and at the same time was a Russian spy.[97]

CHAPTER SIX

Diplomacy: Aftermath of Tehran

ALTHOUGH they were desirous of Soviet assistance, the AK command were also apprehensive about it. Long before the Uprising, there was speculation in AK Headquarters in Warsaw as to appropriate behaviour for AK and the measures it should undertake when the Soviet Army entered Warsaw.

The behaviour of AK membership during 'German–Soviet fighting on Polish territory' was specifically regulated under General Bor's orders concerning Operation Tempest: the AK was to fight the Germans' rearguard as they withdrew under Soviet pressure, by intensive sabotage activities. Tempest was to move westwards, with local AK units rising as the Germans retreated, and local action was to be initiated by local commanders. On the arrival of the Red Army, all AK action should cease. The units should remain in the area when the Soviet Army arrived, avoiding conflict and undertaking counter-measures only 'in self-defence'.[1]

General Bor had official recommendations to follow. The Government's Instruction of 27 October 1943, sent from London, defined AK's role and its behaviour *vis-à-vis* the Soviet Union: If diplomatic relations with the Soviet Government were re-established, the AK should continue to fight Germans, but *should not reveal* itself to the Soviet Army and should not co-operate with the Red Army until the Polish Government had returned to the liberated area of Poland.

If diplomatic relations between the Polish and Soviet Governments were not re-established all these policies were to be effective, with a proviso – in the case of arrests of AK or leaders of the Polish Government, or the persecution of Polish citizens, the AK should undertake 'actions of self-defence'. The implication was that the AK should, in this case, fight the Red Army.[2]

General Bor, however, assumed responsibility for political decisions contrary to the Government's instructions. About .three weeks after receiving these instructions (November 1943), he ordered AK units to 'identify themselves to Russian commanders . . . to manifest by their presence the existence of the Commonwealth of Poland'.[3] He also informed his superiors that he was going to organize another under-

97

ground movement if Polish lands were overrun by Russians.[4] These decisions, put to the Government-in-Exile as a *fait accompli*, were approved after three months.

One measure in particular created anxiety among some members of the staff: the preparation of a list of AK staff members who should identify themselves to the Soviet authorities. At least one member of the AK Headquarters balked at this plan. He was Janusz Bokszczanin, a Polish colonel. He told this author that he had demanded that his name be removed from such a list because he did not trust Communist or Soviet authorities.[5] His demand was resented by his AK superiors, who were *initially* confident that Communists and Soviets would not dare harm the AK in Warsaw and that, even if they tried, they would be forced to yield to the protective pressures of the Western Allies.

That this confidence faltered is indicated in a radio message from General Bor to London after one month of the Uprising. He reported to the Supreme Commander that in case Warsaw was seized by Soviet forces he would only command AK openly; he would not go underground again for two reasons: (1) He would be identified within days, probably hours. To go underground again would undoubtedly provoke immediate arrest and further destruction of the AK men and women by Polish Communists and Soviet authorities. (2) If he were to leave Warsaw and try to continue fighting, the very fact of his going underground would be interpreted as desertion, particularly since his AK subordinates would be exposed to arrest by the Soviets. His message said, 'I am aware of what will be my personal fate at the hands of the Soviets, but I feel that for the welfare of the cause this will be better, and this last card should be put on the table. When thousands of lives are being sacrificed, my own life does not mean much.'[6]

Fearing arrest, Bor assigned leadership of AK to his 'second in command', General Leopold Okulicki, who was already in Warsaw but for reasons of security was 'under cover' during the Uprising. General Bor then ordered that the insurgents' units be kept together, officers with their soldiers. Then, if Soviet or Polish Communists were to begin selective arrests of either officers or civilian administration, he said, 'there will be decisive reaction on our part'.[7]

But the Red Army was using a different script – it was 'their' territory even if the Poles didn't know it; they entered Poland on a very broad front, and the mistreatment of Polish soldiers after the taking of Wilno was a fair sample of what took place in all Polish eastern territories. In eastern Poland, moreover, there were diverse ethnic groups: Polish, Lithuanian, Byelorussian, Ukrainian – each of which had been conditioned by different experiences with the Polish, German and Soviet governments. Their political aspirations differed, and it was into this jungle of ethnic and territorial claims and counter-claims that Armia Krajowa and the Kremlin sent their guerrilla units. In some cases these were engaged in fighting each other as early as March 1944.[8] Fighting was bitter. In some instances, both sides were shooting prisoners.[9]

The Poles, believing that the eastern territories were their own, carried out Operation Tempest whenever the timing was favourable. They attacked withdrawing Germans, often collaborating with the Soviet Union against the common enemy. AK commanders reported with their units to Soviet officers as part of the Polish Army fighting on its own territory. The Soviet command did not see the situation this way. As soon as German units retreated and fighting ceased, the Poles were arrested and disarmed. The officers were separated from their men and dispatched by train in the direction of the Soviet Union. This was a common occurrence, even in central Poland. The 9th AK division in the area of Lublin was arrested and disarmed.[10] The 27th AK division, which had tactically subordinated itself to the Soviet Army, was subsequently ambushed by Soviet forces, disarmed, and herded to a concentration point behind barbed wires.[11] As a rule, the officers were arrested and the rank and file were given a choice: join General Berling's army or be deported.[12] In Lublin, on 26 August, over 200 AK officers and noncommissioned officers were arrested and taken away.[13] Arrests continued long after Operation Tempest. (The arrests of AK units attempting to make their way to Warsaw have already been discussed.) Although many units tried to avoid contact with the Red Army, they were hunted down, encircled, disarmed and imprisoned.

Between 17 and 19 July there were mass arrests of more than 7,000 AK soldiers. Their commanding officers – Colonel Aleksander Krzyzanowski, using the pseudonym General Wolf, and his staff – had been invited to attend a conference with some Soviet officers. During the conference, the Poles were disarmed after a short struggle, and their distinctions were ripped from their uniforms. Then they were arrested as a Soviet officer shouted, 'It is our country! This is our land!'[14] Meanwhile, in the early morning of 17 July, Soviet tanks encircled the Polish units of these commanders. The units, more than 7,000 men, were disarmed and interned in the town of Miedniki, despite the fact that 5,500 of them had risen in Wilno and fought the Germans side by side with the Red Army for six days – from 7 to 13 July.

The importance of the AK presence to the Soviet Government was shown by the fact that General Serov, in charge of Soviet internal security, came to Camp Miedniki to address the men. He told the AK soldiers to give up hope that they would receive assistance from the British or Americans. Seeing no response, he became angry and shouted in Russian, 'This is the end. So you wanted to fight, and that's what you get for it [indicating the barbed wire around the soldiers].' AK Lieutenant Lelewski, calmly smoking his pipe, gestured with his hand at Serov and his staff and responded in Russian, 'Well, for all that – we got[you as] friends.'[15] All the AK officers, among them five generals, were taken to the Soviet Union.[16]

Major Tadeusz Klimowski, Chief of Staff of the 27th AK Division from Wolyn (south-eastern Poland), summarized the motivations of his AK soldiers. The division was composed of local citizens: (1) They were fighting on Polish land, they thought; (2) although knowing about the Katyn Forest Massacre and the policies of the Red Army on Polish territories, they were still following Bor's order to discipline themselves and to show a maximum of goodwill toward the Red Army and to help it as much as they could, and to continue fighting Germans. Ultimately they were arrested.[17]

An AK district commander reported in an interview with the author:

> We were helping, first of all, the Soviet partisans, by providing them a guide. When the front approached Jaslo [his area], I had four companies of AK men behind the German lines. A Red Army patrol got in touch with us and said they would attack Jaslo. Their leader proposed that we should attack the Germans from the rear. The next day another Soviet patrol came to me, and I was told to get in touch directly with the commander of the nearest Soviet regiment. We did so, riding horses under direct German fire. This was what I was told: 'The Polish Government-in-Exile does not exist anymore. The AK [men] should join the Red Army; ultimately it [the AK] will be included in General Berling's units.' Then the Soviet colonel ordered me to call my unit [to him]. I told him I would personally bring my unit, but I couldn't [call them]. They arrested me right on the spot. The next day they put me into a group of Soviet soldiers who were former German prisoners; we were guarded by the NKVD [Security Police].[18]

He escaped and returned to his post. He recalled, 'It was much more difficult [under Soviet occupation] because all of us were marked as AK soldiers. You have to remember that the Communists had their own agents (the German agents we [had discovered and] shot before).'[19]

As a result of such situations, AK soldiers, although still carrying out Operation Tempest, were inquiring through their clandestine radio stations whether the order to reveal their identities and report to the Soviet commanders was still valid. One message to General Bor in Warsaw reported, 'There are intense disagreements about this policy among our officers and noncommissioned officers.'[20]

The Polish General Staff in London were equally at a loss to understand why the Soviets were arresting AK members in eastern Poland, in spite of their joint effort with the Soviet forces against the Germans. At the same time the Americans were giving the Polish Underground millions of dollars to assist Soviet armies. Although, as we have seen, this aid was to be cut off in August 1944, on 18 July, Secretary of State Cordell Hull sent a telegram to Harriman in Moscow, informing him that within the past two years President Roosevelt had authorized the allocation of $10 million to the Polish Government 'to be used for the financing of the operations of the Polish Underground Forces in Poland',[21] and an additional sum of $10 million for this purpose ' on the condition that the Polish Underground Forces will cooperate with the Soviet armies in the struggle against Germany. The [State] Department has been officially informed in this connection by the Polish Ambassador that the Polish Government has recently renewed its instructions to the Polish Underground to cooperate with and assist the Soviet armies in every way, and on the basis of these assurances the $10,000,000 will be made available to the Polish Government.'[22] Mr Hull felt that the Soviet Government should be informed about this 'in order to avoid any possible misunderstanding'.[23] He ends his telegram by saying, 'It is not our intention to request Soviet approval for this action but merely to inform the Soviet Government that this action has been taken.'[24] Harriman responded by vetoing the idea and suggesting that 'If the information must be imparted, then I feel that it should preferably be done informally in Washington.'[25]

The Poles still believed that, if the Polish Home Army (AK) was co-ordinated and commanded directly by the Supreme Allied Command, the intentions of Poles could not be misinterpreted, misjudged, or manipulated by Soviet propaganda in the United States and England. However, British Field-Marshal Brooke informed the Polish Chief of Staff, General Kopanski, that 'The co-ordination of activities of AK with the Allied [command] cannot be done and that [he was] leaving decisions [concerning activities of AK] to the Polish authorities.'[26] The British in this way denied AK soldiers status as part of the Allied forces and left them to face the Soviet Army alone.

Just five days before the outbreak of the Uprising (27 July), Poles decided to appeal to the Americans to approach the Soviet Government '(1) to obtain the release of the arrested [AK] officers [in the Polish eastern territories]; (2) to enable the Polish [Underground] Army to fight in collaboration with Soviet troops against Germany; [and] (3) to obtain from the Soviets recognition of the Polish [Underground] Army in Poland as a co-belligerent Allied army'.[27] The Polish Government-in-Exile requested that the United States send representatives to the AK in German-occupied Poland to see first-hand what was happening. Mikolajczyk also renewed his plea to Churchill to send such liaison. Both Roosevelt and Churchill rejected the request.[28]

In July the Soviet armies were approaching Warsaw. Poles in London and the leaders of AK were now threatened by the Soviet Government not only as representatives of a nation, but also as individuals. The Polish Ambassador notified the British Government that an uprising was to take place in Warsaw, and once again submitted these proposals to the Foreign Secretary Eden 'that His Majesty's Government should intervene with the Soviet Government to prevent any victimisation of Polish units who have been co-operating in the struggle against the Germans'.[29]

When it has been admitted that Anglo-American political attitudes toward Polish affairs directly influenced the Soviet Government's behaviour toward Poland and therefore contributed to the outcome of the Uprising of Warsaw, it remains to be asked: Did American and British military leaders (as distinguished from Roosevelt and Churchill) promise support for, or even encourage, the Polish Home Army, either in a general uprising, or in Operation Tempest, or in the Uprising in the capital?

The answer is an unequivocal NO, and in this context it should be noted that, on 7 July 1944, General Tatar, who was a member of AK Headquarters, and Commander of Section VI (Occupied Poland) or the Polish General Staff in London, made the following statement to General George Marshall, Chief of Staff of the United States Army: 'The capital of Poland, Warsaw, was to be completely eliminated from the plan code named Tempest, [which] meant that no fighting of any kind would take place in Warsaw, even if the original plan for a general uprising of Armia Krajowa [should] occur.'[30]

So the Polish Government in London and evidently the AK Headquarters in Warsaw, as late as 7 July 1944 (about three weeks before the outbreak of the Uprising in Warsaw), had definitely excluded the city of Warsaw from their plans for any military uprising or activities under any conditions!

Neither American nor British military leaders on any level encouraged Poles to initiate action on this scale, and their positions on the issue were clear and are documented beyond any shade of doubt. The best man to provide the evidence is Polish Colonel Leon Mitkiewicz who was, between 1943 and 1945, Deputy Chief of Staff of the Polish forces and representative of the Commander-in-Chief of the Polish forces to the Combined Chiefs of Staff in Washington.

Before the arrival of Colonel Mitkiewicz in March 1943, the liaison officer from the Polish General Staff to the Combined Chiefs of Staff was Colonel Wlodzimierz Onacewicz, who also was the Polish military attaché at the Polish Embassy in Washington. According to Colonel Onacewicz, 'the Combined Chiefs of Staff devoted themselves exclusively to British–American policymaking, and were preparing all strategic planning and decisions without participation from other Allied representatives of other states attached to CCS – China, Canada, Australia, New Zealand and Holland – many of whom were high-ranking generals, had nothing to say and nothing to do. On extremely rare occasions they were asked to state their opinions . . . to maintain the appearance of their usefulness they were often invited to listen to briefings and such.'[31] Sikorski himself selected Colonel Leon Mitkiewicz for this function, and in person gave him these directives: (1) The *general uprising* in Poland should not be undertaken without co-ordination with the Combined Chiefs of Staff in Washington, particularly without assistance in armaments and precise and meticulous synchronization of direct assistance from the Allies. (2) In the event of the German front withdrawing to the line of the rivers Vistula and San still undefeated, it would be impossible for the AK to mobilize on territory occupied by the German Army, and the plan for a general uprising would be abandoned. (3) It was absolutely necessary to ascertain as early as possible whether, if a general uprising against Germans was to be undertaken, the Combined Chiefs of Staff would provide material assistance to the Poles to the degree and at the time requested.[32]

In March 1943, just before his departure for Washington, Colonel Mitkiewicz ascertained again that, in their discussions with the Polish officers, members of the British Imperial Staff insisted the main objectives of Armia Krajowa activities in Poland would be gathering intelligence, sabotage, and diversionary activities. Nothing was said by the British about a general uprising or regaining and holding large cities.[33]

According to Colonel Mitkiewicz, whom the author interviewed, and documents available from him,[34] neither British nor American staff gave any explicit or concrete statements binding them to assist any uprising of Armia Krajowa in Poland. In fact, what the Allied commands expected from Poles was, in principle, 'to carry out sabotage and intensive intelligence work against the Germans'.[35]

As Mitkiewicz talked with members of the Combined Chiefs of Staff it became clear that direct assistance from the United States to Armia Krajowa would not be forthcoming without the approval of the British Imperial Staff in London. By July 1943, Colonel Mitkiewicz had the impression that the United States Joint Chiefs or Staff sincerely wanted to assist Poland, but the British Chiefs of Staff were not as enthusiastic. Colonel Mitkiewicz reported these impressions to General Sikorski and received formal acknowledgment from him on 20 June 1943.[36]

The most definite stand on assistance to AK was taken by the Combined Chiefs of Staff on 23 September 1943. (By this time, General Sikorski had died, and General Kazimierz Sosnkowski had become Supreme Commander-in-Chief of the Polish forces.) The Combined Chiefs of Staff refused to synchronize Allied operations in the west with a general uprising of Armia Krajowa in Poland. Their decision was preceded by directives to the Polish General Staff in London from the British Imperial Staff, informing the Poles that all efforts to secure supplies should go only through the Special Operations Executive in London. These instructions were issued in the second half of 1943, and their meaning was ominously clear. The British Government and Imperial Staff had taken from the control of the Combined Chiefs of Staff decisions about supplying Armia Krajowa, thereby excluding the Americans, who, Mitkiewicz thought, were more apt to have given support. Here are pertinent excerpts from the letter to Colonel Mitkiewicz from the Combined Chiefs of Staff dated 23 September 1943.

The Combined Chiefs of Staff appreciate the great importance that is attached by the Polish Commander-in-Chief to the role envisaged by him for the Polish Secret Army (Armia Krajowa). The operation requirements of active theatres, however, are heavy; the Secret Army could not openly take an active part against the Axis until direct land or sea communication was immediately in prospect; there is also a lack of suitable aircraft for the delivery of large quantities of supplies to Poland. For these reasons the Combined Chiefs of Staff are unable at the present time to see their way to the allocation of the equipment required for the Polish Secret Army.

The supplies requested from U.S. and British sources for sabotage and intelligence activities in Poland have been approved, and the appropriate authorities have been so informed.

The shortage of heavy bomber aircraft continues, and the Combined Chiefs of Staff regret therefore that at the present it is not possible to allocate such aircraft to the Polish Government for delivery to Poland of supplies for sabotage and subversive activities. . . . For the Combined Chiefs of Staff: [Signed] H. Redman, [Signed] J. R. Deane, Combined Secretariat.[37]

Simultaneously with this letter, Brigadier Redman, British Secretary of CCS, explained to Colonel Mitkiewicz semi-officially that the decision had been caused 'by political considerations, especially because of the instability of the Russian – Polish relations and therefore inability to anticipate at this time . . . [how] Armia Krajowa in Poland [would behave] towards the Soviet forces when they entered Polish territory'.[38]

At the end of September 1943, Admiral Leahy, Chief of Staff to the President, saw Colonel Mitkiewicz and emphatically impressed upon him that the Soviet forces would be 'the first Allied forces to enter Polish territory' and also that the Soviet Government under no circumstances desired to have in Polish territory, in addition to its own soldiers, units of Armia Krajowa that would be under the Polish commander in London rather than under Soviet command.[39]

These statements, vital to the fate of Armia Krajowa, were immediately conveyed by Mitkiewicz to Polish Chief of Staff General Stanislaw Kopanski in London.[40] Alarmed by the British and American attitudes towards Armia Krajowa, and by the Polish situation in general, Mitkiewicz returned to London in October 1943 to pressure the Polish General Staff into trying once again to obtain a clear answer from the Combined Chiefs concerning the future and fate of Armia Krajowa. Colonel Mitkiewicz was soon even more disturbed by the prevalent sentiment of the Polish staff in London – a categorical belief that the Western Allies, above all the British, 'will enter Poland first, and they will help Armia Krajowa in the general rising'.[41] He was unable to communicate to the Polish Commander-in-Chief and his Chief of Staff, General Kopanski, the reality of CCS's attitude. He proposed to Kopanski that it would be highly desirable to give instructions, including a clear-cut description of the Allied attitude, to Bor-Komorowski as soon as possible. General Kopanski responded that 'this matter belongs to the Polish Government in London and not to the staff of the Supreme Commander-in-Chief'.[42]

The Combined Chiefs of Staff allotted some equipment and supplies to Armia Krajowa for intelligence and sabotage activities but, although 300 sorties with supply drops were promised, the British Special Operations Executive, which was responsible for their delivery, sent to Poland only thirty between July 1943 and the end of January 1944.[43] Mitkiewicz's representations in London, and the curtailment of the promised assistance to Armia Krajowa spurred the Poles to ask again for a definitive stand by the Combined Chiefs of Staff. The request was submitted on 14 October 1943, and the response came in a letter dated 20 January 1944. The letter is cited here in full because of its importance.

Dear Colonel Mitkiewicz,
The Combined Chiefs of Staff have carefully considered your letter which was presented to them on 14 October 1943.
With regard to the preparation and ultimate equipment of the Polish Forces in Poland, the Combined Chiefs of Staff can only reiterate their remarks as conveyed to you in their letter of 23 September 1943, as they are still unable to see their way to the allocation of the equipment required for the Polish Secret Army. As you are aware, the supplies requested for sabotage and intelligence activities in Poland have been approved and deliveries are and will be taking place in accordance with the availability of aircraft.
With regard to a pronouncement of joint British – American strategic responsibility over Polish territory, the Combined Chiefs of Staff consider that this question is basically political rather than military, and one which can only be determined by the Chiefs of State. It is regretted, therefore, that the Combined Chiefs of Staff, in the absence of any guidance in this matter, do not at present find themselves in a position to discuss this matter conclusively with the Polish General Staff. Sincerely yours, For the Combined Chiefs of Staff, [Signed] H. Redman, A. J. McFarland, Combined Secretariat.[44]

Again, Brigadier Redman was willing to 'supplement' orally what the Chiefs of Staff did not say in writing. He told Mitkiewicz that 'Great Britain and the United States are not assuming any responsibility for the preparation of the general uprising of Armia Krajowa nor for the Armia Krajowa's activities on the Polish territory, because this territory is not in their strategic sphere'.[45]

This, of course, was the direct impact of Roosevelt and Churchill's secret discussions with Stalin concerning Poland several weeks before at the Tehran Conference.

Colonel Mitkiewicz immediately conveyed this by letter to the Polish General Staff in London along with the information he had gathered informally about the outcome of the Tehran Conference.[46]

The Allies were consistent. As early as October 1942, when the Polish plan for the liberation of Polish territory by force was presented, the Combined Chiefs of Staff, the British Imperial Staff, and the Special Operations Executive discouraged the Poles from undertaking a general uprising, and the AK from any major military operations. This position was stated explicitly in writing, reaffirmed verbally by their representatives, and emphatically evidenced by the curtailment of supplies to Poland.

The evidence indicates that Colonel Mitkiewicz fulfilled his duties as the representative of the Combined Chiefs of Staff well. He conveyed all information available to him and reflected the Allied position to his immediate superior, the Chief of the Polish General Staff in London. But was this information conveyed to the Commander of Armia Krajowa, General Bor-Komorowski?

Relationships among the members of the Polish Government and the Polish community in London were complex and tragically ridden with hostility, and sides had been drawn up in an already open feud between Prime Minister Mikolajczyk and Commander-in-Chief General Kazimierz Sosnkowski, Sikorski's equal but separate successors. Each had his loyal supporters and bitter detractors. In this atmosphere no one in the London Polish Government told General Bor precisely what they knew of the attitudes of their British, American and Soviet allies toward the Uprising, and these antagonisms were to bear heavily on the fate of Warsaw. On 12 August 1944, for example (the twelfth day of the Uprising), an extremely sensitive radio message was sent from London to the Government Delegate and General Bor in Poland, of which the substance was agreed by the Prime Minister, Sosnkowski, and by the Minister of Defence, the Chief of Staff of the Polish Forces-in-Exile, the Deputy Chief of Staff of Home Army Affairs, and the Deputy Prime Minister. When this radio message reached Bor the following sentence, concerning the possibility of surrender, *had been deleted*: 'Under these circumstances, with the fullest respect for your heroic achievement so far, we [declare] that *any decision undertaken by you will be accepted by us with the most profound respect*.'[47]

There were a number of odd occurrences within the Polish Government in London.

When Colonel Leopold Okulicki, with the knowledge of General Sosnkowski, parachuted into Poland in May 1944, he assumed an important position in Headquarters of Armia Krajowa. He was strongly in favour of an uprising in Warsaw and was responsible for manipulating the atmosphere around Bor-Komorowski toward that decision.[48] General Monter, Commander of the Warsaw district of AK, asked him, 'Do you think that London will help us in supplies and preliminary bombardment?' Okulicki replied, 'Do you think that it would be otherwise?'[49] (Before his jump Colonel Okulicki was seen by General Sosnkowski, the Polish Supreme Commander-in-Chief in London, and by Sosnkowski's adjutant, Captain Witold Babinski.[50] Either Colonel Okulicki was uninformed about the Allied posture towards the AK or he refrained from telling the AK command all that he knew.)

It is extraordinary, too, to find General Sosnkowski, Commander-in-Chief of Polish Armed Forces, leaving England to visit troops in Italy before the Uprising, and returning *seven days* after its inception, in spite of an urgent message from the Polish President on 2 August requesting that he come back to London at once.

AK Headquarters in Poland had their dissensions too, and General Tatar's departure from Poland was itself the result of political differences and disagreements within the Headquarters.[51]

While in Washington in July 1944, Tatar presented a briefing to the Combined Chiefs of Staff, stating AK's willingness to assume responsibility for combat assignments, and its potential contribution toward defeating the Germans. He also assured the CCS members that AK 'will co-operate with the first Ally who approaches Polish territory, in defeating Germans'.[52] He indicated that AK sabotage, diversion and other military activities resulting in heavy enemy losses caused the concentration of large German units in many areas of Poland to countermand AK activities and he cited an AK action between 6 and 9 April 1944 that disrupted all communication on a railway line for forty-eight hours when the line was being used to bring crucial supplies to the German eastern front, as well as the derailment of twenty-five German military trains within four days (31 March–3 April 1944). With regard to the numbers of Armia Krajowa and its equipment he was specific: as to June 1944, there were 6,500 platoons – more than a quarter of a million people – and their effective armament was sufficient for only 32,000. General Tatar asked the CCS to bring the level of equipment to at least forty-five per cent and to fly 150–200 monthly supply relief flights to Poland. If this number were to be increased to 1300 flights, all the needed equipment could be supplied, and the combat capacity of Armia Krajowa could be fully utilized and synchronized with the Allied operation.[53]

The British were displeased with General Tatar's presence in Washington. Again they reiterated their position. Brigadier Redman, on behalf of his superiors, told Colonel Mitkiewicz that General Tatar's appeal to the Combined Chief of Staff broke the established procedure for handling Polish affairs. Poles were expected to submit their requests to the Special Operations Executive in London, and the CCS would not make any decisions concerning Armia Krajowa in Poland, nor would it respond to General Tatar's pleadings: any such response would be forthcoming to the Polish General Staff in London through Special Operations Office.[54]

Then, Colonel Mitkiewicz writes, Brigadier Redman read to him several documents of great importance concerning Armia Krajowa:

These were the minutes from meetings of the Combined Chiefs of Staff in Washington, and the British Imperial Staff; and also the evaluation of Armia Krajowa in Poland originating from the staff of General Eisenhower. . . .
    These documents indicated that:
    1. The preparation of the general uprising of Armia Krajowa in Poland cannot be assisted by air transports from the west. Such action is only possible by direct assistance on land or by sea, and only in conjunction with the operation of the Soviet Army (Tehran!).
    2. Neither the Combined Chiefs of Staff nor General Eisenhower is in a position to say when the general uprising of Armia Krajowa should take place in Poland. This is a matter for the Polish Government in London, and it should be synchronized with the Government of the Soviet Union since only the Soviet Union is directly interested in such operation. . . .
    3. The disruption of the German communication system in Poland is useful to the Allies in general but specifically most [useful] to the Soviet Government and therefore with that government such actions should be synchronized. . . .[55]

The essence of the conference with Redman as understood by Colonel Mitkiewicz was that the Polish General Staff should ascertain from the British Imperial Staff all decisions made by the Allies about Poland. They should also realize that the activities of Armia Krajowa in Poland including a general uprising, if any, would depend upon co-operation with the Soviet Government, and that the British authorities strongly recommended co-operation and joint decisions with the Soviet Staff and the commander of Armia Krajowa in Poland, rather than between the latter and the Polish Government or General Staff in London; neither the Combined Chiefs of Staff in Washington nor the British Imperial Staff in London should undertake such decisions. This was plain talking.

Colonel Mitkiewicz immediately conveyed this information by radio to General Sosnkowski and his Chief of Staff, General Kopanski, in London.[56] Then, less than a month after General Tatar's unequivocal statement that Warsaw would be excluded when AK units took military action, on the morning of 2 August 1944, the Polish Military Mission in Washington, including Colonel Mitkiewicz himself, learned from the American press that the city of Warsaw was engaged in battle on the order of General Bor-Komorowski. Colonel Mitkiewicz reports 'all officers of our mission were stricken [as] by a thunderbolt . . . and depressed.

'Truly, none of us officers of the mission, knowing the previous sequence of events and the statements of the English and Americans—particularly after hearing the pronouncement of General

Tatar – expected that an uprising by the Armia Krajowa would take place, particularly and especially in Warsaw.'[57]

Colonel Mitkiewicz could only conclude that *the Uprising of Warsaw was planned and activated on the initiative of Polish leadership in Warsaw.*[58]

On the tenth day of the Uprising Colonel Mitkiewicz reported to Polish military headquarters in London that, when on 9 August he had asked for assistance for Warsaw, 'The Combined Chiefs of Staff again took a position that the decision [could] only be made by the British authorities in London. Our requests were conveyed by CCS to London. I was also told that Warsaw [was] within the area of activity of the Soviet Army; and therefore all intervention without knowledge and approval of the Soviet Command [was] impossible.'[59]

There is no evidence, incidentally, that even this message or information therein was conveyed to General Bor in Warsaw by the authorities of the Polish Government-in-Exile!

American and British political positions on Poland were in fact being sifted through five levels of policymaking before they reached the man who gave the order for the Uprising of Warsaw, General Tadeusz Bor-Komorowski. These levels were:

(1) The Heads of State of the Big Three – Churchill, Roosevelt, Stalin and their diplomatic officials;

(2) The Combined Chiefs of Staff (Washington);

(3) The British Imperial Staff (London);

(4) British Strategic Operations Executive (London);

(5) The Polish Government-in-Exile and the Staff of the Commander-in-Chief of the Polish Forces (London); and only then,

(6) The Headquarters of Armia Krajowa and General Bor-Komorowski.

Such was the hierarchy through which political and military information vital to General Bor's planning and direction of AK activities passed, and the available documents indicate that, from the topmost level shared by Roosevelt, Churchill and Stalin, only selected information concerning Poland was passed to lower levels. Bor did not know any more than Mitkiewicz before the Uprising about the most important fact, the ceding of Polish territory east of the Curzon Line to Stalin. (Bor confirmed during the interview with the author (see Appendix B) that he had not known about this, did not learn of it until five months *after* the Uprising, when he was in a German prisoner-of-war camp, and saw an announcement of the Yalta agreement in the German press.)

Information concerning the role the Allies expected the Armia Krajowa to play and the degree of material assistance the Allies would provide was explicitly stated in writing at level two, the Combined Chiefs of Staff, but by the time their policy statement reached General Bor on level six it was no longer explicit. Responsibility for this lies with the Polish political and military *élite* who were in London: somewhere within level five, the Polish Government and the Commander-in-Chief's staff headquarters in London, the information was diluted, distorted or suppressed. This can be blamed in part on the poor relationship between these two bodies and in part on the peculiar structural weaknesses and personal antagonisms within each. The Commander-in-Chief, General Sosnkowski, did not as a matter of routine forward to the Polish President copies of his radio messages to Bor-Komorowski (according to a letter to the author from Pawel Jankowski, Chief of the Chancery of the Polish President, London, 22 November 1968), and indeed it is not clear whether he was obliged to do so. It is difficult to ascertain exactly the degree to which the command of the Polish Armed Forces in Exile and the AK leadership were, in fact, controlled by civilian authorities. Prime Minister Mikolajczyk, for one, maintains that they were not so controlled at all.[60]

By 14 August, Mikolajczyk, back in London, realized that Marshal Stalin was not helping Warsaw in spite of what he had understood to be an expressed promise that such assistance would be forthcoming. That day, too, the Polish Government in London received a blow in the form of a letter from the British Foreign Office. Among other things it said, 'The decision for a general Uprising in Warsaw has been undertaken without previous consultation with His Majesty's Government which, because of that, found itself unable to prepare plans for co-operation in advance.'[61] In fact, of course, Polish Ambassador Edward Raczynski had notified the British Government in a letter dated 27 July 1944, though in fairness it should be pointed out that there had been no previous consultation on that subject. The British also pointed out that the commencement of the Uprising was not co-ordinated with the Soviet Government.

Ambassador Raczynski responded on 16 August, in a letter addressed to Sir Orme Sargent of the British Foreign Office, to the effect that on several occasions the Soviet radio had appealed to the Polish nation to rise against the Germans, and that there had been just such an appeal on 29 July, three days before the Uprising broke out. Moreover, when Prime Minister Mikolajczyk had met Stalin for the first time on 3 August, he had specifically asked for Soviet assistance for the Poles fighting in Warsaw. Prime Minister Mikolajczyk, and the Polish Minister for Foreign Affairs, Tadeusz Romer, had informed members of the British Government on several occasions about the approaching action of the Armia Krajowa in Warsaw, most recently on 25 July 1944, while Raczynski himself had written to Mr Eden on 27 July. The Polish Ambassador therefore maintained that 'Certainly you should agree with me that in the light of the above-mentioned facts, the preparation for armed action by the Polish Home Army against Germans in Warsaw had been submitted in a proper manner to the knowledge of His Majesty's Government.'[62]

It can hardly be argued that the Poles had not consulted the Allies, nor sought their assistance in sufficient time, for the Allies were not co-ordinated either – the Soviet Union was calling for an uprising while the British were discouraging the Poles from such action.

On 22 August, in answer to repeated British and American requests for assistance to Warsaw, Stalin sent this message to both Churchill and Roosevelt.

> Sooner or later the truth about the group of criminals who have embarked on the Warsaw adventure in order to seize power will become known to everybody. These people have exploited the good faith of the citizens of Warsaw, throwing many almost unarmed people against the German guns, tanks and aircraft. A situation has arisen in which each new day serves not only the Poles for the liberation of Warsaw but the Hitlerites who are inhumanly shooting down the inhabitants of Warsaw.
>
> From the military point of view, the situation which has arisen, by increasingly directing the attention of the Germans to Warsaw, is just as unprofitable for the Red Army as for the Poles. Meanwhile the Soviet troops who have recently encountered new and notable efforts by the Germans to go over to the counterattack, are doing everything possible to smash these counterattacks of the Hitlerites and to go over to new wide-scale attack in the region of Warsaw. There can [be] no doubt that the Red Army is not sparing its efforts to break [through] the Germans around Warsaw and to free Warsaw for the Poles. That will be the best and most effective help for the Poles who are anti-Nazis.[63].

Never a word about Soviet broadcasts encouraging the Uprising of Warsaw.

American Ambassador Harriman saw the falsity of the Soviet position. In a radio message on 19 August to the Secretary of State he pointed out that

> Stalin urged Soviet patriots in occupied territory to go underground and wage unremitting war against the Germans. Active resistance movements in occupied countries, such as Tito's in Yugoslavia, have been encouraged and émigré governments have been constantly criticized for counselling a waiting policy. On 16 August in an article on White Russian Partisans, *Izvestia* paid fulsome tribute to their activities, estimáting that they had killed more than half a million German soldiers and officers. . . . The same issue of *Pravda* . . . had laudatory articles concerning the assistance rendered the Allied Armies by French and Italian Partisans.
>
> There was every reason for the Warsaw patriots to anticipate, even without instructions, that the time had come to arise and contribute to their liberation when the Red Army approached the city after its rapid victorious advance through White Russia. . . . Had the Polish Government advocated a waiting policy to the population of Warsaw, it would have doubtless have been excoriated in the Soviet press.[64]

At last, at a meeting of the British War Cabinet on 20 August, Mr Eden referred to the Polish request that their Underground Army should be recognized officially as a fighting force. He was now advised that without using the phrase 'belligerent status' His Majesty's Government, on the basis that it was they who had been supplying the Poles, could make a statement which would give some cover to the Underground Movement. 'It would not, in any event, go beyond what we had said in respect of the Maquis. Nor, he added anxiously, would it be anti-Russian in character.'[65]

On 29 August 1944, after twenty-nine days of fighting, the British and American governments recognized AK as part of the Allied forces, and thereafter insurgents were protected by the Geneva Convention —officially, at least.

CHAPTER SEVEN

Air Assistance

IN JANUARY 1943, four officers of the Polish Air Force were flown from England and dropped by parachute into occupied Poland. A second mission followed in April 1944, and relayed the same message to the AK command: the Polish Air Force under British command was unable to support a general insurgency, and AK Headquarters should guard against any optimism in this matter. Assistance from the Allies was 'practically impossible'.[1] The AK command were as aware then, as after the war, that 'assurances were not given'.[2] AK Chief of Staff, General Pelczynski, weighed the lack of air support against other factors:

> In view of the conviction that Warsaw would inevitably be taken by the Red Army, the problem of assistance from Polish forces in the West and English allies was losing importance as one of the crucial elements in the decision. The command of the AK was aware that the Allied Air Force [sic] from the West could support our fight on the Vistula only after the Allied armies reached the . . . Rhine. The Polish Commander-in-Chief [in London gave] the AK command [precise information] about the conditions of possible Allied support for a general uprising. At that time Warsaw was at the very end of the range of the heaviest Allied planes. Airdrops of combat supplies and armaments sent to Poland from airfields in Italy . . . were not yet reaching the region of Warsaw. . . . [In] making the decision [to initiate the Uprising] the AK command was conscious of the fact that air assistance from the West was uncertain and could only take place with maximum effort on the part of the pilots, because of the pressure of the combat situation in Warsaw. . . . The Red Army was fast approaching the Vistula river without waiting for the Anglo-Saxons to secure air bases on the Continent.[3]

The General reiterated his views five years after the Uprising of Warsaw. '[The initiation by AK of the Uprising in Warsaw] when the front of the Soviet Army was marching toward us was of such high priority that [the lack of air assistance] and other deficiencies in our supplies and preparations did not play a role.'[4]

Yet, in the afternoon of the second day of the Uprising, a message went from AK Headquarters to the Polish Government in London requesting that weapons and ammunition be delivered by air,[5] and General Pelczynski's words seem to imply that the AK command thought it would force the Allies to render assistance. The Polish Underground Trust Archives in London contain a number of the messages concerning air assistance exchanged between military and civilian sections of the Polish Government-in-Exile and their counterparts in Warsaw. Those from Warsaw plead desperately for air support; those from London express despair at the inability to provide it.[6]

The day-to-day operational log book of Squadron 1586, stationed in Italy, indicates that the Uprising came as a surprise to the personnel of the Polish Air Force fighting under British command. This was a Polish squadron of heavy bombers; it was given the special assignment of assisting Warsaw by the British Command. It faced a task beyond its capabilities: the distance was too great for a fighter escort.[7]

On 1 August the squadron had eight planes and five crews; by the thirtieth only one of these original crews survived.

The log book of Squadron 1586 includes these entries:

> 2 August 1944: Atmospheric conditions do not permit flights to Poland. Squadron active over Northern Italy.
> 3 August 1944: Weather prevents flying to Warsaw. Four planes over Italy.
> 4 August 1944: At 2.30 p.m. came an order from the British Command forbidding flights to Warsaw. The squadron leader, upon consultation with the crews, allowed seven planes to take off for Poland (three Liberators plus one Halifax to Warsaw; three Halifax to other dropping zones). The crews volunteered.
> 5 August: No flights owing to bad atmospheric conditions.
> 6 August: No flights, ditto.
> 7 August: No flights to Poland, ditto.
> 8 August:Two Halifax and one Liberator flew to Warsaw.
> The crews reached the objectives and reported the city was on fire.
> 11–18 August: The squardron flew to Warsaw for seven nights in a row.
> [On 12 August, of seven planes, one returned.]
> 19 August: No flights.
> 20–8 August: The squadron flew everynight to Warsaw.
> [On 27 August, of six planes, one returned.][8]

During September, 42 planes of the Squadron flew 17 combat missions to Warsaw, 16 to Italy, 7 to Yugoslavia and 2 to Bulgaria. Eight crews perished in flights to Warsaw. There were no losses in flights to other countries. The last flights to Warsaw were on 20 and 21 September. Total losses of Squadron 1586 for the months of August and

September 1944 were 17 crews, 15 in flight to Warsaw, one crew while delivering supplies to other zones in Poland, and one in northern Italy.[9]

Flight conditions to Warsaw were extremely hazardous, and every plane that returned had been hit.[10] Even parachutes inside the planes were riddled by German bullets or explosives.[11] the Polish Supreme Commander-in-Chief in England, General Sosnkowski, demanded that the pilots fly regardless of weather and losses. On 8 August 1944 he sent a wire to one Colonel Hancza, commander of a Polish liaison base in Italy: 'Because of the situation of the capital and general [policy] considerations, today's operations to Warsaw [must get through]. English maintain that the difficulties indicate impossibility of dropping supplies over Warsaw. We must demonstrate that Polish flights get through. This may have great impact on the prompt initiation of assistance. I told the English: Poles took Monte Cassino, Poles will do impossible in order to help their brothers who fight alone. Signed: Supreme Commander Sosnkowski.'[12]

The Polish airman who commanded Flight 1586 (renamed in September 1944 'Squadron 301 of the Defenders of Warsaw') from June 1944 to May 1945 was Wing-Commander E Arciuszkiewicz, an experienced pilot, who flew a total of eighty-seven combat missions during the Second World War. In a letter[13] to the author, written in 1973, he commented that on the fourth day of the Uprising the British command gave permission for flights to Poland, provided the objective of airdrops was *not* Warsaw. The Polish crews, by agreement among themselves, flew over Warsaw anyway. The next day British Air-Marshal Slessor called Wing-Commander Arciuszkiewicz in to see him, and asked: (1) why the British command had not been informed in advance about the Uprising; (2) with whom it had been co-ordinated; (3) how many insurgents were in Warsaw; (4) how many civilians were in Warsaw; and (5) could planes land east of Warsaw on the territories taken by Soviet armies? The Polish Wing-Commander naturally did not have the information to answer these questions precisely, but in retrospect he did not interpret the questioning as foreshadowing a lack of co-operation on the part of the British, since two air units of more than thirty Liberator-type four-engine heavy bombers, one flown by British crews and the other by South African crews, were assigned to render assistance to Warsaw in mid-August.

Airmen from the British Commonwealth were not happy with their assignment. They openly questioned the purpose for which they were expected to die. After the second flight over Warsaw, their losses were about sixty per cent. They complained bitterly that *Russians* were actually firing at them.

It was the Wing-Commander's impression that his Polish superiors were sending him inexperienced crews and quality-reject planes to be dispatched over Warsaw, and that the Polish Air Force, under pressure from the Polish Commander-in-Chief, General Sosnkowski, acted

'chaotically'. Arciuszkiewicz was in receipt of orders from his Polish
Commander-in-Chief, the Chief of the Polish Air Force, and General
Bor-Komorowski, yet could do only what was permitted by his
immediate British superiors. The demands upon him and his men
bordered on the irrational. He tells of the occasion when

> One day (I don't remember the date exactly), we were informed
> that because of atmospheric conditions, all flights had been
> cancelled. The clouds extended above 30,000 feet. . . . At 1 p.m.
> and again at 3 p.m. the meteorological report [remained the
> same], and we were told that the weather would deteriorate. The
> air base was closed for all flights, including local ones. It was noisy
> in the officers' and noncommissioned officers' canteens. We were
> singing, but in a half-hearted way. . . . we were still living today.
> We didn't know what would happen tomorrow. At 10 p.m. a
> messenger ran into our officers' mess. He gave me a note. It was a
> radio message from London from the Polish Commander-in-Chief:
> 'In spite of atmospheric conditions and objections, the flight to
> Warsaw is to proceed immediately. After reaching its objectives,
> the crew is to jump with parachutes.' This was a demonstration,
> but of what? And who was going to pay for it? . . . We were getting
> orders from someone who was very far from our problems. I
> immediately ordered an alert, but I had to get permission for the
> flight from the [British] commander of the air base. When I phoned
> [to notify him of the order] there was a moment of silence at the
> other end. Then he said, 'Eugene, are you drunk or crazy? Wait a
> minute. I will get you in touch with Slessor . . . you had better . . .
> talk to him.' In a few minutes Air-Marshal Slessor was on the
> phone: 'What is this all about?' Well, I told him about my order,
> omitting the part concerning our parachute jump. He asked me
> whether I had taken note of the atmospheric conditions. I told
> him, 'You know all the conditions better than I do. I am a soldier,
> and I have to comply with my orders.'
>   'When can you start?'
>   'At the earliest, two hours from now.'
>   'I doubt if you can make it.'

Air-Marshal Slessor recognized the Polish officer's dilemma, and his
final order was to 'Have a drink, and go to bed. Tomorrow is another
day. Tonight you will not be flying anywhere. Good night, Wing-
Commander.'

The Wing-Commander later flew several night missions over
Warsaw, and reported that, in the last stages of fighting, the very
outlines of the streets of Warsaw had disappeared. The city was all
rubble, and the stench of smoke and dead bodies permeated the cabin
of the plane. In order to find the drop zone, it was necessary to reduce
speed to 145 miles per hour (when the plane tended to stall), and on one
occasion he saw in the light from burning buildings a small group of
men waving at the plane. Squadron 301 'of the Defenders of Warsaw'
completed a hundred flights during the Uprising. The author has

interviewed two other survivors from this squadron: Warrant-Officer Neciuk, a flight mechanic, and Air-Commodore Rayski, who volunteered to fly as a co-pilot. Neciuk made eighteen flights over Poland; three of them reached the vicinity of Warsaw. His plane, a Liberator, carried a crew of eight men.[14] He recalled that before the flights each member of the crew received an envelope with money and a map, in case they were downed in enemy territory. They also had a large thermos of black coffee and sandwiches of corned beef and bacon: 'We liked the coffee and chocolate, but the sandwiches – not very much.'[15]

The plane used 40 imperial gallons an hour, or 2,300 gallons of gasoline for each flight, which meant 3,500 pounds of weight in fuel alone,[16] and usually carried 1,200 pounds of supplies. The Halifax had six fuel tanks distributed throughout its body, but even so at least one plane returning from Poland ran out of gas as it taxied down the runway. Even with expert navigation it took from fifteen to twenty minutes after reaching Warsaw to locate the drop zone. 'As mechanics, we were under tension watching for red lights on our dashboard. When they appeared it meant either that the fuel was running out or that something was malfunctioning.'[17]

As the Air-Commodore remembers it:

> We took off from the airfield in Brindisi, Italy, while it was still light, around 2 p.m. Our crew was Polish . . . against us were German radar and the Luftwaffe, especially the night fighters. After a while we were flying in darkness and very high. My first pilot's name was Squadron Leader Ladro and the navigator was Flight Officer Chmiel.
>   The first and second times our plane flew [to Warsaw] we flew [alone] because we could not give assistance [in flight] to another plane anyway. We were trying to bypass larger cities. Warsaw was one sea of fire – an eerie red sky. . . . We would pass Warsaw to the right side of the plane. Nobody said anything through the intercom . . . [not even] one word. . . . Sixty miles from Warsaw, on the approach, we could already smell smoke in the plane's cabin and it [remained long after we left] the target. [The height above target was about 450 feet, and our speed during the supply-drop was 135 m.p.h.] Warsaw . . . looked burned out but still glowed with red embers. From time to time there was a pulsation of flames. Towards the north a large complex of buildings was . . . burning with a powerful flame. Smoke hung over all the city. Toward the northern part [Old Town] there were darkening embers. [There were] no movements on the roads.[18]

The planes over Warsaw were inevitably pinioned on beams of anti-aircraft lights for German artillery. German night fighters lurked in the sky. 'The worst time was now – while we were looking for the drop zone. In my first flight we spent half an hour flying around to find it, and we knew we didn't have much gasoline to spare.'[19] (At most, the planes carried one extra hour's fuel.) Finally, the drop.

For those who survived the delivery there was the long journey home. Total flight time was from ten to fourteen hours, depending on weather conditions, the strength of German defences, and the speed with which they located the drop zone. In one flight, 'Of five planes, only one came back. The plane was so shot up that it landed by luck. One member of the crew was wounded. . . . The [Polish] crew of this plane flew over Warsaw six times. Six times! They always returned with the plane . . . shot up.'[20]

The insurgents reported that one of the planes dropped a wreath with the inscription, 'Glory to the heroes of fighting Warsaw.'[21] From a bomber with British insignia, spiralling down in flames, observers saw supplies spilling to the very moment it struck the buildings.

Besides the pilots of Flight 1586, British pilots from the 205th Bombing Group, composed of the 31st South African Wing and the 178th RAF Wing, flew 116 sorties composed of from 4 to 24 planes a night to Warsaw.[22] The shooting-down of a British plane in most tragic circumstances was described by an eyewitness as 'a big burning star . . . coming down from a quiet summer night'.[23] The plane struck a building in the basement of which was a field hospital. Disregarding the flames, Poles – soldiers and civilians – tried to save the crew, but it was impossible. Another eyewitness reported: 'In the billfold of one of the . . . pilots [there was a picture of] two little flags of Great Britain, drawn by a child.'[24]

In London, meanwhile, Polish military and political personalities used all possible contacts, formal and informal, begging, persuading, cajoling, in an effort to obtain planes and supplies for Warsaw. No one was spared – not Churchill, Roosevelt, the British War Ministry, British and American Air Forces, not even King George VI.[25] In a letter dated 14 August 1944, twenty-three Polish pilots of the Polish Fighter Squadron Number 303 serving under British command addressed themselves to the King of England: 'Shall the Luftwaffe, after being swept from the London skies, wreak its vengeance over and spread death in Warsaw? Shall faith in Great Britain be destroyed in the flames which now envelop our capital [Warsaw]?'[26] There were some 200,000 armed Polish soldiers-in-exile under British command. Polish airmen, especially, demanded, within the limits permitted by military discipline, air assistance to Warsaw. They pointed out that Polish Prime Minister Mikolajczyk had informed the British Government in the middle of July 1944 that AK would be in a state of combat readiness between 17 and 25 July. They cited his conversation with Churchill on the evening of 25 July, and the Polish Ambassador's meeting on 27 July with Foreign Minister Eden, when he had submitted a memorandum from General Bor calling for the dispatch to Warsaw of the Polish Paratroop Brigade from England, the bombing by the Royal Air Force of German airfields around Warsaw and the sending of long-range fighter planes. Mustangs or Spitfires, to land on Polish territory that was to be seized by AK.[27]

Obviously, the Polish Government had provided the information.

The British Government had assured the Polish Ambassador with another letter from the British Foreign Office, signed by O. G. Sargent, explaining:

> operational considerations alone preclude us from meeting the three requests you made for assisting the rising in Warsaw.
>
> It would not be possible to fly the parachute brigade over German territory as far as Warsaw, without risking excessive losses. The despatch of fighter squadrons to airfields in Poland would also be a lengthy and complicated process which could, in any case, only be carried out in agreement with the Soviet Government. It could certainly not be accomplished in time to influence the present battle. As regards bombarding Warsaw airfields, Warsaw is beyond the normal operational range of Royal Air Force bombers and the bombing of airfields would in any case be carried out much more appropriately by bombers operating from Soviet-controlled bases. Insofar as your authorities may have had in mind shuttle-bombing, about which there has been some publicity lately, this is carried out by the American Army Air Force and not by the Royal Air Force. I am afraid, therefore, there is nothing that His Majesty's Government can do in this con-nexion. . . .[28]

At the same time Sir Alan F. Brooke of the British War Office reiterated the British Government's position in a personal letter to General Sosnkowski: 'As General Ismay informed General Kukiel [the Polish Minister of Defence] in a letter of 2 August, we had regretfully to decide against sending part of the Polish Parachute Brigade to Warsaw. It is not possible for us to find the necessary transport aircraft to fly in a unit and maintain it in the Warsaw area. Large numbers of transport aircraft would be required for this purpose, and these could not be spared at this critical stage of the campaign in the West.'[29]

The British took this definite stand on 2 August, the second day of the Uprising, but *no one troubled to inform General Bor*, who six days later was still hopeful of assistance: 'Arrival of parachute brigade can decide fate of Warsaw. There are possibilities of landing in the [adjacent] . . . forest, which is in our hands. . . . We demand this effort. . . .'[30]

The soldiers of the Paratroop Brigade stationed in England reacted in their own way on 13 August 1944. The commander of the first battalion, Major W. Tonn, wrote a letter to General Sosnkowski reporting that eighty per cent of the battalion had refused to eat breakfast. When he had asked the soldiers why, they answered: 'I am a Polish soldier. . . . I don't see any assistance from Allies for Poland. . . . This is my way of protesting. . . .' Another paratrooper said: 'I am a soldier, and we fight anywhere; but they [British] . . . should know that I am aware that they are cheating the Polish nation. . . .'[31]

In the files of the Polish Supreme Commander-in-Chief there is another letter marked 2.20 p.m. the same date. It reported the officers, noncommissioned officers, and soldiers still would not eat, but that 'all duties [were] performed'.[32] On the same day the second battalion also refused to eat. The third battalion and the medical company of paratroopers then followed suit. However, they performed all their duties. These men wanted to jump into Poland to assist Warsaw.[33] The commanding general of the paratroopers wrote a letter to General Sosnkowski reporting the unrest and demonstrations among his troops because the Allies were not assisting AK and because the brigade had not been sent to Warsaw.[34]

Ex-Prime Minister Mikolajczyk stated his view in an interview in 1965: 'I was against sending the Paratroopers' Brigade. I wasn't a military man, but I told Sosnkowski, "How can you send these men to their deaths? They will not even get through." But Generals Sosabowski [commander of Paratroopers] and Sosnkowski said that I was against assistance to Warsaw.'[35] Mikolajczyk took this subject to the Polish Council of Ministers in London on 14 August. The minutes of the deliberation noted:

> The Prime Minister explained that he appreciates and under-
> stands completely the motives of Polish airmen and paratroopers,
> but he is [at the same time] compelled to put responsibility for
> these demonstrations on persons [pro-Sosnkowski and anti-
> Mikolajczyk] who are instrumental in this action. [This action] is
> inspired by ill will to foment and sharpen the unrest, so it
> may serve as an attack on the Government . . . in order to blame
> the Government for the Uprising in Warsaw and for the lack of
> proper assistance for the fighting capital.[36]

Internal political and personal disagreements notwithstanding, the Poles were unified in their actions to secure air support. At one point Polish President Raczkiewicz, General Sosnkowski, General Kopanski (Chief of Staff), and General Tabor considered the possibility that 'the Polish Government should resign as an act of political demonstration'.[37] This did not come about but, throughout the sixty-three days of the Uprising, Poles in London continued to press for help through an intensive exchange of correspondence and meetings involving strained confrontations.[38]

The man most directly responsible for a level-headed appraisal of the technical feasibility of air missions to Warsaw was a British Air-Marshal, Sir John Slessor, and so it was he who ultimately became (directly or indirectly) the focus of Polish frustrations. He was re-sponsible for planes, crews, and operational directives, and the demands put to him were complicated, if not impossible. If the Polish Supreme Commander-in-Chief in London considered that the British Government was shirking its duties toward its Polish Allies,[39] the British point of view is well put by Air-Marshal Slessor:

> There was no previous consultation or advanced planning either

with the advancing Russians or with ourselves . . . on the nature of the action to be taken, or the support that could be afforded from the outside. The Poles certainly had good reason for not consulting the Russians. . . . But the failure of the exile Government in London and their Commander-in-Chief, the unhappy General Sosnkowski, to consult us in advance is difficult to excuse in the light of what followed. The first intimation came on July 29 – three days before the rising – in the shape of a letter from General Kukiel, the [Polish] Minister of Defence, to General Ismay, followed on 31st by a visit by General Tabor, the Director of Military Operations of the Polish Secret Army, to the head of S.O.E. They told us that the arrangements had been made for the underground Army to intervene in the imminent battle for Warsaw. Tabor said this might happen any time within the next four or five days – actually it happened the very next day – and presented a series of completely impossible demands from General Bor for various forms of air support. Unfortunately that gallant officer, as also Sosnkowski and Tabor, were land soldiers who had not the remotest conception of what was practicable as far as the air was concerned. Bor made four demands on us for assistance which he described as indispensable and which, for that reason, he should certainly have discussed with us before committing himself to action. . . . It was manifestly impossible for us to intervene with long-range bombers from England in a tactical battle in Poland. It would have not been a practical operation of war in any event, and the habitual refusal of the Russians to give us any information about their own positions or movements made it doubly impossible. . . . They seemed throughout to have ignored the fact that Warsaw was separated from the nearest Allied air bases in the West by over 850 miles, and from those in Italy by more than 750 miles, almost entirely over enemy-held country; even if the squadrons had been able to land safely in the Warsaw area, they could not have been maintained in action. . . . Their last demand was the only one that had a chance of being met, and even that not to anything like the extent they needed; they asked for a substantially increased air supply, particularly of heavy machine-guns, anti-tank weapons, ammunition, and grenades.[40]

The Air-Marshal was then under considerable pressure from his superiors to do the maximum possible for Warsaw. He earnestly tried to do so. On the other hand, the war was still to go on for months to come, and it was his responsibility to husband the resources at his disposal. So, at the end of the first week of the Uprising, on the basis of the heavy losses already accrued, he made a decision almost as painful to him as it was to the Poles.

. . . I had to reluctantly come to the conclusion that air supply to Warsaw was not a practical proposition, even if the weather was favourable; the aircraft would have to fly part of the way out and back in daylight and, with the moon at the full, would be bound to suffer some loss en route; to drop supplies accurately from a low

altitude over a city which was bound to contain AA [anti-aircraft]
artillery and machine-guns would mean that only a few would get
through and much of the drop would fall into the wrong hands. In
general, I said, we should achieve practically nothing and lose a
high proportion of our heavy special duty aircraft. I pointed out
that this project was the equivalent of the Russians attempting
from Poland to support a resistance group in Florence, and urged
that we should exert pressure on them to do the job themselves.
    . . . I was not unconscious of the fact that commanders must
sometimes accept casualties for what are narrowly called 'political'
reasons; and, as the battle dragged on, it was that alone which
precluded me from refusing absolutely to send any more aircraft to
Warsaw. But at the beginning it did not seem to me possible that
the battle could last more than a few days – indeed, but for Russian
treachery, it could hardly have done so.
    The Chiefs of Staff accepted my view and our Mission in
Moscow was told to approach the Soviet General Staff. Then
began a crescendo of political pressure by the Polish authorities in
London of mounting and sometimes almost hysterical intensity. . . . The fault lay with Sosnkowski in initiating, or
authorizing, without any previous consultation or planning, an
operation which could only succeed if it received the outside
support, which the most elementary consideration would have
revealed as impracticable. Even he perhaps may be forgiven for
failing to foresee the depths to which Russian Communist
treachery would descend. . . .
    So the grim story went on. On August 31 Portal [Air Chief
Marshal Sir Charles F. A. Portal, K.C.B., D.S.O, M.C.] informed
me of the political decision that I should permit volunteers to go
to Warsaw whenever I thought they had a chance of success, and
asked me to consider using my British heavy squadrons dropping
from above light flak range with the delayed-drop supply parachutes, of which some had become available.[41]

So the British did continue to send planes over Warsaw.[42]

Twenty years later Sir John Slessor in a letter to the editor of *The
Observer* referred to the period of air assistance to Warsaw as 'the worst
six weeks in my experience'.[43]

The British wanted to assist, but within the framework of reality and
their technical capabilities. It is obvious that the Polish traditional
usage of 'overstatement as means of emphasis'[44] did not complement the
customary British matter-of-fact approach to a problem. The two allies
regarded each other with disappointment.

Meanwhile Polish, South African and British pilots were flying
hundreds of miles over German-held territory to assist Warsaw. Aid
from the Soviets was still not in sight, in spite of the promise given by
Stalin to Mikolajczyk in Moscow. Consequently, on 14 August,
American Ambassador Harriman sent Molotov an urgent letter
requesting 'approval from the Red Air Force for a shuttle mission of

American bombers to drop arms on Warsaw for the resistance forces and then proceed to bases in the Soviet Union'.[45]

The next day Andrey Y. Vyshinsky, First Assistant to the People's Commissar for Foreign Affairs of the Soviet Union, wrote on behalf of Molotov: ' . . . the Soviet Government "could not go along" with this project and that the "action in Warsaw into which the Warsaw population had been drawn was a purely adventuristic affair and the Soviet Government could not lend its hand to it" '.[46]

Harriman discussed this problem with British Ambassador Clark Kerr and decided to approach Molotov jointly and 'endeavour to prevail upon him to change the decision of the Soviet Government'. He reported by radio.

> In Molotov's alleged absence, Vyshinski received us early this afternoon [15 August]. We informed him that we believed the decision of the Soviet Government was a grave mistake and that it would have serious repercussions in Washington and London. We pointed out that Vyshinski's letter did not tally with Stalin's promise to Mikolajczyk to assist the resistance movement in Warsaw. . . . Vyshinski adhered to the statements made in his letter and to the view that the outbreak in Warsaw was ill-advised, not a serious matter, not worthy of assistance, and that it would have no influence on the future course of the war. There were no reasons to reconsider the Soviet position. He said that the Soviet Government had nothing to fear as to public reaction abroad since the exploits of the Red Army and the Soviet people clearly spoke for themselves. I pointed out that we were not requesting Soviet participation in the operation and stated that I could not understand why the Soviet Government should object to our endeavour to assist the Poles even if our attempt to get arms to them should not bring about the desired results. Vyshinski maintained that the landing of the American planes at the Soviet bases constituted participation and the Soviet Government did not wish to encourage 'adventuristic actions' which might later be turned against the Soviet Union. . . .
>
> Clark Kerr inquired whether he understood correctly that there had been a change in Soviet policy from Stalin's promise to Mikolajczyk to assist the Poles in Warsaw. Vyshinski maintained that there had been no change in policy, that it was primarily a matter of the best ways and means of effecting this policy, that the Red Army was helping Poland, and that the question was purely military in character. He was evasive when asked whether the Soviets intended to assist directly the Poles fighting in Warsaw.[47]

This radio message was sent to the President and Acting Secretary of State on 15 August 1944, at 8 p.m. Three hours later, Harriman sent another message: 'For the first time since coming to Moscow I am gravely concerned by the attitude of the Soviet Government in its refusal to permit us to assist the Poles in Warsaw as well as in its policy of apparent inactivity. If Vyshinski correctly reflects the position of the Soviet Government, its refusal is based not on operational difficulties or denial that the resistance exists but on ruthless political considerations.'[48]

Ambassador Harriman on 17 August sent two top-secret radio messages addressed jointly to the President and the Secretary of State in which he took a definite stand on the Soviet attitude toward the Uprising. In the first he said:

I recommend that the President send immediately a strong message to Stalin and instruct me to deliver it personally provided he is in Moscow, otherwise to Molotov (it would be helpful also to receive guidance on the oral explanation desired in order that there may be no doubt Stalin understands the President's views).

In making this recommendation I assume that I am not so out of touch with American opinion but that I reflect your views in believing that we can not (repeat not) accept the Soviet position when they allow the Poles fighting in Warsaw to be killed without lifting a hand and arbitrarily prevent us from making efforts to assist.

My own feeling is that Stalin should be made to understand that American public belief in the chances of the success of world security organization and postwar cooperation would be deeply shaken if the Soviet Government continues such a policy.

. . . Care should be taken however to avoid anything in the nature of a threat, and it should be borne in mind that we have so far no official knowledge that Stalin personally is committed to the decisions Vyshinski expounded as those of the Soviet Government.[49]

In the second message, Harriman reported that he had just seen Vyshinsky who told him, 'We [the Soviet Government] strongly object to English or American aircraft, after dropping arms in the region of Warsaw, landing on the territory of the Soviet Union. . . .' Harriman concluded that 'the Soviet Government has no present intention of attempting to drop arms to the Poles fighting in Warsaw'.[50]

On 17 August the President authorized Harriman 'to make personal representations to Stalin . . . to urge the reconsideration of the Soviet attitude in regard to the use of the shuttle bombing arrangements to drop supplies to the Polish Underground forces in Warsaw . . . to present the position of this Government in such manner as you consider to be most effective'.[51]

Together with the British Ambassador, Harriman saw Molotov that same night at a meeting that lasted three hours. The same arguments came up again on either side with Molotov adding that attempts had been made to take advantage of the Uprising for purposes hostile to the Soviet Government. He was evasive when questioned about the earlier Soviet radio broadcasts exhorting Poles to rise and fight.[52]

On 18 August, Churchill conveyed to Roosevelt, via an American military attaché in London, a copy of a message he had received from

Stalin. Stalin now took a different posture, assuring Churchill that he had given 'orders that the Command of the Red Army should drop arms intensively in the Warsaw sector', but also calling Churchill's attention to the fact that 'the Soviet Command had [not] been informed before the beginning of the Warsaw action. . . . The Soviet Command cannot take direct or indirect responsibility for the Warsaw action.'[53] Stalin, of course, was not being asked to 'assume responsibility'; at this point he was being asked to allow American bombers to land on Soviet-held territory after a shuttle-run over Warsaw – *which he had allowed, for a different purpose, just two months before, in June*, when two American air armadas of 200 and 184 planes respectively did land on the Soviet base at Poltava.[54]

Churchill also cabled Roosevelt his own comments:

The refusal of the Soviets to allow the U.S. aircraft to bring succour to the heroic insurgents in Warsaw, added to their own complete neglect to fly supplies when only a few score of miles away, constitutes an episode of profound and far-reaching gravity. If, as is almost certain, the German triumph in Warsaw is followed by a wholesale massacre, no measure can be put upon the full consequences that will arise. I am willing to send a personal message to Stalin if you think this wise and if you will yourself send a separate similar message.

Better far than two messages would be a joint message signed by both of us. I have no doubt we could agree on the wording.[55]

On 19 August, American Secretary of State Hull assessed Roosevelt's attitude in a radio message to Harriman, as *not willing to go as far as the British* 'in attempting to force Soviet cooperation or participating in sending aid to the [Polish] Underground. . . . Our chief purpose has already been achieved as a result of your representations.'[56]

Harriman responded in radio message No. 3091 of 21 August: ' . . . I do not see how it can be considered that "our chief purpose has already been achieved" and I feel strongly that we should make the Soviets realize our dissatisfaction with their behavior even though this may not bring immediately visible results.'[57]

Roosevelt suggested the following as a joint message to Stalin: 'We are thinking of world opinion if the anti-Nazis in Warsaw are in effect abandoned. We believe that all three of us should do the utmost to save as many of the patriots there as possible. We hope that you will drop immediate supplies and munitions to the patriot Poles in Warsaw, or will agree that our planes should do it very quickly. We hope you will approve. The time element is of extreme importance.'[58] The British Prime Minister approved Roosevelt's draft in its entirety, and on 20 August the joint radio message to Stalin was dispatched.[59]

The American leadership's main objective, however, was expressed by Secretary of State Hull in a telegram to the American Chargé

d'Affaires to the Polish Government-in-Exile, Schoenfeld, in London:
' . . . You might informally indicate to Romer [Polish Foreign
Minister] that, while we deeply sympathize with the feeling of all Poles
in regard to the plight of the heroic Warsaw garrison . . . we feel that
these unfortunate developments should not deter the Polish Government from presenting any reasonable proposals to the National
Committee for a settlement of the Polish question.'[60] The moment had
come when the Polish Government in London was being told not only
to defer to Stalin's demands, but also to come to terms with the
Communist 'Polish' National Committee. Allied insight into the
mutual hostility and suspicion between Polish patriots and the Soviet
Government did not extend beyond the immediate question of aid to
Warsaw, or else the British and Americans were unwilling to confront
the Soviet Government on larger questions related to Poland's future.
Roosevelt's views are seen more clearly in this radio message sent to
Churchill on 24 August:

> My information points to the practical impossibility of our
> providing supplies to the Warsaw Poles unless we are permitted to
> land on and take off from Soviet airfields, and the Soviet
> authorities are at the present time prohibiting their use for the
> relief of Warsaw.
>
> I do not see that we can take any additional steps at the present
> time that promise results.
>
> Stalin's reply . . . to our joint message about the Warsaw Poles
> is far from encouraging to our wishes to assist. [Signed] Roos-
> evelt.[61]

Roosevelt seemed to give up; Churchill did not. On 25 August he sent a
radio telegram to the President:

> Uncle Joe's reply adds nothing to our knowledge, and he avoids
> the definite questions asked. I suggest following reply:
>
> 'We are most anxious to send American planes from England.
> Why should they not land on the refuelling ground which has been
> assigned to us behind the Russian lines without enquiry as to what
> they have done on the way. This should preserve the principle of
> your [government's] dissociation from this particular episode. We
> feel sure that if wounded British or American planes arrive behind
> the lines of your armies, they will be succoured with your usual
> consideration. We do not try to form an opinion about the persons
> who instigated this rising, which was certainly called for re-
> peatedly by radio Moscow. Our sympathies are, however, for the
> "almost unarmed people" whose special faith has led them to
> attack German guns, tanks, and aircraft. We cannot think that
> Hitler's cruelties will end with their resistance. On the contrary, it
> seems probable that that is the time when they will begin with full
> ferocity. The massacre in Warsaw will undoubtedly be a very great
> annoyance to us when we all meet at the end of the war. Unless you
> directly forbid it, therefore, we propose to send the planes.'

If he will not give any reply to this I feel we ought to go and see what happens. I cannot conceive that he would maltreat or detain them. Since signing this, I have seen that they are even trying to take away your airfields at Poltava and elsewhere.[62]

President Roosevelt refused: ' . . . I do not consider it advantageous to the long range general war prospect for me to join with you in the proposed message to U.J. [Uncle Joe].

'I have no objection to your sending such a message if you consider it advisable to do so. Roosevelt.'[63]

Churchill was unhappy. He noted in his memoirs, 'I had hoped that the Americans would support us in drastic action. On 1 September, I received the Polish Premier, Mikolajczyk, on his return from Moscow. I had little comfort to offer. He told me that he was prepared to propose a political settlement with the Lublin Committee, offering them fourteen seats in a combined Government. These proposals were debated under fire by the representatives of the Polish Underground in Warsaw itself. The suggestion was accepted unanimously. Some of those who took part in these decisions were tried a year later before a Soviet court in Moscow.'[64] On 3 September, Churchill and Eden considered sending a message to Roosevelt 'asking him to join Churchill in telling Stalin that the next convoy to Russia would not sail because of his attitude to Warsaw'. This idea too was abandoned.[65]

On 1 September the battle in Warsaw entered its second month. The Old Town Sector was abandoned, and within its ruins the Germans were executing civilian survivors and wounded insurgents who were left behind in hospitals.

The Polish Government-in-Exile was aware of American and British attempts to influence the Soviet Government into giving air assistance; on 2 September 1944, Colonel Onacewicz, who was attached to the Polish mission in Washington, informed the Polish Chief of Staff in London by a coded message of Ambassador Harriman's representations.[66] Stalin's refusal to help seemed particularly cruel when they also knew American and British supplies were going to the Soviet Union. The Poles still believed these allies could exercise more pressure on the Soviet leadership to assist Warsaw.

Mikolajczyk, convinced that all roads to assistance were closed, told Churchill he intended to resign. Churchill's response was:' . . . If you were to resign . . . I would see no other course than to wash my hands of the problem.'[67]

The Polish Commander-in-Chief, General Sosnkowski, had had enough too. On 1 September 1944, he issued Order Number 19, addressed specifically to the soldiers of Armia Krajowa, in which he openly blamed the British for insufficient assistance to Warsaw. He said Poland, with British encouragement, had taken on a lone struggle against the German might in 1939, and the exiled Polish forces had fought during the past five years on sea and on land whenever and wherever the German threat existed. For months the people of Warsaw and Armia Krajowa had been fighting Germans 'alone and abandoned'. It was a

> tragic mystery which we Poles cannot fathom, particularly in view of the technical preponderance of the Allied Forces. . . .
>
> Warsaw is waiting. Not for empty words of recognition, not for words of appreciation, not for assurances of compassion and solicitude. Warsaw waits for weapons and ammunition. [Warsaw] does not beg, like an impoverished member of a family, for crumbs off the table, but demands the means to fight, in recognition of the duties of the Allies and our agreement with them.
>
> If the population of this capital . . . have to perish under the ruins of their homes because of lack of assistance, passive indifference, or cold calculation, it will be a sin of unbelievable magnitude and without precedent. . . . Your heroic commander [Bor-Komorowski] is being charged now with not anticipating the sudden halting of the Soviet offensive at the gate of Warsaw. Only the judgement of history will be able to present a verdict in this matter. And we are quite confident about that verdict. The Poles are . . . blamed for not co-ordinating their initiative with operational planning in Eastern Europe. When it becomes necessary, we shall prove how many times our attempts to achieve that co-ordination were fruitless. For the past five years the Armia Krajowa has been systematically charged with passivity and feigned fighting against the Germans. Today [the Armia Krajowa] is being blamed for fighting too intensely and too well.

And Sosnkowski ended by citing a Polish poet:

> . . . Perfidy, and lies [here dwell]
> I know it, I know it, I know it too well.[68]

Yet Sosnkowski, of all people, was in a position to assess the feasibility of assistance to Warsaw, for he had at his disposal an excellent evaluation by his own staff. General Kopanski, Chief of Staff of the Polish Forces in London, had directed the Operational Department of the Staff of the Supreme Commander to set up plans for air support for a general uprising in Poland, 'to be completed by 1 March 1944'. The specific problems to be worked out were the sending of the Polish Parachute Brigade to Poland, and the provision of strategic and tactical support by the Polish Air Force.

The Operational Department's memorandum, dated 1 March 1944 and signed by Lieutenant-Colonel Protasewicz, indicated that 'weapons and ammunition for one . . . battalion of paratroopers would weigh 33,676 kilogrammes *without men*'.[69] It was augmented by a working-paper from the air force section of the Operational Department, a sensible and empirically validated study prepared by Polish air officers who did not underestimate the difficulties. It specifically stated that 'The German Air Force [had to be] eliminated as a serious and organized fighting force,'[70] as a prerequisite for any air support of an uprising in Poland.

It might be argued that both memorandum and paper were prepared with the view toward a *general* uprising in Poland; they were nevertheless an excellent basis for making a rational decision as to the likelihood of supplying Warsaw by air if a successful uprising depended on air support. It is difficult to believe that such a crucial memorandum prepared at the order of his Chief of Staff, had escaped General Sosnkowski's attention.

A Polish combat flier who served in the Polish Air Force under the British command in the Second World War, in discussing air assistance to Warsaw, put forward the following hypothesis: 'Had the delivery of supplies to Warsaw from the air been planned and prepared by the Allies (and this was obviously possible only if the Poles anticipated such action and in co-operation with the Soviet authorities, assuming their good will), it could have been prepared and organized in the form of mass drops during the day by flights of American and British bombers. [The planes], after dropping the supplies, could have landed on the airfields in Poland which had been seized [from the Germans] by the Soviet Army. Such supply from the air could have given Warsaw great assistance; at the same time, the combat losses in such action would have been considerably lower than normal.'[71] The crucial point was the assumption that the Soviet authorities would show goodwill.

On 4 September the plight of Warsaw was on the agenda of the British War Cabinet again:

> The War Cabinet agreed that it was of the utmost importance that everything possible should be done to help the Poles. It was felt, however, that the only step which we could take which would be likely to be effective, would be that the Prime Minister should invite President Roosevelt to consider the matter again, with a view to the United States Air Force's being authorised to carry out an air operation for dropping supplies on Warsaw, if necessary gate-crashing on Russian airfields.
>
> At the same time, it was felt that Premier Stalin might well not realize how deeply stirred public opinion was in this country about the sufferings of Warsaw and what a shock it would be to public opinion if the Poles fighting in Warsaw were overwhelmed by Germans, without material help having been sent to them from outside. Moreover, the fact that the Russians had refused the use of airfields in their occupation for this purpose was now becoming publicly known. It was, therefore, felt that a telegram should be sent to Premier Stalin in the name of the War Cabinet, warning him of the probable effect of all this on future Anglo-Russian relations.
>
> The War Cabinet accordingly agreed. . . . The Foreign Secretary undertook to prepare drafts.[72]

Once more Churchill entreated President Roosevelt:

Seeing how much is in jeopardy we beg that you will again consider the big stakes involved. Could you not authorize your air forces to carry out this operation, landing if necessary on Russian airfields without their formal consent? In view of our great success in the west, I cannot think that the Russians could reject this *fait accompli*. They might even welcome it as getting them out of an awkward situation. We would of course share full responsibility with you for any action taken by your air force. [Signed] Prime.[73]

He also sent a radio message that day to Stalin, developing the points that had been made at the War Cabinet meeting. He concluded:

The War Cabinet themselves find it hard to understand your Government's refusal to take account of the obligations of the British and American Governments to help the Poles in Warsaw. Your Government's action in preventing this help being sent seems to us at variance with the spirit of Allied co-operation to which you and we attach so much importance both for the present and the future. [Signed] Prime.[74]

Roosevelt's response was, to say the least, astounding. In a radio message to Churchill dated 5 September he said:

. . . I am informed by my office of Military Intelligence that the fighting Poles have departed from Warsaw and that the Germans are now in full control.

The problem of relief for the Poles in Warsaw has therefore unfortunately been solved by delay and by German action, and there now appears to be nothing we can do to assist them.

I have long been deeply distressed by our inability to give adequate assistance to the heroic defenders of Warsaw, and I hope that we may together still be able to help Poland be among the victors in this war with the Nazis. Roosevelt.[75]

In his memoirs Churchill cites that radio message from President Roosevelt in full, but he tactfully refrains from comment.

In the afternoon of 10 September, there could be heard in Warsaw the sound of Soviet artillery, and Soviet planes appeared over the city. This brief flare of activity was remarked upon by Churchill, who later gave his own interpretation of Soviet behaviour:

The Kremlin appeared to change their tactics. That afternoon shells from the Soviet artillery began to fall upon the eastern outskirts of Warsaw, and the Soviet planes appeared over the city. Polish Communist forces, under Soviet orders, fought their way into the fringe of the capital. From September 14 onwards the Soviet Air Force dropped supplies; but few of the parachutes opened and many of the containers were smashed and useless. The following day the Russians occupied the Praga suburb, but went no farther. They wished to have the non-Communist Poles destroyed to the full, but also to keep alive the idea that they were going to their rescue.[76]

Also on 10 September, the British Ambassador, Clark Kerr, showed Harriman a message from the Soviet Government, in answer to the British War Cabinet's plea for aid to Warsaw. Harriman relayed the message immediately to the President and the Secretary of State:

> After a lengthy recital of the circumstances and a statement that the really effective aid will come from the advance of the Red Army, the message states, in paraphrase:
>
> 'In addition there is the form of assistance to the people in Warsaw which can hardly be considered effective; namely, the dropping by airplane of weapons, food and medical supplies. We have dropped both weapons and food for the insurgents in Warsaw on several occasions, but each time we have received information that these supplies have fallen into German hands. If you are so firmly convinced, however, of the efficacy of this form of assistance and if you insist that the Soviet Command organize jointly with the Americans and British such aid, the Soviet Government is prepared to agree to it. It will be necessary, however, to render this aid in accordance with a prearranged plan.'
>
> The message ends by implying that the British were partly to blame for the fact that the Soviet Command was not informed in advance of the Warsaw uprising. Reference is also made to the British failure to prevent the Poles from their action in connection with the Katyn incident.
>
> This message is obviously an extremely shrewd statement for the record, and places the responsibility now on the British and us for the decision whether the dropping of supplies should be attempted at this late date. . . . Harriman.[77]

Harriman was aware of Roosevelt's ideological preferences and sensitive to the demands upon himself in his role as Ambassador that they enforced. Yet he maintained his own integrity and acute perceptions. On 9 September he sent a radio message to Hopkins in which he said, 'I feel that I should report to the President at the earliest convenient time and place,' and pointed out the Soviet Government's 'indifference to world opinion', its 'unbending policy toward Poland', and 'ruthless attitude toward the uprising in Warsaw'. He continued:

> I am convinced that we can divert this trend but only if we materially change our policy toward the Soviet Government. I have evidence that they have misinterpreted our generous attitude toward them as a sign of weakness, and acceptance of their policies.
>
> Time has come when we must make clear what we expect of them as the price of our good will. Unless we take issue with the present policy there is every indication the Soviet Union will become world bully wherever their interests are involved.

At the end of this radio dispatch Harriman insists: 'I feel that I should urgently report personally to the President. . . .'

But Harry Hopkins was instrumental in preventing a meeting between Harriman and Roosevelt at this time.[78]

There is other evidence of the degree to which he affected American policy now in Roosevelt's Presidential Papers. In his memorandum to the President of 11 September 1944, (personal and top secret to the President from Harry Hopkins. Declassified 5 May 1972):

> Have discussed all of the cables relative to Poland with the State Department and Marshall. On the basis of these conferences, would suggest that you send substantially the following messages –
> 1. To the President of Poland, 'This will acknowledge your very urgent wire, and I want to assure you that we are taking every possible step to bring Allied assistance as speedily as possible to the Warsaw garrison. I realize fully the urgent importance of this matter.'
> 2. That you send a message to General Marshall asking him to have Deane explore this matter fully and urgently with the British and Russian military people.
> 3. That the State Department will reply to Harriman's wire to you and the Secretary, coordinating whatever they may say with Marshall's instructions to Deane. Harry.'[79]

Attached to the above was a revealing one-sentence memorandum for Commander Tyree (President's staff), of the same date: 'If you should, by chance, get any message from the President in the next couple of hours, which is crossing this one, will you please hold it before sending to Harriman? [Signed] H.L.H.'[80]

To Jan Ciechanowski, the Polish Ambassador to the United States, Hopkins admitted, 'I have no patience with the human element. I love only F.D.R.'[81]

By 18 September, Anthony Eden was informing the War Cabinet

> that the Russians had now sent help by air to the Polish Underground Army in Warsaw, and had also afforded facilities for the United States Air Force to do likewise. There had in consequence been a very marked improvement in the relations between Russia and Poland, which we could fairly attribute to our persistence. It was most important, however, that . . . Mikolajczyk should now return to Moscow for further consultations; but before this visit could take place, it was essential that General Sosnkowski should resign. The Polish President had twice refused to agree to this course. . . . [Eden] accordingly asked the authority of the War Cabinet to send a message to the Polish President informing him that it was the view of His Majesty's Government that unless General Sosnkowski went, the Polish Government had no chance of reaching a satisfactory agreement with the Russian Government.[82]

General Kazimierz Sosnkowski was the Polish Supreme Commander-in-Chief. He had made public statements about his grave concern over the loss of Polish sovereignty, his fear of seizure of the Polish eastern territories, and the lack of effective support for the Uprising of Warsaw. Now the British Government was instigating his removal.

On the same day as Eden proposed to push for Sosnkowski's removal, American wings at last were over Warsaw. The United States Air Force Narrative of Operations Intelligence Summary Number 283, dated 18 September 1944, tersely relates the story:

EXTRACT
   2. BOMBER REPORT
      COMBAT WINGS (110 B–17S) DISPATCHED TO DROP SUPPLIES AT WARSAW. THREE A/C RETURN EARLY. ALL FORMATIONS DROPPED ON PRIMARY VISUALLY. APPROXIMATELY 1284 CONTAINERS DROPPED WITH FAIR TO EXCELLENT RESULTS. 105 A/C LANDED AT RUSSIAN BASES. FLAK: MODERATE, ACCURATE. E/A OPPOSITION: NIL. CLAIMS: NIL. LOSSES: TWO B–17S, CAUSE UNKNOWN.

In the official history of the United States Army Air Force in the Second World War, this mission is described in more detail.

Although the Americans provided crews and the planes, supplies for this one flight were gathered and loaded by the Polish section of the British Strategic Operations Executive. 'Every flying fortress had a crew of ten members and could take 12 containers. . . . It was necessary to deliver them on four British airfields; Horham, Thorpe, Abbots, and Tramlingham. . . .'[83] The following supplies were packed:

machine pistols, Sten	2,976
light machine guns, Bren	211
bazookas (Piat)	110
revolvers	545
explosives (Gammon)	2,490
explosives (plastic)	7,865 kg.
fuses for explosives	54,400 metres
fuses (others)	8,720 metres
detonating caps	21,990 pieces
meat tins	53,520
hardtack	2,016 tons
margarine	2,016 tons
American soldier's 'K' rations	51,820
milk	5,820 rations
medical equipment	12 containers
ammunition [unspecified]	1,691,400 rounds
ammunition [unspecified]	548,600
shells	2,200
ammunition [unspecified]	27,250
grenades	4,360[84]

In the city itself, news of the approaching American planes was heard on the preceding evening. It was Captain Meadow Lark, the officer responsible for organization and recovery of the air supplies who, in his pillbox at Zlota Street number 7–9, heard a particular Polish melody on the BBC Polish hour the evening of 17 September. According to a prearranged code, the song meant that the next day a major air-supply drop would be coming to Warsaw. The next day at about 10 a.m. there was a confirmation by the BBC. Another musical code signified that the planes were already in the air and should reach Warsaw within three to four hours!

Through a network of messengers, the captain immediately informed the command and fighting units of the approaching planes.[85] Shortly after 1 p.m. the remaining windowpanes of houses in Warsaw began to vibrate from the throbbing engines of the Flying Fortresses and the din of German anti-aircraft artillery shooting at them. Many insurgents disregarded the menace of German snipers and crowded the rooftops, enthusiastically waving their hands and shouting words of gratitude.

Heartbreakingly, because the supplies were dropped from 17,000 feet[86] in a strong wind, many containers floated toward the German positions. Some of the watchers cried; some struck the walls with their fists. Nevertheless, the sight of the white American stars instead of the black German crosses flying overhead was a great boost to morale. One insurgent remembered, 'Immediately we had a spark of hope, hope that somehow all this would end well and that the Western Allies will understand us and our contribution. . . .'[87]

The American planes landed near Poltava in Soviet territory; from there, via Italy, they arrived in England. For the Americans the entire trip took six days.

The AK commander immediately acknowledged delivery of 228 containers, adding that they had fought for another 32 and that 28 more were destroyed because their parachutes were burned. A certain percentage of food containers were, in all probability, retained by the civilian population.

There were surprises in some of the containers that fell into insurgents' hands. For example, part of the ammunition was found to be wooden bullets, the kind used for training exercises.[88] Ammunition was the insurgents' key to life. The AK Commander-in-Chief had previously had to send a radio message to England that he 'did not want money',[89] which planes with British markings had seen fit to drop.

Burdened as he was with the defence of the dying city and its population, General Bor took thought for the crews of Allied planes shot down over Poland. He radioed special instructions out of Warsaw to AK units operating throughout Polish territory, ordering all units to assist and protect surviving crews and to report any information concerning their whereabouts.[90] Responses followed, of which this one is typical:

BASE 11
OPERATIONAL SECTION L.DZ.DEP/191 I/TJ .44. 26 SEPTEMBER
1944. . . .
    SEPTEMBER 18 OVER DABROWA NEAR WARSAW ONE OF OUR
ALLIED PLANES WAS SHOT DOWN. ONE AIRMAN JUMPED WAS
TAKEN PRISONER [BY THE GERMANS]. HIS LEG WAS BROKEN. HE
WAS QUESTIONED WITHOUT MEDICAL ASSISTANCE. HE
SUFFERED TERRIBLY. HIS BEHAVIOUR WAS LIKE THAT OF A
SOLDIER. AFTER QUESTIONING HE WAS SHOT [BY THE GERMANS].
WE COULD NOT ESTABLISH HIS NAME.
    DESCRIPTION: TALL? BLOND? ABOUT TWENTY-TWO YEARS
OLD. HE [CARRIED] A PHOTOGRAPH OF A VERY YOUNG GIRL.
SIGNED OPERATIONAL OFFICER A. SLUZEWSKI.[91]

The commander of a Polish partisan unit operating outside Warsaw
told me in an interview that a British plane with a South African crew
was shot down. One man's parachute did not open. The other man,
upon reaching the ground, opened his eyes for a moment and then lost
consciousness. After a while he opened his eyes again and silently looked
around. Meanwhile the Poles who had come running to give him
assistance completely covered the body of his dead countryman with
flowers. He watched in silence a moment and then died.

    The same informant said that, from one of the American planes shot
down just outside Warsaw, only two men jumped. The unit rushed to
their assistance, but couldn't find them in time. German soldiers arrived
on the scene first. According to reports of the local population, one of the
survivors was of dark complexion, probably a Negro. Near the village of
Dziekanow, he was beaten to death by his German captors.

    In all, 306 planes took off for Warsaw. Of the crews they carried 91
were Polish, 50 were British, 55 South African, and 110 American.
Losses numbered 41 planes and 36 crews. (A crew numbered 7–10
men, depending on the type of plane.) Poles lost 17 planes and 16 crews;
British and South African flyers 22 planes and 19 crews; Americans two
planes and one crew,[92] plus one man in another crew.[93]

    The Russians gave their approval on 11 September and, perhaps
as a concession to the Western Allies, they themselves commenced
dropping supplies on the Polish capital on 13 September. . . .
While at first it appeared that the American mission had been a
great success, and so it was hailed, it was ultimately known that
only 288, or possibly only 130, of the containers [out of 1284] fell
into Polish hands. The Germans got the others.[94]

    A strong disposition remained in Allied circles to send another
daylight shuttle mission to Warsaw. The Polish Premier-in-Exile
Stanislaw Mikolajczyk, made a heart-rending appeal to Prime
Minister Churchill, who telephoned USSTAF on 27 September to
repeat and endorse the Pole's message and to add his own request
for another supply mission, a noble deed, as he called it. From
Washington, President Roosevelt ordered that a . . . delivery to

Warsaw be carried out, much to the discomfiture of the War
Department and its air staff, which regarded such missions as both
costly and hopeless.[95]

The planning for a second relief flight coded operation 'FRANTIC 8'
was undertaken by the Americans on 27 September. Clearance was
received from the Russians on 30 September, and by that time packing
was in advanced stages. The flight was planned for 2 October but,
according to War Department documentation, 'On 1st Oct, we were
notified that the flight plan for 2nd Oct had been disapproved by the
[Soviet authorities] . . . giving as reasons that the Warsaw partisans
had been evacuated.'[96] (This was patently untrue. The defenders were
still there.) The flight was cancelled.

CHAPTER EIGHT

The Battle for Old Town

THE defence of Old Town was crucial to the insurgents. It was because the Germans attacked Old Town Sector that its commander, Colonel Wachnowski, could not follow General Monter's order to attack the 9th German Army's main thrust at Warsaw from the side.

The battle for Old Town can be divided into three phases: (1) the positioning of the insurgents' units in Old Town before Colonel Wachnowski's arrival; (2) Wachnowski's organization, under enemy pressure, of the defence of Old Town; and (3) his attempt, after thirty-three days of fighting, to keep the survivors out of German clutches.[1]

On 7 August the broad avenue linking Old Town and Centre City Sector was covered by German machine guns and controlled by twenty tanks. Old Town was also cut off from Zoliborz Sector – the open fields between the two sectors were commanded by German artillery, machine guns and two armoured trains.

Old Town Sector was encircled by Germans just as Warsaw itself was cut off from outside assistance. Its size was approximately two square miles. During the first week of the Uprising thousands of civilians from Wola and Ochota suburbs had fled there. The numbers of Polish civilians, insurgents, and Germans who fought in Old Town are extremely difficult to establish. Nevertheless, on the basis of sources available in Poland, documentation outside Poland, and research in contemporary German documentation, I have compiled the following statistics: it is estimated that on 1 August 1944 the civilian population in the area of Old Town was between 100,000 and 150,000. Between 6 August and 2 September about 300 persons (civilians and some wounded soldiers) were evacuated through the sewers to the Centre City Sector, and 800 more were evacuated through sewers to Zoliborz Sector. Gravely wounded civilians who were left in Old Town numbered 7,000. On 2 September, when the Germans entered, they established that the population was 35,000, of which 8,000–9,000 were males and one-third lightly wounded. Of the 35,000, they shot 1,309 people and burned 3,695.

The statistics for the insurgents are as follows: on 14 August 1944 there were 9,807 soldiers on the ration-receiving list in the sector. These included 500 members of the Communist AL; right-wing NSZ (Narodowe Siły Zbrojne), and a variety of political organizations and their paramilitary units, all tactically subordinated to AK command.

Colonel Wachnowski faced an impossible task. Here was a citizens' army of volunteers, emerging into action for the first time after five years of underground activities and training. It was a scene of confusion. The lack of uniforms was, for obvious reasons, an additional hindrance to organization and efficiency. Some men were claiming rank or commands to which they were not entitled. One colonel claimed he commanded a motorized brigade – which, in fact, was composed of sixteen officers and two soldiers![2]

Colonel Wachnowski brought some order and discipline to the confusion in Old Town. He began by trying to build with the insurgents under his command a perimeter of defence against the ever-mounting German pressure. I was a part of that perimeter.

But, now that the time for action had come, my thoughts were elsewhere. I felt very much alone. I thought of my girl, who was attached to a unit in another part of town. I worried about my mother and young sister because the district where they lived had already been overrun by the enemy. I envied those families still intact. When an entire family served in a unit, family hierarchies were preserved. One woman was advanced to the rank of corporal, but her young son was private first class.[3] In another unit, the father was the commander; his wife and their twelve-year-old son served under him. Most families were dispersed, so people wrote their names on walls, as, for example, 'Jan Kowal is here.' One sign had obviously been painted in a rush: 'I am here.' There was no signature.

As early as the first week of the Uprising there were two levels of existence in Old Town. One was the life of insurgents, with the civilians who were helping them, fighting on the surface. The other was the subterranean life of the civilians and wounded, who had gone to the deepest basements to escape bombs and artillery shells. On the few occasions when I went through basements, I saw that these people had their own lives – they were eating, sleeping, defecating, delivering babies, and dying. I have been told that many people never emerged from their underground homes during the thirty-three days of the battle for Old Town. Of course, some had to come to the surface for food and water.

Those of us on the surface were not necessarily engaged in shooting. Many people, especially those in the civilian administration, fulfilled important duties and services without having weapons. A girl named Eve, a student of the Warsaw Academy of Fine Arts, was seen going to burning homes and churches in Old Town, dragging *objects d'art* from one place to another, trying to save them from ruins and fire. (She was killed.)[4]

In the first three weeks of battle, human loyalties and family ties were manifested, but with the heightened intensity of the daily struggle for survival they faltered. On many occasions, I saw people praying aloud and huddling together for safety during an air raid, but when the bombs were actually falling the weak were often pushed from the safest places.[5]

Bombing caused the greatest losses and was most demoralizing. German planes with black crosses under the wings passed over our heads every 40–50 minutes, dropping bombs at random from a very low level. They left only to come back again. We knew that some of the bombs weighed over a thousand pounds because our engineers were defusing those that did not explode in order to use the explosives for home-made hand-grenades.

We had no electricity or water delivery, and our area of defence was dwindling daily. After thirty-three days we held only several blocks, within which all buildings were destroyed by air raids, gutted by fires, or both. Graves were scattered over nearly every area that was free of rubble. These conditions made the location of latrines and their use in privacy difficult.

Although it was officially forbidden, hard drinking took its toll. One combat officer reported that within two days seven men died unnecessarily because they were under the influence of alcohol.[6] Poles are a hard-drinking lot in any case. It was considered a display of masculinity to consume a large quantity of alcohol without getting drunk.

On at least three occasions, I was absolutely sure that insurgents from other AK units were shooting at me without provocation. In each instance mistaken identity had to be excluded. Possibly, toward the end of the battle for Old Town, the insurgents were so exhausted, so stretched to the limits of endurance, that hostilities had to spill out in one way or another. Also, some soldiers had delusions in which anyone outside their own units appeared to be the enemy. Some experienced a constant sense of threat. These explanations seem reasonable today, but at the time, when I was shot at from a distance only 20–30 yards from our own positions, my anger was so intense that I barely restrained myself from returning the fire. In one instance I checked the barrel of the offender's rifle – it was still warm. He had shot at me because I 'was moving'.

The need for sleep was always acute. One soldier reported that he had an opportunity to sleep at three o'clock in the afternoon. He lay down on the floor, went to sleep, and awoke at five past three absolutely refreshed and convinced that he had slept for several hours.[7] The average sleeping time for the units was four to five hours. Soldiers slept where and when they could. It was not uncommon to fall asleep from exhaustion in the middle of a sentence.[8]

Fear of a surprise ambush caused the sense of hearing to be so sharpened that, in a sector adjacent to the public gardens, the men who stood night watch reported hearing rabbits moving in the grass and rubble – they knew it was rabbits because they saw them by flashlight.[9]

There was, in general, less sickness than under normal conditions. In one AK doctor's opinion, this was because many of the insurgents were so young, and it was the end of the summer, with good weather. The most common illness was diarrhoea. He had observed no psychic breakdowns among the insurgents who actively participated with weapons in hand during the fighting.[10] I did, however, see one.

The inner strength of some seemed to crystallize, and they emerged with the moral posture of saints. Others became crippled with a variety of neurotic and psychotic traits, including pathological hate. Some volunteered to execute those who were condemned to death by the insurgents' court-martial, particularly SS men and German snipers, or those who had betrayed Gentiles or Jews by collaborating with Germans. One boy executed more than 200 persons. His whole family had been murdered in front of his eyes by men in German uniforms.[11]

Insurgents did not recall night-dreaming during the fighting. I asked many persons about this during action and immediately afterwards in a German prisoner-of-war camp. The responses were the same: no dreams during the Uprising; many dreams immediately after. However, day-dreaming, often aloud to other persons and usually about food, was common throughout the Uprising.

> One was talking about peaches. He counted how many kinds of peaches there are, described how they taste.... We found these images exciting. 'Well, maybe you wish some pears,' he was continuing in a monotonous voice... 'the big ones, kind of gold in colour, juicy, so juicy that they spill on your cheek. We used to call them orange pears, and your teeth can really sink into them like in a beautiful pound cake, and maybe....'
> 'All I want is a piece of pumpernickel,' another interrupted.
> 'And on it a piece of smoked bacon, and a good shot of vodka.'
> 'And I would like to have a pork chop with sauerkraut and lots of bread; the bread has to be there.' . . . The suggestions for menus were boundless in variety and included caviare.[12]

The trees and all foliage were gradually destroyed by artillery and fire. After a few weeks some sectors were left totally barren. Once somebody found one pear with two green leaves still attached to it. Strangely enough, considering their hunger, the insurgents simply sat around looking at it with awe.[13] There were only dead bodies, ruined buildings, black smoke, and dust from the continuous shelling. Some soldiers from Old Town who made the trip through the sewers and emerged in Centre City Sector (less heavily shelled) had a feeling of euphoria upon seeing a tree with leaves. Girls often gave leaves to the soldiers emerging from the dark stinking sewers.[14]

By August, of 1,100 apartment houses in Old Town that were still in the possession of the insurgents, half were in ruins, and 300 more were completely gutted by fire.[15] The stench of unburied bodies and burning homes was sickening. Four days later the field hospitals ran out of anaesthetics, and for the next thirteen days – until evacuation – operations and amputations were performed without them. Since there was no electricity and no water in the pipes, here and there wells were dug. On the black market, a glass of water cost the equivalent of three days of a worker's wages.

All units made two attempts (on 10 August and the night of 21–2 August) to break out of Old Town and establish contact with Zoliborz Sector. Both were unsuccessful. The units bled but fought on, clinging to the ruins. After three weeks, between fifty and eighty per cent of the soldiers – men and women alike – were dead or severely wounded. Combat Group Pine, to which my battalion belonged, lost eighty per cent of its personnel.[16]

The high death toll was not limited to the AK; Socialists, right-wing (NSZ), Peasants' Party and Labour Party members, and Communist units were equally decimated. According to sources printed in Poland after the war, there were in the beginning 500 Armia Ludowa soldiers in combat units in Old Town (from a total of 1,500–2,000 in Warsaw), and approximately the same number in reserve and other services.[17] At the end of August, the high command of AL decided to evacuate its men to Zoliborz Sector. Most of their staff had been killed during bombings. The AK command was informed of the decision and rejected it. Nevertheless, AL units began to leave Old Town on the night of 28–9 August. While in Old Town they defended 2 barricades, and the AK 54.[18]

AK military police stopped the evacuation of one company of the AL under the command of Lieutenant E. Rozlubirski (Gustaw) which consequently held its position in Old Town till 2 September, when they left together with AK units. According to a report of the lieutenant, the company's strength as of 30 August 1944 was 157 persons. Their equipment was five carbines, two pistols, six machine-pistols, and eighteen hand-grenades.[19]

At 12.30 a.m. on 26 August, General Bor and the Delegate of the Government, with their respective staffs, descended into the stinking hostile darkness of the sewers, entering through a manhole 220 yards from German positions. About four hours later they emerged in the Centre City Sector. By that time, the AK held less than half a square mile in Old Town.

Our defence now hinged on about a dozen buildings: they included the Old Arsenal, the Polish Bank, the Bastion of Holy Mary, St John's Cathedral, the hospital for the mentally ill, and Mostowski's Palace. Particularly in the last days, fighting reached an intensity rarely encountered in the history of warfare. In a stand to the death, one building was attacked by the Germans eleven times and actually changed hands seven times.[20] By the end of August, withdrawal was no longer an option – no place in Old Town was further than about 400 yards from the enemy. Colonel Wachnowski's order on 27 August reflected the situation.

> Our position is such that we must commit ourselves to the utmost. Our task is to hold Old Town at any price.
>   . . . Upon us and [the outcome of] this task depends the fate of the AK units [insurgents] fighting in our region, and also that of the civilian population, which will . . . be annihilated by the Germans [if we fail]. Every house and every position we yield diminishes our territory, which may ultimately be so small that our troops will be destroyed. For this reason, the condition for victory and for our survival is the absolute necessity of holding our present positions. . . .[21]

The Colonel had decided to fight to the last soldier. Because we had confidence in his leadership and agreed with his assessment of alternatives, we held. At first the will to fight was strong, and the only evidences of our losing battle were increasing physical exhaustion and the rising death toll. But during these last days, after four weeks of burning hell in Old Town, the spirit, too, began to weaken. The civilian population had had enough. They sent delegations to commanders in their areas, demanding that they be permitted to leave the sector.[22] There were some desertions. One cadet dissolved his platoon and went to the nearest church. When he was found there, he broke into sobs.[23] As it was mentioned, some Communist units also wanted to leave. So did military police.[24]

Early in the afternoon of 30 August, Captain Pine, my commanding officer, ordered me to leave my platoon and go with him to Group North (Old Town) Headquarters, where he reported to Colonel Wachnowski. They immediately left the headquarters, and marched forth, side by side, seemingly oblivious of artillery and mortar explosions. Usually under these circumstances one would move with caution, trying to dodge enemy fire, but my pride compelled me to follow their example, so I marched respectfully several steps behind. Moreover, their lack of concern gave me confidence. We entered a building on Hipoteczna Street and proceeded up a stairway. On the second or third floor they told me to stand guard and not to allow anyone upstairs. I did not know how many floors above me they went, nor the purpose of their meeting. Not until after the war did I find out that they were planning the directions in which our units would try to break through the German positions from Old Town to the Centre City Sector. They were determined that we should not die in the ruins.

It is my understanding that the plan was submitted by General Monter to General Bor, who accepted it and subsequently ordered that Colonel Wachnowski implement it. Our units were to push through the German positions between Old Town and the centre of the city; simultaneously, insurgents units from Centre City Sector, led by Major Zagonczyk, would push in the direction of Old Town. The two groups were supposed to hammer an opening through the German positions by which we would reach the centre of Warsaw.

But General Monter's instructions were not easy to accept, even for such a dedicated soldier as Colonel Wachnowski. Monter had ordered that only those people with weapons and ammunition should be evacuated because they would be needed for further fighting.[25] What about the civilian population and the wounded? Were they to be abandoned in Old Town? Colonel Wachnowski could not believe it, so he sent an officer through the sewers to General Monter for verification. Monter confirmed.[26] I interviewed Colonel Wachnowski about the subject. This is what he said:

> The most difficult moment during the combat, and I remember it very well, was the decision to break through to the Centre City Sector on the surface, not through the sewers. . . .
>
> This was a difficult decision, because I did not believe in its success. Before I decided to carry out this [action], I arranged a special meeting of my commanders: Pine, Rog, and Radoslaw (who came although he was wounded). So did many other younger commanders. I assessed their feelings. They wanted to try to break out of Old Town. I sensed this mood, although I did not believe in the technical feasibility of the action. To maintain the spirit of the soldiers and the commanders, I decided to try, but I didn't have faith in victory. We simply did not have the technical prerequisites for success in such a break-out. . . . This was the most difficult decision in my experience during the battle for Old Town.[27]

The attempt was scheduled to begin at 1.00 a.m. on 31 August, but this was changed to 2.30 a.m. the same day.

It was a terrible experience. Civilians, knowing that the insurgents would be trying to break through, gathered around the bases where we were preparing. Their pushing, screaming and frantic searching for one another in the dark disrupted communications. Our messengers had difficulty in finding their way among the maddened crowds. One platoon could not reach its assigned position because a hysterical crowd was blocking its way. What were they supposed to do? Open fire on Polish women? Soldiers pleaded, begged, pushed to get the civilians out of the way. Finally, their commanding officer ordered them to withdraw and take care of their own wounded.

About 700 yards separated us and the Centre City Sector – the length of seven or eight football fields; but, as Colonel Wachnowski anticipated, most of us couldn't get through – enemy fire-power was simply too great. Only one unit managed to do so.

I interviewed one of its former members. 'We noticed that opposite our jumping-off area was the Church of St Anthony, so from the Bank we attacked in that direction. But it was already getting light. . . . We had four smoke-grenades so we threw them to make a smoke-screen.

Then two men with heavy machine guns crossed the street to the church, and about sixty of us followed.'[28]

The sun rose. There were sixty Polish insurgents in the midst of German positions between Old Town and Centre City Sector. There was no chance of making a break in daylight, so they hid in the basement of the building adjacent to the church. They found there in the ruins bodies of eighty Polish civilians. They had been shot and the corpses partially burned. At regular intervals the Germans threw hand-grenades through the windows and all openings that could lead to AK hideouts. They evidently knew some insurgents were in the area, but didn't want to risk searching for them in the ruins.

At nightfall the Poles formed themselves into a column by threes (in order to look like Germans), and marched in the open through the German positions toward Centre City. A Polish second lieutenant who knew German very well shouted to a German, asking directions. The ruse worked. As they approached Polish positions, the AK men broke into a run and started shouting in Polish. They climbed over the ruins and barricades to the Polish side. Unfortunately, one man was shot by a Polish guard who initially mistook them for Germans. This valiant unit was a part of Company Two (code name 'Redhead') from 'Zophie' Battalion.[29]

Another heroic unit, whose code name was Czata 49, did not make it. Between 93 and 100 men emerged from the sewers *within* the German positions, where they opened fire. The action was intended to divert attention from other AK units making a break toward the security of Centre City. It was a suicidal mission, and these AK men and women knew it.

In preparation, the soldiers filled flasks with water and women gathered all available first-aid kits. They talked about how they would withdraw, fighting, to the Centre City, but considering the conditions and intent of their assignment I doubt that they really believed it. They were aware that the lives of masses of insurgents, wounded and civilians, depended on how well they drew the enemy's fire.

Captain Peter (Stanislaw Zolocinski), the commanding officer, led the way. At the point where they entered a smaller branch of the sewer, they had to crawl in sewage on their hands and knees. Their weapons were their greatest concern. It took ingenuity to keep one's weapon and face up at the same time. When the head of the column reached the proper position, he tried the manhole cover. It seemed to be locked from above. There was still half an hour before the attack on the surface was to start. '[We] heard heavy German boots stamping above us and breaking glass on the street.' The Captain strained and pushed the iron cover with his shoulders. It yielded. Moving it gingerly, he peered out.

His unit had been planned to emerge on the Bank Square. 'He saw all around the tents of German soldiers. Some were smoking pipes or cigarettes. What to do?' This was not simply German-held territory – it

The devastation of Warsaw

General Tadeusz Bor-Komorowski, Commander of the Polish Home
Army

Above, General Antoni
Chrusciel; *below*, Colonel
Karol Ziemski

Emerging from the sewers

The women insurgents. *Above*, girls acting as postmen; *below*, preparing to march into captivity. Note the AK (Home Army) armbands

Above. Children will play at soldiers, even in the gloomiest situation. *Below*, civilians after the capitulation

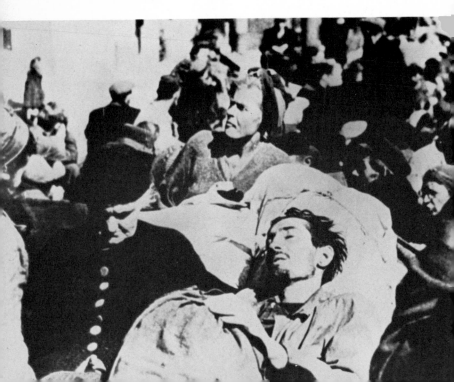

Insurgents' wedding

Exhausted soldiers of the Home Army appear from sewers and basements after two months' grim fighting

was the German camp! 'He discussed the situation with his officers by passing on questions and receiving answers through the soldiers bent in single file behind him.' A decision was made. One lieutenant and a group of men armed with machine pistols would shoot their way out of the manhole, and establish a perimeter to enable the rest to climb out and make a stand. The order was passed down: 'Those who have machine pistols – to the front.' It was about 2 a.m. when several men, gasping for fresh air, emerged slowly from the manhole. 'It was very quiet at this moment. The sky was blue and heavy with stars.' Then, from the nearest tent was heard in German, 'Hans, come here.'

The lieutenant responded with a burst from his machine pistol into the tent, and the fighting exploded in fury, with men shooting wildly at anything that moved. The Germans threw hand-grenades into the midst of the group. Some of the insurgents' machine pistols broke down; others ran out of ammunition. 'One of the boys swore, trying to repair his pistol which was struck. When he was unsuccessful, he threw a hand-grenade into the nearest German tent and ran to a German who was dying.... He grabbed the revolver from his hand and shot into his body again and again.' The few insurgents who survived these bloody minutes realized that they could not form a perimeter. They withdrew into the manhole. One was wounded, and unable to manœuvre on the rungs of the iron ladder in the shaft, so he dived in, on to the heads of those in the sewer. Others followed by desperately jumping down the manhole on top of each other. The lieutenant, still on the surface, was killed.

Then the order was given: 'Those who have hand-grenades – to the surface.' They passed them forward in line since there was no time to change positions. A few attempted to reach the wounded on the surface to drag them to safety, but the palms of their hands were shot through the moment they appeared above the manhole. It was impossible to emerge on to the surface without being shot. Then a bunch of German hand-grenades were thrown into the manhole. The screams of the wounded magnified the terrifying effect of their detonation in such a confined space. The insurgents instinctively fell back, and then, like a field of wheat in the wind, returned to their original positions. There had been no order to withdraw.[30]

On the surface depleted units, carrying their dead and wounded, returned to their barricades and positions once more. Fortunately, the Germans did not attack during this manœuvre. In the action approximately 300 insurgents from Old Town were killed, gravely wounded, or missing. Fifty insurgents from the Centre City Sector had been killed; over a hundred were wounded.[31] In spite of the determination indicated by these figures, breaking through the enemy's position was impossible.

General Monter submitted to Bor another project to save the soldiers of Old Town – evacuation through the sewers. Bor approved. Details

and rigid procedure were established at Group North Headquarters in
Old Town. Only valid passes issued by the commanders of Old Town
and Zoliborz entitled a unit to descend into the sewer, and a time-table
was set up whereby groups, with appointed guides, entered at half-hour
intervals. Also, for safety, the water level in the sewers was regulated (by
closing or opening watertight doors). An order of evacuation was
established: first the wounded; then some of the civilians; next units of
insurgents without weapons, followed by 150 German prisoners of war
(Wehrmacht); last to go would be the armed units, in a predetermined
order. Medics and medical personnel combed basements and ruins for
wounded who could be transported, and led them to the manhole.[32]
The gravely wounded and the majority of citizens had to be left in Old
Town. Dr Pogorski (Morwa) was responsible for a hospital in Old
Town. Since the Germans were not taking prisoners at that time,
anyone left behind would be shot. The doctor knew that, if even one
man should die while going through the sewers, his body might block
the narrow passage and condemn to death the remaining defenders of
Old Town. The wounded were aware, too, that they would not all be
able to make the journey through the sewers. It was up to the doctor to
select those who should go.

> You know, I was aware that if I left them, if I left those human
> beings who with such determination had given everything a
> human being can give for his country, I knew what would happen.
> I shall never forget their eyes – how they looked at me as at
> someone who was passing sentence. The difficulty was that, if there
> was, let's say, a soldier whose arm required a special support, there
> was always a possibility that he might go into shock in the sewer. I
> could not let myself be guided by noble emotions, because I had to
> be responsible for the others who were going to use the sewer. We
> knew that some of the manholes were open and that a scream from
> a wounded man would cause the Germans to throw hand-grenades
> or gasoline, which they would then ignite, into the sewer. These
> were such young boys, such beautifully enthusiastic boys, boys who
> had such a high degree of idealism, especially those who had served
> with the Boy Scouts. They used to identify with the ideals. I tell
> you, the feeling of responsibility was so overpowering that this was
> the most difficult and tragic moment of my life.[33]

Enemy assaults on the insurgents' positions continued relentlessly for
the whole of 1 September; they were particularly ruthless between
5 and 6 p.m. Tanks were firing literally at point-blank range. During
the battle for one building alone, over a hundred Germans were killed;
the death toll for AK men was undoubtedly as high, but could not be
determined with precision. One AK barricade was stormed by seven
heavy tanks. There were onslaughts from all directions – the enemy was
moving in for the final kill.

At nine o'clock that evening Colonel Wachnowski gave an order to commence evacuation. The discipline and consideration shown during these crucial hours were a credit not only to his leadership, but also to the sense of duty and cohesion among the insurgents. When the units of Gozdawa Battalion entered the sewers on 2 September at 2.30 p.m., the Germans were fifty yards away. The last platoon disengaged itself from the enemy at 4.10 p.m. and reached Centre City Sector about four hours later.

When the last insurgents departed from Old Town the Germans poured fire from a flame-thrower directly into the manhole into which they descended.[34]

So, on 2 September, Old Town was abandoned – not without final heartbreaking tragedy. Some civilians, knowing that they would not be allowed to escape through the sewers, in desperation started to dismantle the barricades (bags filled with sand and rubble) protecting the only manhole at that moment available for withdrawal of insurgents. The Germans noticed the commotion. The commander of the AK unit guarding the barricade could not allow the Germans to overrun the manhole. After futile pleading with the civilians, he was compelled to open fire on them. The crowd dispersed; so did the approaching Germans.[35]

One man refused to go into the sewers. It was Colonel Wachnowski. He made a flat and determined statement, 'I will not retreat into sewers.'[36] His adjutant, secretary and courier in one person, Black Barbara, started to cry. The officers of the staff, Majors Majorkiewicz and Kozas, tried to console her. During my interview with her she said that it was General Bor's initiative and pressure that caused General Monter to send an order to Wachnowski personally to withdraw from Old Town with his soldiers.[37] He obeyed reluctantly.

The sewers of Warsaw not only enabled the survivors among the defenders of Old Town to be saved. They proved vital to the insurgents in many ways throughout the Uprising.

According to General Monter, seventy per cent[38] of all liaison and communication between units was via messengers, who transmitted orders, messages and reports, enabling units to maintain some degree of contact with each other. Messengers literally functioned on three levels: on the surface, dodging the German snipers, mortars and artillery through the ruins; through basements, where the population had taken shelter, connected sometimes for several blocks by burrowing through the foundations between houses; and through the sewers.

One had to be prepared to meet and deal with unexpected and strange phenomena in the sewers. The heat from burning houses above them caused some sections to be uncomfortably warm. Once a group encountered a woman who was incoherently shouting orders to an empty passage. One pre-teen boy was found standing in the sewage in a similar state, calling out instructions and offering assistance, oblivious to his lack of audience.[39]

One of the insurgents recalls: 'Evidently we didn't have enough fresh air in the sewers because the candles would not stay lighted. There was a wounded man among us who tore his bandages from his breast and then disappeared under the sewage. People walked over him.'[40]

As is common in situations of great stress, human behaviour in the sewers ran the full gamut from the ridiculous to the heroic. For example, a unit carefully plodding its way in darkness accosted two AK soldiers, an officer and a cadet, who were drunk. They were standing armed in the sewers, turning people back because 'those were their orders'. They were disarmed just as they were about to use their weapons.[41] In another instance an eighteen-year-old girl dragged a telephone cable through the sewers alone in total darkness for ten hours.[42]

Another eyewitness reported that once the customary muted sounds of the gurgling sewage and the rhythmic breathing of people were pierced by the screams of a child being carried by his mother. Those in the immediate vicinity, fearful that the Germans would hear the cries, wanted to kill the child. The mother became hysterical, and the child was not touched. The shuffling line proceeded.[43]

Displays of human compassion (and the lack of it) were boundless. A Boy Scout carried a wounded man on his back through the sewers.[44] If he had fallen, the sewage on that route would have drowned both of them. Of his own free will, a corporal carried a wounded officer for seven hours.[45] Carrying a wounded person increased the possibility of one's own death a thousandfold.

An unusual record of human will to live and endurance was set by two officers and a cadet. They were the last three men to abandon Mokotow Sector. They wandered for twenty-four hours in that underground hell, before they miraculously found their way to the centre of the city, which was still held by insurgents.[46]

Through the sewers, then, we retreated after thirty-three days of fighting for Old Town. When we emerged from the darkness gasping for fresh air in Centre City Sector we did not know that we were to be engaged in street fighting there for another thirty days. And, although Old Town was abandoned, it did not surrender to the enemy.

What did the defence of Old Town accomplish in terms of the objectives of the Uprising?

The tenacity of its defence for thirty-three days enabled the sectors to solidify their defences, and therefore enabled the Uprising to last for another thirty, providing ample time for the Soviet forces to cross the Vistula and come to Warsaw's assistance. Bor said, 'Because of Old Town the Uprising could last for sixty-three days.'[47]

Polish casualties were high so were the Germans'. Losses (killed and wounded) in some German units attacking Old Town were over fifty per cent. Germans sources report that the average of German casualties for Old Town was 150 soldiers a day.[48]

After the war, General Bor said of the defenders of Old Town, 'It is my opinion that ALL the soldiers of Old Town deserve to receive the Cross of Valour.'[49] General Bor's radio message of 3 September 1944 states: 'The heroic defence of Old Town will become a legend.'[50]

As usual with Polish legends, this one also was born in blood.

Approximately 5,000 insurgents (51 per cent, assuming their total number to be 9,807) were killed between 14 August and 2 September; 2,500, or 26 per cent, were gravely wounded. The total casualties among insurgents, then, in my estimate, amounted to 77 per cent.

According to Colonel Wachnowski the insurgents' losses were 33 per cent killed and over 20 per cent gravely wounded, making the total losses 53 per cent.[51]

By 2 September 1944, after 33 days of fighting, 4,800 insurgents remained on the roster.

Of the 4,800, fifteen hundred (1,300 armed, 200 lightly wounded, and auxiliaries), were evacuated to Centre City Sector, and some to Zoliborz Sector. Awaiting the mercy of the enemy, 2,500 gravely wounded were left in field hospitals. About 200 insurgents were unaccounted for after the withdrawal.

In the German units attacking Old Town were approximately 8,000 men. Their losses as of 29 August 1944 were 91 officers and 3,770 rank and file. The Germans lost at least 400–500 more men between 29 August and 2 September. There is no reliable breakdown of the number killed and wounded. Total German losses during the fight for Old Town amounted, then, to 54 per cent.

In summary, the comparative statistics of losses among insurgents and German units during the struggle for Old Town are: insurgents 53 per cent (Wachnowski's estimate) or 77 per cent (my estimate); Germans 54 per cent. In addition, Poles incurred tremendous losses among the civilian population as indicated in the narrative. Let me underscore the fact that these statistics refer only to the battle in Old Town Sector, NOT to the total losses in Warsaw during 63 days of the Uprising.

The respective degree of armament of insurgents and Germans is relevant here. By the end of August only 1,357 insurgents were armed.[52] The word 'armed' should be explained. A soldier with one bottle filled with gasoline was considered 'armed'. One source maintains that on 7 August (after Old Town was cut off from the rest of Warsaw and under siege), the armaments of the insurgents consisted of 8 heavy machine guns, 76 machine pistols and 97 carbines.[53]

CHAPTER NINE

The City under Siege

PROBABLY nowhere else during the Second World War did the combat situation result in this phenomenon: 'One-half of the apartment house, which faced the enemy, was under military rule; the other half was under civilian authority.'[1] Civilians shared the insurgents' fate during the Uprising, but were under the immediate authority of a civilian government.

Polish civilian authorities were extremely important to the Poles because they were the only legal authorities in German-occupied Poland that symbolized the independence for which they were fighting. The first legislative and political body unifying a variety of political parties was locally organized as the Supreme Political Council (10 November 1939–January 1940). Subsequently the Government-in Exile was able to establish direct contact with Polish political parties in Warsaw. Jan S. Jankowski was nominated Delegate of the Government-in Exile from among Poles in the occupied country on 26 April 1943. He was also Deputy Prime Minister. On 3 May 1944, he established the National Council of Ministers (Adam Bien, Stanislaw Jasiukowicz, and Antoni Pajdak). Bien was also a deputy of Delegate Jankowski and Chairman of the National Council of Ministers. (All four men were arrested by Soviet authorities and condemned to prison in the Soviet Union in 1945.)

In February 1940, a corollary political organization called the Political Conciliatory Committee was created. It was composed of three political parties – the Polish Socialist Party, the National Party, and Polish Peasants' Party (PPS, SN, and SL, respectively). After several months the Labour Party (SP) joined this group. The Committee changed its name in 1943 to the National Political Representation of the Polish Nation. In January 1944 it became the Council of National Unity, composed of seventeen members and representing seven Polish political parties, including the clergy and representatives of the Polish co-operative movement. This was the supreme legislative body in occupied Poland. The chairman of the Council of National Unity was Kazimierz Puzak (pseudonym Bazyli), of the Polish Socialist Party. (After the Uprising, he was arrested and imprisoned by Soviet authorities. Later he was released from the Soviet prison, arrested by the Polish Communist authorities, and imprisoned in Poland where he died.)

On 15 March 1944 the Council of National Unity issued a declaration stating its ideological posture. It called for a democratic parliamentary system based on elections and changes of the constitution to ensure a maximum of independence, political freedom, freedom to assert religious and political convictions through the printed word, freedom of assembly, freedom of association, and equality. It also called for the decentralization of administrative functions in favour of territorial local government. This declaration reflected both the aspirations of the populace and those of the leaders and members of AK.

Owing to the difficulties of assembling all the members under combat conditions, a subordinate body, the Supreme Committee of the Council of National Unity, emerged. The Committee was composed of one representative from each of the four major political parties in Poland – the Polish Socialist Party, the Polish Peasants' Party, the National Party, and the Labour Party. (I interviewed three members of the Council of National Unity, one of them the secretary of the Committee during the Uprising.)

The structure of the clandestine civilian government was arranged horizontally and vertically as follows: Horizontally there were two bodies, one executive and the other legislative. The executive was headed by the Delegate of the Polish Government-in-Exile, with the rank of Deputy Prime Minister. This position was held by Jan Stanislaw Jankowski. 'Sobol', 'Doktor' and 'Klonowski' were his pseudonyms at various times. His position was subordinate to the legislative and executive bodies of the Polish Government-in-Exile in London. The Delegate was the highest executive underground authority in occupied Poland. He was superior even to the Commander-in-Chief of the AK in Poland, General Bor-Komorowski, and his staff. In other words, the Delegate had authority in civilian and political matters to encourage or restrain the activities of the Commander-in-Chief. Although the time for the outbreak of the Uprising was chosen by General Bor, his decision required the approval of the Delegate.

Immediately subordinate to the Delegate was the National Council of Ministers, of whom there were three. They supervised the following specialized departments: Foreign Affairs, Agriculture, Education, Social Welfare, Railways, Western Territories, Reconstruction, and Internal Affairs – one of whose branches was the Civilian Resistance Bureau. This last department was reponsible for the clandestine Polish administration of German-occupied Poland. Its network of activities provided the life-force of the underground society-within-a-society. Each department was composed of district delegates elected by counties within each district. All this was, of course, done without the knowledge of the Germans.

Kazimierz Baginski was director of the Department of Internal

Affairs (Secretary of the Interior) until 1 September 1944 when Stefan
Korbonski assumed that position in addition to his duties as Chief of the
Civilian Resistance Bureau. Technically, the Director of the Depart-
ment of Internal Affairs was responsible for the governmental authority
in Poland. Korbonski was not a man to seek power for its own sake.
With tact and consideration, he relied heavily on the judgment of the
Mayor of the city, Marceli Porowski,[2] who was elected by the ministers.

According to one of his associates during the Uprising, the Mayor
worked effectively, quietly, and with devotion for the people of
Warsaw.[3] A well-organized administrative structure permitted him to
have access to every apartment house still standing in the portion of
Warsaw under the control of the insurgents. (After the Uprising,
Porowski was executed by Communist authorities in Poland.)

During the Uprising, Warsaw was divided into six 'regions,' in each
of which there was a delegate directly responsible to the Mayor. Each
region was subdivided into 'blocks' of apartment houses, and each
'block' was further subdivided into individual dwellings. On this very
personal level, residents of a dwelling elected two 'delegates of the
population' to assign responsibility to individuals for security, fire
fighting, sanitation, food distribution, and space allocation, and to
supervise these operations.

I was able to locate and interview one of the six regional delegates,
Konrad Sieniewicz, who at present (1977) lives in Rome. His report for
the first twenty-four days of the Uprising survived. (A copy is in my
possession.) It is evident from this report that the civilian administration of Warsaw was well developed and was actively attempting to
fulfil the needs of the suffering populace. Each of six administrative
regions of Warsaw had the following sections: administration, security,
health, fire control, local government, food delivery, industry, housing,
propaganda.

The highest authority of the legislative branch was the Council of
National Unity. The entire Council, or as many members as possible,
met at least every two or three days. Attendance averaged about twelve
persons, including a representative from the headquarters of the AK.
The majority of the Council were in favour of making early contact with
the Soviet Army.[4] Sessions continued during intensive air and artillery
bombardment. In the instance reported to me, with the windows
breaking, no one went to the basement for protection.[5] One representative recalls that deliberations primarily concerned 'legislation for
the future, apart from immediate orders concerning the Uprising. The
Council of National Unity worked out several decrees that we thought
to be indispensable for the period immediately after the liberation of
Warsaw, when free and independent authority could be asserted. We
could not give up hope for that, in spite of our desperate situation.
Today this looks very naïve. Two issues of Statutes-at-Large [were
printed]. We were able to distribute one; but we did not have time for

dissemination [of the second]. I do not remember whether these decrees were preserved, and I cannot recall the exact substance of the one we distributed . . . but it did contain some rules for free elections in the counties and cities. We wanted to hold these elections immediately after Warsaw was liberated . . . and to have elections to the Polish Parliament at the same time. I prepared the plans on behalf of the Department of Internal Affairs.'[6]

The Council on several occasions called for a reconstruction of Poland based on respect for law and social justice. The last proclamation of the Council of National Unity reaffirmed the ideals of these representatives of the people: 'The Uprising of Warsaw again brought to the surface . . . the problem of Poland, not as a cause for international bargaining, but as a great nation that has fought and bled without compromise for . . . freedom, integrity, and social justice, not only for [itself], but [for these principles to] be implemented in the lives of people and nations, for the noble principles of the Atlantic Charter and everything for which the good people of the world are fighting today.'[7]

Although the immediate future of Warsaw and Poland was foremost in the minds of the Council members, they were also concerned with day-to-day conditions in the city. On 16 August they met to plan for the judicious distribution of foodstuffs, the establishment of field hospitals, and for the welfare needs of those civilians whose homes had been destroyed by bombing or fire.[8]

The Peasants' Party informed the Council that it was organizing within a range of several miles around the city the delivery of supplies to Warsaw for a period immediately after liberation. Their agents had slipped out of Warsaw into the countryside for this purpose.

On the first day of the Uprising, the Delegate of the Government-in-Exile and the President of the Council of National Unity voluntarily moved to General Bor's headquarters to facilitate the decision-making process. This was essential, because of the difficulties of moving about in Warsaw under combat conditions.

The Council of Ministers met every day, and General Bor attended nearly all if its meetings. It was his duty to inform the Delegate and the Council of the combat situation and the progress of the Uprising. The bases for General Bor's reports were the messages and combat reports that General Monter (as Commander of the Uprising) submitted to him twice daily.

The official division of authority between military and civilian leaders was clearly stated on paper. In practice, it was not so clear. Even before the Uprising, AK Headquarters, with the knowledge of General Bor, was building a parallel 'civilian' administration, under its own control.[9] The code name of this operation was Teczka (Briefcase). Its leader had the lively-sounding pseudonym Muzyczka (Pop Music).[10] Political and civilian leaders in Poland were afraid that 'Pop Music' and his military superiors wanted to call the tune for the civilian authorities. The sensitivity of the latter to the possibility of seizure of power by military men was well warranted.

According to Kazimierz Baginski, the AK leadership's bid for power at the expense of the civilian authorities created sufficient alarm for him, as a member of the Council of National Unity and Director of the Department of Internal Affairs until 1 September 1944, to confront General Bor. On 3 August 1944, in the morning, in the presence of the Governmental Delegate, Baginski met Bor and demanded that Bor immediately abolish the position of 'civilian administrator' created by the AK. That position duplicated the post of Mayor of Warsaw already established by civilian authorities.[11] In fact, by 3 August 1944, the 'civilian administrator,' undoubtedly under military control, had already published directives for civilians. Under pressure from Baginski and the Delegate, General Bor agreed to abolish the post in question. Baginski also reminded Bor that, in order to be official, directives to residents of Warsaw must first be signed by the Governmental Delegate and the Chairman of the Council of National Unity, as well as General Bor.[12]

In London, Prime Minister Mikolajczyk was aware that the AK *élite* were surreptitiously duplicating the network of civilian authorities in occupied Poland. He feared that after liberation political complications or civil war would ensue. As one member of the Council of National Unity phrased it, 'The Army was establishing its own civilian administration that reached down to the counties. This was an underground within an underground.'[13]

Karol Popiel, Minister for Reconstruction of Public Administration in the Government-in-Exile, said bluntly that policies of the AK bordered on a *coup d'état* and that some of those in AK Headquarters were using the authority of the AK to 'terrorize' civilian administrators. He maintains that two members of the AK Headquarters in particular were doing so: Colonel Rzepecki and General Okulicki.[14]

Another indication of a power-play by AK leaders was their establishment of a security organization, in addition to the military police, which was known as the KB (Security Corps). During the Uprising, it started to usurp the role of the PKB (State Security Corps). The latter organization, a kind of federal police, was the only legal security agency officially subordinate to the civilian administration.

Reconstruction of facts seems to indicate that the KB was mobilized twenty-four hours *before* the Uprising, that it was provided with food and weapons and already knew which police stations (then under German control) the PKB planned to seize. Not only was the official civilian security organization not so well equipped, it wasn't even mobilized on time. A competing military security organization resulted in some disgraceful incidents that increased the population's anxieties and stresses. For example, at one point a civilian security unit with weapons in hands chased a military security unit that tried to take over its police station.[15] Moreover, the leadership of the KB ultimately sent a message to Soviet Marshal Rokossovsky on the other side of the Vistula, subordinating itself to him![16]

Representatives of political parties in the Council had an additional reason for anxiety: in the first hours of the Uprising men from the propaganda section of AK Headquarters (BIP) led by Colonel Rzepecki took over all the printing presses in the areas seized from the Germans, preventing their use by civilian authorities.[17]

It was not only General Bor's Supreme Headquarters of AK that meddled with civilian affairs, but also the command of the Uprising. On 6 August 1944, General Monter issued Order Number 14 that established the Military Welfare Service. Its first task was 'to organize centres of local government and welfare for the civilian population'.

It is difficult, if not impossible, to establish whether, by duplicating the function of civilian leadership, the intentions of those in command of the AK went beyond the scope of concern for the welfare of Warsaw's population. Such concern would be natural: during the five years of German occupation citizens of Warsaw had given AK military leaders shelter and the lives of their sons and daughters. AK members numbered 40,000, and until the Uprising also led civilian lives.

Was the civilian population really in favour of the Uprising? Did the civilian population reject the AK insurgents at the end of the Uprising as being responsible for the destruction of the city?

It is obvious that in the circumstances it was impossible to take a public opinion sampling or to provide empirically validated data for a scholarly conclusion. However, some facts may indicate the answers.

One undisputed fact emerges from studies, interviews and personal observations during the Uprising: without civilian support the Uprising probably could not have begun, nor, having begun, could it have reached the peak of intensity and determination that it did. Nor could it have lasted for sixty-three days without the affection and respect of the people. If the population had not wanted to assist, no order could have compelled them to do so. The initial enthusiasm when the Uprising began showed where the hearts of the people were. On the streets were heard the words, 'At last, at last!'[18] Women ran into the streets, kissing insurgents, while Polish flags fluttered and everyone sang patriotic songs.[19] Civilians shared their food and water with the insurgents. If flowers could be found, these too were given to them. Women offered to wash soldiers' clothing.[20] Volunteers from among the citizens came to replace losses in AK units and to aid the wounded and carry them to hospitals. Even those who, by virtue of their skills (plumbers, for example), were asked to stay at their civilian posts sought to take up weapons in the nearest unit and participate directly in the battle. A baker, who was so impoverished that he had no shoes, volunteered to make bread in the insurgents' bakery without pay.[21]

Communal kitchens were established in many apartment buildings so residents could contribute whatever they had for mutual survival. It was not uncommon to see nurses from hospitals going from house to house collecting food for the wounded. The public had confidence in the integrity of AK insurgents. One nurse, while collecting food for a hospital, was literally compelled by some civilians to eat food on the spot, because they rightly assumed that she would go hungry in order to take as much food as possible to those who were wounded.[22] Men and women threw their possessions, including furniture, on the barricades. A sense of responsibility toward each other prevailed, especially during the initial period of the Uprising. A nurse, carrying one precious loaf of bread to her soldiers, was approached by a civilian woman who asked for some of it. She refused. Describing that incident twenty-one years later, the nurse expressed a feeling of guilt and discomfort.[23]

The cohesion among civilians and insurgents was sometimes manifested in tragic circumstances. An elderly Polish woman was shot by an insurgent guard when she did not stop at his command. Her husband said, 'I lived with her for forty years, but I do not blame the insurgents for what has happened.'[24] Dramatic evidences of devotion took place as Polish soldiers tried to move the wounded from combat areas after the hospitals had been bombed or burned. When asked to give up their own shelters for the wounded, the people of Warsaw moved out, giving up without complaint the only physical security they had.

Affection even was extended to dead soldiers. An AK soldier recalled seeing a hunchback 'kneeling in front of a dead insurgent and polishing his high boots'.[25]

The insurgents' press helped to build cohesion among civilians. There was a total of 137 publications, excluding papers for children. Many of them were printed at irregular intervals. Some came out every day, others twice a day; some were weeklies. Printing conditions were most difficult as the city had no electric power. Yet civilian volunteers printed and distributed copies of these papers by the thousands.

The general population also was served by the AK Field Postal Services, operated by Girl and Boy Scouts. From 6 August simple makeshift boxes appeared in territory held by insurgents, usually in the vicinity of barricades or hospitals. These were collection points. Some boxes were labelled 'Field Postal Service', but more often they were designated by a lily, the symbol of Polish scouting. Each box was emptied twice a day, unless the postman (none was older than fifteen) was killed. These children had the privilege of wearing the same red and white armbands soldiers wore, and the seriousness with which they went about their business was commendable, if not awesome. There were no postal charges, but it was customary to leave books, papers, or reading material near the box to be taken to insurgents' hospitals. On 2 September stamps printed by the insurgents appeared. If addressed to a location within the same district, the mail was delivered the same day.

However, if the district was isolated by German forces, it took from two to three days to deliver it. Messages were to contain no more than twenty-five words. An average of about 5,000 cards and messages were delivered daily.[26]

In 1967 a batch of undelivered letters was discovered. Each had a stamp on the envelope: 'Scouting Field Postal Service'.[27] Ultimately, with the assistance of the Polish press, television and radio, more than fifty persons claimed them. In some instances the writer or the addressee, or both, were dead, but families sought the letters as precious mementoes.

Here is a description of mail delivery during the Uprising:

> Yesterday a boy between ten and twelve years of age, wearing an insurgents' armband, came to us. . . . He had brought a letter for somebody in the building, but refused to leave it, because his order was 'to deliver', and the addressee was not there. With him was his six- or seven-year-old brother.
> 'Why are you taking him with you?'
> 'Because he is under my protection . . . .!'[28]

Both of them went back through the burning streets taking with them their undelivered letter.

There were less dramatic but equally important instances of the population risking their lives. Civilian authorities arranged to find and care for Christian and Jewish orphans during the Uprising. A special department of the underground civilian administration, 'Protection of Human Beings', was organized to provide for these and for spiritual needs, such as the smuggling of Holy Communion to Polish patriots incarcerated by Germans.[29]

A touching example of the concern of soldiers for civilians occurred in one sector where several milk cows were *not* butchered by insurgents, despite near-starvation, in order that children and mothers who were breast-feeding babies might have milk. This was after Warsaw had been deprived of supplies for over two months and all horses, dogs, and even birds had been eaten.

In all probability the greatest losses were among infants who could not be properly fed. The mothers themselves did not have much to eat, and the people were living under the ruins in airless basements and between walls where humidity and moisture had accumulated for hundreds of years. On the twentieth day of the Uprising the insurgents' paper published this appeal:

> What to Save First! The babies! . . . The youngest ones are dying, our next generation, our hope and assurance of future strength. They are being born, and they die. They are dying because of lack of [food]. Infants must have milk. Undernourished, tormented mothers do not have milk in their breasts. Where it is held by the insurgents, Warsaw is cut off from any supply of milk products. . . . Save the infants, our Polish Warsaw infants. . . . We

shall rebuild our buildings, but the lost generation we will not be able to rebuild. We shall rebuild our churches, even more beautiful ones, to the glory of God, but woe to us if in these churches we shall not hear the clear voices of our children![30]

Four days later the AK radio again broadcast a plea for help for infants and children.[31]

But with the prolongation of war in the streets, constant bombardment, the accompanying misery of starvation, and a growing conviction that all the efforts and sacrifices were futile, civilian behaviour toward insurgents was eventually affected. Now a sober question was asked of the insurgents: 'What have you done to us?' When one unit involved in the fighting was withdrawing through the premises 'of an apartment house, women with small children . . . [were] shouting to insurgents, "Now you bandits are leaving us!" '[32] Incidents such as this one were painful for the soldiers, who remembered when their fellow-townsmen had blessed them with crosses. Toward the end there were instances when civilians refused to give lodging to non-wounded insurgents, something unheard of in the early days of the Uprising. A shoemaker with two children complained to an AK officer about the presence of AK men in his building. He was sure that he and his family would be killed. In fact, he and one of his children were killed later during an aerial bombardment.[33]

The attitude toward the AK was progressively more hostile. Sometimes civilians who were asked to assist by building barricades or attempting to dig out those buried under collapsed buildings refused to help. An insurgent, trying to get medication from a drugstore, attempted to bypass a line of waiting civilians. They stopped him, saying that they had had enough of the Uprising and that he should not have any special privileges.[34] On another occasion, a civilian cut a field telephone-wire in order to tie up a parcel. When accosted abruptly by an insurgent he shouted, 'To hell with you. You will be killed anyhow, so why do you need that?'[35] In a few instances, citizens even misinformed soldiers about safe passages and the direction of German crossfire.[36]

From the small windowless basements of Warsaw complaints were reaching insurgents: 'The military . . . want war. They destroy whole cities. . . . These sons of bitches have caused all human belongings to be burned.'[37]

By the end of the first month of the Uprising the questions were asked, Why does the Uprising continue? Why this bloodbath?[38] The military leaders of the Uprising, committed to its political aims, were consciously sacrificing random individuals in the hope of securing freedom for the whole population, but they were not insensitive to the immediate plight and the frustrations of the people.

As early as the seventh day of the Uprising, General Monter reported, 'In some places panic is beginning to break out among the population. They removed [insurgents'] posters from the buildings in fear of German [reprisals]. . . . White and red armbands and an abandoned machine gun were found standing against a wall.'[39] To counteract the defeatist attitude in the population, the propaganda service 'undertook twenty-one lectures to the population that had escaped from demolished sectors'.[40] Some weeks later Monter reported, 'People in the Powisle area swear at insurgents shooting toward the Germans,'[41] and 'The population in some areas is unfriendly toward insurgents.'[42]

Political party leaders in Warsaw and members of the Council of National Unity, who represented the population, knew that Warsaw's people had been shelled, bombarded, maimed, and killed, and they, too, perceived the changing sentiment. Especially during the second month of the Uprising, civilian authorities appealed directly to Delegate Jankowski to stop the fighting, but he 'did not want even to hear about capitulation'.[43] The Polish Government-in-Exile was informed by radio of the changing civilian attitude. On 4 September four political leaders in Warsaw sent a telegram to Prime Minister Mikolajczyk in London: 'The catastrophic decrease in the amount of territory in our possession, lack of foodstuffs, water, and the complete exhaustion of the population [require that] immediate attention [be given to] the problem of stopping the fighting in Warsaw, particularly in view of the absence of immediate and effective assistance. We are awaiting an immediate reply.'[44] Replies from London were fuzzy and indecisive. So the struggle went on.

Yet, in the last week of September, at the very end of the Uprising, when the civilian population was literally dying from malnutrition, the civilian administration organized a mass collection of clothing and foodstuffs for the AK units still active. About 3,500 pieces of clothing and 2,391 kilograms (5260.2 pounds) of foodstuffs were collected.[45]

The population of Warsaw at the outbreak of the Uprising was estimated at about 1,200,000. A more precise figure cannot be given because of the unusual ebb and flow of the population at that time. Many Poles were hunted by the Gestapo and other German security agencies throughout the occupied country. They came to Warsaw with false identity papers and lived there in hiding from German authorities. Others fled Warsaw for the same reason.

As the city prepared for open rebellion, it faced the necessity of assuring a food supply for its citizens, including the insurgents, during the period of combat, when normal activities would cease. Documents show that the AK set out to solve the problem with an optimistic spirit. The assumption was made by the Chief Quartermaster, Colonel Dolega, that the battle for Warsaw would last no longer than ten days. A resolution was formulated: 'The insurgents would be fed during the first three days from the Underground stores where food was to be hoarded in advance; during the next seven days they would subsist on

German stores . . . which the insurgents planned to capture.'[46]

This plan was stated in an operational order:

(1) For the first three days of the Uprising the entire food supply (except bread) is to be provided by the quartermaster of each district from the district's own reserves; provision of bread [should be allotted] to designated bakeries within each district. (2) Allotments of food supplies (except bread and meat) from the fourth until and including the tenth day [should be taken] from captured German stores by the quartermaster of the area [in which the stores were captured] to the other districts. Bread will be distributed as in (1), above. Meat will be distributed from the central city slaughterhouse. Scheduling of distribution will be announced in the future. The animals are to be fed between first and tenth from purchases, or from stores taken from the Germans.[47]

The Chief Quartermaster reported that on the morning of 1 August 1944 a messenger warned him to collect his subordinate commanders (quartermasters responsible for all the districts of Warsaw) for a special meeting. The meeting lasted till after midnight.[48] Each district quartermaster received five-point instructions: (1) the exact amount of rations per person; (2) a list of insurgents' kitchens within his district; (3) a list of food supplies for his district (to be issued from the secret stores); (4) a tabulation of available foodstuffs in kitchens of the city welfare organization; and (5) a list of bakeries in his district that had supplies of flour.[49]

After the last detail had been agreed upon, 'We shook hands and exchanged warm words of encouragement to do our best and wishes to meet in a free Poland.'[50]

The Quartermaster then reported to General Monter. He noted that Monter and his Chief of Staff, 'Surgeon', were 'both in a very good mood . . . and I was invited to a soldier's lunch. We had hot canned meat, white biscuits, and smoked bacon with bread. These products had been delivered to the headquarters of the district through me as Quartermaster. They were from the Underground stock. We ended the meal with real black coffee and some jam. With the lunch each of us had one shot of vodka for our future, for our fate, and for the alternatives – life or death.'[51]

One has the impression from reading the Quartermaster's report that he had a feeling of duty well performed. He anticipated a supply of slightly over two pounds of sugar per insurgent for the presumably brief period of combat.[52] His satisfaction was a result, in part, of optimism as to the outcome of the fighting, and, in part, of failure to identify the problems of supplying an army engaged in prolonged street fighting. In a conventional army and under normal combat conditions, these supplies probably would be distributed promptly and judiciously. In the Warsaw Uprising such procedures were impossible, especially when the insurgents were compelled to take up defensive positions after several days. German forces began to isolate Polish units throughout the city, and as a result distribution of food became even more haphazard.

In a twenty-four-day period more than 4,000 pounds of bread were baked under the auspices of the civilian administration. It was distributed in one region only to those whose homes were burned and who had no domicile. According to another report, about ninety per cent of the foodstuffs in one region was acquired by official seizure.[53] As a result of these efforts on the part of the civilian administration, every citizen of Warsaw received a small amount of sugar during August. Without a centralized effort, sugar would have been hoarded by those who found it first. When available, horse meat was reserved for hospitals and the military.

But the suddenness with which the food supply in Warsaw deteriorated is illustrated by the fact in the first few days of the Uprising, in one sector, soldiers refused to eat dark bread with artificial marmalade because the civilian population was sharing white bread with them. A week later, in the same sector, one salted herring had to be divided among nine insurgents.[54] Available data indicate that there was a total of twenty-one kitchens in Centre City Sector. These ministered to the needs of the civilian population, one of them preparing food for 8,748 people during the Uprising.[55] (This number may have been underestimated.) In one 'region' there were eleven kitchens cooking for adults and one especially for children.[56]

The names of most of the countless persons who carried supplies to these kitchens under artillery fire, cooked and distributed the food, denying themselves the security of a basement or shelter, are unknown. One, whose name is recorded, is Sergeant Chanuszkiewicz (Cwaniak – 'The Operator'). He repeatedly ventured alone into German-held territory and brought out, by himself, two tons of powdered milk, which he delivered to the civilian administration for distribution to children.[57]

One eyewitness observed, 'Each district had its own "speciality". Stare Miasto [Old Town] had red wine . . . sugar cubes . . . and pumpernickel bread wrapped in cellophane . . . [for a few days]. Powisle [the sector alongside the Vistula river] had chocolate . . . noodles, and marmalade.'[58]

The first area to suffer from lack of supplies was Old Town. By 15 August there were no bread, vegetables or meat for distribution. The insurgents there were pinioned against the river, where they withstood intense German attacks on three sides. They lived mainly on horses, dogs, cats, and grain made into gruel. This grim fare was supplemented occasionally by a drop of red wine discovered in one of the basements.

In Centre City Sector the basic food was wheat grain, which was stored in several places, including the largest brewery in the city. There civilian volunteers delegated by the population and insurgents from each unit went to receive allotments. Ant-like groups converged on the brewery, where the usual procedure was to fill grain sacks about two-thirds full of grain and tie them in the middle. The sacks were more easily carried this way; each weighed about twenty-two pounds. Civilian carriers were permitted to keep one-fifth of their burden as compensation for their labour. Wheat was usually delivered during the night in order to diminish casualties from snipers.[59] Teams of carriers numbered from ten to fifteen persons, predominantly women.

The grain was ground at makeshift mills – trucks with their rear wheels jacked up. The tyres were taken off the rear wheels, and leather belts connected the rims of the wheels to grinders.[60] Soup made from this grain was called 'spit soup', because it was necessary to spit out the outer husk of the grain when eating it. One insurgent, interviewed twenty-five years after the Uprising, said, 'It was my dream that when the war was over I would cook a big pot of that grain soup just to kick it over; then I would eat a piece of sausage.'[61]

As fighting continued, money lost all value, and bartering emerged as the best way to meet individual needs. When Colonel Wachnowski became sick with dysentery, his adjutant decided to secure a piece of white bread for him. She did so by first exchanging a bottle of vodka for a can of meat; then she exchanged the can of meat for three pieces of white bread.[62]

On 14 September 1944 (the forty-fifth day of the Uprising) General Bor noted in a radio telegram to the Government-in-Exile in London: 'We are no longer issuing food.'[63] After fifty days of fighting Bor reported, via radio: 'We are starving.'[64]

The children were the first to die from starvation. Insurgents and civilians scrounged openly for food in ruins and burned-out stores. Two small onions found by a cook were considered 'a miracle'. In some instances, between air raids the insurgents' cooks went to beg the civilian population to share food. Initially, as it was mentioned, it was not necessary to ask for food – the population had shared it most willingly – but, with the prolongation of the Uprising and the diminishing food supply, people, for understandable reasons, gave priority to their families. One of the cooks told her story in an interview: 'I went and asked one of the women in our apartment house [for food]. She told me in great anger, "It is you who should give *us* food now!" But in another apartment I was more lucky. A woman said, "I will share with you everything that I have," and she gave me a whole cup of salt.'[65] This was a treasure, because in this sector there was no salt available.

It might appear that food was as important as ammunition, but in reality this was not so. I observed these priorities when a unit changed position in an emergency: soldiers grabbed weapons, then ammunition, the wounded, and, finally, food. In contrast, the cooks concentrated on food. One of them recalled, 'I grabbed some handkerchiefs and put the pancakes in them; then I picked up medical supplies, also throwing over my shoulder the [sack with] our remaining flour . . . and then [I recalled] the soup! What to do with the soup? I immediately poured the soup into a bucket that was near. I tried to run with the bucket.'[66]

The absence of fats compelled people to improvise. Someone found a bottle of oil: 'It smelled like varnish, so the insurgents took it to their unit's doctor to ask his advice. He was too busy tending the wounded to be bothered with the oil. Hungry as they were, they made some pancakes, fried them in the oil, and ate them. Then they went to the doctor again for advice. He said that on that evidence – the fact that they were still alive – they could use the rest of the oil.'[67]

The same food (quantity and quality) was issued to the lowest-ranking soldier as to the commanding general of the Uprising. There was no preferential treatment, but if someone found food among the ruins – a jar of preserves, for example – as finder, he could claim it.

Our food intake diminished progressively. The soldiers' endurance seemed to be coming from psychic energy, a resource that cannot be empirically verified and that defies statistical analysis. The half-starved men were sometimes so tired that they would go to sleep while eating their gruel.[68] Nevertheless, when awakened by alarm or an order, they collected themselves for action.

Poetry, friend of the abandoned, reflected the feelings of Warsaw's people. It was passionate in its anger. Thematically, it was directed to the people of Warsaw, to Poles in London, to Germans, and even to the Soviet Army across the river.

> The soldier's dream comes true.
> Rise! To duty! As simple as that.
> [Warsaw] is going through fire into golden glory
> Undefeated. Unyielding. [Excerpt][69]

There was a widely known poem directed to the politicians of the Polish Government-in-Exile in London. Its title is self-explanatory: 'We Demand Ammunition.' This verbal hand-grenade was transmitted to London by voice from the insurgent radio station Lightning, on 24 August 1944. This is an excerpt:

> Why do you sing a mourning chorale in London,
> While here we have long awaited a time to rejoice?
> At the sides of their lovers, girls are fighting here,
> And small children join them, and their blood flows proudly.
> Hello. . . . Here is the heart of Poland! . . . Hear Warsaw
>   speaking!
> Throw the dirges out of your broadcasts;
> Our spirit is so strong it will support even you!
> We don't need your applause!
> We demand ammunition!!![70]

Germans captured Polish workers from the Warsaw gasworks and gave them an ultimatum: They must send a special delegation to AK Headquarters to appeal for the fighting to stop, or they would be shot.

The workers refused. In a few days the poem, directed to all Germans, was posted in the city streets. It started with these two sentences:

> The treachery and debasement will mean nothing.
> This sacrifice will not have been in vain, if all Warsaw should burn.[71]

There was also a poem addressed to the Soviet Army across the river.

> A whole month has passed since the Uprising began,
> Sometimes you deceive us
> With the noise of your artillery,
> And you know how hard it will be
> Afterwards for us to say
> 'Again they are making fools of us.'
>
> We are waiting for you
> And you delay and delay.
> You are afraid of us
> And we know it,
> You really want us to be killed here,
> You are awaiting our destruction,
> That's why you stopped in front of Warsaw!
>
> You can do us no harm;
> You have the right to choose:
> You can help us,
> You can save us,
> Or you can wait longer
> And leave us to our death!
> Death is not such a terrible thing –
> We know how to die!
>
> But remember this well:
> From our grave
> The new victorious Poland will arise,
> And you will not be walking
> Upon that free land, you red tyrant!
> Withhold your strength! [Excerpt][72]

Two professional groups – doctors of medicine and priests – deserve mention because of their dedication to the relief of suffering.

The AK Command had anticipated the need to care for the wounded and dying. Before the outbreak of the Uprising every effort was made to secure medicine and equipment for hospitals. The following materials were collected.

(1) 14 sets of surgical instruments for field hospitals and equipment for several field pharmacies;

(2) 5–7 large comprehensive sets of surgical instruments;

(3) about 800 fully equipped medical field kits;

(4) 700 field stretchers; and

(5) approximately 60,000 personal first-aid kits.[73]

These were not enough. About five tons of medical supplies were needed per day – a total of 300 tons for 63 days of fighting. The amount actually commandeered, begged or requisitioned was far below this requirement. However well the medical services might have been planned, they were inadequate in a city where combat conditions isolated entire units. One of the medical officers reported that planning had provided 40 combat nurses per 800 insurgents, but after human losses in personnel and the exhaustion of available medical supplies it was necessary to improvise.[74]

For Centre City Sector eight field hospitals were operational during the Uprising. On an average, each had the capacity to care for 250–300 wounded, two-thirds of whom were insurgents and one-third civilians. 'The mortality [rate] was high – the wounds were located primarily in the areas of abdomen and the limbs.'[75] Besides the field hospitals there were six first-aid points in this sector.

Doctors, unless previously assigned to civilian hospitals, were directly attached to combat units or served near them in temporary military hospitals or first-aid posts. They carried out their duties in difficult, often almost impossible, conditions: in unventilated basements, by electric torch or candlelight, often with makeshift surgical instruments (a handsaw for amputation, for example), very often without anaesthetics,[76] bandages, or disinfectants. They had no fresh water, no toilet facilities, nor even sufficient nourishment for the wounded. In hospitals they slept an average of three hours, 'sometimes four to five, with interruptions as the situation demanded'.[77] They had to put aside their own problems, as this incident illustrates.

A man asked me to help him bury his daughter. She was still alive, so I ran to find the nearest doctor. I told him that she might die. The doctor said, 'She will die within an hour. I cannot leave here, because I have to take care of these wounded.' The wounded were all around him.
I grabbed my revolver and said, 'You must go.'
Then the doctor said to me, 'Listen, mister! Just one moment ago I had news that my whole family was wiped out. I must stay here to do my duty.'[78]

Because 800 Polish doctors of medicine had been murdered by the Soviet Security Police in the Katyn Forest Massacre in 1940, students of medicine were often compelled to assume the roles of fully trained MDs. They did so valiantly.

'An insurgent came for help with a steel splinter in his thigh. So a girl, a second-year student of underground medical school, tried to dislodge the splinter with a razor blade. He survived, but the girl almost didn't.'[79] A young man reported that, although he had only four years of medical school, he had to perform amputations.[80]

Neither the precise number of wounded nor an exact tally of medical facilities available in Warsaw during the fighting will ever be known, since the civilian population often collected wounded insurgents and family members and cared for them in the basements.

In these basements, sometimes with fires raging above them, operations were performed, and the wounded awaited their fate.

> Somewhere at the deep end [of the basement] there was a dim flickering light . . . shining on the faces around it. The wounded lay on mattresses on the basement floor and also in nearby corridors. Another wounded man was brought in. A doctor bent over him examining the wound with a flashlight. The wound was grave . . . and they had to operate immediately. The doctor started to operate; a nurse was assisting. Everybody watched the patch of light concentrated on the wound. The silence was broken by the screams of the wounded man. He became quiet only when consciousness left him.
>
> Outside a hell of explosions was approaching our basement. Then the walls of the basement started to tremble and shake; the entry was being filled with rubble. The dust choked us. Another explosion and a powerful rush of air swept the basement. The flickering light [of the candle] went out. The doctor's flashlight was barely visible through the dust. Somebody shouted, 'We are buried!' The doctor said calmly, 'Several of you should go and try to dig us out. The rest of you sit quietly.' He proceeded to operate, bent over the screaming wounded man. 'Hey, doctor! Why are you tormenting that poor man?' a voice came from the darkened basement. 'We will all be dead. He. You. All of us.' The doctor continued the operation. It seemed as if he did not hear the man's voice. After a moment, without raising his head, he said, 'I know it, but duty has to be done to the very end.'[81]

All reports indicate that nurses and other medical aides followed the same pattern of intense commitment as the doctors. The population and insurgents have unanimously praised the medical profession and the Polish Red Cross for their contribution during the Uprising.[82]

The role of priests in the Uprising was significant and in the tradition of the thousand years of Polish Catholicism. The priests came from all social strata; they had roots among the people, the respect of the people, and a tradition of patriotic service behind them. Nor was that all. Poles traditionally identified the Roman Catholic Church with the freedom and independence of their state. Holy Mary has been called 'the Queen of Poland.'[83]

The Germans fought not only to win, but also to destroy. Both the civilian population and the insurgents knew this. The realization that they faced almost inevitable death was probably one reason religion played such an important part in the lives of Poles during combat.

Throughout the German occupation Warsaw had manifested its profound religious feelings openly. Churches were full. 'Pictures of Holy Mary or Jesus Christ hung in practically every apartment building.

There were also small makeshift altars in front of which all the residents of an apartment building would gather to pray together in the evening. Celebrations of Holy Mass had special meaning during the Uprising. They were the manifestations of faith, hope, and the search for inner strength to overcome human pain and suffering. Mass was initially celebrated in big air-raid shelters, churches, and chapels; when the churches were destroyed, in the ruins, and among the remnants of the buildings.'[84] The prayers were simple and sombrely monotonous, perhaps like the prayers of the early Christians in the catacombs.

The behaviour of priests in combat was impressive, if not always saintly. They not only shared the deprivations, but also rendered greatly needed physical and spiritual assistance. (The same was true of rabbis immediately after the German occupation of Poland in 1939, and before the massacres of Jews in the Ghetto.) Under conditions of such stress much can be said about the strength that comes from spiritual resources. Men with faith seemed to endure harsh conditions much better than those who lacked it. They also had the inner capacity to sustain a certain sense of serenity till the last moment.

Whenever the strength of a man's spirit was tested during the Uprising, whether he was dying in combat, wrestling with his soul, or in physical pain, a priest was there to help. The AK had its own military chaplains. Their preparations for the Uprising had been meticulous: they were equipped with a hundred sets of liturgical accessories and special editions of the Bible for use under combat conditions. When the Uprising broke out, the chaplains were at their posts with their units. Other priests served in their respective parishes. Among these was Cardinal Stefan Wyszynski.[85]

Thanks to the courtesy of one chaplain, I received a comprehensive letter describing the activities of priests in the Old Town Sector. There were eighteen military chaplains in this sector, assisted by the priests and lay brothers of religious orders: Jesuits, Capuchins, Franciscans, and Pallotins. Many of the chaplains received the Polish Cross of Valour, and at least two – Father Rostworowski and Father Warszawski – the highest award for heroism, Virtuti Militari.

Many priests willingly died assisting others. One, in his vestments, braved machine-gun fire to assist some wounded men. Another took Holy Communion to a group of Poles standing against a wall awaiting execution.[86] On many occasions priests were murdered with particular viciousness by SS men. One German SS trooper hanged a Polish priest with the priest's own scarf.

Chaplain Father Pawel's (Warszawski's) service in Old Town went beyond immediate aid to the population and insurgents. He felt that, although the Uprising was a battle against evil, reason should not be abandoned. In an interview Father Pawel, who held the rank of major, reported that on the night of 12 August 1944 he went to Colonel Wachnowski, Commander of North Group and heroic defender of Old

Town, and said, 'You must take the AK men out of Warsaw. This is your last chance.'

Colonel Wachnowski listened, and then asked, 'Father, are you ready to repeat what you said here in front of the AK's Supreme Command?'

I said, 'Yes.'

'Well, then, let's go.'

So we went to AK Headquarters in Old Town, and I talked to them. I told them we had to take the AK soldiers out of Warsaw, that the city would be destroyed, and that we were going to lose the fight, so what we had to do was to save the AK men and the city itself. I told them that the Uprising was nonsense, and that we should stop it immediately. . . . You see, I went there as a chaplain to talk about conscience. I talked for at least an hour.

In fact, we were quarrelling. Bor was silent. Grzegorz [General Pelczynski, Chief of Staff to General Bor] was memorizing what I was saying like a typical intelligence guy. My argument was that it was nonsense. I told them about the disproportion of strength and finally came to the concrete statement that they had made a mistake. The Uprising could not succeed, because we could not get assistance from the West. The German front was stabilized, and the Russians were not assisting. On top of that, we were running out of strength. The Germans had the power and were finishing us off. This was obvious to all of us. . . . Of course, the decision was up to them. When I look at my statements today, twenty-one years after the Uprising, I was correct.[87]

He had not changed the minds of the AK leaders, so he went back to help by encouraging men and saving souls and bodies.

Priests, like doctors, assisted Germans within the area of their personal dedication. Passing by several wounded Germans, Father Paczek, who spoke the German language, offered confession and Holy Sacrament. It was accepted.[88]

Twenty-three years after the Uprising, a woman who had been a fifteen-year-old messenger made this observation about the attitude toward religion and priests during the Uprising: 'Holy Communion used to be distributed outside of churches, in the squares and streets. . . . Before combat, whenever there was an opportunity, the soldiers would take Holy Communion. We used to divide it into very little pieces, because we didn't have enough. Holy Mass was celebrated in the courtyards. People were praying in the basements, and so were soldiers at their posts. Initially, faith was manifested practically all the time.'[89]

Burials during the Uprising were as abnormal as the circumstances of life and death. Access to a cemetery was impossible. The dead were accumulating by the thousand every day, and the warm weather necessitated prompt burials.

Burials were seen to by anyone at practically any time without specific orders. It was a matter of moral obligation. The tenderness displayed by those burying complete strangers was astounding. It was always a hasty procedure because the streets were under artillery or mortar fire, but, as a rule, the body was first searched for identification papers. These papers would then be put in an empty bottle, if one could be found, and the bottle sealed with wax from a candle or possibly with a cork. The bottle with documents was left on the body, and a little cross of sticks was sometimes placed in the hands. If a blanket or sheet could be found, the body would be wrapped in it, but more often the face alone was covered with a piece of uniform, a towel, or whatever was available.

The graves were shallow – a maximum of three to four feet deep. Public squares served as burial grounds, but the dead were also buried wherever soft ground was accessible. Very often pavement was torn from the street and bodies placed in the soil beneath. Usually there was no time to replace the paving, nor did anyone have the inclination. As the Uprising wore on, the streets accumulated a pathetic confusion of rubble from bombed houses, and row after row of graves.

What happens in a city of more that 1,200,000 people when it is deprived of its water supply? Toward the end of the Uprising people in Warsaw drank water from rank puddles and some licked moisture from the walls of basements. Although the insurgents were separated from the civilian population by organization into military units, water supply was a problem requiring joint efforts for solution.

According to the Chief Quartermaster of the Uprising, Colonel Dolega:

> The problems of water and other municipal affairs were in the hands of the Military Service for Protection of the Uprising (WSOP). During the years of German occupation, we had organized personnel to secure from the Germans, to protect, and to operate [the electricity station and the water pumping centre]. However, the day before the Uprising, the Germans commandeered all Polish repair men and kept them (and their tools) at the main pumping station. . . .
>
> On 2 September we created a supplementary technical committee composed of two engineers plus two teams for water emergency repairs. They were attached to the staff of the WSOP. . . . The tools were made in the smithy at the Public Electricity Works.
>
> About 7 September a bomb broke the pipes on the corner of Mazowiecka – Swietokrzyska Streets. Water flooded the streets and basements in the area. By the middle of August, the shortage of water was evident. The Germans controlled the filter stations and pumps, and they gradually shut off the water supply to areas that were in the hands of the insurgents. The rest was done by air bombardment.
>
> At this time a new committee was created. [Its five members were] the quartermaster of the insurgents, the commander of the

WSOP, the commander of the Corps of Engineers, a representative of the Delegate of the Polish Government, and the
personnel of the Warsaw Water Supply Department. The first task
was to check how many wells were registered in the city, how many
were actually producing water, and how much water was
available in each twenty-four-hour period. The committee was
divided into sections for undertaking (1) the building of new wells,
(2) the repairing of deficient wells, (3) the building of wooden
shafts while searching for water, and (4) the requisitioning of all
available hand pumps.

At the same time special orders were issued regulating the
allotment of water for the military and civilians. Among the
insurgents responsibility [for the allotment] rested with the
Quartermaster of the military headquarters; among the civilian
population with the Delegate of the Polish Government.

Meanwhile partially successful attempts were made to repair
the main water station. [At the time it was held by the insurgents.]
At one point the water pressure fell very low . . . and as a result
current from the electric power stations to the pumping stations
was automatically cut off. We contemplated sending to the
Germans under a flag of truce a special team of envoys, to which
our water-specialists would be attached.

We thought the Germans did not have specialists of this nature
and that water was as necessary for them as it was for us. This was
the first [time] the pumps [had been inactive] since their in-
stallation in 1918. . . . Then, suddenly, for reasons we did not
understand, an electric cable [was] activated and we had water
again. It wasn't much, and it didn't rise above ground level. . . .
Unfortunately, shortly afterwards air bombardment destroyed the
system of pipes distributing water in the area outside our
barricades. The cable bringing electricity to the pump station was
also destroyed beyond repair. In some places lakes were formed
from the water . . . flooding basements and shelters. [Then] the
Germans completely shut off the water, [and] the city was left to
rely solely on its own wells. On the average [these] yielded one to
two litres per person [per day], but we could not dream of using it
for fighting the fires.[90]

How did the civilian population cope with the lack of water? How
were they affected? Interviews indicated that they improvised and
clung to life tenaciously.

For example. 'The only receptacle was the bathtub. Into this water,
which we acquired with such difficulty, fell glass, dust and soot as the
result of artillery, mortar and rocket bombardment. We used to filter
the water through linen.'[91]

Soldiers drew water from wells during the night; civilians during the
day.

Black markets emerged in some sections. In Old Town 600 zlotych
was paid for a glass of water.[92] In one case some 'operators' charged $20
in gold for a partially filled bucket of water. The commanding officer of

that region recalled, 'I received a report that the water cost $20 in gold and that the wells were drying up. The hospitals and military units had their own hours to collect water, the water was drying up. People used to wait hours until enough water accumulated in the bottom of the well for them to take their allocation. But we arrested the two sons of bitches [who had organized the black market in water]. We had a military tribunal: military prosecutors and proper proceedings and all. They were found guilty and sentenced to death. The sentence was confirmed by the commander of the region, and in six hours they were shot.'[93]

In the southern region of Warsaw, in the territory held by insurgents, there were fourteen wells plus two artesian wells. From these came the entire water supply for 300,000 people. From the middle of September (in the seventh week of the Uprising) 30,000 people in this region were fed by civilian authorities. They needed water for one bowl of soup a day. By then approximately ten per cent of the population was dying from hunger. In some basements, people had enough to eat and drink; in others they did not. The richer and more enterprising were better off. With the increased viciousness of the struggle, the human instinct for self-preservation (and sometimes greed) asserted itself. The supply of water was diminishing steadily. The springs were polluted, and dysentery was rampant. On 22 September ninety-two wells were serving insurgents and eighty more were in the process of being built.[94]

In a combat report by Lieutenant Peaceful, under the entry of 16 September 1944, there were two sentences: 'Lack of water. Lice appearing.'[95]

CHAPTER TEN

The Red Army at the Gates

IN WARSAW, during the first week of September, the situation was worsening day by day. The Old Town was lost; the Poles were dug in, defending remnants of their positions. The German attacks had new impetus: on 4 September, German units attacked the Centre City Sector; two days later they concentrated on the Powisle Sector, where they overran the insurgent defences. Then they attacked the northern part of the Centre City Sector from three sides. Insurgents' positions were fiercely contested, house by house, sometimes room by room.

AK radio station 'Lightning' was still broadcasting, and a desperate appeal was directed to several hundred thousand Polish soldiers-in-exile, some of whom were under British command, and some under Soviet command:

> All of Poland and Warsaw are carrying on an open battle against the Germans. We are alone. We receive neither weapons nor ammunition. The explanation that it is impossible to give us supplies is not convincing. Prime Minister Mikolajczyk stated that if Warsaw received five tons of ammunition per day we could continue fighting. To deliver five tons of ammunition we need five planes. Pilots . . . remember Warsaw needs five tons of ammunition per day. Sailors, those of you who are guarding convoys to Russia, be aware that Warsaw needs only five tons of ammunition per day. Soldiers . . . remember that the insurgents of the AK need five tons of ammunition per day. Paratroopers, you who recently received the flag from Poland, remember that we have waited for you for the past months and are still waiting. Warsaw is calling you.[1]

A terse speech was made by General Bor's superior in Warsaw, the Government Delegate; the transcript is incomplete because of German interference and atmospheric conditions:

> Poland was created out of struggle. We have counted on our own resources. We did believe in the power and help of our allies. Our armed forces fought beside our allies.
> We believe in the triumph of freedom. We have waited. The

liquidation of the German Reich is definitely anticipated in the West . . . liberation. . . .

In Warsaw . . . uprising. . . . We don't want freedom . . . from anyone . . . freedom. . . . Traditions . . . our own . . . nation. . . . . Warsaw is always ready to do its best. We are sacrificing everything that is most precious – life, blood, and possessions.

On behalf of the National Council of Ministers and the National Council. . . . In Warsaw we are going through a second month of hell without assistance from the outside. . . . Our effort to reach independence. . . . Today with hope . . . will have proved to the world. . . . We are unified in our efforts and fighting. . . . Warsaw became. . . . The combat goes on. We have to be on the ramparts . . . to the ultimate victory. . . . For a democratic Poland . . . free and whole. . . . Long live heroically fighting Warsaw.[2]

There were also short prosaic reports on the participation and morale of the civilian population, informing the Polish Government in London that with each and every day civilians in Warsaw were being murdered in street executions, or forced to walk before German tanks attacking insurgents' positions; further requests for air assistance, medicine and first-aid equipment, details of which combat zones were still able to receive air drops and of what objectives had been won.[3] Bor gave a realistic picture to the outside world of what was happening in Warsaw. One description of combat sent to London read: 'During the past three days our losses have been 100 killed and 300 wounded; nearly all officers have been killed. In one sector alone, on 15 September, the enemy attacked 8 times. . . .'[4]

On the thirty-sixth day of the Uprising this transmission went from Bor's Army Headquarters to London:

> The civilian population is undergoing a crisis that can have a definite impact on the insurgents' combat capacity. We are in crisis and these are the reasons: (1) the town is being bombarded with growing intensity and complete impunity; (2) there is a general conviction that the enemy is attempting to destroy completely the entire territory of Warsaw, including Old Town and central Warsaw; (3) there has been an extension of fighting with no end in sight; (4) smaller and smaller rations, bordering on starvation; (5) great mortality among infants; (6) a stirring-up of the population by unfriendly elements; and (7) lack of water and electricity in all parts of the city.[5]

Then General Bor pointed out that the ammunition was exhausted, and ended with this heart-rending question: 'Is it your opinion that the Allied activities in the West can bring the end of the war in the next few days? We do not count on fast gains by the Soviets.'[6]

Again on 6 September, Bor and the Delegate of the Polish Government sent a wire to the Polish Prime Minister and the Commander-in-Chief in London reporting the critical situation in

Warsaw and the ebbing of the insurgents' resilience. They envisaged three possible courses of action: after obtaining agreement from Germans, to remove the civilians, and then fight to the death; to surrender unconditionally; or to capitulate sector by sector as and where the Germans attacked them, which would allow further time for the Soviet army to cross the river, but would result in wholesale destruction of the city.

> We think that the defeat of the Uprising of Warsaw will have not only military effects after the war, but political ones. If both the Polish Government and its allies could appreciate this now, it might be useful during political bargaining. It is obvious that, after the Uprising in Warsaw collapses, power will pass into Communist hands not only in Warsaw, but also in the whole country. Immediate assistance from you in the form of bombardments and supplies can improve the situation and slightly delay the crisis.[7]

At the end of September Bor sent this message simultaneously to the Polish Prime Minister and the Commander-in-Chief in London: 'The food situation for the army and civilian population is catastrophic. For some time we have not been eating enough, and within a few days the rest of the stock will be exhausted. We are facing famine, complete exhaustion, and epidemic. Mortality among the children is still on the upswing, cases of death from starvation are occurring among adults. The Uprising will collapse for lack of food. . . .'[8]

General Bor's appeals were useless. He received neither assistance for the city nor instructions as to which course of action he should choose. His frustration is reflected in this message to London: 'The fighting insurgents and the community expect concrete decisions; not only assistance for Warsaw, but also a clear statement on ways of recovering Poland's independent existence and sovereignty threatened by the aggressive policy of the Soviet Union. . . .'[9]

Left to himself to choose among grim alternatives, he continued to do what his concept of duty and his political posture dictated. He, as the commander of AK, and General Monter, commander of the Uprising of Warsaw, decided to fight by all means to the last house.[10]

The Government Delegate in Warsaw, who had participated in the decision to start the Uprising, was also sending messages to the Government in London, asking the same questions: 'What does the Government intend to do, and what are we supposed to do, after one month of such a lonely fight?'[11]

In August the Delegate had demanded of the office of Prime Minister Mikolajczyk that a message be forwarded to Roosevelt and to Churchill, which is revealing of the way the Polish leadership in battle-ravaged Warsaw perceived the role and moral obligations of the United States and Britain:

Gentlemen, we are approaching you for the second time. For the past three weeks we have been carrying on a bloody fight completely alone, insufficiently supplied with weapons and ammunition, and without air assistance. At the same time, all reports that reach us from Polish territory occupied by the Soviets, from territories that are disputed by the Soviet Union and those that are not, inform us that the Soviet authorities intern, arrest, or detain in Camp Majdanek Armia Krajowa civilian administrators. This is the AK that so successfully assisted them in fighting the German forces. In this way, after five years of incessant and bloody resistance against the Germans, the Polish nation is being cruelly enslaved by one of its allies. Is it true that the great nations of the United States of America and Great Britain can passively watch this new tragedy overtaking Poland . . . their ally? Is it true that even the Polish Air Force under British command is not allowed to come to the assistance of dying Warsaw? Is it true that Poland is going to be a victim of partition based on spheres of interest? We are declaring in the most solemn manner that we are fighting on the ruins of burning Warsaw, and we shall fight . . . for independence, and . . . defend that independence against any sort of imperialist. In this fight we have united peasants, workers, and intelligentsia. The Polish nation, seeing the passivity of both great allies toward dying Warsaw and also their silent approval of the outrages committed under the Soviet occupation, cannot understand and is reacting with bitter disappointment. Signed: the Delegate of the Polish Government.[12]

The fact was that neither Roosevelt, nor Churchill nor, above all, the Polish Government-in-Exile assisted General Bor or the Government Delegate in their search for alternatives to end the combat. General Bor and his insurgents were left alone.

General Bor and his Headquarters, of course, expected assistance from still another source – the Red Army, commanded by Marshal Rokossovsky. Several divisions were encamped on the other side of the Vistula in Praga in September. The insurgents could see them with binoculars from Warsaw's side. In the last two weeks of fighting a shallow river separated their forces from the insurgents, and each side could see the other across it.

Whatever the bitterness between German and Soviet armies during the Second World War, the forces surrounding Warsaw seemed to have, until the middle of September, at least a silent agreement for mutual noninterference during the Uprising. General Bor's combat report of 7 September 1944 remarked: 'The characteristic feature of the combat situation is the practically complete cessation of fighting between Germans and Russians. Moreover, we have observed . . . sun-bathing by both sides on their front lines, although the distance between their positions is only 300 metres.'[13]

But perhaps the Vistula before Warsaw was impassable for units with heavy equipment?

Just one year before the Uprising, the same units of the First

Byelorussian Front had been able to concentrate about 2000 heavy artillery pieces, mortars, and 500 rocket artillery to liberate Kiev; approximately 400 artillery pieces and mortars covered each half-mile of the front line.[14] For the attack on German positions just outside Kiev, soldiers of the Front constructed fifty bridges and footbridges alongside 240 miles of the Dnieper.[15] Soviet combat photographs show Soviet troops forcing that river, which was two to three times wider than the Vistula. When it was necessary, the commander of the Front engaged his second line of troops and his reserves in battle.[16] The Soviet armies were able to cross even larger and better defended rivers than the Vistula at will. They were masters of improvisation. On another occasion, a single battalion of the First Polish Army, the 6th Engineers, built 200 boats for crossing a river in six days![17]

It *was* possible to cross the Vistula. In the fifth week of Uprising, Germans ferried tanks *from the eastern shore to Warsaw*.[18] Obviously, smaller and lighter objects such as anti-tank artillery for insurgents could also be ferried across. During the Uprising, two AK noncommissioned officers (Shark and Wodniak) transported one heavy machine gun and thirty carbines from the Soviet-held shore and delivered them to AK insurgents. According to an eyewitness report published in present-day Poland, the Vistula river adjacent to one insurgent position was so shallow that 'the First Company . . . of the 8th Infantry Regiment literally pushed their boats across the river with water up to their knees'.[19] So the river was not impassable.

It is also clear that Marshal Rokossovsky's Headquarters was receiving information and pleas for assistance through radio contacts and messengers sent by Bor, Monter, and other AK officers as early as 8 August. On 17 September, General Bor sent a radiogram to Marshal Rokossovsky via Polish Headquarters in London, offering Rokossovsky the opportunity to establish direct telephone contact between them. It would have been relatively simple to do so, as AK engineers had discovered a telephone cable under the Vistula to which both parties could be connected. General Bor explained the precise location of the cable and the manner in which the connection could be made.

Realising the importance of setting up direct contact between the two military leaders, Prime Minister Mikolajczyk asked an aide, Mr Zaranski, to deliver this radio message immediately to Soviet Ambassador Viktor Z. Lebiediev at the Soviet Embassy in London. (The aide's report on the mission is still in Prime Minister Mikolajczyk's private archives, signed 'Zaranski', where the author found it.)

Zaranski telephoned the Soviet Embassy at midnight on the day Bor's radio message reached London, and informed the man on duty that he wished to deliver immediately an urgent telegram concerning the liaison between General Bor and Marshal Rokossovsky. He was told that there was no one in the Embassy because it was Sunday, and to phone the next day. He did so at 11 a.m. He repeated his story and asked to see someone to whom he could deliver this important telegram. He was told that the Secretary of the Embassy would see him right away. The report continues:

> I went immediately to the Soviet Embassy, where I was greeted by the Secretary, and after an exchange of greetings I sat down in front of him and took from my coat pocket the letter from the Prime Minister to which the telegram from General Bor was attached. I said, 'Allow me, sir, to translate into Russian the text of the telegram from General Bor to Marshal Rokossovsky concerning the manner in which telephone communication can be established. . . .' At that moment, as I began to read General Bor's telegram, I was interrupted by the Secretary saying, 'Dear sir, I am to communicate to you on the order of Ambassador Lebiediev that Ambassador Lebiediev will not accept any further telegrams or letters from the Polish Prime Minister or from Warsaw. It would have been quite different at the beginning of this affair, where the problem of liaison was concerned. . . . The Polish Government should be aware of the fact that there are no diplomatic relations between my Government and the Polish Government.' I responded by telling him that what was most important was to facilitate co-operation in a common fight to defeat the Germans, and that the Polish Government was very grateful to the Soviet Government for its desire to be in radio contact; however, since such radio communication was far from perfect and since the radio stations were not synchronized precisely . . . I was bringing word of the simplest solution . . . the telephone cable, which had not been destroyed and which could be activated at any moment. Therefore, I proposed that I would wait as long as he would like me to, and I suggested that meanwhile he should report to Ambassador Lebiediev . . . the whole matter, and I expressed hope that Mr Ambassador would change his opinion. The Secretary responded that he had such precise and detailed instructions that he considered this matter to be definitely closed. So I pocketed the letter from the Prime Minister and said goodbye.[20]

Tension pervaded Bor's and Monter's Headquarters. The ever-present questions were: Will the Red Soviet Army come to our assistance? How long can we hold out? Should we capitulate? In the second week of September (after six weeks of the Uprising) the Warsaw Council of Nationality Unity, representing the feelings of the populace and its civilian administration, proposed that Warsaw capitulate.[21] The military leaders refused not only because they were still counting on diplomatic efforts to move the Soviet Army to their assistance, but also because they were fearful that both civilians and insurgents might be completely annihilated by the Germans after surrender. So the fight raged on. Priests were giving absolution. Love-making had the tenderness and despair of being together for the last time. No longer were cries of infants and small children heard in the basements and air-shelters; most were already dead from starvation. The barricades and ruins were defended by ever-smaller bands of insurgents.

On the fiftieth day of the Uprising, General Monter issued an order that said in part, 'Today we are standing on the threshold of victory. Because of your heroic sacrifices, tenacity, discipline, and perseverance, Warsaw has received assistance and succour. The moment is approaching when the victorious and heroic Red Army will come to give the last blow to the German barbarians.'[22]

It is disconcerting to read the orders and statements issued by both generals to the insurgents throughout the fighting: they were much more optimistic than the correspondence that circulated between the headquarters. Now, after fifty days of fighting, the rank and file of insurgents were virtually assured by their two highest leaders that the Soviet Army would come to their assistance. But still the Red Army did not come.

Did General Bor and General Monter have any basis for their continued anticipation of Red Army assistance? Earlier in September the AK command had believed Red Army units were consciously stalling for political reasons on the outskirts of Warsaw. But, according to Soviet intelligence, a powerful concentration of German forces (the 5th Viking SS Panzer Division, the 3rd Totenkopf SS Panzer Division, the 19th Division, and about two infantry divisions) was blocking access to Warsaw. The Soviet command assigned the 47th and 70th Armies and units of the First Polish Army, supported by the 16th Air Army, to combat these forces.

General Heinz Guderian, who was then Inspector-General of the German armoured troops as well as Chief of the Army General Staff, saw the situation:

> The question has frequently been asked why the Russians, who knew about the Warsaw Uprising, did not do more to help it, and, indeed, stopped their offensive along the line of the Vistula. . . . It may be assumed that the Soviet Union had no interest in seeing these elements owing allegiance to the Polish Government-in-Exile strengthened by a successful uprising and by liberating their capital. Doubtless the Soviets wanted the credit for such actions to go to their dependent Poles in the Lublin camp. But this is a matter for the former allies to sort out among themselves. All that concerned us was that the Russians did not then advance beyond the Vistula, and we were consequently granted a short breathing spell.[23]

Another high-ranking German general, F. W. Von Mellenthin (Chief of General Staff, Fourth Panzer Army; Russian Front, 15 August to 14 September 1944), put it this way:

> Meanwhile the general situation in Poland had improved considerably. The Uprising in Warsaw had looked very threatening,

but tension eased when the Russians failed to push through to link up with the insurgent Poles. The German 9th Army, which was fighting in this sector, formed the impression that the Russians had outrun their supplies of gasoline and ammunition and were too weak to break our line. However this may be, the Red Army did nothing to help the Poles. . . .[24]

After six weeks of observing the Red Army's activities on the outskirts of Warsaw (across the Vistula), Hitler's commanders in Warsaw concluded that the Soviets did not plan to attack Warsaw.[25] This conclusion represented a German appraisal of the Soviet government's attitude toward Polish patriots, rather than an evaluation of the Red Army's real alternatives.

Still, the German command remained apprehensive about what one German authority called 'the nightmare of combined action'[26] – the Soviet Army and the AK pitted against Germans. Polish units attached to the Red Army did make sporadic attempts to cross the Vistula river in September; Soviet co-operation with AK units in the Kampinos Forest north-west of Warsaw was also a possibility. Several thousand armed Polish partisans were poised in its cover. All they needed in order to slash through German defences and reach the city was strong Soviet artillery and air support. The massive United States Air Force raid in September may have given the German command the impression that an American–British–Soviet co-operation to help insurgents had begun. The Germans feared that the Uprising might also explode in western Poland, becoming the general uprising for which Poles had been preparing. This anxiety is evident in the battle log of the 9th German Army and is confirmed by postwar documents.[27] But the Red Army remained inactive.

German leadership sought a political purpose behind the Uprising of Warsaw – 'to estrange the Soviets from the British'.[28] The 9th German Army was ordered to suppress the Uprising as soon as possible in order to show how ineffectual was the Allies' help to the insurgents. During the Uprising and after the war, many politically sophisticated Germans considered the Soviet Union's refusal to assist the insurgents in any significant manner a betrayal of its allies.

On 11 September, though, the Soviet offensive resumed, and within three days they had smashed their way through to the Warsaw suburb of Praga. Rokossovsky later remarked: 'This was when the Uprising in the Polish capital should have started. A joint strike by the Soviet Army from the east and the insurgents from Warsaw, taking the bridges, could have succeeded in liberating and holding Warsaw, though, even in the most favourable circumstances, that would have been just about all the Front's troops could do.'[29]

Two days earlier, on 9 September, General Monter had already written to General Bor suggesting that the First Polish Army and the Polish Committee of National Liberation in Lublin be approached and a promise of loyal co-operation be extended to the Commander-in-Chief of the Polish Communist forces. He maintained: 'We should be more elastic. Anybody who can give us assistance deserves gratitude.' General Bor responded that appealing to the Commander-in-Chief of the Polish Communist forces (General Michal Rola-Zymierski) 'is, in my opinion, betrayal'.[30]

A few days later he issued a statement to the soldiers: 'We all want good, neighbourly relations with the USSR, but under one condition: under the condition that the Soviet Government recognizes our right to a completely independent existence as a nation and as a state. . . .'

Bor was fearful that the Communists would seize control of Poland. The Polish Communist Committee of National Liberation (organised in Moscow), which had arrived in the town of Lublin, ninety-three miles south-east of Warsaw, with the Red Army, a few days before the outbreak of the Uprising, had many distinctive, if not peculiar, features – its composition, sources of support, and its grandiose claims to represent the people of Poland. They were predominantly Polish Communists, but some (for example, Boleslaw Bierut and Wanda Wasilewska) were Soviet agents. How shallowly this subversive organization was rooted in Polish society is demonstrated by the fact that, while in Lublin this group of people, already claiming to be the 'Polish Government', still had to be fed by the Red Army.[31] The Committee's propaganda, however, was alarming to the AK command.

The paper printed by the Polish Communists, even before they were officially organized as the Polish Committee of National Liberation, forcefully and vociferously called on Poles to fight against the Germans, while charging the AK with passivity toward the Germans.[32] *Free Poland* was published in Moscow and appeared for the first time on 1 March 1943. An excerpt from the lead editorial takes this position: 'We consider Polish passivity and waiting a betrayal of Poland. The role of the country is to fight on the broadest possible scale.'[33] The appraisal of the AK propagated by *Free Poland* obviously reflected the Soviet position: 'The AK . . . has weapons and could fight, but it does not want to. We want to stress this fact emphatically – it could fight, but it does not want to.'[34]

As the Soviet Army approached Warsaw, the Polish Communists' call to rise, whether in publications or in broadcasts in Polish from Soviet radio stations, had grown ever more shrill: 'Every Polish homestead must become a stronghold in the struggle against the invaders. . . . Faithful sons of the nation, rise to the last battle! Not a moment is to be lost!'[35] one broadcast said. Just four days before the Uprising, the Polish Communists issued this proclamation: 'Fellow-countrymen! The hour of liberation has struck. . . . The Polish Committee of National Liberation exhorts you to do your utmost for the speedy liberation of our country and the defeat of the Germans. Poles, to arms. . . .'[36] Several hours after the outbreak of the Uprising, at 8.15

p.m. on 1 August, they broadcast in Polish: 'After five years of terrible bondage, five years of blood and tears, our beloved city will again be free . . . those who sincerely desire to serve the Fatherland ought to be standing in the same ranks.'[37] The Committee also made this proclamation through its Commander-in-Chief of Polish forces under Soviet command, General Michal Rola-Zymierski, (then in Lublin), in Order Number 6 issued 13 August 1944: 'Soldiers. The time for liberation of our capital has come. . . . I order . . . soldiers of the First Polish Army . . . to storm Warsaw,'[38] which call was repeated in Order Number 23 of 15 September 1944.[39] Since Rola-Zymierski would not publish such orders without the consent of the Polish Committee of National Liberation, one can conclude that the Committee, though mindful of its desire to take over political power from AK, yet wanted to help the population of Warsaw.

There was, too, among the units of the First Byelorussian Front commanded by General Rokossovsky, the First Polish Army, organized in the Soviet Union and composed of Polish deportees from the eastern Polish territories, supplemented by volunteers and soldiers drafted after the Red Army entered Poland. Its strength as of 1 July 1944 was 90,972 soldiers.[40] This army was in one respect similar to the Army of the Polish Government-in-Exile – in that it, too, was equipped by a foreign government. But, while the soldiers of the Polish Forces-in-Exile took oaths to protect the Constitution, Law, and the President of the Polish Commonwealth,[41] the soldiers of the First Polish Army under Soviet command swore 'to be faithful to the Soviet Union . . . to maintain the brotherhood of arms with the friendly Red Army'.[42]

To my knowledge, this was the only contemporary soldiers' oath in which soldiers of a sovereign state were required to swear an oath of loyalty to a foreign country and to a foreign army. It harks back to 1814, when Polish soldiers were forced to pledge, 'I swear to Almighty God and the Holy Trinity to be faithful to the flag given by the Most Enlightened Tsar of All Russia, the Polish King, My Benevolent Lord. . . .'

There were other differences. The First Polish Army was predominantly officered by Soviet officers who wore Polish uniforms, and it was heavily staffed with Communist political officers, many of whom were not Polish. Since the latter could charge a soldier with 'political unreliability', punishable by immediate imprisonment at least, these political officers wielded the power of life and death over the men.

On 15 September 1944, the Commander of the First Polish Army, Major General Zygmunt Berling, undertook to force the Vistula river at last, and link with insurgents in the region of Czerniakow and Zoliborz.[43] According to both Soviet and Polish sources, the staff of the First Byelorussian Front allotted the First Polish Army these additional Soviet forces: five brigades of artillery, one regiment of mortars, three battalions of engineers and one battalion of amphibious cars. In addition, six units of artillery and the Red Air Force were to support the action.

The forcing of the Vistula started on the night of the fifteenth, according to the Soviet General Jerzy Bordzilowski, but it was not successful, because of poor organization, German artillery fire, and insufficient strength in the first wave.[44] Many of the amphibious cars could not 'overcome shallow spots in the river'.[45] In his judgement, the units that did cross to the insurgents' side of the river 'sustained heavy losses and could not achieve . . . success'.[46]

General Berling's intention was to send the 3rd Polish (Kosciuszko) Infantry Division forward to link with AK units at Czerniakow: and, indeed, the first boats from the eastern shore of the Vistula touched the western shore in Czerniakow Sector in an area defended by 400 AK soldiers, who, though cut off from the rest of the insurgents, were still holding the shore for the expected Soviet support. Morale was high among General Berling's soldiers even while forcing the river under German fire. One woman platoon commander had placed flowers in the barrels of her platoon's mortars before the crossing.[47]

The first group that crossed the Vistula returned to the 'Soviet' shore (though why they returned is not clear), accompanied by AK Major Kmita, assigned as liaison officer to the First Polish Army. They also brought with them a letter from AK Colonel Radoslaw (Jan Mazurkiewicz), commander of Czerniakow Sector, to the Soviet command: 'We are involved in heavy fighting. My sector is attacked by tanks. Help me in defence. . . . If you have radio contact with Monter . . . inform him of my situation.'[48]

By 19 September the following units of the First Polish Army were positioned on the insurgents' shore of the river: in the area of Zoliborz, two battalions of the 6th Infantry Regiment; near Kierbedz Bridge, one platoon of the 3rd Cavalry Regiment; near Poniatowski Bridge, two battalions of the 8th Infantry Regiment; in Czerniakow Sector, two battalions of the 9th Infantry Regiment. To the south, three infantry companies from the 7th and 2nd Infantry regiments were feigning an attack to distract the Germans.[49]

Then the Czerniakow bridgehead collapsed under German pressure, and Berling's Polish soldiers, who were not supported by other Soviet units, withdrew to the eastern shore of the Vistula. Losses suffered by the First Polish Army in this eight-day engagement amounted to 3,764. (If losses incurred in the battle for approaches to the river are included, the total casualties amounted to 5,662 soldiers.)[50]

It is a matter for conjecture why the Polish soldiers who crossed the river and held the bridgehead for eight days were not supported by the Soviet command. With support they could have fanned out into other areas held by the insurgents. But other units of the First Byelorussian Front were not sent to the assistance of the Polish units. Historians in contemporary Poland treat this lack of Soviet support delicately, if they treat it at all. It seems likely that this was a political rather than a military decision; Stalin later commented to Ambassador Harriman that General Berling's action 'went against the better judgement of the Red Army'.[51]

There was a witness to the fact that, on 13 September 1944, Stalin, after talking on the telephone to Rokossovsky, suggested to Marshal G. K. Zhukov that Berling's forces be used 'in forcing the Vistula',[52] but the discrepancy between General Berling's action and the support made available by Stalin suggests a rift in their solidarity. Stalin himself, at a meeting with representatives of the Polish Committee of National Liberation, urged that Warsaw be taken only after very strong preparation: 'We cannot take it with artillery. We would have to destroy [it] section by section.' He proposed encirclement, 'Otherwise you cannot [take the city] unless you want to destroy [it].'[53]

A sergeant in the First Polish Army commented during an interview in 1972 that on the east side of the river his soldiers and he were convinced that they were going to liberate Warsaw, until he witnessed the following incident. His company had gone down to the shore of the Vistula, to help load heavy pieces of artillery to be ferried across the river; the artillery did not come, however, and at dawn they took cover in the bushes near the river so as not to be visible from the western shore. 'Sometime around four or five o'clock in the morning, a group of high-ranking Russian officers, including generals, came into the area shouting, implying that we had created a mess, and asking us where our commander was, We knew that something had gone wrong.' General Rokossovsky was among the officers who wanted to know why the Poles had not told them that they were going to cross the river. The officers said that, had they known, they would have provided artillery and air assistance.[54] The sergeant's impression was that this Polish action in crossing the river was without Soviet approval, and there is strong supporting evidence, for many commanders of units within the First Polish Army were removed from their positions by the Soviet command after this action, among them General Galicki, commander of the 3rd Division, and General Berling.

It is possible, perhaps, that the action was unsuccessful because General Berling's desire to help the insurgents drove him to force the Vistula without sufficient preparation, and that in the fervour of battle, and out of human compassion for the insurgents, the Polish Commander eluded the tight reins of the Soviet command, counting on its assistance once he had crossed the river. Military experts in present-day Poland are not in agreement on this subject. Some maintain that General Berling received an order from the Soviet command for action by the First Polish Army, but that the order did not mention taking Warsaw. Some interpret Berling's move to the insurgents' shore as a local reconnaissance mission that was not intended to proceed into the centre of the city.

There is no doubt whatever of General Berling's genuine intention to come to the assistance of the insurgents. As late as 29 September he was offering to help an isolated group of AK soldiers in Zoliborz Sector cross the Vistula to the eastern shore, who with their commander Colonel Mieczyslaw Niedzielski (pseudonym Zywiciel) had held off attacks by the 19th Panzer Division and other German units from four sides for an entire week. The Colonel, however, refused to surrender or to evacuate the area until he was finally ordered to do so together with all other AK units by General Monter. The story persists, too, that General Berling wrote a special letter to Stalin in connection with the Uprising, though the General denies this in his letter to me.[55] Perhaps reliable data will be available in the future that will permit a definite assessment of the circumstances within which General Berling and his Polish soldiers operated in relation to Marshal Rokossovsky's command.

The Soviet command itself afforded the insurgents assistance in three other ways during the period between 13 September and 29 September. In the first place, there was sporadic artillery support, in some instances at the request of the AK command, whose effectiveness could not be ascertained. Secondly, Soviet fighters were observed over the city, sometimes engaged in dogfights with German planes. Lastly the insurgents received supplies from the Polish Air Force attached to the First Polish Army and also from Soviet Air Force planes. A total of 589 planes participated. They flew 2,243 sorties and spent 2,501 flight hours in the air over Warsaw.

The first plane to come over Warsaw with supplies from the east was piloted by Alexander Danielak, a Pole.[56] Drops were made during the night from a very low altitude. Small and rather slow biplanes were used so that the insurgents' positions could be most accurately pinpointed. Supplies from these planes hit the designated drop zones with precision. I witnessed the delivery of several bags of ammunition dropped from a dark sky to a space indicated by a triangle of several bonfires made by insurgents as a recognition sign. I was near the triangle when two bags fell about 10–20 feet from me. The contents of one bag spilled open on hitting the pavement, but the other bag remained intact. It contained ammunition for machine pistols.

Soviet sources describe the quantity and type of supplies sent to the insurgents: one artillery piece (45 mm); 1,378 machine pistols; 159 mortars (50 mm); 505 anti-armour rifles, 170 carbines; 522 short carbines; 350 German carbines; 300 of 45 mm shells; 37,260 mortar shells (50 mm); 57,640 rounds of ammunition for anti-armour rifles; 1,312,600 pieces of ammunition for carbines; 1,360,984 rounds of ammunition (type not given); 75,000 rounds of ammunition (7.5 and 7.7 mm); 260,600 rounds of ammunition for Mausers; 312,760 pieces of parabellum ammunition; 18,428 hand-grenades; 18,270 German hand-grenades; 515 kilograms of medical equipment; 10 field telephones; 9,600 metres of telephone cables; one field telephone station; 10 batteries for field telephone; 22 batteries (BAS-AT); 126,681 kilograms (278,696 pounds) of foodstuffs.[57]

Poles made much of the fact that the supplies were dropped without parachutes. I saw a beautiful new Soviet long-barrelled anti-tank rifle bend into a pretzel when it hit the ground. Some insurgents claimed it was part of a devilish two-faced plan: on one hand, the Soviet Army could claim it was helping insurgents; on the other hand, most of the supplies they dropped were utterly useless by the time they were picked up. It is my opinion that the circumstances limited effective supply drops. At that time the areas held by insurgents were small and encircled by Germans. German anti-aircraft artillery was strong and active. To locate the recognition signals in the burning city and to descend just above the rooftops to drop the loads called for heroism on the part of the Polish and Soviet pilots. To have carried out the operation with parachutes would have been equally ineffective, if not harmful to the insurgents, because wind conditions would have most certainly carried many parcels right into German hands, supplying them instead. Some measures had been taken to prevent damage. Some supplies were in bags made of sailcloth. Many were wrapped in two such bags, between which thoughtful hands had packed straw, chips of wood, or sawdust.[58] But most of the ammunition dropped was Soviet-made, whereas the insurgents were equipped mainly with German weapons, so frustration ran high among insurgents. The utility of the Soviet supply drops was questionable, but the insurgents were desperate. Any assistance, however slight, was welcome among units racing for the drops.

There were a number of clashes among units competing for supplies. As a result, General Monter's staff ordered me to be responsible for registering and delivering to General Monter's Headquarters supplies dropped in the Centre City Sector. This was the most unrewarding duty I had to perform during the Uprising. My platoon went from one spot to another at night to secure whatever we could find and transport it to headquarters. (Soviet planes were dropping supplies only at night.) Failing that, we took the names of commanding officers of the units who had taken the supplies but had refused to part with them. Restraint, persuasion, and sometimes threats were required to dislodge supplies from units that had found them. A policy of 'finders keepers' was ridiculous in these circumstances, because some units found mortars and, inevitably, others found ammunition for them. The units frequently attempted to deal with each other instead of conveying all supplies to the command for the most effective distribution. Many disputes, brawls, and military court proceedings resulted from this problem. Supply drops were interrupted between 18 and 21 September, after which they were resumed; the last supplies were dropped on the night of 28 September.

In the meantime General Bor could see from radiograms sent from the eastern territories by underground stations a clearly emerging pattern in Soviet policy toward the legal Polish Government and AK soldiers. In the eighth week of the Uprising, he evaluated the intentions of the Soviet Government in a radio message to his Supreme Commander-in-Chief in London. He complained that the Red Army was arresting members of the AK and that the Soviet Government was using a variety of 'committees' to seize power in Poland. It was his opinion that 'the Bolsheviks will complete the process in Warsaw after they seize it. We have to assume that it is here [in Warsaw] . . . that the Soviet Government will make the decision as to whether there is a place for the Armia Krajowa and its Government-in-Exile in London or not.'[59] If Armia Krajowa were not tolerated, he saw no other way than to demobilize AK in all territories seized by the Soviet Army.

In the second week of September, General Bor had sent General Monter 'Instructions for Behaviour upon Entry of the Soviet Armies into Warsaw', in which he ordered Monter to hold the regions in the insurgents' possession; to clear the thoroughfares through Warsaw so the Soviet units could pursue Germans; and to call AK partisans outside Warsaw to come to the city. Territories held by insurgents were to be clearly identified by Polish flags.[60] Attached to these instructions was an enclosure entitled 'How to Parley with the Red Army'. General Monter subsequently issued Special Order Number 83, dated 13 September 1944, calling for the seizure and holding of as much of the city as possible.[61]

The man responsible for putting these instructions into operation, Colonel Stanislaw Weber (pseudonym Surgeon), Chief-of-Staff to General Monter, described to me Monter's posture toward Soviet entry into Warsaw, stated to him by Monter between 20 and 25 September 1944. General Monter wanted to continue to fight the Germans beside the Red Army as soon as possible, but in a separate unit, to be called 'The AK Warsaw Corps'. For this purpose he intended to ask the Soviet command for weapons and equipment; under no conditions was he willing to allow the incorporation of AK units into the First Polish Army commanded by General Berling. He wanted to have liaison officers ready and a Russian-speaking translator attached to each AK unit in preparation for the entry of Soviet forces into Warsaw. All AK units were actively to help clear the east–west thoroughfares, so that the Soviet Army could go through Warsaw toward Germany. Insurgents were to be tightly grouped in regions so as not to block the passage of Soviet troops; they were to place themselves in good defensive positions in order to defend themselves against any attempt to disarm or arrest them. They were also to provide protection to the civilian population and to give immediately 'every technical and combat assistance to the Soviet armies'.[62] General Monter ordered the implementation of these instructions, but that they be conveyed to the commanders of the units orally, not in writing.[63] In report Number 60 he said, 'I am counting on the entry of the Soviet Army. . . .'[64] Even at the end of September, General Monter felt sure that the Soviet armies would cross the Vistula and come to the insurgents' assistance. He was particularly optimistic after two Soviet artillery observers were dropped in Warsaw.[65]

A comparison of three separate incidents that occurred on 17 September within the areas held by insurgents shows the complexity of cross-currents and political issues troubling the command of AK toward the end of the Uprising. On that day, two representatives of 'The Combined Military Forces' (Communist), Colonel Julian Skokowski and Major Sek, went to see General Monter. With them General Monter was less optimistic. He told them, 'The Soviets are not trying to help us; that is why we are going to be compelled to capitulate.'[66] The two men implored Monter to take over the command of AK and not to listen to directives of the Polish Government-in-Exile.[67] Their intent was to drive a wedge between AK and its legal government, but also to save Warsaw.

The same day General Bor sent a radio message asking the Supreme Commander-in-Chief in London and the Polish Government-in-Exile what he should do if the Soviet Army, after seizing Warsaw, began to persecute the soldiers of Armia Krajowa.[68] Also on 17 September, a curious editorial appeared in *Biuletyn Informacyjny*, the official publication of AK in Warsaw. For the first time AK leaders *played down the importance of the Warsaw Uprising*, referring to it as only one of the 'leaves' of military history, 'not the first and not last' and 'just as a fragment of this war'.[69]

My speculation is that the reason for this editorial was that the AK command was still anticipating Soviet entry into Warsaw, and it had decided to play down, if possible, the importance of the Soviet seizure of Warsaw. The unfortunate effect of this policy was that, since they had access to this freely distributed publication, the Communists and therefore the Red Army undoubtedly concluded that the Poles were trying to rob the Soviet Army of credit for victory during their expected entry into Warsaw.

Three days later, on 21 September, General Monter sent a radio message to the commanding officer of Zoliborz Sector, ordering the colonel to expand and fortify his territory and to invite Soviet commanders to him, but *not to go to them*.[70] This was hardly a proper attitude toward Soviet commanders coming to the rescue, particularly after two months' imploring them to come. But this scenario was not peculiar to General Monter alone; it was endorsed by the Polish political leaders in Warsaw, including the Delegate. This was the Delegate's plan:

> In the Centre City Sector there [will] be Polish civilian and military authorities. The Deputy Prime Minister the Delegate, as rightful host of the city and of the country, will welcome the Red Army. The Armia Krajowa will be concentrated in the same

region to provide security in the case of unfriendly activities or provocation. The Government Delegate of the city of Warsaw will undertake the civilian administration of the city as temporary mayor. The preconceived attitude toward the Red Army [will] be one of friendship and willingness to co-operate, on condition [that] the Polish authorities are respected.[71]

In one building held by insurgents there were stored large portraits of Prime Minister Stanislaw Mikolajczyk. With these, the insurgents were to assume the role of host and display them to the incoming Soviet Army![72]

When Harriman and Kerr delivered messages about the Quebec Conference on the evening of 23 September, *after* the failure of General Berling's attempts to cross the Vistula in strength, Harriman found

that for the first time Stalin spoke with sympathy for the insurgents. He said that the Red Army was in contact with each of the groups in isolated parts of the city both by radio and by men going back and forth. It was now understood why the insurrection had been started prematurely. The Germans had threatened to deport all of the male population from Warsaw, and it [had become] necessary for the men to fight. They had no choice, as they faced death either way. The men, therefore, who were organized had started resistance, and other men had gone underground, hiding themselves in sewers. Stalin never mentioned the Government in London but said they had not found General Bor, who had evidently left the city and was 'commanding a radio station' in some unknown place. . . .

Stalin showed understanding and concern for the Poles in Warsaw and none of his previous vindictiveness. He explained that after Praga had been taken it was possible to judge the situation more clearly.[73]

The AK soldiers still fighting in the ruins suspected that the battle was lost. Now the problem was how long they would survive. If Stalin felt sympathetic towards them at this point, they didn't know it; there was nothing to indicate a change in Soviet attitude. They were wiped out. They knew it, and Stalin knew it. There were five Red Army short-wave stations operating in Warsaw in September, reporting to Soviet HQ; there was a Russian officer by the name of Captain Kalugin, with the AK command in Warsaw since the beginning of the Uprising, and still able to send messages to Stalin via AK short-wave stations; Soviet planes were flying at will over the fires of Warsaw for reconnaissance purposes, while the Polish Communists in Warsaw intermingled with the population and with the AK, with free access to their sentiments and sufferings and information which they imparted through messengers and other means of communication to the 'Lublin Committee', which in turn was in direct contact with Stalin. There were also innumerable messages, reports, and requests conveyed by the AK command by short-wave radio and personal messengers to the Soviet forces on the other side of the Vistula (see the next chapter for evidence).

Stalin did not send sympathetic messages to the insurgents, the civilians in Warsaw or the AK command: he had a less informed and much more gullible audience in the British and American allies. At the meeting of the British War Cabinet on 25 September, Eden said that in his judgement Marshal Stalin now had a more favourable attitude toward Poles. He also noticed that 'the population of Warsaw was in sore straits and very short of food', so the War Cabinet requested that the Chiefs of Staff 'suggest to the United States Air Command that they should consider undertaking a further flight to Warsaw, dropping mainly food supplies'.[74] All that was needed now to weaken the attitude of the Polish Government *vis-à-vis* Stalin's demands was to dangle in front of it the prospect of further assistance to Warsaw.

At the same time, this government was split from within by British pressure for the removal of General Kazimierz Sosnkowski from his post as the Polish Commander-in-Chief. The British were evidently able to bring over to their view the Polish Cabinet, Mikolajczyk, and even General Anders, the victorious leader of the battle of Monte Cassino, who according to Eden's report to the War Cabinet had said that 'General Sosnkowski's retention, or otherwise, was a matter of indifference to the Polish Army'.[75]

There were men of conscience in the British Parliament who saw the injustice of their own government's appeasing Stalin as once it had appeased Hitler. On 27 September, Mr McGovern, MP, asked Eden,

Does the right hon. Gentleman think that there is anything to be gained by covering up the fact that an Ally of ours is both deporting and shooting Nationalists and Socialists in Poland?
Mr Eden: The hon. Gentleman talks about covering up matters, but I must tell the House that not only are these affairs of delicacy between Allies, but also that there is some difficulty in ascertaining the facts. Therefore, we should treat these matters with caution and with reserve at the present time.
Earl Winterton: Could my right hon. Friend not make it clear, in reply to my question, that His Majesty's Government can be responsible only for the conduct of His Majesty's Government, and cannot be responsible for the conduct of other nations?
Mr Eden: My right hon. Friend is absolutely correct. That is why I explained that I was asked a question about affairs which concern two of our Allies, for which my responsibility is not direct.
Commander Sir Archibald Southby: While it is true that these are matters of delicacy, are not matters concerning our responsibility to our Ally, Poland, also matters of principle?
Mr Eden: Yes, Sir, and our responsibility has been fully, and I might add gallantly, discharged.[76]

In a Confidential Annex to the British War Cabinet Minutes it is noted that, on 2 October, Eden announced that General Sosnkowski 'had now been removed from his post as Commander-in-Chief. In his place the Polish Government had appointed General Bor-Komorowski.'[77] Eden remarked that this, too, was 'unfortunate' because the Polish Communist Committee of National Liberation 'regarded General Bor as a criminal'.

'The Minister of Information was invited to [talk to] the Governors of the BBC, and to inform them that the War Cabinet hoped that in [the] future less emphasis [would] be given in news bulletins to the Polish political difficulties.'[78]

CHAPTER ELEVEN

Capitulation

THERE were, and still are, conflicting views within the Polish community in Poland and abroad as to the ultimate responsibility for the decision that Warsaw rise against the Germans. Opinion also is divided over responsibility for continuing the insurrection long after it was clear that there was no hope for success. It is surprising that even the Polish Government-in-Exile has never made an official inquiry into the latter aspect.

In London, as early as the sixth day of the Uprising, a member of the Polish Labour Party Council urged that the Ministers be asked to inform AK Headquarters of all information they had about the political situation and that the Ministers recommend that Bor consider the surrender of Warsaw, Operation Tempest to be continued in the Polish countryside as originally planned. The Ministers rejected the proposal, however.[1]

In Warsaw the struggle wore on into the second month. In September, General Bor misjudged Soviet action for the second time. On 11 September, hearing Soviet artillery from the east shore of the Vistula, and having been informed that the Soviet Union was co-operating with the United States to assist Warsaw, he again expected that the Russians would come to the assistance of the insurgents by forcing the river. On these premises he broke off negotiations with the Germans for surrender.

There were other reasons for General Bor's reluctance to surrender. He believed he could not afford to surrender to the Germans too early because then Soviet and Communist propaganda would call the Uprising a mere demonstration and charge him and the insurgents with collaboration with Germans. (They did so many times, in any case.) So far as Bor knew, the Government-in-Exile was making every effort to bring pressure for a Soviet attack on Warsaw. Bor's staff assumed, wrongly, that Churchill and Roosevelt would bring sufficient pressure on Stalin to compel Soviet troops to cross the river. Unfortunately, although Bor's government was conveying news of its efforts in this direction to him, it did not tell Bor the minimal results the efforts had achieved.

This is not to say that some of the hopes for Soviet intervention were not also the irrational hopes of men at the end of their psychological resources. An example is the proclamation issued by General Monter on 7 September 1944, the thirty-eighth day of the Uprising, in which he promised the insurgents, 'Help from the outside will come within a maximum of four to five days.'[2] (In 1959, fifteen years after the Uprising, the source for this optimistic statement was finally traced. AK Colonel Jozef Szostak, a member of AK Headquarters, simply invented the notion of assistance in four to five days. The information was conveyed to General Monter, who in turn repeated it in his proclamation to the insurgents and entered it in Situational Report Number 43, dated 7 September, issued at 10 a.m.)

On 7 September the Council of National Unity recommended that the fight for Warsaw be terminated.[3] General Bor then responded to German offers to negotiate a surrender (see Table No. 3) and on 10 September, with the knowledge of Government Delegate Jankowski,[4] he sent AK delegates to German General von dem Bach. However, as it was mentioned, on 11 September, General Bor changed his mind and persuaded the Council of Ministers to break off negotiations with the Germans. His arguments were specific: he felt that 'there were sounds of artillery to the north and east of Warsaw [the Soviet Army, was again, in fact, struggling with the Germans for access to the river]; the spirit of the insurgents has improved and therefore, surrender would not be very popular'.[5] In Bor's evaluation, fifty per cent of the insurgents would be against it. Moreover, since he believed that the Allies and the Soviets were collaborating in defence of Warsaw (the flight of the American Air Force planes to Warsaw with supplies and their subsequent landing in the Soviet Union), capitulation should not take place. During a discussion the Ministers decided that negotiations should not be broken off until the effectiveness of the assistance to Warsaw had been ascertained.[6] According to one Polish source, General Monter, General Pelczynski and Colonel Szostak were very much against capitulation at that time. Monter said, 'This would be the depths of tragedy!'[7]

On 18 September, Monter sent a radio message to Marshal Rokossovsky, explicitly offering collaboration of AK insurgents with General Berling's Army and the Soviet Army in fighting for Warsaw.[8] Both he and General Bor had sent such messages before and, as before, received no reply.

At the end of September all reserves of ammunition and food ran out. Some insurgents and civilians were dying from exhaustion and starvation.

On 29 September, Bor sent a radiogram to his Commander-in-Chief in London informing him that what little food was left would suffice for only the next three days, that he had informed Marshal Rokossovsky of this and would ask him for assistance again. He was explicit: if he did not receive substantial help, he would be compelled to capitulate.

However, in the last sentence the General said, 'In the case of attack by the Red Army within the next few days . . . I will resume fighting.'[9]

The fate of Warsaw's insurgents and population was not the only responsibility resting on Bor's shoulders. He was also commander of the AK outside Warsaw. On 1 October he sent a special radio message to them: 'Fighting in Warsaw no longer has any chance of success, and I have decided to terminate it.'[10] Bor nominated General Okulicki as the next commander of the AK. He ordered that action of Operation Tempest be held to a minimum and that all efforts be focused on defence of the population.[11]

The AK rank and file did not want to capitulate. Whole units were refusing to surrender. When one AK second lieutenant, a shoemaker by profession, received news that the AK had been ordered to surrender, he grabbed a revolver and shouted that he would 'not allow anybody to surrender'. Then his commanding officer, Colonel Zywiciel, handed him his own revolver and said, 'Then you have to start with me and shoot me, because I am responsible for conveying that order to my soldiers.' The lieutenant broke into incoherent sobs.[12] Reactions to capitulation varied. Two soldiers of my company committed suicide just before we were to go into German captivity. Several AK insurgents in one unit informed their commanding officer that they did not intend to go to a German prison camp, but would leave Warsaw with the civilian population and go back into the underground to fight.[13] General Bor and other AK officers were fully aware of the intense feelings among the insurgents, and this knowledge was reflected in their orders. An example is this order I received from my battalion commander on 2 October: 'Immediately instruct all your positions and those of your neighbouring units that they should not open fire nor act aggressively.' It was true – after two months of battle the insurgents were still 'aggressive'.

All his misgivings notwithstanding, General Bor ultimately decided to capitulate.

During negotiations, German and Polish officers talked. The Chief of Staff to General von dem Bach complained to one of the Poles, 'I lost six officers who went towards insurgents' positions with white flags to encourage you to surrender. All of these men were killed.'[14] A tough Polish combat officer, AK Major Kazimierz Szternal, who had jumped with a parachute into German-occupied Poland, when he met the German Commander of Warsaw, General von dem Bach, said, 'You, the nation which gave Goethe and Schiller to the world, have tried through terror to take away from us the rights of existence and freedom.' To this, von dem Bach responded, 'This is war.'[15]

When General von dem Bach and General Bor met on 4 October, von dem Bach continued to pressure Bor. He demanded that Bor issue an order to *all* AK members, including those who were outside Warsaw, 'to cease underground activities against German forces'.[16] He also insisted that insurgents who were members of Communist organizations be excluded from the agreement of fair treatment.[17] Bor's response was on both points unequivocally negative.[18]

Himmler, Chief of German Police, ordered the total destruction and levelling of Warsaw.

On 3 October the insurgents' daily, *Biuletyn Informacyjny*, declared: 'Nobody in Poland, or in Warsaw, or in the world, can . . . say that we [surrendered] too early.'[19]

There was a sense of cohesion among the insurgents that survived beyond prospects of success. Nothing would have been easier than simply to take off one's AK armband and merge with the population. In this way, the chances of going to a German prison camp would have been decreased. But very few did so. There was an overpowering feeling of elation and duty well done; 15,378 insurgents, including 922 officers, of whom 2,000 were women, marched out of the city as German prisoners.[20]

Here and there along the streets, civilians fell to their knees as our columns passed by.[21] This was an unforgettable, almost shocking scene, because in Poland one kneels in reverence only to the Holy Sacrament.

After sixty-three days, it was over. As the soldiers walked into German captivity, they were there, on both sides of the streets covered by the rifles of the German police: thousands and thousands of emaciated, dirty, bandaged, bloodstained men and women of Warsaw, who within hours would be herded into the camps themselves. They were crying, shouting, singing the Polish national anthem. They ran from behind the police, hugging, kissing, and giving the insurgents gifts.

Anyone not familiar with Polish culture or its values might ask why, then, did the civilian population voluntarily subject itself to such suffering? It seems to me the answer lies in Polish national history. The insurgents had standards to measure up to, standards of their ancestors who for literally a thousand years bled to secure and maintain Polish independence. Their kings, their martyrs and their soldiers were the models and the symbols of ideals against which they measured their own behaviour. Within the past 300 years alone Warsaw itself had fought against Swedes, Russians, Austrians, Germans, and the armies of the Soviet Union (which in 1920 were as near as six miles from the city gates). And, of course, in 1939 the German Army, although, in conjunction with the Soviet Army, it had overrun the whole of Poland, had still been forced to fight for three weeks to get to the centre of Warsaw. Their city had a tradition and a past that they were proud of. It was the Warsaw style of behaviour remembered and recounted to them by their grandfathers and fathers. They had something to live up to, or die for.

How did the civilians react to the surrender? Undoubtedly they were relieved that the constant hail of explosives and bombs would stop. Yet a reliable first-hand report of the behaviour of representatives of the population during a meeting at which the evacuation of the city was announced shows another aspect.

On 3 October the Government Delegate instructed Stefan Korbonski, the Secretary of the Interior, to announce that civilians should leave Warsaw immediately, but Korbonski was not to tell the population that the AK was also surrendering and would go into German internment camps. More than a hundred representatives of the population gathered for the meeting. They accepted the order to abandon Warsaw in silence. Then, when they realized that nothing had been said about the fate of insurgents, one delegate asked, 'And what will happen to the AK?' When they received no answer about the fate of the AK the meeting was interrupted with the cry: 'If the AK is to stay, so will we! If the [AK is] to die, then we shall die together.'[22]

The meeting broke up. The Government Delegate had to organize another meeting at which the Warsaw residents' representatives were informed that the AK was to capitulate and go into German prisoner-of-war camps. Ultimately, this was accepted.[23]

One possible reason why Polish authorities didn't tell the population about the fate of the AK in the first place may have been that, while the Government Delegate and General Bor wanted to spare the population further suffering, they were ready to break off the temporary truce and negotiations with the Germans for capitulation should the Soviet forces suddenly start an offensive.

The best evidence for this hypothesis is an appeal broadcast from an insurgent radio station in Warsaw one hour and twenty minutes before the formal signing of the official surrender. The message from the dying city, monitored by Polish receiving-stations in London,[24] was barely audible:

> Hello, Warsaw speaking. . . . We are still fighting, Warsaw. . . . Warsaw is not yet defeated. . . . This town of one million people is being wiped out. . . . We have given more than we could. . . . Give us immediate assistance! This assistance is due to us! . . . We are today the conscience of the world. We . . . have confidence and are still waiting for your help.
>
> We were called 'the inspiration of the fighting nations and the inspiration of the world'. . . . We, as a nation, have a right to live. We demand that right! . . .[25]

That was all that could be distinguished. It was 7.40 p.m., 2 October 1944. The Poles would continue to fight if given support.

To describe the physical condition of the population and insurgents at the time of surrender is beyond my capability. They had endured two months of house-to-house street fighting, incessant artillery and air bombardment, and were deprived of normal amounts of water and food.

When the time came to leave the ruins, the half-starved survivors took with them only what they could carry, presumably what was most valuable to them. Some carried their wounded or sick loved ones on their shoulders; many departed empty-handed, walking in a daze. Here is the list of civilians who had crossed voluntarily into German captivity:

August	8	7,000
	9	2,000
	10	100
September	8	Number unknown
	9	,,
	29	,,
	30	,,
October	1	7,000–16,000
	2	Number unknown
	3–7	Total evacuation of civilian population. At least 155,000 left through German checkpoints. Many avoided German control.

After capitulation, on 4 October 1944, at 7.30 p.m., the AK station Lightning broadcasted for the last time.[26] 'Rudnicki signed off for the Polish Radio and . . . the manager of the radio station Lightning for its staff.'

'That was the end. . . . Silence. The lamps were still warm for a moment after the current was cut off . . . then . . . the manager approached the console. He struck it with a heavy hammer. . . .'[27] It was all over. Two Soviet and five German radio stations, all broadcasting in Polish, commanded the air waves over the abandoned city.[28] Warsaw was not a Polish city anymore, except perhaps in the hearts and memories of those who had fought there. It was an expanse of desolate ruins in which several hundred Germans (four battalions) were carrying out police duties.

On 17 January 1945, five and a half months after the Soviet forces had arrived in the vicinity, they entered Warsaw. Germans abandoned the ruins to the Soviet soldiers without much of a fight.[29]

The Soviet Government established a special medal for its soldiers: 'For the liberation of Warsaw'.[30] The German Government honoured its soldiers who fought in Warsaw by creating a special metal badge to be worn on their uniforms.

On 3 October, the day the insurgents prepared to march into German captivity, Churchill sent a wire message to Roosevelt with this comment: '. . . About the Poles . . . you and I think so much alike about this that I do not need any special guidance as to your views.'[31] Two days later, Churchill sent this letter (on his official stationery) to Polish Prime Minister Mikolajczyk:

My dear Excellency, I received with deep sorrow your letter telling me that resistance had ceased in Warsaw. As you know, we were anxious to do everything in our power to bring assistance to General Komorowski's forces and nothing but insuperable difficulties of weather and geography prevented our assistance being more effective. . . .[32]

(In 1957 I dined with Mr Mikolajczyk, and the subject of this letter came up. When I asked what his reaction had been, he simply turned his face from me, but I saw that his eyes were filled with tears.)

It was just one week after the surrender of Warsaw that the President of the Polish Roman Catholic Union of America, John Olejniczak, wrote to President Roosevelt, enclosing resolutions of the Union's plenary session in Chicago: '. . . unanimously proclaiming and expressing their faith in judgement and decisions of [the President] relative to [the] future of Poland'.[33] Roosevelt responded:

I am deeply grateful for your letter of October tenth, with which you enclosed a copy of a resolution adopted by the Board of Directors of the Polish Roman Catholic Union of America. Please convey to your fellow members my heartfelt appreciation and thanks for their expression of faith and confidence. I need not reassure you that I shall continue to take unfaltering interest in the future of Poland.[34]

The Soviet Government continued to remove the remaining elements of Polish opposition, one by one. They had destroyed forty-two per cent of the Polish Officers' Corps in the Katyn Forest Massacre and other places still undiscovered; they had the eastern territories, actually half of Poland, in their hands; they had stood by as the Germans destroyed the backbone of any remaining resistance. The intellectual *élite* who had survived the occupation, Poland's scientific and cultural backbone, were now under the ruins of Warsaw.

The only Polish adversary still standing was the Polish Government-in-Exile.

On 28 October 1944, Soviet Ambassador to the United States Andrei Gromyko wrote a letter to Secretary of State Cordell Hull. Mr Gromyko was instructed by the Soviet Government to inform the United States Government that the Communist Polish Committee of National Liberation insisted that they, not the Polish Government-in-Exile, should represent Poland at the Conference on Internal European Transport in London. Further, 'The Soviet Government declares that without the participation of the Polish Committee of National Liberation in the Conference on Internal European Transport, it [the Soviet Government] will not find it possible to take any further part in the work of the above-mentioned Conference.'[35] Under-Secretary of State Stettinius, in a special memorandum for the President on the subject, noted, 'This is the first time that the Soviet Government had made its participation in any United Nations conference or discussions

dependent upon what amounts to the enforced recognition of the
Lublin Committee as the only legal representative of the Polish
nation.'[36]

The unrelenting pressures on the Polish Government-in-Exile continued after the surrender. For example, on 27 November 1944, Eden
received Mikolajczyk and Polish Foreign Minister Romer in London
and 'warned them that the British intended to cut off our [Polish] air
and cypher communication with Poland and to cancel the plan to
appoint a military mission to the Home Army [AK]'.[37] But the Armia
Krajowa in the rest of Poland was still fighting Germans!

In Poland, meanwhile, the terror of the Soviet police was reaching its
climax, and AK men were being hunted. According to Stalin, by
December 1944 'the Polish National Committee has achieved
significant successes in strengthening the Polish state and the apparatus
of state power on the territory of Poland'.[38] How they were going about
it only their Polish victims knew.

On 12 August, Mikolajczyk had reported from London to Bor in
Warsaw that it was his impression that the Soviet Government had
decided not to Sovietize Poland at this time, reserving the timing and
final decision for the future. He continued, 'On the other hand, the
Polish Communists are determined to take this opportunity to com-
munize Poland.' The message ends with this paragraph:

> I submitted to the Council of Ministers one paramount question:
> Which ways, which means, should be chosen in order to save
> Poland from Sovietization? What should the Polish Government-
> in-Exile do? Continue its fight [and] remain in exile? Or, by taking
> advantage of its own contacts abroad, should [it] return to Poland,
> exposing itself [and] all the political parties [that] are the bases for
> its existence, to all the dangers [of a return], and then admit
> Communists into the ranks of the government to prevent Poland
> from Sovietization? At the same time [a coalition government]
> should be concerned to establish sincere Polish–Soviet col-
> laboration in the future.[39]

The importance of this statement should not be underestimated.
Mikolajczyk felt that there was no way except to admit Communists
into his own government. On 16 August, Stalin informed him that his
personal conviction was that the Uprising was a 'thoughtless adventure', that the Soviet command should not and could not assume any
responsibility for the Uprising, and would dissociate itself from that
action.[40]

Meanwhile, Mikolajczyk tried another way of approaching the
Soviet Government. On 22 August 1944, with his knowledge, General
Izydor Modelski, Deputy Minister of National Defence in the Polish
Government-in-Exile, handed a note to the Soviet official Volkov in
London. In this note Modelski informed the Soviet Government that
Mikolajczyk intended to form a government in Warsaw in which Polish

Communists would participate.[41] According to the note, at that moment Mikolajczyk already had the support of three Polish political parties and the 'Majority of Socialist Ministers' for this idea.[42]

The hopelessness of the Warsaw situation was recognized by some of the members of the Polish Government-in-Exile. According to General Modelski, effective assistance for Warsaw could come only from the Soviet Union. He called the attention of Soviet authorities to the fact that their abandoning Mikolajczyk now and their refusal to assist Warsaw would only strengthen the political position of General Sosnkowski's group, which was considered to be anti-Soviet. The Modelski memorandum ends on this note: 'Minister Popiel [of the Polish Government-in-Exile] states, in addition, that Prime Minister Mikolajczyk will agree to the departure of Deputy Minister Modelski either for Moscow or with the team of ministers for Warsaw.'[43]

Neither in the archives of Prime Minister Mikolajczyk nor of General Modelski was there any response to this Polish proposition.

Meanwhile, as the result of an intensive exchange of radio messages between Mikolajczyk and the Governmental Delegate in Poland, the Council of National Unity (the Polish Underground Parliament) consented, with some reluctance, to Mikolajczyk's attempts to work out a *modus operandi* with the Soviet Government.[44] Not so General Bor. In a radio message directed to 'the Commander-in-Chief and Prime Minister' he assumed the role of political leader and policymaker. He commented, 'This plan means complete capitulation and foresees a number of most important political actions based solely on Soviet good will. . . . This plan is a departure from the present political line and a descent from our position of independence.' General Bor charged his government with 'complete capitulation' to Russia, bending under the pressure of circumstances, and having a submissive attitude. The radiogram also contained this sentence, 'Should the necessity arise, we are ready to repeat our proof in the face of anybody who would wish to destroy our independence.'[45]

Mikolajczyk's position among Polish exiles was threatened as there was considerable opposition within the Polish Government to his attempt to work out some accommodation with the Soviet Government. Opponents charged him with softness, with a tacit agreement to give up Wilno to the Soviet Union, and with recognition of the Polish Committee of National Liberation.[46] Mikolajczyk's anxious awareness of the possibility of 'intrigues' against him is revealed in his radio messages to the Government Delegate in Warsaw.[47] He proceeded to narrow the base of his government.[48]

The Polish Communists also had troubles of their own. There are available the minutes of four meetings (15, 18, 24 and 27 September 1944) of the Polish Committee of National Liberation at which political implications of the Uprising of Warsaw were discussed. At the meeting of 15 September one member stated, 'The political battle for Warsaw is

starting . . . now.'⁴⁹ Another (Stanislaw Radkiewicz, who, as commander of the police, was responsible for the bloody terror in the
postwar years in Poland) came to the point: 'If we are driving for
Warsaw . . . we are driving with the purpose that already in Praga we
should establish the political centre of power. It is unthinkable for us to
allow somebody else to take power now. We have four divisions at our
disposal. Our army will capture everything. Any attempt to take power
from us unlawfully [sic] should be squashed with the assistance of
General Kieniewicz.'⁵⁰ The members of the Polish Committee of
National Liberation participating in these proceedings knew General
Kieniewicz as commander of the Soviet artillery just outside Warsaw.
(Brigadier-General Boleslaw Kieniewicz, a Soviet officer, was at that
time attached to the Polish 4th Infantry Division. From May 1945 to
December 1946, he wore a Polish uniform and was Commander of
Internal Security Forces in Poland.) In essence, Radkiewicz was
proposing that if the Polish Committee of Liberation could not seize
political power from the Polish Government and the AK, then Soviet
artillery should be called upon to concentrate its fire on Warsaw and the
AK insurgents.

Among these men were some of conscience. One of these, Rzym-
owski, also had courage. He asked, 'I would like . . . an explanation
why the Red Army [has] delayed its march on Warsaw so much? There
is information from Warsaw which indicates that a month ago, just
before the Uprising, there was a moment when Warsaw was practically
open and undefended by the Germans. Everyone in Warsaw could see
them [the Germans] fleeing the city. This was one of the reasons why the
insurgents decided to attack. . . . This problem is very important,
because one can draw the conclusion that the Red Army's progress was
affected by political considerations. We should equip ourselves with
solid evidence to explore the question: Was the Red Army able to come
earlier?'⁵¹

Not until all documentation from the Polish Communist Party
Archives is available (at this time it is not, even for rank-and-file Polish
Communists) will the interaction among the Polish Communists in
Poland, those imported from the Soviet Union, Rokossovsky, and
Berling be fully known. These relationships were extremely complex.
The possibility that they contributed to General Berling's downfall
cannot be excluded. If there is one statement from an authoritative
source that provides a key to the explanation of Soviet behaviour *vis-à-
vis* the Uprising of Warsaw, it is that of Stalin to Marshal Zhukov:
'Churchill wants the Soviet Union to barter with a bourgeois Poland,
alien to us, while we cannot allow this to happen. . . .'⁵²

That General Bor didn't tell the Red Army about the Uprising is not
a valid argument for withholding assistance unless other considerations
than fighting Germans were involved. Both Paris in 1944 and Prague in
1945 initiated fighting against Germans without agreeing upon a

time-table with the approaching Allies; yet they were liberated by Allied forces within a few days.

In 1969 Marshal Rokossovsky's book, *A Soldier's Duty*, appeared in an English translation; *Memoirs*, by Marshal Zhukov, followed in 1971. Both books refer to the Uprising of Warsaw, and both blame General Bor for more than not informing them of the date and time of the outbreak of the Uprising. Marshal Zhukov says Bor did not make 'any attempt[53] to co-ordinate the insurgents' actions with those of the First Byelorussian Front'.[54] Marshal Rokossovsky alleges that General Bor 'never even tried to establish direct contacts with the Front HQ'.[55] Another Soviet military historian of the postwar period adds another accusation: that General Bor not only did not get in touch with the Soviet authorities, but 'he [also forbade] others to do so'.[56] The Soviet charges are crucial for an assessment of responsibility for the aftermath of the Uprising, and they must be considered.

It is true that General Bor did not inform the approaching Soviet Army about the timing of the Uprising. As early as May 1944, the AK command ordered that contacts with the Polish Communists in Warsaw be terminated.[57] But, immediately upon commencement of the Uprising, General Bor sought help.[58] The first Polish appeal for assistance to Soviet authorities was sent on 1 August (actually on 2 August, but dated 1 August), via London, and, according to a Soviet source, was conveyed by the British Military Mission in Moscow to the Soviet General Staff on 2 August 1944 at 1.10 p.m.[59] There is explicit evidence that General Bor, General Monter, and several AK sector commanders were in direct contact with Marshal Rokossovsky's and General Berling's headquarters on many occasions during the Uprising. (See Tables No. 1 and No. 2.)

There were five radios, in addition to the stations attached to the AK Headquarters, conveying messages directly between the insurgents and Soviet forces on the east shore of the Vistula. Four were Soviet-made and serviced by Soviet officers, and the fifth one belonged to AK being temporarily attached to General Berling's HQs described below.

From 18 September, Soviet Lieutenant Wurdel operated a Soviet radio transmitter in Zoliborz Sector that conveyed messages between his command post and the AK commander of this sector, Colonel Zywiciel. Wurdel crossed the Vistula to insurgents on the order of a local commander of either a Russian unit, or a Polish unit under Russian command.

From 20 September, Captain Wieckowski (AL) operated a Soviet radio transmitter in Zoliborz Sector.

On 21 September two Soviet soldiers (Captain Kolos' mission) parachuted into Warsaw with Soviet radio transmitters.

From 21 September, Soviet Major Chernuhin and his radio set served as a communication bridge between the AK commander of Mokotow Sector and a Soviet artillery post.

From 24 September, there was an AK officer with a radio set in General Berling's headquarters conveying messages between the AK Headquarters in Warsaw and General Berling.

There is further proof of the intensity of contacts between AK and Soviet forces. The information in the following tables has been collated from a variety of Polish and Soviet sources. Contacts with Soviet forces that were *initiated by AK Headquarters* are listed in Table No. 1. Table No. 2 indicates *the initiative from the Soviet authorities*. Both tables are incomplete because some contacts and messages were never recorded and because copies of others are not available. Nevertheless, the tables indicate that AK Headquarters sought direct assistance and offered to co-operate. Moreover, the records show that the Soviet command began responding by radio on 21 or 22 September. Bor reported that he received the first radio message signed by General Berling on 28 September. In the light of this, the statements by Soviet Marshals Rokossovsky and Zhukov that Bor declined communication with them appear untrue, unless they refer to the period before the Uprising began. There is no evidence either way for this.

TABLE NUMBER 1

PARTIAL ENUMERATION OF CONTACTS WITH THE SOVIET COMMAND INITIATED BY THE AK COMMAND IN WARSAW DURING THE UPRISING

Date	Sender	Medium	Intended Recipient
1 Aug	Gen. Bor	Radio message via London	Soviet General Staff Moscow
5(7) Aug	Soviet Captain Kalugin (he was not delegated in any way by the Soviet authorities)	Radio message with Bor's knowledge, if not editorial help	Stalin
8 Aug	Gen. Bor	Radio message via London	Marshal Rokossovsky
8 Aug	Gen. Monter	Radio message	Marshal Rokossovsky
8 Aug	Gen. Monter	Radio message	Marshal Rokossovsky
9 Aug	Gen. Monter	Radio message	Marshal Rokossovsky
16 Aug	Armia Ludowa	Two women messengers	?
10 Sept	Armia Ludowa	Two women messengers	Personally reported to Rokossovsky and then to National Liberation Committee in Lublin

Date	Sender	Medium	Intended Recipient
10 Sept	Gen Bor	Radio message via London	Marshal Rokossovsky
12 Sept	Armia Ludowa	Three women messengers	Marshal Rokossovsky
14 Sept	AK Col. Zywiciel	An AK officer and woman messenger	Marshal Rokossovsky
15 Sept	AK Col. Zywiciel	Messenger with a letter	Soviet command
15 Sept	AK Col. Radwan	From 3 to 5 AK soldiers	General Berling
15 Sept	Gen. Bor	Radio message via London	Marshal Rokossovsky
15 Sept	AK Col. Daniel	Patrol calling for help	Soviet command
16 Sept	Three AK Soldiers crossed the Vistula on their own initiative. One reported to General Berling. He stressed the gravity of the situation and pointed out artillery targets to him.		
17 Sept	Gen. Bor	Radio message via London	Intended for Marshal Rokossovsky (discussed)
18 Sept	Gen. Monter	Three messengers with a field radio set	Gen. Berling
17 Sept	Gen. Bor	Radio message via London	Marshal Rokossovsky
18 Sept	AK Col. Radwan	Radio message	Gen. Berling
18 Sept	Field telephone contact between insurgents in Czerniakow Sector and the Polish (Communist)		
20 Sept	Gen. Bor	Radio message	Marshal Rokossovsky
21 Sept	Gen. Monter	Radio message describing situation in Warsaw	Marshal Rokossovsky
22 Sept	Gen. Monter	Radio message via Soviet Captain Kolos' radio offering synchronized action	Marshal Rokossovsky. Acknowledged, but not answered
28 Sept	Gen. Bor	Radio message informing that AK can fight only till 1 Oct	Marshal Rokossovsky

Date	Sender	Medium	Intended Recipient
29 Sept	AK Col. Zywiciel	Soviet radio operated by Lt Wurdel (stationed with insurgents) and radio managed by Captain Wieckowski (AL); both begged for immediate assistance	Gen. Berling and/or Soviet command
30 Sept	Gen, Bor	Warsaw situational Reports Numbers Three and Four transmitted by radio messages via London	Marshal Rokossovsky
30 Sept	Gen. Bor	Radio message via London relaying signal code	Marshal Rokossovsky

(In all probability, the last two messages were not forwarded by the Polish HQ in London.)

It is possible that messages sent by Bor via the Polish Command in London, via the British Mission in Moscow and via the Soviet Supreme Command in Moscow, to Rokossovsky were stopped by the Soviet Command in Moscow. On the other hand, as the table shows, Marshal Rokossovsky received radio messages directly from General Bor. It was impossible to ascertain in all cases whether messages were actually acknowledged or answered.

TABLE NUMBER 2

PARTIAL ENUMERATION OF CONTACTS WITH THE INSURGENTS IN WARSAW DURING THE UPRISING INITIATED BY SOVIET MARSHAL ROKOSSOVSKY'S AND/OR GENERAL BERLING'S HEADQUARTERS OR THEIR SUBORDINATE UNITS

Date	Sender	Medium	Intended Recipient
13 Sept	Soviet command	Message dropped from Soviet plane.	?
14 Sept	Soviet command	Message dropped from Soviet plane.	AK Col. Zywiciel

Date	Sender	Medium	Intended Recipient
14 Sept	HQ of 125th Soviet Corps	Patrol of 5 Polish soldiers	AK Col. Radwan
19 Sept	Soviet Command	Soviet Lt Wurdel and radio operator with a radio crossed the Vistula to insurgents. Messages sent and received.	AK Col. Zywiciel
19 Sept	Gen. Berling	Soviet radio station given to AL Capt. Wieckowski, a 2nd Lt, and a private, who crossed the Vistula to the insurgents' shore. Messages sent and received.	AK Col. Zywiciel
20 Sept	Soviet command	Soviet artillery Maj. Chernuhin from 2nd Artillery Regiment reached AK Sector Mokotow to direct artillery fire. Messages sent and received.	
21 Sept	Soviet General Staff in Moscow	Via Marshal Rokossovsky, with a field radio set sent Soviet Capt. Kolos and a Soviet radio operator. They parachuted into Warsaw and established liaison with AK Headquarters.	AK Headquarters
22 Sept	Captain Kolos maintained radio contacts between Marshal Rokossovsky's Headquarters and General Bor's Headquarters. Messages sent and received.		

TABLE NUMBER 3

GERMAN–POLISH CONTACTS LEADING TO THE SURRENDER OF WARSAW

18 Aug	The German command proposes capitulation to the Polish command, threatening that otherwise 'the city and its population will be completely destroyed'. The proposal includes a promise of combatant status for AK insurgents. The Polish command does not respond.
27 Aug	The 9th German Army command instructs Hungarian General Lengyell formally to contact General Bor and encourage him to stop fighting, reaffirming the insurgents' status as combatants.
7 Sept	German General Rohr invites representatives of the Polish command to discuss the possibility of surrender. Via the Polish Red Cross General von dem Bach also invites representatives of the Polish command for similar discussion.
9 Sept	General Bor cautiously responds to the German offer by sending two AK officers through the Polish Red Cross to General Rohr, to ascertain conditions. At 6 p.m. Bor sends a message to Rohr telling him that he will reply on 10 September.
10 Sept	At 7 a.m. General Bor sends a letter to General Rohr demanding written assurance of fair treatment of insurgents, civilians, and Polish authorities. Rohr responds at 11 a.m., agreeing to give such assurance. He also expresses his expectations that Bor will agree to capitulate by 4 p.m. General Bor hears Soviet artillery from the other side of the Vistula. He is still expecting American air assistance. At 3 p.m. Bor sends a message to the German command in which he demands that the above-mentioned assurance of fair treatment be given personally by the commander of the German Army Group Centre, General Reinhardt, and that it be broadcast over German radio. General Rohr responds. He promises to go to Reinhardt, convey the message to him, and deliver an answer to Bor by 8 p.m. He also says that he expects the Poles to surrender by 10 p.m. Around midnight General Rohr informs Polish Headquarters that General Reinhardt approves the conditions, and that he expects Polish approval of surrender by 1 p.m. on 11 September.
11 Sept	At 1.30 p.m., General Bor writes to Rohr blaming him for breaking off negotiations. Fighting continues.
18 Sept	The German command proposes surrender to Colonel Niedzielski, AK commander of Zoliborz Sector. In response, the Colonel asks the Germans to surrender to him. The battle continues.
20 Sept	The Germans again propose surrender. Bor declines.
21 Sept	The Germans propose surrender to Czerniakow Sector. The insurgents decline.
25 Sept	The German command proposes surrender to the AK commander of Mokotow Sector. The Pole does not respond. The struggle goes on.
26 Sept	The German command proposes surrender to the AK commander of Centre City Sector. The commander does not reply. Insurgents there, too, continue battling Germans.
27 Sept	The German command again proposes surrender to the AK

commander of Zoliborz Sector. The Pole does not answer. His
units literally fight for every yard of ground.

28 Sept   General von dem Bach again proposes capitulation to General
Bor. After informing Marshal Rokossovsky that Warsaw can fight
only until 1 October, General Bor begins negotiations with the
German command.

30 Sept   The AK delegation meets the Germans in the German Headquarters. A cease-fire is set for 1 and 2 October, between 5 a.m. and 7
p.m., and the evacuation of 200,000 civilians is agreed upon.

1 Oct   Because he has not heard from Marshal Rokossovsky about
assistance to Warsaw, General Bor decides to capitulate. He
informs von dem Bach that Polish envoys will arrive at German
headquarters near Warsaw at 8 a.m.

2 Oct   The capitulation agreement is signed at German Headquarters
outside Warsaw at 9 p.m. Only one and a half hours before the
signing, General Bor's radio station was still calling the Allies for
'immediate assistance'.

Finally, the last Soviet charge should be examined. Rokossovsky
maintained in his memoirs that when, on 16 September, units of the
First Polish Army crossed the Vistula 'they landed at points on the bank
supposedly held by insurgent units, that being the assumption upon
which the whole plan had been based. But then these footholds were
found to be in Nazi hands! . . . Soon we learned that, on instructions
from Bor-Komorowski and Monter, the AK units had been withdrawn
from the river-front suburb into the heart of the city. Their place had
been taken by Nazi troops.'[60] It should be stated that this is not true.

How frustrating these statements must have been to the Polish
Communists, especially to those who fought and helped to hold that
particular insurgents' position; and what a suppressed fury they must
have created among the several hundred valiant soldiers of the First
Polish Army who live in Poland today, who landed on the AK-held
side of Warsaw and were welcomed there by 400 insurgents, with whom
they desperately held the bridgehead there for eight days! Ideological
differences notwithstanding, soldiers from the two armies stood together
in combat against the ferocity of German attacks, and shared a bond as
Poles struggling for their city. Hundreds of these AK men, Communist
insurgents, and men from units of the First Polish Army under Soviet
command are alive today and could testify that the Soviet Marshal
distorted the truth. (I interviewed one of these men, 2nd Lieutenant
Xen, Boleslaw Stanczyk, an executive officer of a company AK.
Interview: Chicago, 18 May 1966.)

On 23 February 1965 I dined in a quiet London restaurant with
General Tadeusz Bor-Komorowski. We discussed the Uprising. I asked
him whether he was still sure that Marshal Rokossovsky really could
have come to his assistance. In his calm and pensive fashion he said,
'Rokossovsky could not have taken Warsaw before 10 August 1944, but
afterwards he could have entered Warsaw.' His original opinion that
the Red Army could have taken Warsaw within two or three days after

the outbreak of the Uprising on 1 August had changed. After twenty-one years, having studied the Soviet, German and Polish battle reports, he had modified his view and was honest about it. But this quiet man with sad eyes, sitting across from me, held Warsaw for *sixty-three days* in the sincere belief that, if the Red Army could not cross the river in three, seven, or ten days, it might still do so within sixty-three days.

After the war, Konstantin Rokossovsky, commander of the First Byelorussian Front, became simultaneously Polish Deputy Prime Minister, Polish Minister of National Defence, Member of the Polish Politbureau, and Marshal of Poland in 1949. The Communist Government also bestowed upon him the extremely rare and coveted Polish Order Virtuti Militari, First Class. This order was established in 1792 by the last Polish king for heroism in battle against Russia.

What happened at the gates of Warsaw was a misfortune for both Poland and the Soviet Union. Were it not for Soviet policies and territorial demands during the Second World War, the Katyn Forest Massacre and the Uprising of Warsaw, Polish public opinion would have been more affected by the fact that 600,000 Soviet soldiers had died on Polish soil fighting Germans, and there might have been an interruption in the long history of enmity and bitterness between Poland and Russia.

While Poland has a Communist government bound to the Soviet Union by economic, political and military considerations, the role played by the Soviet Government in the Uprising will be discreetly discussed and Poles in exile have no real audience except each other. But memories in Eastern Europe are painfully long and these events have been entered in the balance sheets that keep alive mutual mistrust between Poland and the Soviet Union.

The epitaph to the Warsaw Uprising was in effect written at Yalta, four months after its final suppression. During the tri-partite dinner meeting on 4 February 1945, the real heart of the matter came under consideration. The topic was the 'Voice of Smaller Powers in Post War Peace Organization'. Charles Bohlen took the minutes: 'Marshal Stalin, the President and the Prime Minister appeared to be in a very good humor throughout the dinner.' And then, during the last half-hour of the dinner,

> Marshal Stalin made it quite plain on a number of occasions that he felt that the three Great Powers which had borne the brunt of the war and had liberated from German domination the small powers should have the unanimous right to preserve the peace of the world. . . . He said that it was ridiculous to believe that Albania would have an equal voice with the three Great Powers who had won the war and were present at this dinner. . . .
>
> Marshal Stalin said that he was prepared in concert with the United States and Great Britain to protect the rights of the small powers but that he would never agree to having any action of any

of the Great Powers submitted to the judgment of the small powers.

The President said he agreed that the Great Powers bore the greater responsibility and that the peace should be written by the Three Powers represented at this table.

The Prime Minister said that there was no question of the small powers dictating to the big powers but that the great nations of the world should discharge their moral responsibility and leadership and should exercise their power with moderation and great respect for the rights of the smaller nations.[61]

Poland was physically a small nation in 1944. The AK insurgents and supporting population of Warsaw assumed that their fight would influence Poland's political fate. They erred in that assumption. But the chief handicap of the Poles, for which neither they nor their allies were responsible, was the fact that their country lay directly between two giants – Germany to the West and Russia to the East. In August 1944 they would have been damned if they fought and damned if they didn't.

In their own concept of honour and duty, they chose to fight rather than to wait passively for events to overtake them. They reaped destruction, but in their own cultural style, defending their homes and national independence.

From a distance of thirty years, it appears that the end would have been the same, in any case. If Warsaw had not fought, the unsympathetic would have said that Poles did not deserve their freedom, that they had assented to or abetted Nazi tyranny, and that they had been unwilling to fight for the common cause. The Poles fought, and the unsympathetic say that they fought alone because they refused to 'co-operate' with the Soviet Union. This is simply misinformation. Except for a pitiful minority of Cummunists, Poles did not want to be absorbed by the Soviet Union or dominated by it.

Research in all the available primary documents, including German, made it clear that all parties shared the same handicap – incomplete knowledge – and that this was partly because they (even the Allies) wilfully concealed information from each other. There was a lack of communication among all the Allies and among the Poles themselves. In the best diplomatic tradition, no one told anyone else the truth, or even as much of it as he knew. Misunderstandings were compounded.

Documents and memoirs show the diplomats and statesmen of the time to have been completely human. They safeguarded their own nations' interests as they saw the situation. Upon reflection, what else could we expect? Nor is it surprising that from the perspective of thirty years the means by which national self-interests were served seem shoddy, if not shameful.

The tragedy of Poland was not only that her enemies destroyed Warsaw, but also that her friends did not fully understand what was taking place and why. What really happened? I have attempted to answer that question.

APPENDIX A

Comparative Statistics[1]

1. POLISH STATISTICS FOR THE UPRISING OF WARSAW

(Numbers are approximate)

(a)   Insurgents in combat: 40,000

During 63 days of fighting (including actions in Kampinos Forest):

Killed	10,200
Missing (killed?)	7,000
Gravely wounded	5,000
Total losses	22,200
Insurgents sent to German prisoner-of-war camps	15,900

(b)   Civilians in Warsaw:

Killed	200,000–250,000
Evacuated during and after the Uprising	700,000

The figures include losses incurred during the battle for Old Town Sector.

Old Town Sector

(c)   Insurgents killed between 14 August and
        2 September   5,000 at least
        (The number of insurgents killed between
        1 and 14 August has not been
        established.)
        Insurgents gravely wounded   2,500

(d)   Civilians killed   100,000–120,000
        Civilians gravely wounded   7,000 at least

In my estimation, casualties among insurgents fighting for Old Town were 77 per cent.

(e)   Insurgents imprisoned in German prisoner-of-war camps:

> 900 officers (including 6 generals)
> 2,000 women soldiers of AK
>
> 13,000 rank and file
> _____
> 15,900

(f)   About 3,500 AK soldiers merged with the civilian population.

It is my considered judgement that the human losses mentioned above as compiled from a variety of sources are underestimated.

(g)   General Berling's First Polish Army   90,972 (on 1 July 1944)
        Losses in fighting for Warsaw   5,662
        (Killed, missing and wounded)

(h)   Material losses in Warsaw

Destroyed:

> 10,455 buildings
>   923 historical buildings (94 per cent)
>   25 churches
>   14 libraries
>   64 high schools
>   81 elementary schools

2.   *GERMAN STATISTICS FOR THE UPRISING OF WARSAW*

(a)   German forces in combat:

> On 1 August 1944   13,000
> After 20 August 1944   21,520

The strength of German forces fluctuated greatly. On some days, it reached 40,000 men.

(b)   During 63 days of fighting:

> Killed   10,000
> Missing (killed?)   7,000
> Wounded   9,000
>   Total losses   26,000

(c)   Approximately 1,000–2,000 Germans were captured by insurgents. About 1,000 were returned to German authorities after the Uprising.

(d)   Material losses (equipment) including those sustained in the

fighting in Kampinos Forest and armament captured by insurgents:

  3 planes
310 tanks, self-propelled artillery, armoured cars
  4 rocket launchers
 22 artillery pieces (calibre 75 millimetres)
340 trucks and cars

The number of smaller personal weapons has not been established.

APPENDIX B

Interview between Major-General Tadeusz Bor-Komorowski, Commander-in-Chief of Armia Krajowa (The Polish Home Army) during the Uprising of Warsaw, 1944, and Professor J. K. Zawodny

THE interview took place at 42, Emperor's Gate, London, England, on 17 May 1965. Conducted under controlled conditions, it was open-ended and lasted two hours. Instead of tape-recording the interview, I decided in this case (and in many others) to make notes. Immediately after the interview, I re-read the notes to General Bor. He corrected my interpretation of the Polish word *dezawuowac*. I then asked him to write in his own hand his personal data, including the pseudonyms which he used in the underground.

He did not request any further proof-reading or verification of my notes. Subsequently, he invited me for tea at the adjacent coffee house. There he gave me, as a memento, a ribbon of the Polish order Virtuti Militari (5th Class), which he had originally worn on his uniform. (The ribbon is now in my possession.) The General remembered me from the time of the Uprising. I saw him on numerous occasions in London in 1964–5, when I was doing research on the Uprising of Warsaw. I found him always straightforward, modest, and devoid of arrogance.

This interview was in the Polish language, and it is printed here with the permission of the Institut Littéraire, Paris. It was originally published as 'Wywiad z Gen. Bor Komorowskim', *Kultura*, Paris, No. 11 (229), 1966.

ZAWODNY: *What was the basic objective of the Warsaw Uprising?*
BOR: The Warsaw Uprising was a continuation of Operation Tempest in the expectation that the Russians, under their own impetus and as a consequence of their losses, would be forced to take Warsaw.
ZAWODNY: *What was the basis for General Monter's report that a Russian drive on Warsaw was a fait accompli? Have I phrased my question correctly?*
BOR: I questioned him about the basis of his report. Monter told me that his information came from 'forward patrols in no-man's-land'. His report mirrored the situation correctly. You have only to look at the *Soviet History of the War*. The attack on Warsaw was initiated [by the Soviet Army].

ZAWODNY: *Did General Monter present the material preparedness of the AK*
for action pessimistically, in accordance with the facts, or was he in an optimistic
mood?

BOR: I am not going to disown Monter. That is always very easy. His
evaluation of the situation was to the point. However, you have to
consider the arms distribution among the units and the tactics of
attacking fortified objects and strongpoints; you will find that that is
another story. Objects that presented heavy obstacles for our units
would have been easy targets for one anti-tank gun if the Russians had
entered the fight.

ZAWODNY: *Had you been under pressure to initiate the action in Warsaw*
earlier? If so, who pressured you?

BOR: Yes, there was some pressure. Some members at Staff Headquarters of the AK such as Rzepecki and Okulicki, especially Okulicki,
were in favour of earlier action. However, I did not have [the General
stressed this by the tone of his voice and then repeats] I did not have
sufficient proof of an imminent drive on Warsaw. Not until the Soviets
were attacking Warsaw was the moment ripe for an order to initiate
action within the city. The only way to achieve victory would have been
a co-ordinated effort from without and within. I would like to say that
we made continuous efforts to secure such co-ordination. However, the
Soviets arrested all radio-operators and commanders of the AK in the
east. And also our government in London did everything they should
and could in the political arena.

ZAWODNY: *General, why didn't General Sosnkowski return to London,*
although he was informed of the situation in London and Warsaw and was asked
by the President to do so?

BOR: He left, so as not to be here [in London]. I find this a difficult
matter to talk about. His relations with Mikolajczyk and the matter of
the Uprising played a part. However, the fact that he left is not as
important as the fact that he did not come back at the President's
demand. This is a problem. . . . Sosnkowski should have foreseen that
the fight for Warsaw would turn into an uprising. In fact, it was only
after eight to ten days' fighting that the Russians' attitude really
determined the fate of the Uprising.

ZAWODNY: *General, did Rettinger have any influence with the AK Headquar-*
ters, or did he influence the decision about the Uprising?

BOR: Absolutely not. He had no influence whatsoever on the decision
to start the Uprising. This was never even discussed with him. We
discussed the internal political situation but never the Uprising.

ZAWODNY: *Why did you not capitulate earlier?*

BOR: I waited for a better turn of events. Unconditional
surrender – no! I was counting on the Russians occupying Warsaw from
the moment that they started their offensive on Praga. Well, as it turned
out, later, their attitude became clear.

ZAWODNY: *General, did you know – and, if so, when did you learn – that the*

Allies had already turned over eastern Poland to the Soviet Union in Tehran? Was it in November [December] 1943?

BOR: I heard about this only after the Uprising, when I was a prisoner of war. The instruction of the Commander-in-Chief gave some inkling, but there were no details. I would like to state categorically that at the start of the Uprising I did not know that the Allies had agreed to hand over our territories. I knew that the Russians wanted them but I did not know that [the territories] were already promised to them.

ZAWODNY: *General, if you had known that the Allies had already surrendered eastern Poland to the Soviet Union and that the Allies would not give any effective help to fighting Warsaw, would you still have made the decision to fight in Warsaw?*

BOR: I would have continued the Tempest operation as long as there were Germans in our country. If not, the Communists would have suspected us of co-operating with the Germans. No, I would not have stopped fighting even in Warsaw, since for a long time the Germans did not recognize us as soldiers, and there would have been a massacre.

ZAWODNY: *Looking back on the Warsaw Uprising after twenty-one years, what do you think of it now?*

BOR: I would say that it is still too early to say whether the Uprising was good or bad for the Polish cause. Future generations will make that judgement. Even in the case of defeat, such a moral and physical effort will be remembered by the nation. This effort brought forth cultural and moral values and strength that could not have come from a passive attitude. We cannot know at present what influence the AK's struggle will have on the formation of the Polish nation's spirit and positive values. This, of course, is my personal opinion.

ZAWODNY: *Which criticism has been most painful to you?*

BOR: The criticism of people who lived in Poland under German occupation and should know what things were like then – and yet now they present them in another light. I can understand that the Communists and people abroad have lots to say. [At this point the General became lost in thought for a few minutes. It was evident that what he was going to say next was painful for him.] Sosnkowski's reproach that I was disloyal toward the Commander-in-Chief and that I acted contrary to the Commander-in-Chief's orders. That is what hurts. It will not cover him with glory, and it obscures the picture. And, you know, another thing that hurts me very much – the people who called our AK soldiers arsonists. This was said even in the West.

ZAWODNY: *In the 'West'? Could you be more precise?*

BOR: I am thinking of what happened in the Armoured Division and the Second Corps [the units of the Polish Forces-in-Exile].

ZAWODNY: *General, which subjects do you consider have not yet been covered in the history of the Uprising of Warsaw, and which have not yet been properly treated by historians?*

BOR: Soviet and German sources should be used and quoted more often. It would also be useful to give full consideration to the subject: What was the purpose of the Uprising? Certain malicious opinions, especially, need to be corrected. You see, the difference between the Uprising of Warsaw and the general uprising has not been explained properly.

This Uprising has been one of the greatest efforts of our nation in many years and has had an influence on the formation of spiritual values. This is an aspect that should also be treated.

ZAWODNY: *General, if you will allow me a personal opinion — when you consider Warsaw's history throughout the ages, it is a very heroic city and it has its own tradition of solving its problems. Has this city been honoured in any way?*

BOR: Warsaw was decorated in 1939 with the Virtuti Militari, 5th Class. I know of no precedent of decorating cities with a higher class of this order. As far as I am concerned, I have refused the order Virtuti Militari, 2nd Class, with which I was to be decorated after the war.

ZAWODNY: General, thank you very much for this interview.

BOR: Please call on me for any information that you may need at any time.

APPENDIX C

Interview between Professor George F. Kennan[1] and Professor J. K. Zawodny[2]

30 MAY 1972

ZAWODNY: This is Professor Zawodny speaking. I am at the office of Professor George Kennan at the Institute for Advanced Study, Princeton. Today is . . . 30 May 1972.

Professor Kennan has been kind enough to answer some questions pertaining to his period of service in Moscow in 1944; specifically, in August 1944, when Mr Mikolajczyk[3] was present in Moscow.

Now, the first question, Professor Kennan, which I have, is this:

What do you remember about Prime Minister Mikolajczyk?

KENNAN: I don't recall talking with Mikolajczyk myself during his visit there. I think I saw him on at least two occasions. One was some sort of reception. Another was a dinner, as I recall it; I can't remember who gave the dinner, it was in the building of the old Russian Supreme Court, if I remember it correctly, but I can't remember who was his host on that occasion: whether it was the Russians themselves. There was, of course, no Polish Embassy there and it was not, as I recall it, at *our* Embassy. It may figure in my diary notes, but I don't think so.

I remember, in any case, that there was a dinner there, and I was included, for it was a big dinner. It was perhaps thirty or forty people, at least; and I, being fairly senior in rank (I was the Number Two in our Embassy) was included, not in the top group, but just below it. I sat next to one of the Poles in Mikolajzyk's entourage, or between two of them. And on that occasion I saw him. He responded, if I am not wrong, to a toast. I think there was one other occasion, but I can't remember what it was. He may have paid a call at our Embassy; I think that's likely; and I may have assisted there when he came; but if so, again, he came with a considerable entourage, and Ambassador Harriman[4] conducted the discussion, I did not. I remember him only – well, you know his physical characteristics better than I do; he was not a tall man; I wouldn't say he was stout, but he was stocky. He had a real peasant's figure. I remember him with sort of sandy hair. He was composed, but serious. I realized of course that he was in a very tragic position, and saw him that way. I felt

217

intensely sorry for him. As you know, I could see no hope for him. I saw even less hope than he did, and that was very little.

ZAWODNY: *On which grounds did you base your feelings that there was no hope for him?*

KENNAN: I was convinced that the Soviet regime proposed to get rid of his government and to dominate Poland. I had been surprised, in 1943 and in the months thereafter, at the violence of the Soviet reaction against the Polish Government-in-Exile – surprised at how difficult they were for the Western Allies to deal with on this subject. I had, before leaving Washington, spent an evening with the Counsellor of the Polish Embassy there – Wszelaki.[5] It was at Bill Bullitt's[6] house. Bill Bullitt had been our Ambassador in Moscow earlier and was, at that time, a good friend of mine. I often stayed at his home in Washington. He was a great friend of Ciechanowski[7] and the Poles, and he had Wszelaki over for an evening.

I was leaving for Moscow, and I suppose Bullitt thought, correctly, that it would be useful for me to talk with one of the Poles. Wszelaki was an intelligent man, and we both knew something about the Soviet Union. So we put our heads together to try to analyse what it could be that made this Soviet reaction so sharp, and we both came to the conclusion that there was something the Russians were not talking about which accounted for their position. I think we both strongly suspected that this was the Katyn massacre[8] and the deportations of 1939[9] – that this was very important to them.

Well, we simply came to the conclusion that there must be some factor playing a role here which was not visible on the outside. We were not so surprised at the territorial claim, but we were surprised at how difficult the Soviet Government was being with regard to the Polish Government-in-Exile.

Now, for this reason, I had no sympathy with the action of the United States Government and the British Government in suggesting to Mikolajczyk that he come to Moscow. I did not think that this was right. This was only a way of washing their own hands of the subject. If they were not able to get a decent agreement out of Stalin, they should have faced the music right there and not pushed poor Mikolajczyk over to deal with him.

ZAWODNY: *That brings me to another question. In my research in Mr Mikolajczyk's papers, I found the following letter,[10] which I would like to show you. You might be useful, first of all, in deciphering for me this signature. Do you have any idea whose it is? It is on a letter from the British Embassy in Moscow. It isn't Kerr, is it?*

KENNAN: That is Clark Kerr.[11] He was the Ambassador (ZAWODNY: Of the British Government).

ZAWODNY: This is a very curious, very interesting document. It never has been, so to speak, brought to light yet. It's from the British Embassy in Moscow and it's signed by the British Ambassador (KENNAN: Yes) and it's dated 2 August 1944.

This letter is written to Tadeusz Romer, who was Minister for Foreign Affairs of the Polish Government-in-Exile, and who was at that time with Mikolajczyk in Moscow. (KENNAN: Right.)

Let me read to you some pertinent parts:

My dear Minister:

You asked me last night to put on paper the speculations I was making about Mr Mikolajczyk's negotiations with the Russians. Here they are:

What you may expect the Russians to ask:

1. The remodelling of the Polish Government. . . . [Then he goes into specifically what they want.]

2. The acceptance of the Curzon Line as a basis of neg otiations. . . . [He elaborates.]

3. Some kind of withdrawal from the suggestion that the killing at Katyn was done by the Russians. About this there is very strong feeling here. I am sure that you do not need to be reminded of that. For myself, I think that the easiest way out of this difficulty would be the acceptance of the findings of the Soviet Commission that inquired into the crime.

[An additional four points follow dealing with the demands on the part of the Soviet Union. Then the last page of this letter is under the heading, 'Now for what you may expect in return', and here he says:]

1. The re-establishment of diplomatic relations.

2. The fullest assurances about:

(a) The territorial and administrative integrity of the new Poland. Stalin has said again and again that he wants to see 'a strong, independent and friendly Poland'.

(b) The territorial compensation to be given to you in the North and in the West.

(c) The fullest co-operation of the Soviet government in the ejection of the German population from the regions you are to take over.

(d) Soviet support in keeping Germany in her place thereaf- ter. . . .

3. Adherence to the Soviet – Czech Treaty.

4. The homing of all the Polish exiles scattered about the Soviet Union.

This is very blunt language. *I want to know if you recall whether the American personnel of the American Embassy had at any time put pressure on Mr Mikolajczyk?*

KENNAN: No, I think we put much less than did the British.

ZAWODNY: I see.

KENNAN: The State Department and the President, for different reasons, were more sceptical about the Russian attitude. The British had, of course, a special problem with the Polish Army in England,[12] and were under great embarrassment.

I wonder whether this letter was ever shown to our Embassy, there. I don't recall seeing it before. It may well be that Ambassador Clark Kerr showed it personally to Harriman, but asked him to keep it quiet.

I don't know, also, how much Clark Kerr may have agreed with what he was writing here. He may have written it under instructions from his government. He may have been following faithfully the line given him by the Foreign Office.

ZAWODNY: This might give you some insight, because he ends the letter in this way:

> You will understand that all this is speculation, not in any sense advice. But I think that you should bear in mind the consistency of the line Stalin has taken from the beginning and that it is based most of all on reasons of security.

KENNAN: This was where he was wrong. It was not military security. It was, rather, internal security. The British never understood – our people never fully understood – the extent to which this was a police operation, in Poland, an operation of the Soviet Secret Police. After all, the Polish section, I believe someone told me, had been headed by Bierut[13] for eight years. These were the people who were being placed in charge of Poland. This Polish government was a stooge government of the police. It wasn't really even a representative government of the Polish Communist Party, because most of that Party, as you know, had been destroyed. They had to dig Poles out of the bowels of the Police Department in Moscow to scrape up a group of people that they could present as a Polish government. They were afraid of political security. They were afraid that a scandal might be made over the Katyn massacre, over the deportations. This was, I think, something that they were very much afraid of, and it played a strong part here. They were determined they would not have any government to make an issue of these things.

ZAWODNY: You mention Ambassador Harriman. I have in front of me a telegram from Ambassador Harriman to the US Secretary of State. I would like to read to you some excerpts from it and ask your opinion about certain matters here.

> When Mikolajczyk arrived in Moscow he told me that it was his belief that the Soviet Government intended to communize and Sovietize Poland and the National Council [Committee] for Liberation was an instrument for this purpose. At our first talk the British Ambassador and I told him that our evidence did not conform to this opinion and shortly after when he expressed the same opinion to a group of American newspapermen several of the more responsible took strong exception to it.

Following this paragraph, Mr Harriman evaluates the role of Mikolajczyk and presents him as a rather suspicious man who doesn't have much faith in the Committee.

KENNAN: A man suspicious of others.

ZAWODNY: Yes. And then, he says this:

> I am spelling this out in such detail as it is my impression that
> Mikolajczyk's deep-seated suspicions and fears of Communism
> will play a part in the decision that he and his associates take on his
> return to London. Although it is impossible to foresee how events
> will develop in Poland I believe that at this time Mikolajczyk and
> his associates must put suspicion aside and earnestly attempt to
> make a reasonable settlement. . . .

And then he finishes the telegram by saying this – and this is a crucial
sentence:

> It is my earnest hope that the British Government bring full
> pressure on Mikolajczyk and his associates to act quickly and
> realistically and I recommend that we support this position.
>   [Signed] Harriman[14]

KENNAN: Well, this was, of course, not my view. I never wrote that
telegram, and I don't recall seeing it. It may be that he did not show it to
me, knowing that my views were different. (ZAWODNY: I see.) But I
think that this outlook was completely misconceived. Nothing that
Mikolajczyk could have done at this point, other than offering to make
himself an agent of the Secret Police against his own government, could
have saved him personally, and nothing could have saved Poland from
Soviet domination. This was the situation; and it made no difference,
really, what he did. Yes, if he'd wanted to become a Soviet agent to
report on his colleagues, then he might have saved himself.

ZAWODNY: That's exactly what Mikolajczyk said at a certain point.
*But what puzzles me here is on which grounds do you think Mr Harriman had
such a strong feeling, abandoning poor Mikolajczyk? Whose view was he reflecting
here?*

KENNAN: Mr Harriman's views changed during the course of the
war. Of course, he was a man very loyal to the President, and he tried
always to reflect the President's views and policies. He was still, at that
time, trying to achieve the ideal of Big Three unity. He felt that the
position of the Polish Government-in-Exile was an obstacle in this. I
think that during the next year his opinions changed very rapidly.

ZAWODNY: Are you referring to 1945?

KENNAN: Yes, the time between September 1944 and September
1945. I think Mr Harriman saw other evidence, and changed his view.
This was, if I am not mistaken, two days before the final meeting that he
had with Molotov[15] over the flying-in of supplies.[16]

ZAWODNY: I think it was earlier.

KENNAN: I think that meeting was the fourteenth.

ZAWODNY: Yes, it could be. I don't recall now.

KENNAN: And I think that perhaps even a week later he would have
written a little differently.

ZAWODNY: I see.

KENNAN: But this reflected what we, the old Russian hands in the
State Department, always called, in the governmental slang of the time,
'the starry-eyed view' of the Soviet Government and of their relations
with Poland. Harriman and Clark Kerr were making, here, the same
mistake. They supposed that the Polish government in London, i.e.,
Mikolajczyk and some of his colleagues, could save themselves and
Poland by conceding the military security interest of the Soviet Union
in Poland. This was not, really, the issue. The issue was: who should run
Poland? The Soviet Government had it already within its power to
assure it own military security interest in Poland. The question now
was: who was going to speak for the Polish people? And what that voice
would sound like. The Soviet leaders wanted to make sure that this was
a voice that echoed the Moscow line.

That was where the British and American Governments made their
mistake. The things that Clark Kerr by implication led Mikolajczyk to
hope that he could receive in return for these concessions were, I think,
quite misconceived.

ZAWODNY: *Do you have any evidence that Mr Harriman or other members of
the Embassy were swaying Mikolajczyk in the same way as the British
Ambassador seemed to?*

KENNAN: Well, you see this from the telegram. They were pressing
him to make an agreement at any cost with the Soviet Government. But
this statement, for instance, that they could have the repatriation of the
Polish exiles in the Soviet Union was a very rash statement. Half of them
were dead.

ZAWODNY: Well, and of course the uncritical reference to Stalin's
statement about 'the free and democratic Poland'.

KENNAN: Of course. Of course.

You know, I think probably Mr Harriman had not shown me this,
because you will recall that among the papers that I showed you there
was a memorandum I had given him at an earlier date calling attention
to the significance of an article by, I think it was, Jedrychowski[17] about
the border problem, pointing out that the borders Jedrychowski
mentioned would place Poland at the mercy of the Soviet Union
indefinitely. Now, of course, it was correct when Clark Kerr told him
'You'll get compensation in east Prussia and in eastern Germany.' The
Russians were very much aware that, if the Poles accepted these great
areas of Germany and expelled the German population of them, they
would compress a spring which they would never dare to release, and
they would thenceforth always be dependent on Russian help to keep it
compressed.

ZAWODNY: Mr Kennan, I have here an excerpt from your own
Memoirs stating:

It has been my opinion, ever since, that this was the moment when,
if ever [KENNAN: I was referring primarily to the fact that the

Soviet Government had not taken an active part in aiding the uprising], there should have been a full-fledged and realistic political showdown with the Soviet leaders: when they should have been confronted with the choice between changing their policy completely and agreeing to collaborate in the establishment of truly independent countries in Eastern Europe or forfeiting Western-Allied support and sponsorship for the remaining phases of their war effort.[18]

KENNAN: Yes.

ZAWODNY: *Did you make your view known to Mr Harriman or anybody else?*

KENNAN: I can't remember stating it to him specifically in that way. All of us who were the old Russian hands – Loy Henderson[19] in the State Department, Durbrow,[20] myself – we all worried all through the war about the misunderstanding that we felt was growing up. We thought that there ought to be a frank talk with the Soviet Government about these matters. We recognized the difficulty that our people were in so long as they were not able to establish a second front and so long as the Russians were still fighting for the liberation of their own territory. But, you see, what had happened in that summer of 1944 had removed both of those obstacles. We had invaded the Continent. Our invasion was proceeding successfully. The Russians at this point had freed all of Soviet territory. The issue was no longer the liberation of Soviet territory and the repulsion of the German invasion. The issue now was what the Russians were going to do with the areas that they were overrunning in eastern Europe. And what I meant by this statement was that I thought that, instead of pushing poor Mikolajczyk to make what would have been a disgraceful sell-out of his own country to the Russians, we should have gone to the Russians and have said: 'Look here, if you people are going to behave this way in eastern Europe – if you're going to pin foreign-inspired dictatorships on these people, and deprive them, really, of all national and individual freedom – then it is simply not worth it for us to give you assistance to enable you to do that for the remainder of the war. If that's the way you're going to act, you will have to be on your own, and we will be on our own, and we will each do what we feel is necessary. We can't stop you from doing this, but we also will not take responsibility for it. You will have to do it on your own responsibility. And you will have to take the blame before the world opinion. We will not help you.' You see?

In which case, I would have curtailed or stopped the Lend-Lease, and said, 'We have no interest in helping you to do what you are evidently going to do.' And if the Russians had said, 'Well, how do you know we're going to do these things?' well, now after the Uprising we had the argument for it. We could have said, 'Look at your reaction to the Warsaw Uprising. It's quite clear that you were quite prepared to have these fellows slaughtered off. It is clear to us that the Polish Underground, the Home Army, have in you an enemy just as bitter as they have in the Germans on the other side. Well, we can't go along with this hypocrisy. The Poles have been our allies. If you're going to treat them that way, it is a great blow to Allied solidarity, for we cannot support you in it. We're not going to make war on you. The world has had enough of war. Europe can't stand any more. But we also are not going to support you in those policies.' Now, it seems to me that it would have been possible to say this to Stalin.

ZAWODNY: It appears to me, Professor Kennan, that in contrast to the great respect for law and legal commitments which Anglo-Saxons traditionally have, with reference to Poland, the pressures and deals into which Mikolajczyk was literally pushed were a violent disregard of the Atlantic Charter.[21]

KENNAN: Well, of course it was. The British, more than ourselves, had already compromised their position much earlier in the war. Eden[22] had done it at the end of 1941 and the beginning of 1942 when, in effect, he agreed, as you know, that the Baltic states and eastern Poland should go to the Soviet Union. Well, at that time, the position of the British was so desperate that they were willing to make this sacrifice. But, again, even with the problem of the borders, I think at this time (1944) we could have said to them: 'Well, all right, we see now what you're going to do. In this case, borders are meaningless, and we will have no responsibility for what you do about them. If you're going to appoint a Soviet Police agent as the President of Poland, it makes no difference where the border lies between that country and your country. We are now helpless to affect this situation and we are going to take no position on it.'

ZAWODNY: Mr Kennan, it is evident from your book that the position which you are taking now is consistent with your earlier views. (KENNAN: That is correct.) *Since a considerable number of people shared your views and they were located in strategically important positions, as you were, could you enlighten me and provide the answer to this question: Why weren't these views implemented into policy? Who, or what, was preventing these views from being formalized and from having some impact?*

KENNAN: Well, policy was not being conducted from the State Department, where many people sympathized with the views I've just stated.

ZAWODNY: *Who was making the policy?*

KENNAN: The White House. Harry Hopkins[23] and Henry Morgenthau[24] were both very important in that respect. Incidentally, the Morgenthau papers and the Roosevelt papers are now available. Have you been through the Morgenthau papers at Hyde Park?

ZAWODNY: No.

KENNAN: You can go through them.

But I think that the President had made such extravagant promises about the Great Power collaboration that we were going to have after the war that he was embarrassed now to recognize the full depths of the dilemma that we were in over Poland. He didn't realize the significance of the extension of the Soviet borders there, or of the term that Russia wanted a 'friendly' Poland, or a 'friendly' Romania, and so forth. He didn't realize that this didn't mean 'friendly' in our sense. This meant 'friendly' in the sense of being absolutely under the very jealous and very cruel authority of the Kremlin and of the Soviet apparatus of power.

I put it that way, because you know there's one very interesting thing that I was thinking of, reading these materials that you gave me to read: Nobody knows, I think, exactly what were the channels of liaison and command between Moscow and even the Polish Committee and the Lublin Poles.[25] They were certainly not through the Soviet Foreign Office. The Foreign Office was only a façade here. It dealt with the Lublin Poles on the formal level, you see, as an independent government, after this period. But, the real lines of command went either through the party or through the Soviet Police. The Comintern had been abolished, and the party didn't normally give orders officially to another Communist party – it gave guidance. I think what happened was probably that there was a Party channel for ideological communication with the Polish Communists, but that the enforcement went through the Soviet Secret Police; and that if, for instance, one of Bierut's entourage had objected, in a way that was inconvenient or embarrassing for the Soviet Union, to any of the advice that they got on the Party level, some excuse would have been found to arrest him, just as Bierut said to Mikolajczyk: 'I would arrest you'.

I was interested to recall that it was Bulganin who was sent as Soviet Commissar for Civil Affairs in this area. Bulganin[26] was an old Chekist. He had been a Chekist back in the twenties. Now, whether these people ever really divested themselves of this status or whether they were merely loaned for other jobs, but retained their affiliation and their disciplinary relationship to the Police establishment, I don't know.

ZAWODNY: Most interesting.

KENNAN: It is interesting, because it is possible that they were merely loaned to other organizations for a time. This was true of all the big Politburo-level Commissars, I think, in the newly occupied territories. They were, I believe, all former Police officials – Chekisti. Suslov[27] was, I think.

ZAWODNY: *Mr Kennan, I have a question which you may decline to answer, if you wish. It concerns Mr Harry Hopkins, his influence on Roosevelt with regard to eastern Europe, in particular. Do you have any comments on that?*

KENNAN: Well, I think that Harry Hopkins *was* the man most responsible for this policy toward Poland.

ZAWODNY: *Why?*

KENNAN: He was devoted to Franklin Roosevelt. He was very liberal. He didn't understand the Russians. He had the particular, special, American liberal view of Russia. I think he very much wanted to see realized the collaboration between the three great powers which the President had been promising the American people during the war.

Also, I suspect that he was affected by the characteristic American liberal view . . . [that] the prewar Polish government was practically a Fascist government – very far to the right – very reactionary – very anti-Soviet. People like Harry Hopkins thought that Stalin's reaction to Poland was one of unrequited love, that Stalin was severe with the Poles because the Poles had taken an antagonistic attitude towards him and towards Russia in the past – that had the Poles taken a friendly view of Russia, it would have been all right. This, you see, was their deepest misunderstanding. They didn't understand that you couldn't have this kind of relationship with the Soviet Union in the twenties and the thirties. Can you name me one non-Communist country on the borders of Russia that had a pleasant or a friendly relationship with the Soviet Union, one which was a relationship of confidence? I can't see that you can. The Finns didn't; the Estonians didn't; the Latvians didn't; nor did the Lithuanians. The Poles didn't; the Romanians didn't; the Turks didn't, really. The Turks had perhaps the best relationship, because the Russians had an interest in supporting them, up to a certain point, against the Western powers; but still, it was a relationship always full of suspicion. I remember old Budenny,[28] the Cavalry general, making a toast – in the presence of the Turkish Ambassador: 'Here's to the Americans. They're our only friends. They're so far away.'

This is what Harry Hopkins didn't understand. He thought – and I think FDR thought – that all these countries along the western border of Russia had only themselves to blame for their poor relations with the Soviet Union – that, had they taken a more friendly attitude towards Russia, things wouldn't have been this way. This was really nonsense.

. . . What Harry Hopkins and these people didn't understand was the full extremism of the Stalin regime in its foreign relations – both the Lenin and the Stalin regimes. It was a question, as Lenin said, of *kto kogo*.[29] The leaders of these regimes believed in power. They wanted to know who had power. And, if they didn't have power over someone else, they regarded him as an enemy.

You will remember that in one of my dispatches from Moscow, at this time (I think that it has now been published in the *Foreign Relations Series*; it was published in any case, in the Annex to my *Memoirs*) I said something to the effect that the jealous eye of the Kremlin is capable of distinguishing only vassals and enemies, but nothing between. This is what Harry Hopkins didn't understand. The Kremlin leaders were sort of colour-blind to any gradations of relationships to them: either you obeyed them, in which case you were their vassal, or you refused to obey them, in which case you were the enemy.

ZAWODNY: *How could you explain the fact that the Poles, knowing that from experience, and trying to convey that to the Western Allies, were not listened to? Was the Polish Government-in-Exile so discredited? It was a legal government.*

This was an ally whose 200,000 soldiers were bleeding on all fronts, starting from September 1939. The Anglo-Saxon leaders were cultivated people, with a conscience. How could they become suddenly blind to the fate of the country which was, as Roosevelt said at one time, 'the inspiration of the nations'?

KENNAN: Yes, and the country for the defence of which England went to war.

ZAWODNY: Yes.

KENNAN: Well, that's a very profound question and it goes back to the very essence of the war itself. It gets back, Jay, to something that I have often had occasion to say: that the Allied victory in this war was mortgaged from the very beginning by the fact that the Allies were not strong enough to defeat Hitler alone and had to take advantage of the power of the Soviet Union. And, that being the case, they were unable to take a clean position with relation to their initial war aims. They had to compromise with the political aims of the Stalin regime. This placed them in a false and hypocritical position. And Poland was the place where this became most evident. And in a way, the reason why they were less sympathetic to the Poles was precisely that the Poles did work so hard to defend their independence, which was an embarrassment to them. They wanted the Poles to oppose the Germans but to give themselves up to the Russians. The Czechs, who gave themselves up to the Russians right on through – who invited the Russians to do what they pleased with Czechoslovakia – the Czechs were much more popular in the West.

I don't think this was the only explanation. I think, also, that the influence of left-wing elements in the United States was important. The whole temper of intellectual leftist opinion in the United States was, let us say, indulgent with regard to the Soviet Union in a way that it was not indulgent with regard to Poland. Pilsudski[30] was regarded as a Fascist. The German–Polish Pact of 1934[31] gave people the impression that these two states were close.

Not only that, but you know great damage was done to thinking in this country by the inability of people to realize that Hitler was not an extension of the Kaiser's regime. There was a belief among these people in the radical left, or the intellectual left, in this country that Hitler's regime was just another conservative regime, and that all conservative regimes were Fascist. They never realized that the Nazi regime was a lower-middle-class movement and not one of the aristocracy. These same misunderstandings applied to Poland. If there was a conservative regime in Poland, and a conservative Catholic regime, especially, this meant, in liberal eyes, that the Poles were practically like the Nazis.

The Czechs got by, because of Huss and the fact that the Church – most of it – was not Catholic. But, the Austrians – Schuschnigg[32] and these people – gained little sympathy in the West.

ZAWODNY: If you have explored this question to your satisfaction, could I move on?

KENNAN: Well, this was all relevant to why Harry Hopkins had these prejudices.

ZAWODNY: Herbert Feis, in his book *Churchill, Roosevelt and Stalin*, makes this observation with regard to the Uprising of Warsaw with particular reference to the position of the Soviet Army:

> . . . the final decision to halt before Warsaw may have been either
>
> 1) because, as the Poles in London and Churchill came to believe, Stalin wanted to wait until the Poles in Warsaw were wiped out; or
>
> 2) because the Soviet advance in the northern part of the line was stopped early in Autust, thus not completing the swing through East Prussia north of Warsaw to cut communications to the west; or
>
> 3) because, as Stalin said, the Red Armies had to stop at the Vistula in front of Warsaw to bring up weapons, and German defense strength in Warsaw was far too strong.[33]

Do you have any views on those three alternatives?

KENNAN: I think it's impossible to say which of these weighed most prominently in the minds of the men in the Kremlin. Remember that Stalin seldom did anything from one reason alone.

ZAWODNY: *Could you give me an example?*

KENNAN: Well, we noticed all through the history of the Stalin regime that, in almost any move Stalin made, several considerations came to bear on it which favoured it. And, from all that we can find out, he was very careful never to reveal, even to his own comrades, which of these considerations was dominant in his mind.

ZAWODNY: I see.

KENNAN: He kept *them* guessing. He would merely approve the decisions, but he wouldn't say which of these things was influencing *him*. Now, it may have been that all of these things played a part. I would suggest, however, that if it had been Polish Communists who were in a state of uprising against the Germans, and ones which were under the control of the Kremlin, the Russians would not have waited on the other side of the river.

APPENDIX D

Selected Documents

Number 1

The British (and French) Guarantee Polish Independence, 31 March 1939

The Prime Minister (Mr Chamberlain): The right hon. gentleman the leader of the Opposition asked me this morning whether I could make a statement as to the European situation. As I said this morning, His Majesty's Government have no official confirmation of the rumours of any projected attack on Poland and they must not, therefore, be taken as accepting them as true.

I am glad to take this opportunity of stating again the general policy of His Majesty's Government. They have constantly advocated the adjustment, by way of free negotiation between the parties concerned, of any differences that may arise between them. They consider that this is the natural and proper course where differences exist. In their opinion there should be no question incapable of solution by peaceful means, and they would see no justification for the substitution of force or threats of force for the method of negotiation.

As the House is aware, certain consultations are now proceeding with other Governments. In order to make perfectly clear the position of His Majesty's Government in the meantime before those consultations are concluded, I now have to inform the House that during that period, in the event of any action which clearly threatened Polish independence, and which the Polish Government accordingly considered it vital to resist with their national forces, His Majesty's Government would feel themselves bound at once to lend the Polish Government all support in their power. They have given the Polish Government an assurance to this effect.

I may add that the French Government have authorised me to make it plain that they stand in the same position in this matter as do His Majesty's Government.

[Great Britain. *Documents Concerning German–Polish Relations and the Outbreak of Hostilities between Great Britain and Germany on September 3, 1939. Presented by the Secretary of State for Foreign Affairs to Parliament by Command of His Majesty.* London: His Majesty's Stationery Office, Misc. No. 9 (1939), Cmd. 6106, 1939, p. 36.]

Number 2

President Roosevelt and Stalin agree on the changes in Polish frontiers. The President also disclaims interest in the political integrity of Lithuania, Estonia, and Latvia in favour of the Soviet Union. (Roosevelt did not inform Churchill about this conversation.) Tehran, 1 December 1943.

ROOSEVELT - STALIN MEETING, DECEMBER 1, 1943, 3.20 P.M., ROOSEVELT'S QUARTERS, SOVIET EMBASSY

PRESENT

UNITED STATES	SOVIET UNION
President Roosevelt	Marshal Stalin
Mr Harriman	Foreign Commissar Molotov
Mr Bohlen	Mr Pavlov

Bohlen Collection

Bohlen Minutes

SECRET

The President said he had asked Marshal Stalin to come see him as he wished to discuss a matter briefly and frankly. He said it referred to internal American politics.

He said that we had an election in 1944 and that while personally he did not wish to run again, if war was still in progress, he might have to.

He added that there were in the United States from six to seven million *Americans of Polish extraction, and as a practical man, he did not wish to lose their vote. He said he personally agreed with the views of Marshal Stalin as to the necessity of the restoration of a Polish state but would like to see the Eastern border moved further to the west and the Western border moved even to the River Oder.* [Author's italics.] He hoped, however, that the Marshal would understand that for political reasons outlined above, he could not participate in any decision here at Tehran or even next winter on this subject and that he could not publicly take part in any such arrangement at the present time.

Marshal Stalin replied that now the President explained, he had understood.

The President went on to say that there were a number of persons of Lithuanian, Latvian, and Estonian origin, in that order, in the United States. He said that he fully realized the three Baltic Republics had in history and again more recently been a part of Russia and jokingly added that when the Soviet armies re-occupied these areas, he did not intend to go to war with the Soviet Union on this point. [Author's italics.]

He went on to say that the big issue in the United States, insofar as public opinion went, would be the question of referendum and the right of self-determination. He said he thought world opinion would want some expression of the will of the people, perhaps not immediately after their re-occupation by Soviet forces, but some day, and that he personally was confident that the people would vote to join the Soviet Union.

Marshal Stalin replied that the three Baltic Republics had no autonomy under the last Czar who had been an ally of Great Britain and the United States, but that no one had raised the question of public opinion, and he did not quite see why it was being raised now.

The President replied that the truth of the matter was that the public neither knew nor understood.

Marshal Stalin answered that they should be informed and some propaganda work should be done.

He added that as to the expression of the will of the people, there would be lots of opportunities for that to be done in accordance with the Soviet constitution but that he could not agree to any form of international control.

The President replied that it would be helpful for him personally if some public declaration in regard to the future elections to which the Marshal had referred, could be made.

Marshal Stalin repeated there would be plenty of opportunities for such an expression of the will of the people.

After a brief discussion of the time of the President's departure and that of Marshal Stalin, the President said there were only two matters which the three of them had not talked over.

He said he had already outlined to the Marshal his ideas on the three world organizations but he felt that it was premature to consider them here with Mr Churchill. He referred particularly to his idea of the four great nations, the United States, Great Britain, the Soviet Union, and China, policing the world in the post-war period. He said it was just an idea, and the exact form would require further study.

Mr Molotov said that at the Moscow Conference, in accordance with the Four Power Declaration, it had been agreed that the three governments would give further study to the exact form of world organization and the means of assuring the leading role of the four powers mentioned.

During the conversation, in reply to the President's question, Marshal Stalin said that he had received the three papers which the President had handed him the day before yesterday, one in regard to air bases, and the other two in regard to secret contacts involving the Far East, but said he had not had time to study the documents carefully, but would take it up in Moscow with Ambassador Harriman.

At this meeting, Stalin referring to his conversation with the President on November 28 [29] on the world organization, said that after thinking over the question of the world organization as outlined by the President, he had come to agree with the President that it should be world-wide and not regional.

[FRUS, *The Conferences at Cairo and Tehran, 1943*, pp. 594–6.]

Number 3

The Soviet radio appeal to the people of Warsaw for 'direct, active struggle in the streets of Warsaw' against 'Hitlerites', on 29 July at 8.15 p.m. Repeated by the Polish Communist radio network on 30 and 31 July 1944. Translated from Polish.

No doubt Warsaw already hears the guns of the battle which [are] soon to bring her liberation. Those who have never bowed their heads to the Hitlerite power will again, as in 1939, join battle against the Germans, this time for the decisive action. The Polish Army, now entering Polish territory, trained in the USSR, is now joined to the People's Army to form the Corps of the Polish Armed Forces, the armed core of our nation in its struggle for independence. Its ranks will be joined tomorrow by the sons of Warsaw. They will, together with the Allied Army, pursue the enemy westward, drive the Hitlerite vermin from the Polish land, and strike a mortal blow at the last of Prussian imperialism. For Warsaw, which did not yield, but fought on, the hour of action has already arrived. The Germans will no doubt try to defend themselves in Warsaw and add new destruction and more thousands of victims. Our houses and parks, our bridges and railway stations, our factories and our public buildings will be turned into defence positions. They will expose the city to ruin and its inhabitants to death. They will try to take away all the most precious possessions and turn into dust all that they have to leave behind. It is therefore a hundred times more necessary than ever to remember that in the flood of Hitlerite destruction all is lost that is not saved by active effort, that by direct, active struggle in the streets of Warsaw, in its houses, factories, and stores, we not only hasten the moment of final liberation, but also save the nation's property and the lives of our brethren.

[Bor-Komorowski, *The Secret Army*, p. 212.]

Number 4

Address by General Bor-Komorowski, Commander-in-Chief of the Polish Home Army (Armia Krajowa) to his troops on the first day of the Uprising, 1 August 1944. Translated from Polish.

Soldiers of Warsaw!

Today I have issued the order you have been waiting for, the order to begin open battle against Poland's age-old enemy, the German invader.

After nearly five years of uninterrupted and heavy fighting underground, today you will carry your arms in the open in order to free your Country again and to render exemplary punishment to the German criminals for the terror and crimes committed on Polish soil.

Warsaw, 1 August 1944

Chief Commander of the AK

Bor

[AK, p. 874.]

Number 5

Letter of British Ambassador Archibald Clark Kerr to Tadeusz Romer, Minister of Foreign Affairs of the Polish Government, on the subject of Prime Minister Mikolajczyk's negotiations with the Russians. Moscow, 2 August 1944.

XVI

BRITISH EMBASSY,

MOSCOW.

August 2nd, 1944

His Excellency
Monsieur Tadeusz Romer,
Minister of Foreign Affairs of the Polish Government
Moscow

My dear Minister:

You asked me last night to put on paper the speculations I was making about Mr Mikolajczyk's negotiations with the Russians. Here they are: *What you may expect the Russians to ask:*

1. The remodelling of the Polish Government so as to exclude certain elements here believed to be reactionary and anti-Soviet, and to include fresh elements drawn from amongst Poles in Poland and in the USSR, with perhaps one or two of the Professor Lange colour from the United States.

2. The *acceptance of the Curzon Line as the basis of negotiations.* This need not preclude your people from making a special appeal for Lvov and Vilna on ethnographical grounds and indeed on sentimental grounds. My feeling (it is no more than a feeling) is that Lvov, in spite of great pressure from Kiev, may still be in the balance, but that there is little or no hope about Vilna, which, when recently taken, was proclaimed as the capital of the Soviet Republic of Lithuania.

3. *Some kind of withdrawal from the suggestion that the killing at Katyn was done by the Russians. About this there is very strong feeling here. I am sure that you do not need to be reminded of that. For myself I think that the easiest way out of this difficulty would be the acceptance of the findings of the Soviet Commission that enquired into the crime.*

4. *Some kind of working arrangement with the Polish Committee of National Liberation.* If Mr Mikolajczyk had managed to get to Moscow a little sooner it might have been possible to escape the present embarrassment of the setting up and of the recognition by the Soviet Government of this Committee. But there is nothing to be gained by regretting the past. The Committee is there. It has acquired some importance and some recognition. It is one of the most formidable factors in the situation. As you know you are expected to get into touch with it and Mr Mikolajczyk told me last night that he had already made an appropriate move in that direction. Much, if not nearly all, of the success of his mission will depend upon how this question is handled.

5. *You must, I think, foresee a determined suggestion that the 1921 Constitution be re-established without delay.*

6. Some rearrangement of the supreme military command, so as to get General Anders' army and General Berling's under one head – a man who is acceptable to both sides. But you told me last night that your proposed solution for this was to abolish the post of Commander-in-Chief.

7. Some arrangement about the functions of the official underground movement. The Russians have never been convinced of the effectiveness or the good faith of this movement. They prefer the partisans, what Mr Morawski calls 'The People's Army'.

Now for what you may expect in return:

1. The re-establishment of diplomatic relations.

2. The fullest assurances about:

   (*a*) The territorial and administrative integrity of the new Poland. Stalin has said again and again that he wants to see 'a strong, independent and friendly Poland'.

   (*b*) The territorial compensation to be given to you in the North and in the West.

   (*c*) The fullest co-operation of the Soviet Government in the ejection of the German population from the regions you are to take over.

   (*d*) Soviet support in keeping Germany in her place thereafter. No difficulties about all this.

3. Adherence to the Soviet–Czech Treaty.

4. The homing of all the Polish exiles scattered about the Soviet Union.

You will understand that all this is speculation, not in any sense advice. But I think that you should bear in mind the consistency of the line Stalin has taken from the beginning and that it is based most of all on reasons of security.

Yours sincerely
ARCHIBALD KERR

[Mikolajczyk Papers, Files Moskwa I and II; author's italics.]

Number 6

Proclamation of the Polish Committee of National Liberation – Communist (PKWN), 'To Fighting Warsaw', in which they announce help for the insurgents. Lublin, 13 August 1944. Translated from Polish.

To fighting Warsaw!
To all the fighters of Warsaw!
To all the inhabitants of Warsaw!

The day of the liberation of Warsaw is near. Your torture and suffering are coming to an end. The Germans will pay dearly for the bloodshed and ruins. The First Division 'Tadeusz Kosciuszko' has entered Praga. The Polish Army is fighting side by side with the Red Army. Fight on! Whatever the intentions of the agitators who led you into the Uprising prematurely and without consultation [or] co-ordination with the Red Army – we are with you all the way. The whole Polish nation stands behind you. A decisive battle is being fought on the Vistula. Help is coming. Gather all your strength! Hold on!

> Polish Committee of National Liberation
> (on Radio Lublin)

['Bulletin of Sub-District No.2 of the People's Army' 1944, No. 41, p. 1.
(KPP, pp. 185–6.)]

Number 7

Letter from Communist Central People's Committee (CKL) to the Communist Country's National Council (KRN) in Warsaw [still in a state of insurgency] containing a resolution recognizing the Polish Committee of National Liberation – Communist (PKWN) as the temporary government of Poland and declaring an intention to collaborate with it. 21 August 1944. Translated from Polish.

Central People's Committee [CKL]

> Warsaw, 21 August 1944

To the National Council [Communist]
in Warsaw.

The Central People's Committee is submitting the text of the resolution taken at the plenary meeting of the CKL on 21 August 1944:

The Central People's Committee, recognizing the National Liberation Committee as representing the vital interests of the Polish nation, herewith declares its intention to consider that committee as the temporary government, and to collaborate with it.

Until an agreement concerning detailed guidelines for this collaboration is reached, the temporary guidelines discussed with the representatives of KWN and KRN will be observed.

These guidelines should, above all, deal with collaboration in the following fields: (*a*) political, (*b*) military, (*c*) administrative, (*d*) propaganda.

In order to secure the widest co-operation in the creation of the Polish state, it is the opinion of the CKL that the basis of the present government coalition represented in the KWN should be broadened to include all democratic factions, and, above all, the Peasants' Party as a whole.

[Signatures]

[KPP, pp. 138−9.]

Number 8

German forces employ criminals to suppress insurgency in Warsaw. An organizational order, 9 September 1944. Translated from German.

Teletype:

1) Main office, SS-Court, Munich
2) SS-Main Office, Berlin
3) SS-Economic Administration Office, Berlin
4) SS-Obergruppenfuehrer von dem Bach.

handwritten: Danzig-Matzkau.

The Reichsfuehrer-SS ordered that 1500 prisoners *from the penal camp Matzkau* [author's italics]−the figure established after consultation between SS-Ostubaf Grothmann and SS-H'Stuf. Beelitz−are to be formed into a battalion for the Dirlewanger Regiment. Immediately this battalion is to be given food, clothes, and to be armed with hand weapons and ammunition. Marching orders to be given after three days. Destination: Fighting Stand Corps Group v.d. Bach, Warsaw. *Purpose of assignment: holding the front line in suppressing the Uprising in Warsaw.* [Author's italics.]

The Main Office of SS-Economic Administration is herewith requested to provide everything with regard to clothing, in direct consultation with the *penal camp Matzkau* [author's italics].

The SS−Fuehrungshauptamt is requested to arrange for the provision of equipment and arms and to prepare the battalion to march. Please inform me about departure and arrival of the battalion.

Chief of Command Staff RFSS
Signed Rode
SS Brigadefuehrer and Major-General
of the Waffen SS

20.9.1944
Be/Bn

[Krannhals, p. 393.]

Number 9

TASS [Soviet Press Agency] Communiqué, charging that the insurgents had made no attempts to co-ordinate their action with the Soviet Supreme Command. 13 September 1944. Translated from Russian. (See General Bor's response, Document No. 10.)

Reports originating from the Polish radio and Polish press have recently appeared in the foreign press, regarding the uprising in Warsaw which, on the orders of Polish émigrés in London, began on August and is in progress. It is hinted by the Polish press and radio of the government-in-exile in London that the insurgents in Warsaw contacted the Soviet Command and that that Command did not send them any help. The Soviet agency TASS has been authorized to state that these reports of the foreign press are either the result of a misunderstanding or else they are a slander against the Soviet Command. It is known to TASS that the Polish circles in London which are responsible for the Warsaw uprising have made no attempts to inform in advance and to co-ordinate the action with the Soviet Supreme Command. Responsibility for the consequences of the Warsaw events, therefore, rests exclusively with the Polish émigré circles in London.

[*Pravda*, 13 Sept 1944, No. 194 (9651), and *Izvestia*, 13 Sept 1944, No. 192 (8494).]

Number 10

Telegram sent by General Bor-Komorowski, in response to TASS charges that no advance notice of uprising was given to the Soviet Army. He explains and tells of Polish attempts to establish contact with the Soviet Army after the Uprising began. Warsaw, 14 September 1944. Translated from Polish.

Telegram from the Chief Commander of the AK to London: data in reply to the TASS communiqué of 13 September [1944]. AK units established communication with the Soviet command from the time that the Soviet armies entered Polish territory, in January 1944. This was the case in Wolyn and in the province of Wilno, in eastern Malopolska, in Bialystok province, and around Lublin. All these contacts resulted in sad experiences for AK. After profiting from our help on the battlefields, the Soviet army arrested the leaders of all AK units, and the units were disarmed.

On the basis of these experiences we did not immediately seek communication with the Soviet command, but rather waited for a sign of their good will. [However] when, on 3 August, Soviet Army Captain Kalugin approached AK units he was received and lodged with the Staff of the Commander-in-Chief of AK in Warsaw. Through Captain

Kalugin we transmitted to the Soviet command on 7 [5?] August our needs for armaments and the bombing of indicated objectives in Warsaw. Moreover, on 8 August, the Commander of the Uprising in Warsaw also sent a wireless cable via London to Marshal Rokossovsky in which he suggested co-ordinating their actions and help for Warsaw; unfortunately, neither Captain Kalugin nor the Commander of the Uprising have yet received an answer to their cables.

[AK, p. 833.]

Number 11

Farewell address of General Bor-Komorowski, Commander-in-Chief of Armia Krajowa, to the insurgents, issued after signing the act of surrender. Warsaw, 3 October 1944. Translated from Polish.

Soldiers of Fighting Warsaw!

The heroic deeds of Polish soldiers which constitute two months of fighting in Warsaw are proofs, however full of horror, of our desire for freedom – our strongest desire. Our battle in the capital, in the face of death and destruction, stands in the forefront of famous deeds of Polish soldiers during this war. They will be a lasting memorial to our spirit and love of freedom. *Although we were not able to gain a military victory over our enemy (since the general situation in our country was not favourable to our endeavour), those two months of fighting for every foot of Warsaw's streets and walls have fulfilled a political and ideological goal. Our struggle will influence the fate of our nation, since it is a contribution without equal in its heroism and sacrifice to the defence of our independence.* [Author's italics.]

Today, when the enemy's technical superiority has forced us into the central sector of our city – the only sector still under our control – when the city's ruins are crowded with soldiers and the heroic civilian population, suffering from unbearable conditions of living on the battlefield, when we have not enough of even the most primitive food, and when there is virtually no chance of defeating the enemy, we have to confront the problem of complete destruction of the population by the enemy and the chance of having most of the fighting soldiers and hundreds of thousands of the civilian population buried under the ruins.

I have decided to call a halt to the fighting.

I thank all the soldiers for their military bearing that never wavered under the most difficult conditions.

I pay homage to the dead for their suffering and sacrifice.

I want to express the admiration and gratitude of the fighting units to the population, and their affection for it. I would also like to ask their forgiveness for the transgressions, which no doubt occurred more than once in the course of this long fight.

During the cease-fire discussion I have done my best to assure our soldiers of all the rights due to them, to create the best possible living conditions and care for the civilian population so that they might be spared as much as possible of the suffering caused by the war.

I hereby ask of all soldiers, my very dear comrades during these two months of fighting, whose will to fight was unbroken to the last moment, to obey in good order all commands that will be issued as a consequence of our decision to stop fighting.

The civilian population is to obey all evacuation orders issued by me, the commanding officer of the city and the civilian administration.

With faith in the final victory of our just cause, believing in our beloved, great and happy country, we will continue to be the soldiers and citizens of Free Poland, pledging allegiance to the flag of the Republic.

Supreme Commander-in-Chief AK Bor-Komorowski,
Major-General
Warsaw, 3 October 1944

[AK, pp. 883–4.]

Number 12

Manifesto issued by the Polish Council of National Unity and the Home Council of Ministers of the Legal Polish Government after the surrender of Warsaw. Warsaw, 3 October 1944. Translated from Polish.

To the Polish Nation:

. . . On 1 August 1944, we began an open struggle against the Germans in Warsaw. We chose this moment because Russian troops were on the outskirts of Warsaw, because our Western Allies had begun their decisive march to Berlin, because owing to the large numbers involved it had become impossible for the Home Army to remain concealed, because desire for freedom, accumulated during the long years of occupation, had become impossible to restrain any longer, and lastly because behind the German front we were threatened with mass round-ups, the deportation of Polish youth, and the destruction of our capital city.

When we openly took up the struggle in Warsaw, we did not suppose that we could beat the Germans alone. We were too weak in numbers and equipment for that. We counted on the aid of Russia and our Western Allies.

We had the right to count on such help at a time when detachments of the Home Army fighting in Wolyn, the Wilno area, in Lwow, and Lublin had contributed vitally to the successes of the Russian army, at a time when Polish divisions were fighting and bleeding for the common cause on the fields of Italy and France, on the land, on the sea, and in the air.

We were deceived. We did not receive proper help. The supplies dropped by our Western Allies, the Soviet Army's capture of Praga, Russian air cover, food supplies, arms and ammunition dropped by the Russians – none of this came in time nor did it come in any proportion to our requirements. It was not effective. Enormous quantitative and technical superiority enabled the Germans to reconquer one after another the districts we had won, and our situation gradually became hopeless. That is the truth. We have been treated worse than Hitler's allies: Italy, Romania, Finland.

So we fought alone for nine weeks. We fought on the ruins of Warsaw, on the ruins of all that we love, all that is a memorial of our centuries-old past. Rivers of our blood have soaked into our sacred Polish earth.

But now, when our soldiers have fired their last shells captured from the enemy, when the mothers of our children have no more food to give them, when the long queues of people can no longer draw water from the exhausted wells, when we have begun to drag the starved dead from cellars, we have no possibility of continuing the struggle, and we must stop.

For want of serious assistance, the Warsaw August Rising is going under at the very moment when our Army is helping France, Belgium and Holland to their liberation. We refrain today from judging this tragic affair.

May the just God estimate the terrible wrong which the Polish nation has suffered, and let Him deal justly with those who have committed that wrong. . . .

[DPSR, pp. 398–9.]

Number 13

Eight days after the fall of Warsaw (on 11 October 1944 during the Moscow talks) Churchill, Stalin, Eden and Harriman conversed about the Uprising. Reported by Anthony Eden, British Secretary for Foreign Affairs.

Anthony Eden to Sir Orme Sargent: Telegram (Extract)
MOSCOW, 12 October 1944
F.O. 371.   C14115/8/55

In conversation after dinner at the Embassy last night Marshal Stalin was at great pains to assure the Prime Minister that failure to relieve Warsaw had not been due to any lack of efforts by the Red Army. The failure was due entirely to the enemy's strength and difficulties of terrain. Marshal Stalin could not admit this failure before the world. Exactly the same situation had arisen at Kiev* which in the end had only been liberated by outflanking movement. The Prime Minister said he

[*See reference to Kiev p. 176.]

accepted this view absolutely and he assured Marshal Stalin that no serious persons in the United Kingdom had credited reports that failure had been deliberate. Criticism had only referred to the apparent unwillingness of the Soviet Government to send aeroplanes. Mr Harriman who was present said that the same was true of the people in America.. . .

[Antony Polonsky, *The Great Powers and the Polish Question 1941–1945; A Documentary Study of Cold War Origins*. London: London School of Economics and Political Science, 1976, p. 220.]

List of Persons Interviewed

A Note on the Interviews

The interviews were carried out under controlled conditions. Depending on the respondent's reaction to the use of a tape recorder, some interviews were taped; others were taken down in handwriting by me. In all instances respondents were previously informed as to the purpose of the interview (to collect data for a book or articles on the Uprising of Warsaw); and were asked to submit a handwritten summary of basic personal data. When requested, the interview was read or played on the spot to the respondent for amendments, or submitted for proofreading.

The transcripts of three interviews were lost in the mail. I was able to repeat two of them, but the third could not be repeated because the respondent, Mr Jan Hoppe, died.

One interview was withdrawn from my data at the request of the interviewee after he visited Poland. His name was removed from the list.

One interview was not used on grounds of unreliability; therefore, the name of the respondent has not been included.

Professor Zbigniew Pelczynski of Oxford University is quoted in the book. However, since our conversation did not take place under controlled conditions, he is not listed either.

Name (Pseudonym)	Rank and Functions at the End of the Uprising	Place and Date of Interview
Anders, Wladyslaw	Major-General. Commander 2nd Polish Corps, 8th British Army, Italy.	London: 17 May 1965
Baginski, Kazimierz	Vice-President of the Council of National Unity, Warsaw; Director, Dept of Internal Affairs attached to the Delegate	Phoenix, Arizona: 17–18 April 1966

of the Polish Government-in-Exile in Warsaw.

Baranowski, Antoni (Alan)	Captain. Officer of Section I, Supreme HQ of the Polish Home Army, AK.	Paris: 20 May 1965
Biega, Boleslaw (Sanocki)	Secretary the Council of National Unity, Warsaw	New York: 31 March 1968
Bisping, Maria (Ola)	Lieutenant. Internal Communication Section, Supreme HQ of the Polish Home Army, AK.	London: 26 March 1965
Blaszczak, Stanislaw (Rog)	Major. Commander of Rog Sector, Old Town; Commander of the 36th Infantry Rgt, AK.	Chicago: 21 May 1966
Bokszczanin, Janusz (Obar, Sek)	Colonel. Chief of Operations, Supreme HQ of the Polish Home Army, AK.	Paris: 21 May 1965
Bor-Komorowski, Tadeusz (Lawina, Znicz, Bor)	Major-General. Commander-in-Chief of the Polish Home Army, AK. Complete interview in Appendix B.	London: 17 May 1965
Braun, Jerzy	Member of the Council of National Unity, Warsaw.	Philadelphia: 29 January 1966
Bregman, Aleksander	Polish political commentator and writer	London: 13 May 1965
Broner, Adam	Noncommissioned officer. Deputy platoon commander and political instructor, 8th Infantry Rgt, 1st Polish Army (under Soviet command.)	Princeton; 2 August 1972
Bukowska, Ewa Maria (Wawa)	2nd Lieutenant. Instructor, Women's Auxi-	London: 26 March 1965

liary, Polish Home
Army, AK.

Chalko, Zbigniew (Cyganiewicz I)	Cadet. Platoon Commander, Polish Home Army, AK.	Chicago: 17 May 1966
Chrusciel, Jadwiga (Kozak)	Cook, · Polish Home Army, AK.	New York: 27 November 1966
Chrusciel, Wanda (Kalina)	Hospital aide, Polish Home Army, AK.	New York: 27 November 1966
Ciolkosz, Adam	Former Member of Polish Parliament. Member of National Council, London. Polish political leader, writer and commentator.	London: 10 May 1969
Degorska, Halina (Iga)	2nd Lieutenant Messenger, Old Town, Polish Home Army, AK.	Philadelphia: 23 February 1967
Depta, Pawel (Sokol)	Private, Polish Home Army, AK.	Harvard: 7 May 1968
Dziubinski, Franciszek (Dolega)	Corporal, Polish Home Army, AK.	Chicago: 19 May 1966
Furka, Wladyslaw (Emil)	Private, Polish Home Army, AK.	New York: 1 April 1968
Gac, Jadwiga (Jadzia)	Private. Combat nurse and messenger, Polish Home Army, AK.	Philadelphia: 7 May 1968
Grygo, Klementyna (Zabka, Borowka)	Private. Messenger and clandestine press distributor, Polish Home Army, AK.	New York: 31 March 1968
Iranek-Osmecki, Kazimierz (Makary, Heller, Kazimierz)	Colonel. Chief Section II (Intelligence), the Supreme HQ of the Polish Home Army, AK.	London: 13 May 1965
Janczewski, George H. (Glinka)	Cadet. Section leader, Polish Home Army, AK.	Philadelphia: 2 January 1968
Juszczakiewicz, Stanislaw (Kornik,	Lieutenant-Colonel. Commander, Kuba Sec-	London: 12 May 1965

Kuba)	tor, Old Town, Polish Home Army, AK.	
Kennan, George F.	Professor, The Institute for Advanced Study, Princeton. Minister-Counsellor, US Embassy, Moscow 1944–6. US Foreign Service Officer 1927–53.	Princeton, NJ: 30 May 1972
Kopanski, Stanislaw	Major-General. Chief of Staff to the Commander-in-Chief Polish Army-in-Exile.	London: 10 May 1965
Korbonski, Stefan (Zielinski)	Captain. Director of the Department of Internal Affairs attached to the Delegate of the Polish Government-in-Exile in Warsaw.	Washington, DC: 1 January 1968
Kozlowski, Vladimir L. (Jastrzebiec)	Lieutenant. Company Commander, Old Town, Polish Home Army, AK.	Chicago: 21 May 1966
Kukiel, Marian	Major-General. Minister of National Defence, Polish Government-in-Exile.	London: 10 May 1965
Kukla, Zofia (Krystyna, Krystyna-Zofia)	Corporal. Combat messenger-nurse, Polish Home Army, AK.	London: 26 March 1965
Kwiatkowska-Komorowska, Irena (Baska)	2nd Lieutenant. Adjutant, Secretary and liaison co-ordinator to the Commander of Old Town and 2nd in Command of the Uprising of Warsaw Col. K. Ziemski.	Toronto: 26 August 1966
Kwiatkowski, Bohdan (Lewar)	Major. Chief of Staff of Warszawa-Srodmiescie Sector. The last officer for special assignments to Gen. Okulicki (the last	Chicago: 21 May 1966

Commander-in-Chief of the Polish Home Army, AK).

Larys, Kazimierz (Adwokat)	Major. Chief of Communication Warsaw District, Polish Home Army, AK.	New York: 31 March 1968
Lukomska, Irena (Dziembowska)	2nd Lieutenant. Commander of a women's auxiliary unit, Polish Home Army, AK.	Chicago: 17 May 1966
Mikolajczyk, Stanislaw (Stem)	Prime Minister, Polish Government-in-Exile.	Princeton, NJ: 31 March 1957; Washington, DC: 26 June and 14 December 1965
Milko-Wieckowska, Irena (Wierzbicka)	2nd Lieutenant. Combat Messenger, Polish Home Army, AK.	Philadelphia: 10 November 1966
Miszczak, Franciszek (Bogucki)	Major. Chief of Intelligence Section 'Eastern Front', the Supreme HQ of the Polish Home Army, AK.	London: 13 May 1965
Mitkiewicz, Leon (Prus)	Colonel. Representative of the Commander-in-Chief of the Polish Forces to the Combined Chiefs of Staff in Washington, DC, and Deputy Chief of the Polish Forces.	New York: 30 March 1968
Modrzejewski, Jozef (Sep, Leon, Karol, Lis, Prawdzic)	Major. Commander of Jaslo District, Inspector of Krosno District, Polish Home Army, AK.	Philadelphia: 27 February 1967
Neciuk, Jerzy	Warrant Officer. Flying Engineer, Polish Air Forces in Great Britain. Flew to assist the Polish Home Army, AK.	London: 27 May 1967
Niedzielski, Mie-	Colonel. Commander of	Chicago: 18 May

czyslaw (Zywiciel)	Zoliborz Sector, Polish Home Army, AK.	1966
Nowak, Jan (Jezioranski Zdzislaw, Janek, Zych)	Captain. Liaison Officer of the Supreme HQ of the Polish Home Army, AK, to England. Chief editor of broadcasts in English by the Polish underground radio station Lightning.	Munich: 25 May 1965
Olczak, Henryk (Zolw)	Corporal, Old Town, Polish Home Army, AK.	Toronto: 26 August 1966
Papee, Kazimierz	Polish Ambassador to the Holy See, Vatican.	Rome: 14 June 1967
Pelczynski, Tadeusz (Grzegorz, Robak)	Brigadier-General. Chief of Staff of the Supreme HQ of the Polish Home Army, AK.	London: 14 May 1965
Pierre – Skrzynska, Janina (Krystyna)	2nd Lieutenant. Combat Messenger, Old Town, Polish Home Army, AK.	London: 23 February 1969 Brussels: 22 April 1969
Pogorski, Tadeusz (Morwa)	MD. Commandant of a field hospital in the Uprising, Old Town.	Cleveland: 27 August 1969
Pomian, Andrzej (Mikolaj Dowmuntt)	Captain. Chief of Propaganda Section (AK press) in the Bureau of Information and Propaganda of the Supreme HQ of the Polish Home Army, AK.	Washington, DC: 17 January 1968; Addendum: 12 November 1969
Popiel, Karol	Minister of Reconstruction of Public Administration in the Polish Government-in-Exile.	Rome: 14 May 1967
Pronaszko – Konopacka, Janina (Janina)	Lieutenant. Combat Liaison and Secretary to the last Commander-in-Chief of the Polish Home	London: 13 May 1965

	Army, AK, Gen. Leopold Okulicki.	
Rayski, Ludomil.	Air-Commodore. Pilot, Polish Air Force in Great Britain. Flew to assistance of the Uprising.	London: 25 May 1967
Romer, Adam	Director, Bureau of the Council of Ministers, Polish Government-in-Exile.	London: 17 May 1965
Rostworowski, Tomasz (Tomasz)	Major. Chaplain to the Supreme HQ of the Polish Home Army, AK.	Rome: 15 June 1967
Sawicki, Kazimierz (Opor)	Brigadier-General. General Staff of the Polish Home Army, AK.	London: 13 May 1965
Sieniewicz, Konrad	Cadet. Commander of a barricade. Government-Delegate for Region I, Warszawa–Powisle.	Rome: 14 May 1967
Sienkiewicz, Aniela (Elzbieta)	Cadet. Actually fighting with weapons but also used as a combat messenger and nurse, Polish Home Army, AK.	London: 9 April 1965
Stanczyk, Boleslaw (Xen)	2nd Lieutenant. Executive officer of a company, Polish Home Army, AK.	Chicago: 18 May 1966
Szmajdowicz, Boleslaw Jozef (Blysk)	2nd Lieutenant. Commander of two parachute supply-receiving stations in Poland, Polish Home Army, AK.	Philadelphia: 7 March 1967
Szternal, Kazimierz (Zryw)	Major. Deputy Commander of Mokotow Sector, Chief of Staff of Region VI, Polish Home Army, AK.	Chicago: 17 May 1966
Tuleja, Casimir W. (Goral)	MD. 2nd Lieutenant. Battalion medical officer,	Chicago: 17 May 1966

	Old Town, Polish Home Army, AK.	
Turkowska, Irena Danuta (Danka)	Combat Nurse, Old Town, Polish Home Army, AK.	Hamilton, Canada: 27 August 1966
Warszawski, Jozef (Ojciec Pawel)	Major. Chaplain to Radoslaw unit, Polish Home Army, AK.	Rome: 13 June 1967
Weber, Stanislaw (Chirurg, Popiel)	Lieutenant-Colonel. Chief of Staff to the Commander of the Uprising of Warsaw, Polish Home Army, AK.	London: 15 May 1965
Wieckowski, Jan J. (Drogoslaw)	2nd Lieutenant. Executive officer of a company, Old Town, Polish Home Army, AK.	Philadelphia: 29 March 1967
Zadrożny, Stanislaw (Pawlicz)	2nd Lieutenant. Manager of the underground radio station Lightning, Polish Home Army, AK.	Munich: 25 May 1965
Zaleski, August	Minister of the Polish Government-in-Exile.	London: 15 May 1965
Zawadzki, Tadeusz (Zenczykowski, Kania)	Captain. Chief of Propaganda, Bureau of Information and Propaganda of the Supreme HQ of the Polish Home Army, AK.	Munich: 25 May 1965
Ziemski, Karol Jan (Wachnowski)	Colonel, Deputy Commander of the Uprising of Warsaw; Deputy Commander of the Warsaw Corps of the Polish Home Army, AK; Commander of the Defence of Old Town. Subsequently promoted to the rank of Brigadier-General.	London: 11 May 1965. Also conversations, London: 13 April 1965; 6 and 17 Jan 1972
Zipser, Grażyna (Grażyna)	Combat messenger, Polish Home Army, AK.	New York: 31 March 1968

Zlotnicki, (Witold)	Witold	2nd Lieutenant. Company Commander, Polish Home Army, AK.	London: 20 March 1965
Żorawska, (Joanna)	Janina	Lieutenant. Combat messenger and commander of women's auxiliaries in Lesnik unit, Polish Home Army, AK.	London: 26 March 1965

Notes

Abbreviations

AK: Poland. Komisja Historyczna Polskiego Sztabu Glownego W Londynie. *Polskie Sily Zbrojne w Drugiej Wojnie Swiatowej.Armia Krajowa* [*Polish Armed Forces in the Second World War. The Home Army*]. London: Instytut Historyczny im. Gen. Sikorskiego, Vol. 3. 1949–1951, 972 pp.

AMD USSR: Archives of the Ministry of Defence, USSR.

APUMST: Archives of the Polish Underground (1939–1945) Study Trust, London.

Bor Reports: Majorkiewicz Felicjan. 'Meldunki Sytuacyjne Dowodcy Armii Krajowej Gen. Dyw. Tadeusza Bor-Komorowskiego z Okresu Powstania Warszawskiego 1944, Do Wladz Naczelnych w Londynie Z Przypisami Opracowanymi Przez Autora' ['General Bor's Combat Reports for the Period of the Uprising of Warsaw, 1944, dispatched to the Polish authorities in London. With Author's Annotations']. *Dane Nam Bylo Przezyc*. Warsaw: Pax, 1972, pp. 181–232.

CHPPR: Chancery of the President of the Polish Republic, London.

DPSR: Sikorski Historical Institute. *Documents on Polish–Soviet Relations, 1939–1945*. London: Heinemann, Vol. 2, 1967, 866 pp.

FRUS: Foreign Relations of the United States. Washington: United States Government Printing Office.

German Army: Bundesarchiv-Militararchiv: H-12-9/3 bis H-12-9/9-'Kriegstagebuch der 9. Armee mit Anlagebanden, Kartensammlungen und diversen Einzelaktenstucken' ['Daily War Reports of the 9th Army with Supplements, Collections of Maps and Diverse Single Documents']. Microfilm: Records of German Field Commands, Armies, T-312, Roll 343–9. Washington, DC: The National Archives of the United States.

Hopkins Papers: Harry L. Hopkins Papers, Franklin Delano Roosevelt Library in Hyde Park, New York.

IVOVSS: Moscow. Institut Marksizqma-Leninizma. *Istoria Velikoi Otechstvennoi Voiny Sovetskogo Soiuza* [*History of the Great Patriotic War of the Soviet Union*]. 1960–5. 6 Vols.

KPP: Komunistyczna Partia Polski. Komitet Centralny. Zaklad Historii. [Polish Communist Party. Central Committee. Historical Office.] Przygonski, Antoni. *Udzial PPR i AL w Powstaniu Warszawskim* [*Participation of PPR and AL in the Uprising of Warsaw*].Warsaw: Ksiazka i Wiedza, 1970, 265 pp.

Mikolajczyk Papers: Collection of Documents, Papers and Photographs of the Former Prime Minister of Poland, Stanislaw Mikolajczyk. In private hands.

Mitkiewicz Dossier: Col. Leon. Mitkiewicz. Z-ca SSNW w Washingtonie. *Dossier: The Combined Chiefs of Staff.* Documents. Typescript in Polish made available by Col. Mitkiewicz to author: n.d., n.p. Col. Mitkiewicz was the Representative of the Polish Commander-in-Chief of the Polish Forces-in-Exile to the Combined Chiefs of Staff in Washington, DC, and Deputy Chief of Staff of the Polish Commander-in-Chief of the Polish Forces-in-exile.

Monter Reports: Jerzy Kirchmayer, *et al.*, 'Meldunki Sytuacyjne "Montera" z Powstania Warszawskiego' ['General Monter's Combat Reports of the Warsaw Uprising']. *Najnowsze Dzieje Polski: Materialy i Studia z Okresu II Wojny Swiatowej*, Warsaw: Vol. 3. 1959, pp. 97–180.

Morgenthau Diary: Henry J. Morgenthau Presidential Diary at the Franklin Delano Roosevelt Library in Hyde Park, New York.

PISM: The Polish Institute and Sikorski Museum, London.

Romer Report: Tadeusz Romer. 'Report of the Minister of Foreign Affairs miles of shelving'. Consult bibliography for the Guide.

Public Record Office: British records for the period 1939–45 cover 'seven of the Polish Government-in-Exile, T. Romer, Concerning the Diplomatic Activities in London with Regard to Assistance to Fighting Warsaw.' File of the Polish Minister of Foreign Affairs, Position 172, pp. 262–79. Typescript in Polish. Copy: Polish Underground Study Trust, London.

Roosevelt Papers: Collection of Manuscripts and Archives in the Franklin Delano Roosevelt Library in Hyde Park, New York.

Introduction: Warsaw Erupts

1. Tadeusz ˙ Bor-Komorowski (Lawina, Znicz, Bor), Major-General, Commander-in-Chief of AK. Interview: London, 17 May 1965. For full transcript see Appendix B. See also Poland. Komisja Historyczna Polskiego Sztabu Glownego w Londynie. *Polskie Silyzbrojne w Drugiej Wojnie Swiatowej: Armia Krajowa [Polish Armed Forces in the Second World War: The Home Army]*. London: Instytut Historyczny im Gen. Sikorskiego, Vol. 3, 1950–1, pp. 651–928. To be cited in this book as AK.

(a) Territorial organization of insurgents in Warsaw in July 1944, prior to the Uprising.

   I. Srodmiescie Sector: 4 regions
   II. Zoliborz Sector: 3 regions

   III. Wola Sector: 3 regions
   IV. Ochota Sector: regions
   V. Mokotow Sector: 6 regions
   VI. Praga Sector: 5 regions
   VII. 'Koleba': area around Warsaw divided into 8 regions
   IX. Okecie: an independent region including a German airfield.

(b) On 6 Aug 1944 this organization was changed by Gen. Monter and adapted to combat conditions.

1. Command Centre Polnoc. Lt-Col. Karol Ziemski (Wachnowski), Commander. Fiercest combat for Old Town till 2 Sept. These units did not surrender; they withdrew through sewers and continued to fight in other parts of Warsaw.

II. Command Centre Srodmiescie. Lt-Col. Edward Pfeiffer (Radwan), Commander.

III. Command Centre Poludnie. Lt-Col. Kaminski (Daniel), Commander until the middle of Aug; then Lt-Col. Jozef Rokicki (Karol), Commander; and ultimately Maj. K. Szternal (Zryw), Deputy Commander, took command on 26 Sept 1944, while simultaneously commanding Baszta region.

(c) On 20 Sept 1944 Gen. Bor-Komorowski reorganized the insurgents into regular units of the Polish Army – the Warsaw Corps of Armia Krajowa, Gen. Chrusciel (Monter); Commander; Col. Ziemski (Wachnowski), Deputy Commander. The Corps was composed of three infantry divisions:

8th Inf. Div. (infantry regiments 13, 21 and 32)
28th Inf. Div. (infantry regiments 15, 36 and 72)
10th Inf. Div. (infantry regiments 28, 29 and 30)

2. Jan Stanislaw Jankowski (Sobol, Doktor, Klonowski), the Delegate of the Polish Government for German-occupied Poland (also Deputy Prime Minister) in his radio message from Warsaw during insurgency on 1 Sept 1944. AK, pp. 880–8. A copy of this message and voluminous radio correspondence between the AK command and the Polish Government-in-Exile (London) have been secured from the archives of the Polish Underground Movement (1939–1945) Study Trust in London. These archives will be cited as APUMST.

3. AK, pp. 666 70.

4. Stanislaw Weber (Surgeon, Popiel), Lieutenant-Colonel, Chief of Staff to the Commander of the Uprising of Warsaw, AK. Interview: London, 15 May 1965; compare with Antoni Chrusciel (Monter), *Powstanie Warszawskie* [*The Warsaw Uprising*].

London: n.p., 1948, p. 15.

5. Ibid.

6. Jerzy Kirchmayer *et al.*, 'Meldunki Sytuacyjne "Montera" z Powstania Warszawskiego' ['Monter's Combat Reports of the Warsaw uprising'], *Najnowsze Dzieje Polski: Materialy i Studia z Okresu II Wojny Swiatowej*. Warsaw: Vol. 3, 1959, pp. 97–180. To be cited as Monter Reports.

7. Ibid. p. 100.

8. Tadeusz Dolega-Kamienski (Badacz), 'Powstanie Warszawskie: Kwatermistrzostwo' ['The Warsaw Uprising: The Quartermaster'], typescript. The author was the Chief Quartermaster of the Uprising. Jozef Pilsudski Institute of America, New York, p. 2.

9. Kazimierz Baginski, 'Wspomnienia a Pierwszego Okresu Powstania' ['Memories from the First Part of the Uprising'], *Nowy Swiat*, New York, 2 Aug 1950, p. 4.

10. Tadeusz Zarzycki, 'Relacja Dotyczaca Przebiegu Akcji Powstanczej Na Odcinku IV Rejonu I Obwodu: Odcinka Srodmiescie, Polnoc-Zachod' [Combat Report], copy of the typescript made available to the author. England: 1947, pp. 2 and 26, passim.

11. Monter, Report No. 6, 4 Aug 1944. Chronological phases of the fighting were as follows:

(1) Polish initiative and attack, 1–4 Aug.

(2) Polish defence, 5 Aug to 2 Oct.

(3) The sequence of German pressure on insurgents:

(a) Wola, 1–11 Aug.
(b) Old Town, 1 Aug to 2 Sept.
(c) Powisle and Srodmiescie-Polnoc, 3–10 Sept.
(d) Czerniakow Gorny, 11–23 Sept.
(e) Mokotow Gorny, 24–7 Sept.
(f) Destruction of 'Kampinos' Group, 29 Sept.

(g) Zoliborz, 29–30 Sept.
Kirchmayer, op. cit., pp. 179–80.

Incisive criticism of the insurgents' planning and tactics has been provided in an interview with Stanislaw Juszczakiewicz, a high-ranking AK officer who participated in the fighting. It can be summarized as: (a) chaotic improvisation, (b) operational plans that did not establish priorities as to which areas *had* to be seized *v.* those areas in which fighting should be held to a minimum only in order to distract the Germans from priority areas, and (c) no manpower reserves were planned for or

established. Stanislaw Juszczakiewicz (Kornik, Kuba), Lieutenant-Colonel, Commander of Kuba sector, Old Town, AK. Interview: London, 12 May 1965.

12. Hans von Krannhals, *Der Warschauer Aufstand 1944* [*The Warsaw Uprising, 1944*], Frankfurt am Main, Bernard and Graefe Verlag Fur Wehrwesen, 1964, passim.

13. Monter, Report No. 15, 12 Aug 1944.

14. Monter, Report No. 13, 10 Aug 1944.

15. Monter, Report No. 11, 8 Aug 1944.

Chapter 1. AK: Leadership and Resources

1. *Kazimierz Pluto-Czachowski,* 'Godzina "W" na Woli' ['Hour "W" in Wola'], *Stolica*, No. 39, 1969, p. 6; Kazimierz Pluta-Czachowski, 'Z Woli na Starowke; Na Posterunku Powstanczym KG AK' ['From Wola to Old Town at the Command Post of the Supreme HQ of AK'] *Zai Przeciw*, No. 36, 1969, p. 7 and No. 38, 1969, pp. 14, 16.

2. Antoni Chrusciel (Monter), *Powstanie Warszawskie* [*The Warsaw Uprising*]. London: n.p., 1948, passim.

3. Leslaw M. Bartelski, *Powstanie Warszawskie* [*The Warsaw Uprising*]. Warsaw: Iskry, 1965, p. 195.

4. APUMST, Monter to Colonel Karol, radio message, Order No. 92, dated 26 Sept 1944.

5. During the Uprising, under pressure of German attacks Gen. Bor changed his headquarters three times.

6. Bartelski, op. cit., p. 77.

7. Adam Borkiewicz, *Powstanie Warszawskie 1944: Zarys Dzialan Natury Wojskowej* [*The Uprising of Warsaw 1944: Military Aspects*]. Warsaw: Instytut Wydawniczy Pax, 1964, p. 204 n. 343.

8. General Berling's forces began

their attempt to force the Vistula river on 13 Sept 1944. For details, see chs 10 and 11.

9. APUMST, Bor's radio message L. dz. 6314/44, 4 Aug 1944.

10. APUMST, Bor's radio message O.VI. L. dz. 6436/44, 6 Aug 1944.

11. APUMST, File Warszawa-Srodmiescie; Historia Batalionu Chrobry II, p. 13.

12. Irena Danuta Turkowska (Danka), combat nurse, Old Town, AK. Interview: Hamilton, Canada, 27 Aug 1966.

13. Milko-Wieckowska Irena. (Wierzbicka). 2nd Lieutenant. Combat Messenger. The Polish Home Army AK. Interview: Philadelphia, 10 Nov 1966.

14. M. I. Semiriaga, *Antifashistskie Narodnye Povstaniia* [*National Uprisings against Fascists*]. Moskva: Nauka, 1965, p. 82.

15. Borkiewicz, op. cit., p. 58; *Biuletyn Informacyjny*, No. 55, 18 Aug 1944, p. 2.

16. *Biuletyn Informacyjny*, No. 58, 21 Aug 1944, p. 1.

17. Komunistyczna Partia Polski. Komitet Centralny. Zaklad Historii Partii. Antoni Przygonski, *Udzial*

PPR i AL w Powstaniu Warszawskim [*Participation of PPR and AL in the Uprising of Warsaw*]. Warsaw: Ksiazka i Wiedza, 1970, pp. 92–3.

18. Letter to the author from Mr S. Krakowski, YAD VASHEM Martyrs' and Heroes' Remembrance Authority, Jerusalem, Israel, 9 May 1952.

19. Borkiewicz, op. cit., pp. 188, 154, 179, 544.

20. Krakowski, letter, cited above.

21. Borkiewicz, op. cit., p. 179.

22. Krakowski, letter, cited above.

23. Szternal, interview.

24. Krakowski, letter, cited above.

25. Ibid.

26. Ibid.

27. Ibid.

28. Mikolajczyk Papers, File Ml, vol. 64.

29. Letter from Mr Michael Borwicz to the author, 12 May 1972. A scholarly study should be made of the contribution of Jews to the Uprising of Warsaw. The following sources should be useful: Zydowski Instytut Historyczny, Warsaw; Centralna Zydowska Komisja Historyczna, Warsaw; YAD VASHEM Martyrs' and Heroes' Remembrance Authority, Jerusalem; Kibbutz Lahomei Hagetot, Israel; YIVO Institute for Jewish Research, New York; Polish Underground Movement (1939 –1945) Study Trust, London; Polish Institute and Sikorski Museum, London.

For their assistance in my research in Jewish materials sincere thanks are due to Mr Zee Ben Schlomo of the Institute of Contemporary History and Wiener Library, London; Dr Michael Borwicz, Paris; Dr Lucjan Dobroszycki of YIVO, New York; and Mr S. Krakowski of YAD VASHEM, Jerusalem.

30. Niedzielski Mieczyslaw (Zywiciel). Colonel. Commander Sector 'Zoliborz'. The Polish Home Army AK. Interview: Chicago, 18 May 1966.

31. Bronislaw Tronski, *Tedy Przeszla Smierc: Zapiski z Powstania Warszawskiego* [*Death Passed Through Here: Notes from the Warsaw Uprising*]. Warsaw: Czytelnik, 1957, pp. 250–1.

32. Kazimierz Baginski, Vice-President of the Council of National Unity, Warsaw; and Director of the Department of Internal Affairs attached to the Delegate of the Polish Government-in-Exile in Warsaw. Interview: Phoenix 17 and 18 Apr 1966. However, notice that fighting for Warsaw was not the 'general uprising'.

33. Antoni Chrusciel (Monter), *Powstanie Warszawskie* [*The Warsaw Uprising*]. London: n.p., 1948, p. 11.

34. At its peak (prior to the Uprising) the AK contained 380,175 underground soldiers, including 10,756 officers, 7,506 cadets, and 87,886 noncommissioned officers. Fully staffed platoons numbered 627. In addition, there were 2,633 'skeleton platoons'. Prior to the Uprising a full combat platoon had 50 soldiers and a 'skeleton platoon' had 25 soldiers. Poland, Komisja Historyczna Polskiego Sztabu Glownego w Londynie. *Polskie Sily Zbrojne w Drugiej Wojnie Swiatowej. Armia Krajowa* [*Polish Armed Forces in the Second World War. The Home Army*]. London: Instytut Historyczny im. Gen. Sikorskiego, 1950–1, Vol. 3, pp. 119–25; see also Chrusciel, op. cit., p. 3. Weapons: Jerzy Kirchmayer, *Powstanie Warszawskie* [*The Warsaw Uprising*]. Warsaw: Ksiazka i Wiedza, Czwarte Wydanie, 1964, pp. 140–94; AK, pp. 679–83, 799–801; Aleksander Skarzynski. *Polityczne Przyczyny Powstania Warszawskiego* [*Political Determinants of the Warsaw Uprising*]. Warsaw: Panstwowe Wydawnictwo Naukowe, 1965, p. 339; Adam Borkiewicz *Powstanie Warszawskie 1944: Zarys Dzialan Natury Wojskowej* [*The*

Uprising of Warsaw 1944: Military Aspects]. Warsaw: Instytut Wydawniczy, 1964, p. 35.

35. Kirchmayer, op. cit., p. 144.

36. Ibid. pp. 140–6.

37. Ibid. p. 143.

38. Stanislaw Blaszczak (Rog), Major, Commander of Rog Sector, Old Town; Commander of the 36th Infantry Regiment, AK. Interview: Chicago, 21 May 1966.

39. Mieczyslaw Niedzielski (Zywiciel), Colonel, Commander of Zoliborz Sector, AK. Interview: Chicago, 18 May 1966.

40. Jerzy Braun, Member of the Council of National Unity, Warsaw. Interview: Philadelphia, 29 Jan 1966.

41. Stanislaw Komornicki, *Na Barykadach Warszawy* [*On the Barricades of Warsaw*]. Warsaw: MON, 1964, p. 20.

42. Tadeusz Kubalski, *W Szeregach 'Baszty'* [*The Rank and File of 'Baszta'*]. Warsaw: Wydawnictwo Ministerstwa Obrony Narodowej, 1969, p. 151.

43. Franciszek Dziubinski (Dolega), Corporal, AK. Interview: Chicago, 19 May 1966.

44. Casimir W. Tuleja (Mountaineer), 2nd Lieutenant, battalion medical officer, Old Town, AK. Interview: Chicago, 17 May 1966.

45. APUMST, File Stare Miasto, Roman Patynowski's testimony, p. 5.

46. Ibid., Feliks Jeziorek's testimony, p. 1.

47. George H. Janczewski (Glinka), Cadet, section leader, AK. Interview: Philadelphia, 2 Jan 1968.

48. Janusz K. Zawodny, 'Raport Dowodcy Plutonu A.K. z Powstania Warszawskiego' ['Report of a Platoon Commander in the Uprising of Warsaw'], *Zeszyty Historyczne*, Paris, Instytut Literacki, No. 176, 1969, p. 176.

49. Emil Kumor, 'Powstancza Fabryka Granatow' [Insurgent's Hand-grenade Factory'], *Kierunki*, Warsaw, No. 34, 25 Aug 1957.

zycki, D. Taczanowski's testimony, pp. 3, 6–7.

51. Zawodny, *Zeszyty Historyczne*, No. 176, 1969, pp. 183–4.

52. APUMST, File Warszawa-Srodmiescie, Part II, Mariusz Westfal's testimony, p. 1.

53. Ibid., File Colonel Uszycki, 'Historja Batalionow Chrobry I and Chrobry II', p. 9.

54. Kazimierz Sawicki (Opor), Brigadier-General, General Staff of AK. Interview: London, 13 May 1965.

55. Waclaw Zagorski, *Wicher Wolnosci: Dziennik Powstanca* [*Wind of Freedom: Diary of an Insurgent*]. London: Nakladem Czytelnikow-Przedplacicieli, staraniem SPK Kolo No. 11, 1957, pp. 133, 135.

56. APUMST, File Warszawa-Srodmiescie, Part II, Edward Kowalczyk's testimony, p. 3.

57. Bartelski, op. cit., p. 69.

58. APUMST, File Praga, Leon Kraszka's testimony, p. 2.

59. Ibid., File VI, L. dz. 6541/44, 8 Aug 1944.

60. Antoni Przygonski, 'Armia Ludowa w Dniu Wybuchu Powstania Warszawskiego i jej Walki na Woli od 1 do 7 Sierpnia 1944' ['People's Army on the Day of the Warsaw Uprising: Its Battles at Wola from 1–7 August 1944'], *Najnowsze Dzieje Polski: Materialy i Studia z Okresu II Wojny Swiatowej*, Warsaw, Vol. 5, 1961, p. 54; Antoni Przygonski, 'Armia Ludowa w Powstaniu Warszawskim na Starym Miescie' ['The People's Army in the Warsaw Uprising in the Old Town'], *Wojskowy Przeglad Historyczny*, Warsaw, No. 3, 1965, pp. 96–138.

61. Stanislaw Weber (Surgeon, Popiel), Lieutenant-Colonel, Chief of Staff to the Commander of the Uprising of Warsaw, AK. Interview: London, 15 May 1965.

62. P. Kraczkiewicz, Lieutenant-Colonel, *Clandestine Production of Arma-*

ments and Sabotage Equipment.
(Chronological development, organizational table, technical drawings and specifications. Also attached notes concerning sabotage of the German war efforts in occupied Poland during the Second World War. Typescript in Polish, 68 pp. Unpublished. Given to the author by Lt-Col. Krac-Kzkiewicz, who was the technical manager of the production of sabotage equipment for AK Headquarters (1940–4), and also Deputy Chief for the Clandestine Production of Armaments of the AK. (Mar 1944 to 1 Aug 1944). He also participated in policy formulation and operations with regard to sabotage units; AK, pp. 323–49; Dolega, op. cit., passim.

63. Letter from Mr Zygmunt Byczynski (AK member) to the author, 16 Oct 1958.

64. Tadeusz Bor-Komorowski, *Armia Podziemna* [*The Secret Army*]. 3rd ed.; London: Nakladem Katolickiego Osrodka Wydawniczego Veritas, 1950, p. 148.

65. Kirchmayer, op. cit., p. 144.

66. Bor-Komorowski, *Armia Podziemna* [*The Secret Army*], p. 148.

67. Ibid.

68. Janina Pronaszko-Konopacka (Janina), Lieutenant, combat liaison and secretary to the last commander-in-chief of AK, Gen. Leopold Okulicki. Interview: London, 13 May 1965.

69. Kirchmayer, op. cit., p. 142.

70. Dolega, op. cit., passim.

71. Julian Miklaszewicz, 'Gospodarka Pieniezna AK' ['Fiscal Management of the Home Army'], *Biuletyn Informacyjny Kolo AK*, London, No. 2, Feb–Mar 1948, pp. 4–5, No. 3, Apr–May 1948, pp. 4–5.

72. Ibid., No. 2, p. 5.

73. Ibid.; see also AK, pp. 343–9.

74. Stanislaw Mikolajczyk (Stem), Prime Minister, the Polish Government-in-Exile. Interview: Princeton, 31 Mar 1957

75. AK, p. 346.

76. Mikolajczyk, interview 3 Mar 1957; see also articles concerning Colonel Hancza's death in *Kultura* (Paris), issues 1963, 1964, passim.

77. Dolega, op. cit., p. 20.

78. AK, p. 682.

79. Ibid. p. 796.

80. Stanislaw Zadrozny, *Tu-Warszawa: Dzieje Radiostacji Powstanczej Blyskawica* [*Warsaw Calling: A History of the Uprising Radio Station Lightning*]. London: Nakladem Ksiegarni Orbis, 1964, passim.

81. Stefan Korbonski, *Fighting Warsaw: The Story of the Polish Underground State 1939–1945*. London: George Allen & Unwin Ltd, 1956, passim; Stefan Korbonski, *Warsaw in Chains*. London: George Allen & Unwin Ltd, 1959, passim; see also by the same author *W Imieniu Kremla* [*On Behalf of the Kremlin*]. Paris: Instytut Literacki, 1956, 381 pp.; and *Warsaw in Exile*. New York: Frederick A. Praeger, 1966, 235 pp.

82. Wanda Pelczynska, 'Rozglosnie Walczacej Warszawy' ['The Radio Stations of Fighting Warsaw'], *Tydzien Polski*, London, 5 Dec 1964, p. 3.

83. Stanislaw Mikolajczyk (Stem), Prime Minister, the Polish Government-in-Exile. Interview: Princeton, 31 March 1957.

84. Z. S. Siemaszko, 'Powstanie Warszawskie: Kontakty z ZSRR i PKWN' ['The Uprising of Warsaw: Contacts with the USSR and PKWN']. *Zeszyty Historyczne*, Paris, Instytut Literacki, No. 12, 1969, p. 15.

85. Borkiewicz, op. cit., p. 495.

86. AK, p. 796.

87. Jozef Garlinski, *Miedzy Londynem i Warszawa* [*Between London and Warsaw*]. London: Gryf Publication Ltd, 1966, p. 26 n.

88. Malinowski, *Najnowsze Dzieje Polski*, Vol. 7, 1963, pp. 39–56, passim.

89. Z. S. Siemaszko, 'Lacznosc Radiowa Sztabu N.W. w Przede Dniu Powstania Warszawskiego' ['Radio Communication of the Commander-in-Chief's Staff on the Day Preceding the Beginning of the Warsaw Uprising'], *Zeszyty Historyczne*, Paris, Instytut Literacki, No. 6, 1964, p. 74.

90. Registered in full by Capt. Andrzej Pomian. See Pomian's letter to APUMST, 18 Dec 1959, L. dz. 424/5 9, cited in full in Andrzej Pomian, *The Warsaw Rising: A Selection of Documents*. London: n.p., 1945.

91. Zadrozny, op. cit., passim.

92. 'On 17 Aug 1944 about 10.00–10.15 a.m. the station [Lightning] from Warsaw was heard [in London] for the first time on frequency 9129.' Report of the Chief of Communication, Special Branch, Polish General Staff, London. APUMST, File VI Special Branch.

93. Tadeusz Bor-Komorowski, *Armia Podziemna* [*The Secret Army*]. 3rd ed. London: Nakladem Katolickiego Osrodka Wydawniczego Veritas, 1950, p. 305.

94. Halina Auderska and Zygmunt Ziolka, ed., *Akcja N* [*Action N*]. Warsaw: Czytelnik, 1972, pp. 734–41.

95. Bor, *Armia Podziemna* [*The Secret Army*] p. 306.

96. Ibid.

97. Stefan Korbonski, 'Listy do Redakcji' ['Letter to the Editor'], *Zeszyty Historyczne*, Paris, Instytut Literacki, No. 16, 1969, pp. 227–31.

98. Zenon Kliszko, *Powstanie Warszawskie: Artykuly, Przemowienia, Wspomnienia, Dokumenty* [*The Warsaw Uprisings: Articles, Speeches, Recollections, Documents*]. Warsaw: Ksiazka i Wiedza, 1967, p. 17; Malinowski, *Najnowsze Dzieje Polski*, Vol. 7, 1963, pp. 43–4.

99. Pelczynska, *Tydzien Polski*, 5 Dec 1964, p. 3.

100. Ibid.

101. Ibid.

102. Janusz Laskowski, 'Radiostacja Swit' ['The Radio Station Swit'], Parts I and II, *Zeszyty Historyczne*, Paris, Instytut Literacki, Vol. 9, 1966, pp. 101–30; No. 10, 1966, p. 221.

103. Siemaszko, *Zeszyty Historyczne*, No. 6, 1964, p. 71.

104. Ibid., passim.

105. Stanislaw Kopanski, General, 'Concerning Radio Communication between the Chief of Staff of the Polish Forces in Exile (General Kopanski) in London, and the Supreme Commander of the Polish Forces, General Sosnkowski, while on Inspection Tour of the Polish Forces in Italy', typewritten memo kindly given by Gen. Kopanski to the author on 17 May 1965, pp. 1–2.

106. APUMST, radio message from Stefan Korbonski (Nowak), L. dz. 4585/44, 12 Aug 1944.

107. Ibid., radio message to Prime Minister Mikolajczyk, L. dz 113, part 2; see Zygmunt Nagorski, *Wojna w Londynie: Wspomnienia, 1939–1945* [*War in London: Memories, 1939–1945*]. Paris: Ksiegarnia Polska w Paryzu, 1966, p. 275.

108. PISM, File Prezydium Rady Minstrow, No. 26, Tomasz Arciszewski's speech from London to AK in Warsaw, 13 Aug 1944.

109. APUMST, Kwapinski in London to the Chairman of the Council of National Unity in Warsaw, radio message VI, No. 6526, 9 Aug 1944.

110. Garlinski, *Miedzy Londynem i Warszawa* [*Between London and Warsaw*], p. 46, n. The problem of radio communication between AK in Poland and the Polish authorities in London is controversial and needs further study. Apart from Mr Garlinski's book the following sources should be consulted (they include a broad spectrum of views): Jozef Srebzynski, Deputy Commander of Communications of AK, *Zagadnienie Lacznosci Krajowej i Zagranicznij w Okresie*

Konspiracji 1940–1944 [*The Problem of Communications in the Underground and with Contacts Abroad during the years of Conspiracy 1940–1944*]. Typescript in Polish, 133 pp. including supplement 'Organizacja Lacznosci' ['Organization of Communication'], 37 pp. Original in the Polska Akademia Nauki, Warsaw. Copy: Archives of the Polish Underground (1939–1945) Study Trust, London; APUMST, Colonel Uszycki's archives, passim; Stefan Korbonski, *W Imieniu Rzeczypospolitej* [*On Behalf of the Polish Commonwealth*]. 2nd ed,; London: Gryf, 1964, pp. 63–107, 139–56, 187–98, 279–88, 364, et passim; Zadrozny, op. cit., passim; Z. S. Siemaszko, *Zeszyty Historyzne*, Paris, Instytut Literacki, No. 6, 1964, pp. 64–116; also by Z. S. Siemaszko, 'Lacznosc i Polityka' ['Com/munication and Politics'], *Zeszyty His-toryczne*, Paris, Instytut Literacki, No. 8, 1965, pp. 187–207; Popkiewicz, 'Szczegoly Lacznosci Radiowej Miedzy Londynem i Warszawa' ['Details of Radio Communication between London and Warsaw'], *Zeszyty Historyczne*, Paris, Instytut Literacki, No. 13, 1968, pp. 215–20; also by the same author 'List do Redakcji' [Letter to the Editor'], *Zeszyty Historyczne*, Paris, Instytut Literacki, No. 7, 1965, pp. 211–15; 'List do Redakcji' ['Letter to the Editor'], *Zeszyty Historyczne*, Paris, Instytut Literacki, No. 9, 1966, p. 235; 'List do Redakcji' ['Letter to the Editor'], *Zeszyty Historyczne*, Paris, Instytut Literacki, No. 15, 1969, pp. 249–251; Stefan Korbonski, 'List do Redakcji' ['Letter to the Editor'], *Zeszyty Historyczne*, Paris, Instytut Literacki, No. 19, 1971, p. 233; also AK, p. 681.

Chapter 2. Insurgents In and Outside Warsaw

1. Antoni Przygonski, *Z Problematyki Powstania Warszawskiego* [*Among the Problems of the Warsaw Uprising*]. Warsaw: Wydawnictwo Ministerstwo Obrony Narodowej, 1964, p. 31, n. 47.

2. Ibid.

3. Ibid.

4. Wojskowy Instytut Historyczny. Zaklad Historii Partii Przy KC PZPR. *Dowodztwo Glowne GL i AL: Zbior Dokumentow z Lat 1942–1944.* [*Supreme Command of the GL and AL: Collection of Documents for the Years 1942–1944*]. Warsaw: Wydawnictwo M.O.N., 1967, passim; Polska Zjednoczona Partia Robotnicza. Komitet Centralny. Zaklad Historii Partii. *Konumikaty Dowodztwo Glownego Gwardii Ludowej i Armii Ludowej.* (Dockumenty). Wyd. 2, opr. Ed. Markowa *et al.* [*Communiques of the Supreme Command of the People's Guard and of the Peoples' Army*]. Warsaw: Wydawnictwo Ministerstwa Obrony Narodowej, 1961, passim.

5. Antoni Przygonski, *Z Problematyki Powstania Warszawskiego* [*Among the Problems of the Warsaw Uprising*], pp. 47–8.

6. Ibid. p. 48; see also Komunistyczna Partia Polski. Komitet Centralny. Zaklad Historii Partii. Antoni Przygonski, *Udzial PPR i AL w Powstaniu Warszawskim* [*Participation of PPR and AL in the Uprising of Warsaw*], pp. 19–20.

7. Ibid., p. 20.

8. Przygonski, *Z Problematyki Powstania Warszawskiego* [*Among the Problems of the Warsaw Uprising*], p. 52.

9. Ibid.

10. AK, p. 703.

11. Ibid.

12. Franciszek Miszczak (Bogucki), Major, Chief of Intelligence Section

'Eastern Front', the Supreme HQ of AK. Interview: London, 13 May 1965.

13. Stanislaw Mikolajczyk (Stem), Prime Minister, the Polish Government-in-Exile. Interview: Washington, DC, 26 June 1965.

14. *Contra*: Komunistyczna Partia Polski. Komitet Centralny. Zaklad Historii. Antoni Przygonski, *Udzial PPR i AL w Powstaniu Warszawskim* [*Participation of PPR and AL in the Uprising of Warsaw*], p. 22. In fact, on 30 July 1944, Colonel Jozef Pienkos from the Communist organization PAL approached AK Col. Jan Rzepecki from AK HQ to synchronize their co-operation 'in the approaching fight', Jan Rzepecki, 'Letter to Editor', *Wojskowy Przeglad Historyczny*, No. 1, 1966, pp. 427–8.

15. Tadeusz Bor-Komorowski, *The Secret Army*. London: Victor Gollancz, 1951, p. 246.

16. *Pamietniki Zolnierzy Baonu Zoska: Powstanie Warszawskie* [*Diaries of Soldiers of Group Zoska: Warsaw Uprising*]. Warsaw: Nasza Ksiegarnia, 1957, p. 280.

17. Ibid. p. 316.

18. APUMST, Bor's radio message No. L. dz. (?), 14 Aug 1944.

19. Adam Borkiewicz. *Powstanie Warszawskie 1944: Zarys Dzialan Natury Wojskowej* [*The Uprising of Warsaw: Military Aspects*]. Warsaw: Instytut Wydawniczy Pax, 1964, pp. 249–50, n. 556.

20. APUMST, Bor's radio message O.VI. L. dz. 7276/44, 22 Aug 1944.

21. Bartelski, op. cit., p. 127.

22. Ibid. p. 124.

23. Borkiewicz, op. cit., p. 551; see also APUMST, radio messages from Major Okon. No. 107/VV/999, 19 Sept 1944; L. dz. 8403, 14 Sept 1944; L. dz. 13562/44, 17 Aug 1944; L. dz. 13611/44, 19 Aug 1944; and No. 88/VV/999, 31 Aug 1944.

24. Halina Czarnocka, 'Udzial Kobiet w Armii Krajowej' ['The Participation of Women in the Home Army'], *Biuletyn Informacyjny, Kolo AK*, London, No. 36, Dec 1958 and Feb 1959, p. 3.

25. The following source is indispensable as an overview of Polish women's participation in the Second World War. Wanda Nesteruk, 'Sesja Popularno-Naukowa Poswiecone Udzialowi Kobiet Polskich w II Wojnie Swiatowej w Latach 1939–1945' ['The Conference on the Subject of the Participation of Polish Women in the Second World War, 1939–1945'], *Wojskowy Przeglad Historyczny*, Warsaw, No. 3, 1971, pp. 363–8.

The Communist forces (Armia Ludowa) had a plan to organize combat units composed solely of women. When the woman who conceived the idea, Janina Bier, was arrested and murdered by Gestapo the project collapsed. Nevertheless, Communist women served with their units in the same capacities as AK women – as medics, liaison, etc. See: Wojskowy Instytut Historyczny. Zaklad Historii Partii Przy KC PZPR. *Dowodztwo Glowne GL i AL: Zbior Dokumentow z Lat 1942–1944* [*Supreme Command of the GL and AL: Collection of Documents for the Years 1942–1944*]. Warsaw: Wydawnictwo M.O.N., 1967, pp. 313–18.

26. Zofia Wankowiczowa, 'Kombatantki (Powstanie Warszawskie)' ['Women Combatants'] *Kultura*, Paris, Instytut Literacki, No. 10, 1954, p. 85.

27. Ibid. p. 79.

28. Boleslaw Jozef Szmajdowicz (Blyst), 2nd Lieutenant, Commander of two parachute supply-receiving stations in Poland, AK. Interview: Philadelphia, 7 Mar 1967.

29. Czarnecka, op. cit., p. 2.

30. Jan Karski, *Story of a Secret State*. Boston: Houghton Mifflin Company, 1944, p. 281.

31. Wankowiczowa, op. cit., p. 93.

32. APUMST, radio message L. dz.

K.4687/44.

33. APUMST, radio message L. dz. K. 4713/44.

34. APUMST, File No. 1240; Maria Jasinkowicz, p. 1.

35. Ewa Maria Bukowska (Wawa), 2nd Lieutenant, Instructor of women's auxiliaries, AK. Interview: London, 26 Mar 1965; also Grazyna Zipser (Grazyna), combat messenger, AK. Interview: New York, 31 Mar 1968, passim.

36. APUMST, radio message from Warsaw, 18 Aug 1944 at 6.30 p.m.

37. Tadeusz Dolega-Kamienski (Badacz),*Powstanie Warszawskie: Kwatermistrzostwo* [*The Warsaw Uprising: The Quartermaster*]. The author was the Quartermaster of the Uprising. Typescript. Jozef Pilsudski Institute of America, New York, passim.

38. Karol Jan Ziemski (Wachnowski), Colonel, Deputy Commander of the Uprising of Warsaw, Deputy Commander of the Warsaw Corps of the AK, Commander of the Defence of Old Town. After the war he was promoted to the rank of brigadier-general. Interview: London, 11 May 1965.

39. Mieczyslaw Niedzielski (Zywiciel), Colonel, Commander of Zoliborz Sector, AK. Interview: Chicago, 18 May 1966.

40. Jadwiga Gac (Jadzia), Private, combat nurse and messenger, AK. Interview: Philadelphia, 7 May 1968.

41. Wankowiczowa, op. cit., p. 79.

42. Vladimir L. Kozlowski (Jastrzebiec), Lieutenant, Company Commander, Old Town, AK. Interview: Chicago, 21 May 1966.

43. Kazimierz Szternal (Zryw), Deputy Commander of Mokotow Sector, Chief of Staff of Region VI, AK. Interview: Chicago, 17 May 1966.

44. Irena Lukomska (Dziembowska), 2nd Lieutenant, Commander of a women's auxiliary unit, AK. Interview: Chicago, 17 May 1966.

45. Niedzielski, interview.

46. Casimir W. Tuleja (Mountaineer), 2nd Lieutenant, battalion medical officer, Old Town, AK. Interview: Chicago, 17 May 1966.

47. Gac, interview.

48. Tadeusz Pogorski (Morwa), MD, commandant of a field hospital in Old Town. Interview: Cleveland, 27 Aug 1969.

49. Bronislaw Tronski, *Tedy Przeszla Smierc: Zapiski z Powstania Warszawskiego* [*Death Passed Through Here: Notes from the Warsaw Uprising*]. Warsaw: Czyt lnik, 1957, p. 54.

50. Niedzielski, interview.

51. Turkowska, interview.

52. Halina Degorska (Iga), 2nd Lieutenant, messenger, Old Town AK Interview: Philadelphia, 23 Feb 1967.

53. Gac, interview.

54. Zipser, interview.

55. Gac, interview.

56. Jozef i Maria Czapscy, *Dwuglos Wspomnien* [*Reminiscences in Two Voices*]. London: Polska Fundacja Kulturalna, 1965, pp. 153−4.

57. Andrzej Czarski. *Najmlodsi Zolnierze Walczacej Warszawy* [*Fighting Warsaw's Youngest Soldiers*]. Warsaw: Pax, 1971, p. 7.

58. Leslaw M. Bartelski, *W Kregu Bliskich: Szkice Do Portretow* [*In the Circle of Comrades: Sketches for Portraits*]. Krakow: Wydawnictwo Literackie, 1967, p. 106.

Chapter 3. The German Army

1. Jozef Warszawski (Ojcie Pawel), Major, chaplain to Colonel Radoslaw's unit, AK. Interview: Rome, 13 June 1967.

2. The Polish Institute and Sikorski Museum, London (to be cited as PISM). File: Prezydium Rady Ministrow, Ref. No. K.4018/1944.

Radio message from Poland (Korbonski), 6 July 1944.

3. Tomasz Rostworowski(Tomasz), Major, chaplain to the Supreme HQ of AK. Interview: Rome, 15 June 1967.

4. United States. General Staff. *General Marshall's Report: The Winning of the War in Europe and the Pacific Biennial Report of the Chief of Staff of the US Army July 1, 1943 to June 30, 1945 to the Secretary of War.* New York: Simon & Schuster, 1945, p. 30.

5. Herman Gackenholz, 'Der Zusammenbruch der Heeresgruppe Mitte 1944' ['The Collapse of the Army Group Centre, 1944'], *Entscheidungsschlachten des Zweiten Weltkrieges*, Frankfurt am Main: Verlag für Wehrwesen Bernard and Graefe, 1960, passim.

6. Hanns von Krannhals, *Der Warschauer Aufstand 1944* [*The Warsaw Uprising, 1944*]. Frankfurt am Main: Bernard and Graefe Verlag für Wehrwesen, 1964, p. 162, to be cited as Krannhals.

7. Ibid. See also Martin Broszat, *Nationalsozialistische Polenpolitik 1939–1945* [*National Socialist Policy towards Poles, 1939–1945*]. Frankfurt am Main: Fischer Bücherei, 1961, passim; Hans Roos, 'Polen in der Besatzungszeit' ['Poland during the Occupation'], *Osteuropa-Handbuch Polen*, Köln: Boehlau Verlag, 1959, pp. 167–93.

8. Ibid.

9. Kurt Tippelskirch, *Geschichte des Zweiten Weltkrieges* [*A History of the Second World War*]. Bonn: Athenaeum Verlag, 1951, p. 545.

10. Bundesarchiv-Militärarchiv: H-12-9/3 bis H-12-9/9 'Kriegstagebuch der 9. Armee mit Anlagebänden, Kartensammlungen und diversen Einzelaktenstücken' ['Daily War Reports of the 9th Army with Supplements, Collections of Maps and Diverse Single Documents']; film: Records of German Field Commands, Armies, T-312, Rolls 343–9. The National Archives of the United States, Washington, DC. To be cited as *German Army*; Bundesarchiv-Militärarchiv. Smilo Frhr. von Lüttwitz, Der Kampf der 9. Armee vom 21. September 1944 bis 20. Januar 1945. (1948.) ['The Battle of the 9th Army from 21 September 1944 to 20 January 1945']. H-08.10/6; see also Gackenholz, op. cit., pp. 455–78 and Krannhals, passim.

11. Emanuel Halicz, 'Doswiadczenia Powstania Styczniowego w Ujeciu Naczelnych Wladz Hitlerowskich' ['Experiences in the January Uprising as Interpreted by the Supreme German Authorities'], *Wojskowy Przeglad Historyczny*, Warsaw, No. 3, 1965, p. 358.

12. Krannhals, op. cit. pp. 308–9.

13. Ibid., pp. 135, 309.

14. Jerzy Sawicki, *Przed Polskim Prokuratorem: Dokumenty i Materialy* [*Before the Polish Prosecutor: Documents and Materials*]. Warsaw: Iskry, 1958, Von dem Bach testimony, p. 29; Stanislaw Ploski, 'Relacja Von dem Bacha o Powstaniu Warszawskim' ['Report of von dem Bach on the Warsaw Uprising'], *Dzieje Najnowsze*, No. 2, April–June 1947, Vol. 1, pp. 295–324.

15. *Hitler's Lagebesprechungen: Die Protokollfragmente seiner militärischen Konferenzen 1942–1945*. Herausgegeben von Helmut Heiber. [*Hitler's Situation Reviews: Fragments of Records of His Military Conferences, 1942–1945*. Edited by Helmut Heiber.] Stuttgart: Deutsche Verlagsanstalt, 1962, p. 425, 627; Walter Warlimont, *Im Hauptquartier der Deutschen Wehrmacht 1939–1945* [*Inside the German Army Headquarters, 1939–1945*]. Frankfurt am Main: Bernard and Graefe Verlag für Sehrwesen, 1962, conference on 1 Sept 1944. Verified with the original document at the University of Pennsylvania Library,

Rare Book Collection, Code No. 46M – 20, pt. 7, fragment No. 43, pp. 8 – 10.

16. Krannhals, op. cit., p. 265.

17. Ibid. p. 320.

18. Ibid. pp. 260, 320.

19. Ibid. p. 308; see also Alan Clark, *Barbarossa: The Russian – German Conflict 1941 – 1945*. New York: Signet Book published by New American Library, 1966, p. 432, n. 3.

20. Krannhals, op. cit., p. 314.

21. Ibid. p. 320.

22. Glowna Komisja Badania Zbrodni Niemieckich w Polsce. *Zburzenie Warszawy: Zeznania Generalow Niemieckich przed Prokuratorem Rzeczypospolitej* [*Destruction of Warsaw: German Generals' Testimonies to the Prosecutor of Poland*]. Warsaw: Ministerstwo Obrony Narodowej, 1946, p. 45.

23. Krannhals, op. cit., p. 320.

24. Ibid. p. 135.

25. *Zburzenie Warszawy*, op. cit., passim.

26. Krannhals, op. cit., p. 260.

27. Komisja Historyczna Polskiego Sztabu Glownego w Londynie. *Polskie Sily Zbrojne w Drugiej Wojnie Swiatowej. Armia Krajowa.* [*Polish Armed Forces in the Second World War. The Home Army*]. London: Instytut Historyczny im. Gen. Sikorskiego, Vol. 3, 1950–1, p. 687. Cited as AK.

28. Krannhals, op. cit., passim.

29. Ibid., passim.

30. Tadeusz Bor-Komorowski, *The Secret Army.* London: Victor Gollancz, 1951, pp. 277–8.

31. Mieczyslaw Niedzielski (Zywiciel), Colonel, commander of Zoliborz Sector, AK. Interview: Chicago, 18 May 1966.

32. Marian Glowacki (Peaceful), Lieutenant, 'Notes Bojowy' ['Combat Notes'], manuscript in Polish made available to the author. London, spring, 1969.

33. Casimir W. Tuleja (Mountaineer), battalion medical officer, Old Town, AK. Interview: Chicago, 17 May 1966.

34. Krannhals, op. cit., p. 357.

35. Vladimir L. Kozlowski (Jastrzebjec), Lieutenant, company commander, Old Town, AK. Interview: Chicago, 21 May 1966.

36. Irena Milko-Wieckowska (Wierzbicka), 2nd Lieutenant, combat messenger, AK. Interview: Philadelphia, 10 Nov 1966.

37. Tuleja, interview.

38. Lucjan Fajer, *Zolnierze Starowki: Dziennik Bojowy Kpt. Ognistego* [*Soldiers of Old Town: The War Diary of Captain Ognisty*]. Warsaw: Iskry, 1957, p. 234.

39. Henryk Grzymala-Rosiek, 2nd Lieutenant, AK. *Wspomnienia z Okresu Powstania w 1944 roku* [*Memoirs from the Time of Uprising, 1944*], typescript in the possession of Col. M. Niedzielski, Chicago, p. 5.

40. Monter Reports, Report No. 17, 15 Aug 1944; Report No. 29, 29 Aug 1944.

41. APUMST, File Stare Miasto, Col. Zywiciel to Col. Wachnowski, radio message, L. dz. 7997/44, 6 Sept 1944.

42. Monter Reports, Report No. 18, 16 Aug 1944.

43. Stanczyk Boleslaw. (Xen). 2nd Lieutenant. Executive officer of a company. AK. Interview: Chicago, 18 May 1966.

44. Jan Gozdawa Golembiowski, 'Koszta w Akcji' ['Koszta in Combat'], typescript in possession of the author, pp. 1–11.

45. Peter Aurich, 'Der Verrat an der Weichsel' ['Betrayal of the Vistula'], *Deutsche Soldatenzietung*, No. 21, 2 July 1954, p. 12.

46. Monter Reports, Report No., 12 Aug 1944.

47. APUMST, File Daniel-Baszta, p. 118.

48. The basic source is *Documenta Occupationis Teutonica*, voluminous studies published in Poland. Consult

also Wladyslaw Bartoszewski, *Erick von dem Bach*. Warsaw-Poznan: Wydawnictwo Zachodnie, 1961, 109 pp.; Wladyslaw Bartoszewski, *Prawda o Von dem Bachu* [*The Truth about vondem Bach*]. Warsaw-Poznan: Wydawnictwo Zachodnie, 1961, 144 pp.; Szymon Datner, Janusz Gulowski, Kazimierz Leszczynski, *Genocide 1903–1944*. Warsaw-Poznan: Wydawnictwo Zachodnie, 1953, 334 pp.; Kazimierz Leszczynski, *Heinz Reinefarth*. Warsaw-Poznan: Wydawnictwo Zachodnie, 1961, 98 pp.; Jerzy Sawicki, *Ludobojstwo: Od Pojecia do Konwencji, 1933–1948* [*Genocide: From the Idea to the Convention, 1933–1948*]. Cracow: L. J. Jaroszewski, 1949, 224 pp.; Jerzy Sawicki, *Przed Polskim Prokuratorem: Dokumenty i Materialy* [*Before the Polish Prosecutor: Documents and Materials*]. Warsaw: Iskry, 1958, 345 pp.; Jerzy Sawicki and Boleslaw Walawski, *Zbior Przepisow Specjalnych Przeciwko Zbrodniarzom Hilterowskim i Zdrajcom Narodu z Komentarzem* [*Collection of Special Regulations against the Hitler Criminals and the Traitors of the Nation, with Commentary*]. Warsaw: Czytelnik, 1945, 63 pp.; Edward Servanski *et al.*, *Zbrodnia Niemiecka w Warszawie 1944: Zeznania–Zdiecia* [*German Attrocities in Warsaw, 1944: Testimony and Photographs*]. Poznan: Wydawnictwo Instytutu Zachodniego, 1946, 246 pp.

49. Krannhals, op. cit., p. 310.

50. Kazimierz Leszczynski. *Heinz Reinefarth*. Warsaw-Poznan: Wydawnictwo Zachodnie, 1961, p. 26.

51. APUMST, File No. 1240, Maria Jasiunkowicz's testimony.

52. Report of Col. Alexander Björrlkund, former Finnish Military Attaché in Warsaw. PISM, Gabinet Naczelnego Wodza A.XII. 1/64.

53. Leslaw M. Bartelski, *Powstanie Warszawskie* [*The Uprising of Warsaw*]. Warsaw: Iskry, 1965, pp. 81–2.

54. Ibid. p. 81.

55. Interview by a journalist with

Gen. von dem Bach, *Kurier Codzienny*, 2 Feb 1947, p. 2; Krannhals, p. 135.

56. Krannhals, op. cit., pp. 133–4, 321.

57. Ibid. pp. 308, 325.

58. Ibid. p. 324.

59. Rostworowski, interview, cited above.

60. Ibid.

61. Leslaw M. Bartelski. *Powstanie Warszawskie* [*The Uprising of Warsaw*]. Warsaw: Iskry, 1965, pp. 85–6.

62. Peter Aurich, 'Der Verrat an der Weichsel' ['Betrayal of the Vistula'], *Deutsche Soldatenzeitung*, No. 21, 2 July 1954, p. 12.

63. Krannhals, op. cit., p. 323.

64. Ibid. pp. 304–5.

65. Casimir W. Tuleja (Mountaineer), 2nd Lieutenant, battalion medical officer, AK. Interview: Chicago, 17 May 1966.

66. Krannhals, op. cit., pp. 134–5.

67. Ibid. p. 323.

68. Bor-Komorowski, op. cit., p. 235.

69. Janusz K. Zawodny, 'Raport Dowodcy Plutonu AK z Powstania Warszawskiego' ['Report of a Platoon Commander in the Uprising of Warsaw'], *Zeszyty Historyczne*, Paris, Instytut Literacki, No. 176, 1969, pp. 186–7.

70. For details, see Wilfried Strik-Strikfeldt, *Against Stalin and Hitler: 1941–45*. New York: The John Day Company, 1973, pp. 1–270.

71. (1) Kaminski's 'Russian' SS Brigade; (2) Cossack Regiment of Police Number 3; (3) Muslim SS Regiment Number 1 (minus the 3rd Battalion); (4) Cossack Battalion Numbers 579 and 590 (General von dem Bach's reserves); (5) Dirlewanger's Brigade, composed of (a) the Azerbaijani 1st Battalion of the 3rd Regiment and the 2nd Battalion of Bergmann's Regiment, both later attached to the Reck and Schmidt Groups; (b) the 4th and 572nd Battalions of the 57th Cossack

Security Regiment; (c) the 6th and 9th squadrons of the 3rd Cossack Cavalry Brigade.

In addition, the following German units fighting in Warsaw during the Uprising were composed of several ethnic and national groups: (1) Operational Command of Security Police Unit Number 7A, with the 9th Army: (2) guards of the Warsaw Ghetto prison, Pawiak, under command of the Security Police; (3) a group of Security Police and SD, composed of German security forces from Warsaw and Poznan, who were commanded by Captain Spilker. Sources: AOK 9, Ia 449 geh. v. 26.8.44. Bumi, H-12-9/9, as cited by Krannhals, op. cit., pp. 311–19.

72. Ibid. p. 321. Without condoning the atrocities, one could remind Poles that, historically speaking, the Ukrainian nation, too, has as a national group undergone much the same fate as Poland. For Ukrainian views on their participation in the Uprising, see Borys Lewickyj, 'Ukrainska Likwidacja Powstania Warszawskiego'

['Ukrainians Suppress the Uprising of Warsaw'], *Kultura*, Paris, Instytut Literacki, No. 6, 1952, pp. 74–87; Lubomyr Ortynskij, 'Prawda o Ukrainskiej Dywizji' ['Truth about the Ukrainian Division'], *Kultura*, Paris, Instytut Literacki, Vol. 11, 1952, pp. 109–16; L. Shankovskyi, 'Varshavska Povstannia i Ukraintsi u Svitli Dokumentiv' ['Warsaw Uprising and Ukrainians in Documents'], *Vyzvolnyishliakh*, London, No. 2 (227), 1967, pp. 152–9.

73. Monter Reports, Report No. 25, 23 Aug 1944; Report No. 26, 24 Aug 1944.

74. Felicjan Majorkiewicz, 'Kontakty z Wegrami w Czasie Powstania Warszawskiego' ['Contacts with Hungarians during the Warsaw Uprising'], *Wojskowy Przeglad Historyczny*, Warsaw, No. 1, 1971, p. 409.

75. Ibid.

76. *German Army*, op. cit., 27 August 1944, p. 445.

77. Ibid.

78. Aurich, op. cit., p. 12.

79. Krannhals, op. cit., p. 196.

Chapter 4. The Red Army

1. St Antony's College, Oxford University, 'Proceedings of a Conference on Britain and European Resistance 1939–1945, Organized by St Antony's College, Oxford', 10–16 1962. Official position of the Soviet Government as voiced by the Soviet Delegate Mr Rosanoff, passim.

2. APUMST, File Deportacje.

3. Ibid.

4. For details, consult J. K. Zawodny, *Death in the Forest: The Story of the Katyn Forest Massacre.* Notre Dame, Indiana: University of Notre Dame Press, 1962 and 1972, 235 pp. Also by Macmillan (London), 1971.

5. It was necessary to rely on citations of these documents in other official Soviet sources, the writings of

the Soviet generals directly involved in Polish campaigns, and those of Polish writers in Poland who had partial access to Soviet archives. The most important source, however, was the official *History of the Great War of the Soviet Union 1941–1945*, particularly Vol. 4. There are two reasons for reliance on this last source. First, all the distinguished Soviet scholars and military men who wrote and edited this work had access to original documents, to which they refer in footnotes. Second, in describing the activities of the Soviet Army in Poland during the Second World War, all Soviet scholars and military men refer consistently to the *History* as the basis for their studies. (It is expected that a new, revised history of the Second World War will soon be published in the Soviet Union.)

The dates given here are from Soviet sources, and are referred to here to give the official Soviet point of view.

6. The Archives of the Ministry of Defence of the USSR. The Archives to be cited as AMD USSR. Set 233, No. 2307, Vol. 50, p. 312. Instytut Marksizmu – Leninizmu. *Historia Wielkiej Wojny Narodowej Zwiazku Radzieckiego, 1941 – 1945* [*History of the Great Patriotic War of the Soviet Union, 1941 – 1945*]. Warszawa: Wydawnictwo Ministerstwa Obrony Narodowej, Vol. 4, 1965, pp. 224 – 6. For other official Soviet sources consult: Akademiia Nauk SSSR. Institut Istorii. *SSSR v Velikoi Otechestvennoi Voine 1941 – 1945: Kratkaia Khronika* [*The USSR in the Great Patriotic War, 1941 – 1945: A Short Chronicle*]. Moskva: Voennoe Izdatel'stovo Ministerstva Oborony SSSR, 1964, 866 pp.; Akademiia Nauk SSSR. Institut Slaviaovedeniia. *Istoriia Pol'shi* [*A History of Poland*]. Moskva: Nauka, Dopelnitel'nyi tom, 1965, 582 pp.; Robert Beitzell, ed., *Tehran, Yalta, Potsdam: The Soviet Protocols*. Hattiesburg, Mississippi: Academic International, 1970, 349 pp.; *Bol'shaia Sovetskaia Entskilopediia*: 1955, Vol. 34; *Istoriia Velikoi Otechestvennoi Voiny Sovetskogo Soiuza 1941 – 1945*. [*A History of the Great Patriotic War of the USSR, 1941 – 1945*] Vol. 4. Moscow: Voennoe Izdatel'stvo Ministerstva Oborony SSSR, 1962, 736 pp.

7. Ibid. p. 225.

8. Ibid.

9. A. A. Grechko, *Osvoboditel'naia Missiia Sovetskikh Vooruzhennykh Sil vo Vtoroi Mirovoi Voine* [*Liberation Mission of the Soviet Armed Forces in the Second World War*]. Moskva: Politizdat, 1971, p. 90 and passim.

10. IVOVSS, vol. 4, p. 194.

11. Ibid.

12. For example: Rokossovsky, op. cit., passim; M. I. Semiriaga, *Antifashitskie Narodnye Povstaniia* [*National Uprisings against Fascists*]. Moskva: Nauka, 1965, pp. 49 – 93; S. G. Poplavskii, *Tovarishchi v Bor'be* [*Comrades in Battle*]. Moskva: Voennoe Izdatel'stvo Ministerstva Oborony SSSR, 1963, passim.

13. IVOVSS, Vol. 4.

14. AMD USSR, Set 'KGND, No. 178 542 SS. Vol.12, pp. 21 – 2' as cited by Kazimierz Sobczak, 'Kilka Uwag o Zamierzeniach Dowodztwa Radzieckiego w Rejonie Warszawy w Lecie 1944' ['Some Comments Concerning the Intentions of the Soviet Command in the Region of Warsaw in the Summer of 1944'], *Najnowsze Dzieje Polski*, Warsaw, Vol. 11, 1967, p. 90.

15. Ibid.

16. Ibid. n. 20.

17. A. M. Samsonov, *Osvobozhdenie Belorussii, 1944* [*Liberation of Byelorussia, 1944*]. Moscow: Nauka, 1970, p. 98. I am grateful to Mr. Andrzej Pomian for calling my attention to Marshal Vasilevsky's statement.

18. Sobczak, *Najnowsze Dzieje Polski*, Vol. 11, 1967, pp. 91 – 2.

19. Makarenko in *Pravda*, 2 Aug 1944.

20. Adam Broner, Polish noncommissioned officer, deputy platoon commander and political instructor, 8th Infantry Rgt, I Polish Army (under Soviet command). Interview: Princeton, 2 Aug 1972.

21. Letters from General Zygmunt Berling to the author, 14 May 1969; 28 Oct 1969.

22. V. I. Vysotskii *et al.*, *Gvardeiskaia Tankovaia* [*The Guard Tank Unit*]. Moscow: Voennoe Izdatel'stvo Ministerstva Oborony SSSR, 1963, pp. 128 – 34; Akademiia Nauk SSSR. Institut Istorii. *SSSR v Velikoi Otechestven-*

noi Voine 1941–1945: Kratkaia Khronika [*The USSR in the Great Patriotic War, 1941–1945: A Short Chronicle*]. Moskva: Voennoe Izdatel'stvo Ministerstva Oborony SSSR, 1964, pp. 354–5; 380–4.

23. IVOVSS, Vol. 4, p. 244.

24. Combat Order No. 23, 2nd Guard Tank Army, dated 1 Aug 1944 at 4.10 a.m. AMD USSR, Set 307, No. 4178, vol. 31, pp. 46–7. Cited in Wlodzimierz Woloszyn, *Na Warszawskim Kierunku Operacyjnym: Dzialania 1 Frontu Bialoruskiego i 1 Armii WP 18.VII—23.IX. 1944* [*On the Operational Sector of Warsaw: Actions of the First Byelorussian Front and the First Polish Army, 18 July to 23 September 1944*]. Warsaw: Wydawnictwo Ministerstwa Obrony Narodowej, 1964, p. 66, n. 91.

25. For a detailed discussion based on Soviet primary data concerning the struggle of the Soviet Second Armoured Army in the approaches to Warsaw, see ibid. pp. 70–3.

26. IVOVSS, Vol. 4, p. 244.

27. Ibid. For supporting statistical data concerning difficulties and achievements of the Byelorussian Front see Wincenty Iwanowski, 'Operacja Bialoruska Armii Radzieckiej 1944 r.' ['Byelorussian Operations of the Soviet Army in 1944'], *Wojskowy Przeglad Historyczny*, Warsaw, No. 1, 1960, particularly p. 90 explaining difficulties in supplies; *contra* Soviet Marshal Konev, Commander of the First Ukrainian Front on Polish soil, emphasized the efficiency and sufficiency of supplies. I. S. Konev, *Zapiski Komanduiushchego Frontom, 1943–1944* [*Memoirs of the Front Commander, 1943–1944*]. Moskva: Nauka, 1972, passim.

28. IVOVSS, Vol. 4, p. 244.

29. Ibid. p. 232.

30. AMD USSR, Set 233, No. 2307, Vol. 34, pp. 1–2, as cited by Sobczak, *Najnowsze Dzieje Polski*, Vol. 11, 1967, pp. 93–4. See also Woloszyn, op. cit.,

pp. 78–9, n. 117.

31. *Pravda*, No. 194, 13 Aug 1944; *Izvestia*, No. 192, 13 Aug 1944.

32. Andrzej Pomian (Mikolaj Dowmuntt), Captain AK. Interview: Washington, DC, 17 Jan 1968. Addendum: 12 Nov 1969.

33. Alexander Werth, op. cit., pp. 876–8.

34. Ibid. p. 878.

35. Rokossovsky, op. cit., p. 262.

36. Ibid. p. 261.

37. Marshal Rokossovsky's statement, *Le Monde*, 27 April 1955. General Bor referred to this statement as a 'lie'.

38. Boris Olshansky, 'The Rokossovski Enigma: Ten Years after the Tragic Warsaw Uprising', *The New Leader*, 27 Sept 1954, pp. 20–1.

39. Radio Free Europe, Special Programme, No. 2580, 8 Aug 1964.

40. Chuikov, op. cit., passim.

41. S. Shtemenko, General, 'Na Drodze Do Zwyciestwa' ['On the Road to Victory'], *Zeszyty Historyczne*, Paris, Instytut Literacki, No. 19, 1971, pp. 36–63; S. Shtemenko, 'Pered Udarom w Belorussii' ['Before the Offensive in Byelorussia'], *Voenno-istoricheskii Zhurnal*, Moscow, No. 9, 1965, pp. 44–59.

42. Shtemenko, *Zeszyty Historyczne*, No. 19, 1971, pp. 36–63; For Soviet view see: Akademiia Nauk SSSR. Institut Istorii. *SSSR v Period Velikoi Otechestvennoi Voiny (1941–1945gg): Ukazatel' Dissertatsii i Avtoreferatov* [*The Soviet Union during the Time of the Great Patriotic War (1941–1945): Guide to Dissertations and Reports*]. Moskva: 1963, 41 pp.; Akademiia Nauk SSSR. Institut Slavianovedeniia. *Istoriia Pol'shi* [*A History of Poland*]. Moskva: Nauka, Dopelnitel'nyi tom, 1965, 582 pp.; Ivan Dmitrievich Kuntiuba, *Sovetsko–Pol'skie Otnosheniia 1939–1945gg.* [*Soviet–Polish Relations 1939–1945*] Kiev: Izdatel'stvo Kievs-

kogo Universiteta, 1963, 206 pp.; Komisariat Ludowy Sprawiedliwosci ZSRR. *Sprawozdanie Sadowe w Sprawie Organizatorow, Kierownikow i Uczestnikow Polskiego Podziemia w Zapleczu Armii Czerwonej na Terytorium Polski, Litwy oraz Obwodow Zachodnich Bialorusi i Ukrainy* [*Minutes of the Court Proceedings Concerning the Organizers, Leaders, and Participants of Polish Underground in the Rear of the Red Army on the Polish and Lithuanian Territory and Western Areas of Byelorussia and Ukraine*], passim; Polska Zjednoczona Partia Robotnicza. Komitet Centralny. Zaklad Historii Partii. *Pol'skoe Rabochee Dvizhenie v Gody Voiny i Gitlerovski Okkupatsii* [*Polish Workers' Movement: During the War and Hitler's Occupation*]. Moscow: Izd-vo Polit. Lit-ry, 1968, 454 pp.; Stalin, *Perepiska Predsedatelia Soveta Ministrov SSSR s Prezidentami SSha i Prem'er Ministrami Velikobritanii vo Volikoi Otechestvennoi Voiny 1941–1945gg.* [*Correspondence Between the Chairman of the Council of Ministers of the USSR., the President of the United States, and the Prime Minister of Great Britain during the Great Patriotic War of 1941 – 1945*], 2 vols, passim; *Vneshniaia Politika Sovetskogo Soiuza v Period Otechestvennoi Voiny: Dokumenty i Materialy* [*Foreign Policy of the Soviet Union During the Patriotic War: Documents and Materials*]. Moskva: Gospolitizdat, 1944 – 1947, 3 vols.

For the view of the Polish Government-in-Exile see: Poland. Ministerstwo Informacji. *Territory, Population, and Legal Status of the German and Soviet Occupations of Poland.* Angers, France: March 1940, 11 pp.; Poland. Ministerstwo Spraw Zagranicznych. *Stosunki Polski – Sowieckie od Wrzesnia 1939 do Kwietnia 1943: Zbior Dokumentow* [*Polish – Soviet Relations from September 1939 to April 1943: Collection of Documents*]. Najscislej tajne – Top secret.) London: 1843, 317 pp.; Poland, Polish Government-in-Exile, Council of Ministers. *Facts and Docu-*

ments Concerning Polish Prisoners of War Captured by the USSR During the 1939 Campaign. (Strictly confidential.) London: 1946, 454 pp.; Polish Government-in-Exile, Ministry of Foreign Affairs. *Stosunki Polski – Sowieckie od Kwietnia 1943 – Wrzesnia 1946* [*Polish – Soviet Relations from April 1943 – September 1946*]. Top Secret. Collection of Documents: 399 documents, telegrams, statements, etc. London: The Archives of the Polish Underground Movement (1939–1945) Study Trust, London. Deposit No. 11; Poland, Polish Government-in-Exile. *Official Documents Concerning Polish – German and Polish – Soviet Relations 1933–1939.* London and Melbourne: Hutchinson & Co. Ltd, 1940, 222 pp.; *Protocols from Discussions at the J. Pilsudski Institute in London on the Subject of the Uprising of Warsaw, Fighting of AK and the Attitude of the Soviet Union.* In Polish. Mimeographed. 1950, 4 sets. File B II, The Archives of the Polish Underground Movement (1939–1945) Study Trust, London; Sikorski Historical Institute. *Documents on Polish – Soviet Relations, 1939–1945.* London: Heinemann, Vol. 1, 1961, and Vol. 2, 1967.

For the Polish People's Republic view, see: Polska Akademia Nauk. Wydzial Nauk Spolecznych. *Sesja Naukowa Poswiecona Wojnie Wyzwolenczej Narodu Polskiego 1939–1945* [*Scientific Session Dedicated to the War of Liberation of the Polish Nation, 1939–1945*]. Warsaw: Wydawnictwo Ministerstwa Obrony Narodowej, 1959, 651 pp.; Polska Zjednoczona Partia Robotnicza. Komitet Centralny. Zaklad Historii Partii. *Ksztaltowanie sie Podstaw Programowych Polskiej Partii Robotniczej w Latach 1942–1945: Wybor Materialow i Dokumentow* [*Polish United Workers Party. Central Committee. Department of the Party's History. The Forming of the Fundamental Programme of the Polish Worker's Party During the Year 1942–1945: A Selection of Materials and Documents*]. Warsaw: Ksiazka i Wiedza, 1958, 590 pp.; Polska Zjednoczona Partia Robotnicza. Komitet Centralny. Zaklad Historii Partii. *Publicystyka Zwiazku Patriotow Polskich, 1943–1944: Wybor* [*The Political Journalism of the Union of Polish Patriots, 1943–1944: A Selection*]. Warsaw: Ksiazka i Wiedza, 1967, 445 pp.; Wojskowy Instytut Historyczny. *Wojna Wyzwolencza Narodu Polskiego w Latach 1939–1945* [*The War of Liberation of the Polish Nation 1939–1945*]. Warsaw: Wydawnictwo Ministerstwa Obrony Narodowej, 1966, Vol. I, 881 pp., and Vol. II, Maps and Tables.

For scholarly analysis, see: Jan M. Ciechanowski. *Powstanie Warszawskie* [*Uprising of Warsaw*]. London: Odnowa, 1971, 399 pp.; Jan M. Ciechanowski, 'The Political and Ideological Background of the Warsaw Rising, 1944', University of London Doctoral Dissertation, 1968; Matthew Philip Gallagher, 'Soviet Interpretations of the Second World War: The Official Line and Unofficial Views', Harvard University Doctoral Dissertation, 1959–60; Nish A. Jamgotch, Jr, 'Eastern Europe as a Soviet Core Interest', Claremont Graduate School Doctoral Dissertation, 1963–4; Kastsaros Thomas, 'Anglo-Soviet Relations During World War II with Special Reference to Europe', New York University Doctoral Dissertation, 1963–4; Benjamin Mackall May, Jr, 'Themes of Soviet War Propaganda 1941–45', Yale University Doctoral Dissertation, 1957–8; Benjamin Frederick Misse, Jr, 'The Loss of Eastern Europe, 1938–46', University of Illinois Doctoral Dissertation, 1964–5; Edward J. Rozek, *Allied Wartime Diplomacy: A Pattern in Poland*. New York: John Wiley & Sons, Inc., 1958, 481 pp.; Edward Jozef Rozek, 'Soviet–Polish Relations, 1939–47: A Case Study of Soviet Foreign Policy', Harvard University Doctoral Dissertation, 1955–6; Andrzej J. Wojcik, 'Attitudes of Certain Western Public Communication Media Toward the Polish Frontier Issues, 1939–44', Columbia University Doctoral Dissertation, 1960–1.

43. Shtemenko, *Zeszyty Historyczne*, No. 19, 1971, pp. 36–63.
44. Ibid.
45. Ibid.

Chapter 5. Diplomacy: Tehran

1. Irena Milko-Wieckowska (Wierzbicka), 2nd Lieutenant, combat messenger, AK. Interview: Philadelphia, 10 Nov 1966.

2. Great Britain. *Documents Concerning German–Polish Relations and the Outbreak of Hostilities between Great Britain and Germany on September 3, 1939. Presented by the Secretary of State for Foreign Affairs to Parliament by Command of His Majesty*. London: His Majesty's Stationery Office, 1939, Misc. No. 9 (1939), Cmd. 6106, p. 36.

3. US House of Representatives. *Message of President Roosevelt to the Congress, August 21, 1941. Embodying Text of the Atlantic Charter*. 77th Congress, 1st Session, 1941. Washington: Government Printing Office, 1941, Doc. No. 358.

4. Count Edward Raczynski, *In Allied London: The Wartime Diaries of the Polish Ambassador Count Edward Raczynski*. London: Weidenfeld & Nicolson, 1962, p. 100.

5. Ibid p. 111.

6. Anthony Eden, *The Reckoning*. London: Cassell, 1965, pp. 335–45.
7. Ibid. pp. 370–2 (via Lord Halifax).
8. Winston S. Churchill, *The Second World War: The Hinge of Fate*. Boston: Houghton Mifflin Company, 1950, p. 327. See also Churchill–Stalin exchange, pp. 328–9, for evidence that all Soviet frontiers in the west were involved, including Poland.
9. Eden, op. cit., p. 432.
10. US Department of State. *Foreign Relations of the United States Diplomatic Papers: The Conference at Cairo and Tehran 1943*. Washington, DC: United States Government Printing Office, 1961, no vol., Publication No. 7601, p. 15. To be cited as FRUS.
11. Leon Mitkiewicz, *Z Gen. Sikorskim na Obczyznie* [*In Exile with General Sikorski*]. Paris: Dokumenty, Instytut Literacki, 1968, p. 127.
12. Eden, op. cit., pp. 380–1.
13. Churchill, *The Hinge of Fate*, p. 327.
14. Raczynski, op. cit., pp. 140–1.
15. Eden, op. cit., p. 468.
16. Ibid. p. 482.
17. Ibid.
18. Ibid.
19. Ibid. p. 496.
20. Ibid. pp. 489–90.
21. Ibid. p. 496.
22. FRUS, 1943, no vol., Publication No. 7601, pp. 594–696.
23. In all, more than 50 items that appear in the American version are absent from the Soviet version. Robert Beitzell, ed., *Tehran, Yalta, and Potsdam: The Soviet Protocols*. Hattiesburg, Mississippi: Academic International, 1970, p. iv.
24. Charles E. Bohlen. *Witness to History 1929–1969*. New York: W. W. Norton & Company, Inc., 1973, pp. 144, 152.
25. Edward R. Stettinius, *Roosevelt and the Russians: The Yalta Conference*. Garden City, New York: Doubleday & Co. Inc., 1949, pp. 269–71. According to Charles Bohlen who was present, 'At Teheran Hopkins' influence on Roosevelt was paramount.' Charles E. Bohlen, *Witness to History 1929–1969*, p. 148.
26. Robert E. Sherwood, *Roosevelt and Hopkins: An Intimate History*. New York: Harper & Brothers, 1948, pp. 280, 216.
27. Harry L. Hopkins Papers, Box 142 at the Franklin Delano Roosevelt Library in Hyde Park, New York. To be cited as H. L. Hopkins Papers.
28. Ibid.
29. See Dr Lubin's letter to Roosevelt, 31 Jan 1945, concerning Mr Jan Stanczyk, former Minister of Labour in the Polish Government-in-Exile in London. Roosevelt Papers, Pres. Sec. File, Executive office, Lubin, Dr Isadore.
30. Presidential Secretary File, Box 51, Poland folder 1–44 at the Franklin Delano Roosevelt Library in Hyde Park, New York. To be cited as Roosevelt Papers.
31. Ibid.
32. Ibid.
33. Ibid.
34. Ibid
35. Ibid.
36. The quotation is from Professor Kennan's letter of 8 July 1973 to the author, cited here with his permission.

George F. Kennan, Professor, Institute for Advanced Study, Princeton. Minister-Counsellor, US Embassy, Moscow, 1944–6; US Foreign Service Officer 1927–53; Ambassador to Yugoslavia, 1961–3. Interview: Princeton, 30 May 1972 (see Appendix C).

For other relevant statements by Kennan on the subject of the Uprising, consult George F. Kennan, *Memories 1925–1950*, pp. 199–215. For background and interpretation of the American–Soviet relations, see the following by the same author: *American Diplomacy 1900–1950*. Chicago, Illinois: University of Chicago

Press, 1952, 154 pp.; *On Dealing with the Communist World.* New York: Harper & Row, 1964, 57 pp.; *Realities of American Foreign Policy.* Princeton, New Jersey: Princeton University Press, 1954, 120 pp.; *Russia, the Atom and the West.* New York: Harper & Brothers, n.d., 116 pp.; *Russia and the West under Lenin and Stalin.* Boston: Little, Brown & Company, 1961, 411 pp.; *Soviet Foreign Policy 1917–1941.* Princeton, New Jersey: D. Van Nostrand Company, Inc., 1960, 192 pp.; and pertinent articles.

37. For a summary of the attitudes of all parties involved, see, J. K. Zawodny, *Death in the Forest: Story of the Katyn Forest Massacre.* Notre Dame: Notre Dame University Press, 1962 and 1972, 235 pp. Also published under the same title, London: Macmillan, 1971.

38. Eden, op. cit., p. 508.

39. Ibid.

40. 397 H. C. Deb (5th ser.) 697–698 (1944).

41. Marian Kukiel, Major-General, Minister of National Defence, the Polish Government-in-Exile. Interview: London, 10 May 1965.

42. Ibid.

43. Sir Owen O'Malley to Mikolajczyk, 3 Jan 1944, Mikolajczyk Papers, File Rozmowy Polityczne 'E i RWB'.

44. Raczynski, op. cit., p. 207.

45. Ibid. p. 218.

46. Council of National Unity and the Government Delegate in Poland to Prime Minister Mikolajczyk, radio message, 9 Mar 1944. Mikolajczyk Papers, File Kraj.

47. Raczynski, op. cit., p. 198.

48. Mikolajczyk Papers, File Rozmowy K. 1944, Prof. Grabski's handwritten notes, also loose typewritten pages. See also Stanislaw Kirkor, 'Urywek Wspomnien' ['Fragments of Memories'], *Zeszyty Historyczne,* Paris, Instytut Literacki, No. 18, 1970, pp. 99–108; Stanislaw Kirkor, 'Rozmowy Polsko-Sowieckie w 1944 Roku' ['Polish–Soviet Discussions in 1944'], *Zeszyty Historyczne,* Paris, Instytut Literacki, No. 22, 1972, pp. 41–64.

49. Stanislaw Mikolajczyk, *The Pattern of Soviet Domination.* London: Samson Low, Marston & Co. Ltd, 1948, p. 72.

50. Mr Hull told this to Mr Henry J. Morgenthau, Jr, the US Secretary of the Treasury. Subsequently Morgenthau reported this to Roosevelt on 19 Aug 1944. Morgenthau's Presidential Diary, p. 1386, at the Franklin Delano Roosevelt Library in Hyde Park, New York. To be cited as Morgenthau Presidential Diary.

According to Charles Bohlen, Roosevelt's interpreter at Tehran, 'Roosevelt had no position papers on questions that would be discussed. It was my first experience with Roosevelt's informal method of operation. He did not like any rules or regulations to bind him. He preferred to act by improvisation rather than by plan.' Bohlen also mentioned that there was no possibility of Stalin's misunderstanding Roosevelt. Bohlen, op. cit., pp. 136, 138, n. 1.

51. *Dziennik Ustaw RP, 1944* [*Statutes at Large of Polish Government, 1944*], No. 1, enclosure, 22 July 1944.

52. Ibid.

53. Ibid.

54. Ibid.

55. Wojskowy Instytut Historyczny, Centralne Archiwum Wojskowe. *Organizacja i Dzialania Bojowe Ludowego Wojska Polskiego W Latach 1943–1945: Wybor Materialow Zrodlowych* [*Organization and Combat Activities of Polish People's Army, 1943–1945: Selected Materials*]. Warsaw: Ministerstwo Obrony Narodowej, vol. 4, 1962, pp. 272–3.

56. Ibid. pp. 273–5.

57. Ibid. p. 275.

58. Ibid. p. 273.

59. Harriman to the President and the Secretary of State, radio message,

7 June 1944. Declassified 18 Feb 1972. Roosevelt Papers; Pres. Sec. File No. 53; Diplomatic Correspondence, Russia 1944–1945.

60. Ibid.

61. Ibid., Harriman to the President and the Secretary of State, radio message, 12 June 1944. Declassified 18 Feb 1972. Roosevelt Papers; Pres. Sec. File No. 53; Diplomatic Correspondence, Russia 1944–1945. See also W. Averell Harriman and Elie Abel, *Special Envoy to Churchill and Stalin 1941–1946*. New York: Random House, 1975, pp. 336–8, 333–4, 338–49.

62. Roosevelt Papers; Pres. Sec. File No. 53; Diplomatic Correspondence, Russia, 1944–5.

63. Ibid.

64. Ibid.

65. Ibid.

66. Ibid.

67. FRUS, 1944, Vol. 3, pp. 1364–5. See Appendix D for the full citation of Roosevelt's statement concerning his abandonment of Lithuania's independence.

68. For summary of this meeting on 18 July 1944, see Polish Institute and Sikorski Museum, London, File Prezydium Rady Ministrow, L. 49. The Institute to be cited as PISM.

69. Lord Moran, *Churchill: Taken from the Diaries of Lord Moran*. London: Constable; Boston: Houghton Mifflin Company, 1966, pp. 213–15.

70. Stanislaw Mikolajczyk (Stem), Prime Minister, the Polish Government-in-Exile. Interviews: Princeton, 31 Mar 1957; Washington, DC, 26 June 1965 and 14 Dec 1965. Also Mikolajczyk, op. cit., pp. 78–9. Translation from Mikolajczyk Papers, File Moskwa I, vol. 64.

71. Mikolajczyk, op. cit., pp. 78–9.

72. Mikolajczyk Papers, File Moskwa I, vol. 64.

73. Ibid., Romer.

74. Ibid.

75. Ibid.

76. Ibid.

77. Harriman to the President and the Secretary of State, radio message, Moscow, 1 Aug 1944. Roosevelt Papers, Pres. Sec. File, Box 51, Poland.

78. FRUS, 1944, Vol. 3, pp. 1313–15.

79. Ibid.

80. Sikorski Historical Institute. *Documents on Polish–Soviet Relations, 1939–1945*. London: Heinemann, vol. 2, 1967, p. 309. To be cited as DPSR.

81. British Ambassador Sir Archibald Clark Kerr to Polish Minister of Foreign Affairs Tadeusz Romer, letter, Moscow, 2 Aug 1944. Mikolajczyk Papers, File Moscow I and II.

82. FRUS, 1944, Vol. 3, p. 1428.

83. During his visit to Washington, Mikolajczyk presented a memorandum to the American Government requesting $97 million to supply Armia Krajowa. FRUS, 1944, vol. 3, p. 1363, n. 67; Mitkiewicz Dossier, encl. 70 L. dz. 620/44.

84. Ibid. p. 1370.

85. DPSR, p. 323.

86. Ibid. p. 324.

87. FRUS, 1944, Vol. 3, pp. 1373–4.

88. Ibid.

89. DPSR, p. 339.

90. Harriman to the President and the Secretary of State, radio message, 10 Aug 1944. Declassified 18 Feb 1972. Roosevelt Papers; Pres. Sec. File No. 53; Diplomatic Correspondence, Russia 1944–5.

91. Ibid.

92. President to Under-Secretary of State, memorandum, 13 Aug 1944, on White House stationery signed 'FDR'. Roosevelt Papers, Map Room Papers, Box 6.

93. Mikolajczyk Papers, File Moskwa I, vol. 64.

94. Ibid.

95. Ibid.

96. Mikolajczyk, interview.

97. For details, see Hugh Trevor-Roper, *The Philby Affair: Espionage, Treason, and the Secret Service.* London: William Kimber, 1968, pp.

15–100. (British assistance to the American flight to Warsaw in Sept 1944 was known in British circles by the codeword 'Philby'. Was that a coincidence?)

Chapter 6. Diplomacy: Aftermath of Tehran

1. APUMST, Bor's enclosure No. 1 to radio message L. dz. 2100, ibid., dated 20 Nov 1943.

2. APUMST, the Polish Government's Instruction to General Bor, radio message L. dz. 5989, dated 27 Oct 1943; dispatched 1 Nov 1943.

3. APUMST, Bor to Commander-in-Chief, radio message L. dz. 2100/44, 24 and 26 Nov 1943; see also Bor's radio message to AK units in eastern Poland L. dz. 5060/44, 28 Nov 1943.

4. Ibid. L. dz 2100.

5. Janusz Bokszczanin (Obar, Sek), Colonel, Chief of Operations, Supreme HQ of AK. Interview: Paris, 21 May 1965.

6. APUMST, Bor to Commander-in-Chief, radio message L. dz. 7648/44, 31 Aug 1944.

7. Ibid.

8. Z. S. Siemaszko, 'Najwyzszy Czas Mowic Glosno' ['It's Time to Speak Aloud'], *Kultura*, Paris, Instytut Literacki, Nos 1 and 2, 1972, p. 202. Compare with Nikola Prokopiuk, 'Z Dzialalnosci Radzieckich Oddzialow Rozpoznawczo-Dywersyjnych na Terenie Polski w Latach 1944–1945' ['Combat Activities of the Red Army Intelligence-Sabotage Units on Polish Territory, 1944–1945'], *Wojskowy Przeglad Historycznny*, Warsaw, No. 1, Jan – Mar 1968, pp. 235–65.

9. Ibid., Siemiaszko, p. 202.

10. AK, pp. 627–8.

11. PISM, File Prezydium Rady Ministrow No. 7, radio message from the commander of the 27th AK Division. Arrests took place on 21 Sept 1944.

12. AK, passim.

13. APUMST, File Soviet Attitude toward AK; see also Bor to Commander-in-Chief in London, radio message L. dz. 8114, 9 Sept 1944.

14. Jozef Garlinski, *Miedzy Londynem i Warszawa* [*Between London and Warsaw*]. London: Gryf Publications Ltd, 1966, p. 89.

15. Z. Szyleyko, 'Meldunek z Kresow' ['Report from Eastern Poland'], *Biuletyn Informacyjny*, London, No. 49, Aug 1972, p. 8.

16. Ibid.

17. T. Klimowski, ' "Powstanie Warszawskie" J. Ciechanowskiego' ['J. Ciechanowski's "Warsaw Uprising" '], *Biuletyn Informacyjny*, London, No. 49, Aug 1972, p. 14.

18. Jozef Modrzejewski (Sep, Leon, Karol, Lis, Prawdzic), Major, commander of Jaslo District, inspector of Krosno District, AK. Interview: Philadelphia, 27 Feb 1967.

19. Ibid.

20. APUMST, File Soviet Attitude toward AK, Zywiec to Prom, radio message No. 88/XXX/555, 12 Sept 1944.

21. FRUS, 1944, Vol. 3, pp. 1363–6.

22. Ibid.

23. Ibid.

24. Ibid.

25. Ibid. p. 1366.

26. PISM, File Oddzial Specialny Sztabu Naczelnego Wodza, Kolekcja 17/2, f. 1/4. 21 June 1944.

27. Memorandum by the Assistant Chief of the Division of Eastern European Affairs Elbridge Durbrow. FRUS, 1944, Vol. 3, pp. 1369–70.

28. Top Secret, Mikolajczyk · to

Churchill, letter, 21 Feb 1944. Mikolajczyk Papers, File VI.

29. Tadeusz Romer, 'Report to the Minister of Foreign Affairs of the Polish Government-in-Exile, T. Romer, Concerning the Diplomatic Activities in London with Regard to Assistance to Fighting Warsaw, 6 October 1944.' File of the Polish Minister of Foreign Affairs, Position 172, pp. 262–79. Typescript in Polish. Copy: APUMST, London. To be cited as Romer.

30. Mitkiewicz, *W Najwyzszym Sztabie Zachodnich Aliavtow* [*With the Combined Chiefs of Staff of the Western Allies*], p. 190. It was impossible to secure the original transcript of the Tatar–Marshall conversations. (United States of America, General Service Administration, National Archives and Records Service, letter, 26 March 1973; also George C. Marshall Research Foundation, letter, 28 Nov 1972.) Gen. Tatar wrote that he was against 'fighting in large cities.' Yet, he continues . . . when the decision was made in Warsaw, I did everything possible, in my post [in London] to support it. . . .' Letter from Gen. Stanislaw Tatar to the author, 1 Nov 1969.

31. Wladystaw Onacewicz. 'Komentarze. . . .' *Zeszyty Historyczne*, 1970, No. 18, p. 178.

32. Leon Mitkiewicz, 'Kulisy Powstanie Warszawskiego' ['Informal Background of the Uprising of Warsaw'], typescript in Polish made available to the author by Col. Mitkiewicz. New York, 1967, pp. 18–19.

Leon Mitkiewicz (Prus), Colonel, Representative of the Commander-in-Chief of the Polish forces to the Combined Chiefs of Staff in Washington, DC, and Deputy Chief of Staff of the Polish Forces. Interview: New York, 30 Mar 1968.

33. Mitkiewicz, interview.

34. A dossier concerning Poland and the Combined Chiefs of Staff that contains photostatic copies of 99 documents dated between 1 Apr 1943 and 3 Aug 1944 was given to the author by Col. Mitkiewicz.

35. Reaffirmed to Col. Mitkiewicz in personal conversation on 7 July 1944 by Brig.-Gen. H. Redman of the Combined Secretariat of the Combined Chiefs of Staff. Mitkiewicz, 'Kulisy Powstania Warszawskiego' ['Informal Background of the Uprising of Warsaw'], p. 58.

36. General Sikorski to Colonel Mitkiewicz, radio message, 20 June 1943. Ibid. p. 31.

37. Combined Secretariat, the Combined Chiefs of Staff, Washington, to Col. Leon Mitkiewicz, Polish Embassy, letter dated 23 Sept 1943 signed by H. Redman and J. R. Deane. Mitkiewicz Dossier, Enclosure 43 to L. dz. 620/44.

38. Leon Mitkiewicz, 'Powstanie Warszawskie: Z Mojego Notatnika w Washingtonie' ['The Warsaw Uprising: From My Diary in Washington'] *Zeszyty Historyczne*, Paris, Instytut Literacki, No. 1, 1962, pp. 95–156.

39. Ibid. pp. 124–5.

40. Mitkiewicz, interview and Dossier. No contradiction in interview with Gen. Kopanski: Stanislaw Kopanski, Major-General, Chief of Staff to the Commander-in-Chief, Polish Army in Exile. Interview: London, 10 May 1965. It was Gen. Kopanski's view that the Government-in-Exile was responsible for dissemination of information to AK leaders. See also Stanislaw Kopanski, *Wspomnienia Wojenne 1939–1946* [*War Memoirs, 1939–1946*]. London: Nakladem Katolickiego Osrodka Wydawniczego 'Veritas', n.d., passim.

41. Ibid. pp. 126–7.

42. Ibid. pp. 127–8.

43. Jozef Garlinski, *Politycy i Zolnierze* [*Politicians and Soldiers*]. London: Polska Fundacja Kulturalna, 1968, passim; Jozef Garlinski,

Miedzy Londynem i Warszawa [Between London and Warsaw]. London: Gryf Publications Ltd 1966, passim.

44. Combined Secretariat, the Combined Chiefs of Staff, Washington, to Col. Leon Mitkiewicz, Polish Embassy, letter dated 20 Jan 1944 signed by H. Redman and A. J. McFarland. Mitkiewicz Dossier.

45. Brig.-Gen. H. Redman of the Combined Chiefs of Staff speaking to Col. Mitkiewicz on 18 Jan 1944 in Washington, DC. Mitkiewicz, *Zeszyty Historyczne*, No. 1, 1962, p. 129.

46. Mitkiewicz, interview.

47. In 1973 *Zeszyty Historyczne* (Paris) published in several consecutive editions a series of radio messages exchanged between Generals Sosnkowski and Bor. Mr Jerzy Giedroyc (the editor of *Zeszyty*) and Mr Witold Babinski (the author of the series) were kind enough to send me the galleys in advance of publication. Thus, although acknowledging thereby *Zeszyty* as the source, I am unable to say at the time of writing in which volume the given radio message will appear. The reader should be guided by its heading and date: Babinski, Witold. *Zeszyty Historyczne* No. ?, 1973, Heading: 'Uprising', Gen. Sosnkowski to the President of Poland, letter dated 13 Aug 1944.

48. Very strongly confirmed on three occasions by Prime Minister Mikolajczyk. Stanislaw Mikolajczyk (Stem), Prime Minister, the Polish Government-in-Exile. Interviews: Princeton, 31 Mar 1957; Washington, DC, 26 June and 14 Dec 1965. Also Gen. Bor said, ' . . . Rzepecki and Okulicki, especially Okulicki, were in favour of earlier action [in Warsaw].' See author's interview with Gen. Bor in Appendix B.

49. Wladyslaw Pobog-Malinowski,- *Najnowsza Historia Polityczna Polski 1864–1945. Tom Trzeci. Okres 1939–1945 [The Latest Political History of Poland, 1864–1945. Vol. 3. Years 1939–1945]*. London: n.p., 1960, p. 612, n. 73a.

50. Capt. Babinski responded to Prof. Zawodny's query about this matter: ' . . . After seeing the Commander-in-Chief, General Okulicki acquainted himself with the documents in my possession.

'Today I am unable to enumerate all the documents that General Okulicki studied. In addition, he also had access to materials of Departments of the Commander-in-Chief's General Staff, and to those of the Command of the [Polish] Air Force [in London].

'I was not present during General Okulicki's report to the Commander-in-Chief. . . .' Letter to the author from Capt. Witold Babinski, Montreal, 24 Apr 1973.

Before his death, Gen. Kazimierz Sosnkowski *declined* to be interviewed by Prof. J. K. Zawodny on the subject of the Warsaw Uprising. (Letter from Gen. Sosnknowski from Grenada, West Indies, 18 Feb 1966.) Since the General was travelling between the West Indies and Canada at that time, Prof. Zawodny offered to meet him for an interview in New York, Washington, or Philadelphia. In fact, the General was in New York in June 1966. Gen. Sosnkowski was the only member of the Polish Government-in-Exile and of the Polish Armed Forces who refused to be interviewed. What, then, Gen. Sosnkowski told Gen. Okulicki before the latter's jump in Poland could not be ascertained. Gen. Okulicki died 24 Dec 1946. His widow was unable to shed any light on the subject (telephone conversation with the author, London, 9 Jan 1972). No one else has come forth with information. Consequently, the author does not take a position on the issue because of lack of evidence. The degree to which Generals Tadeusz Pelczynski and Leopold Okulicki influenced Gen. Bor's decision to commence the fighting in Warsaw requires further inquiry. So do the reliability and origin of Gen. Monter's initial report about Soviet presence near Warsaw. Such inquiry is chronologically beyond the scope of this study. However, see: Jan M. Ciechanowski, *Powstanie Warszawskie* [*Uprising of Warsaw*]. London: Odnowa, 1971, 399 pp.

51. Letter from Gen. Stanislaw Tatar to the author, 1 Nov 1969, Warsaw.

52. Mitkiewicz Dossier, L. dz 620/44.

53. Minutes of Special Meeting held in Room 240 of the Combined Chiefs of Staff Building on Monday, 12 June 1944 at 2 p.m. Also Memorandum: Most Secret from the Office of the Polish Representative to the Combined Chiefs of Staff, 'On the present activities of the Polish Secret Army and the German military situation on the Eastern Front presented by General Tabor, Deputy Commander-in-Chief of the Polish Secret Army, to the Combined Chiefs of Staff at the meeting held on Monday, June 12, 1944.' Also enclosure 68. Mitkiewicz Dossier, L. dz. 620/44. Also Mitkiewicz, interview; also Mitkiewicz, *Zeszyty Historyczne*, no. 1, 1962, pp. 133–4.

54. Leon Mitkiewicz *W Najwyzszym Sztabie Zachodnich Aliantow, 1943–45* [*With the Combined Chiefs of Staff of the Western Allies, 1943–45*]. London: Katolicki Osrodek Wydawniczy 'Veritas', 1971, pp. 181–2.

55. Ibid. pp. 183–5.

56. Mitkiewicz, 'Kulisy Powstania-Warszawskiego' ['Informal Background of the Uprising of Warsaw'], p. 61.

57. Mitkiewicz, *W Najwyzszym Sztabie Zachodnich Aliantow, 1943–45* [*With the Combined Chiefs of Staff of the Western Allies, 1943*], p. 195.

58. Mitkiewicz, interview; also ibid. pp. 194–5.

59. Mitkiewicz to the Chief of Staff of the Commander-in-Chief, radio message, 10 Aug 1944 (the tenth day

of the Uprising APUMST, File Gabinet Naczelnego Wodza, No. 383, L. dz. 808/44. Some constitutional questions ought to be unravelled by Poles: Who was responsible for informing Bor–his military or civilian superiors in London? It appears that neither did the job with the clarity and incisiveness which a commanding general had every right to expect. In any case Gen. Kopanski undoubtedly submitted radio messages from Col. Mitkiewicz to Gen. Sosnkowski. Intense direct radio communication was maintained by the Commander-in-Chief Gen. Sosnkowski and Gen. Bor. For explanations reflecting Gen. Sosnkowski's view consult Witold Babinski, *Przyczynki Historyczne od Okresu 1939–1945* [*Historical Supplements to the Period 1939–1945*]. London: B. Swiderski, 1967, 712 pp. Also by the same author numerous articles and documents in *Kultura; Zeszyty Historyczne* (both published in Paris) and *Wiadomosci* (London) in the post-Second World War period. For Gen. Kopanski's views consult Kopanski, *Wspomnienia Wojenne, 1939–1945* [*War Memoirs, 1939–1946*], passim; Stanislaw Kopanski, 'Concerning Radio Communication between the Chief of Staff of the Polish Forces in Exile (Gen. Kopanski) in London, and the Supreme Commander of the Polish Forces, Gen. Sosnkowski, while on Inspection Tour of the Polish Forces, Italy', typewritten memo given to the author by Gen. Kopanski on 17 May 1965, 2 pp.; Stanislaw Kopanski, 'Uwagi Gen. Kopanskiego do Ksiazki W. Babinskiego' ['General Kopanski's Comments Concerning W. Babinski's Book'], typewritten notes made available to the author by Gen. Kopanski, n.d., 15 pp. See also Jozef Srebrzynski, Deputy Commander of Communications of AK, 'Zagadnienie Lacznosci Krajowej i Zagranicznej w Okresie Konspiracji, 1940–1944' ['The Problem of Communications in the Underground and with Contacts Abroad during the Years of Conspiracy 1940–1944'], typescript in Polish, 133 pp., including supplement 'Organizacja Lacznosci' (37 pp.). Original in the Polska Akademia Nauki, Warsaw, copy in the Archives of the Polish Underground Study Trust, London.

60. Interview with Mikolajczyk, Princeton, 31 Mar 1957.

61. T. Romer, *Report of the Minister of Foreign Affairs of the Polish Government-in-Exile, T. Romer, Concerning the Diplomatic Activities in London with Regard to Assistance to Fighting Warsaw, 6 October 1944*. File of the Polish Minister of Foreign Affairs, Position 172, pp. 262–79. Typescript in Polish. Copy: Polish Underground Study Trust, London; for an excellent summary of Polish and British diplomatic efforts

concerning assistance to Warsaw see Count Edward Raczynski, *In Allied London: The Wartime Diaries of the Polish Ambassador Count Edward Raczynski*. London: Weidenfeld & Nicolson, London, 1962, pp. 303–19.

62. Romer, op. cit.

63. FRUS, 1944, Vol. 3, pp. 1385–6.

64. Ibid. pp. 1382–3.

65. British Cabinet Papers CAB 65/43; WM (44), 3. Minutes of the meeting 21 Aug 1944 at 5.30 p.m. Public Record Office. See also Secretary's Standard Files (SSF) in Cabinet Papers 65/47 and 48; also F.O. 371/39385–421; 371/39422 –433; 39434–436. For guidance see Public Record Office. *The Second World War: A Guide to Documents in the Public Record Office*. London: Her Majesty's Stationery Office, 1972, 303 pp.

Chapter 7. Air Assistance

1. Jozef Garlinski, 'Z Perspektywy 24 Lat' ['From the Perspective of 24 Years'], *Wiadomosci*, London, 24 Mar 1968, p. 4; Josef Garlinski, *Politycy i Zolnierze [Politicians and Soldiers]*. London: Polska Fundacja Kulturalna, 1968, p. 196.

2. Statement by Col. Kazimierz Iranek-Osmecki, Chief of Section II (Intelligence) of the Supreme HQ of AK at Josef Pilsudski Institute, London, 15 Sept 1950. APUMST, File BII.

3. AK, p. 661.

4. Gen. Pelczynski's statement at Jozef Pilsudski Institute, London, 15 Sept 1950. APUMST, File BII; see also Garlinski, *Politycy i Zolnierze [Politicians and Soldiers]*, p. 190.

5. Andrzej Pomian, *The Warsaw Rising: A Selection of Documents*. London: n.p., 1945, p. 1.

6. For radio messages concerning air supplies to Warsaw, consult APUMST, Files I and II, 'Radio

Messages for the Period of the Uprising of Warsaw', L. dz. 13517–83. See also n. 38 of this chapter.

7. Franciszek Kalinowski, *Lotnictwo Polskie w Wielkiej Brytanii, 1940–1945 [Polish Air Force in Great Britain, 1940–1945]*, Paris: Instytut Literacki, 1969, p. 272.

8. Ibid. pp. 267–76.

9. Ibid. p. 272. For pertinent letters to editor, see Kalinowski in *Zeszyty Historyczne*, No. 15, 1969, pp. 238–40; Garlinski, pp. 237–8; another Polish source gives the number as 16 crews and 17 planes. See Garlinski, *Politycy i Zolnierze [Politicians and Soldiers]*, p. 252.

10. Ibid. p. 277; Antoni Wejtko, 'Lotnik Poludniowo–Afrykanski o Polsce' ['A South African Flier Talks about Poland'], *Wiadomosci*, London, No. 16, 16 Apr 1961, p. 1.

11. Gen. Ludomil Rayski's oral report to Gen. Wladyslaw Anders on 5 Sept 1944 at 3 p.m. APUMST, Ar-

chive No. 2357/2.

12. APUMST, File Gabinet Naczelnego Wodza, L. dz. 6492/44, 8 Aug 1944.

13. Letters from Wing-Commander Eugeniusz Arciuszkiewicz to the author dated 28 Feb 1973 and 14 May 1973. This officer was Commander of Flight 1586 (Squadron 301) from 14 June 1944 till 6 May 1945; see also Kalinowski, op. cit., pp. 266–81.

14. Jerzy Neciuk, Warrant-Officer, Flight Engineer, Polish Air Force in Great Britain. Flew to assist the AK. Interview: 27 May 1967.

15. Ibid.

16. Capt. J. L. van Eyssen, 'Jak Lotnicy Afrykanscy Niesli Pomoc Warszawie' ['How South African Pilots Helped Warsaw'], Orzel Bialy, London, Part 1: No. 22, 1 May 1958, p. 2; No. 23, July 1958, p. 2.

17. Neciuk interview.

18. Ludomil Rayski, Air-Commodore, Pilot, Polish Air Force in Great Britain. Flew to assistance of the Uprising. Interview: London, 25 May 1967; see also Ludomil Rayski, Royal Air Force Pilot's Flying Log Book of Air-Commodore L. Rayski. (Original Log Book) in Rayski's possession.

19. Rayski, interview.

20. APUMST, File Zestaw Naczelnego Wodza pos. 210. Gen. Rayski's radio message L. dz. 7480/44, 28 Aug 1944; see also Gen. Wladyslaw Anders, 'Sprawa Powstania Warszawskiego' ['In the Matter of the Warsaw Uprising'], Wiadomosci, London, 3 Oct 1948, pp. 1–4.

21. APUMST File Stare Miasto, Tadeusz Kopszywa's testimony, p. 12.

22. Kalinowski, op. cit., pp. 272–3.

23. Leslaw M. Bartelski, Powstanie Warszawskie [The Uprising of Warsaw]. Warsaw: Iskry, 1965, pp. 109–10.

24. Mr Dobraczynski's testimony as reported, ibid.

25. PISM, File Gabinet Naczelnego Wodza.

26. Ibid.

27. APUMST, Minister of Foreign Affairs Tadeusz Romer: Report concerning assistance of Warsaw, 6 Sept 1944, p. 262.

28. APUMST, File Zrzuty Powietrzne.

29. British War Office, Top Secret letter from Sir Alan Brooke to Gen. Kazimierz Sosnkowski dated 12 Aug 1944. APUMST, File Interwencja I, pos. 38.

30. APUMST, Bor's radio message, L. dz. 6490/44, 4 Aug 1944.

31. Ibid., File Zestaw Gabinetu Naczelnego Wodza, pos. 154.

32. Ibid.

33. Ibid.

34. PISM, File Prezydium Rady Ministrow, No. 26.

35. Stanislaw Mikolajczyk (Stem), Prime Minister, the Polish Government-in-Exile. Interview:Washington, DC, 26 June 1965.

36. Minutes of the meeting of the Council of Ministers of the Polish Government (in London), 14 Aug 1944. PISM, File Posiedzenia Rady Ministrow, No. 47, p. 2.

37. Ibid., File Prezydium Rady Ministrow, No. 27.

38. For primary documentation concerning this controversial subject, consultation of the following sources is indispensable: Mikolajczyk Papers, File R M Rozmowy Polityczne Nos. 156–290, pos. 281; PISM, File Prezydium Rady Ministrow No. 27, APUMST, Polish Minister of Foreign Affairs Tadeusz Romer: Report concerning assistance to Warsaw, 6 Sept 1944; also File Interwencja: Warszawa RI and RII. For efforts of the Polish Ambassador to the British Government see: Count Edward Raczynski, In Allied London: The Wartime Diaries of the Polish Ambassador Count Edward Raczynski. London: Weidenfeld & Nicolson, 1962, pp. 303–21, 328–41. Efforts of the Polish Commander-in-

Chief Gen. Kazimierz Sosnkowski CHPPR, File 'Akcja Sztabu Naczelnego Wodza w Aprawie Pomocy Warszawie. . . .' No. 4/d; PISM, File A.XII. 1/64; Stanislaw Sosabowski, *Najkrotsza Droga [By the Shortest Route]*. London: Komitet Wydawniczy Polskich Spadoshroniarzy, 1957, pp. vii–xxix; Kazimierz Sosnkowski, *Materialy Historyczne [Historical Materials]*. London: Gryf Publications Ltd, 1966, passim.

39. APUMST, File Interwencja, Gen. Sosnkowski's radio message to Gen. Bor, 11 Aug 1944 at 4 p.m.

40. Sir John Slessor, *The Central Blue: The Autobiography*. London: Cassell, 1956; New York: Frederick A. Praeger, 1957, pp. 613–14.

41. Ibid. pp. 614–19.

42. Ibid. p. 619.

43. Air-Marshal Sir John Slessor's letter to the editor. *The Observer*, 16 Aug 1964, p. 9.

44. This expression was coined by Prof. Alicja Iwanska, an American sociologist (of Polish origin) of great sensitivity and competence in cross-cultural analysis.

45. FRUS, 1944, Vol. 3, pp. 1374–6.

46. Ibid.

47. Ibid.

48. Ibid. pp. 1376–7.

49. Harriman to the President and Secretary of State, radio message, 17 Aug 1944. Declassified 15 Feb 1972. Roosevelt Papers, Pres. Sec. File, Box 51, Poland.

50. Ibid.

51. US Secretary of State to US Ambassador Harriman in Moscow, radio message, 17 Aug 1944. Declassified 18 Feb 1972. Roosevelt Papers; Pres. Sec. File No. 53; Diplomatic Correspondence, Russia 1944–5.

52. FRUS, 1944, Vol. 3, pp. 1386–9.

53. Churchill to Roosevelt conveying Stalin's message, radio message, 18 Aug 1944. Roosevelt Papers, Map Room Papers, Box 6.

54. US Air Forces, *The Army Air Forces in World War II*, pp. 312–13.

55. Churchill to Roosevelt, radio message, 18 Aug 1944. Roosevelt Papers, Map Room Papers, Box 6.

56. Hull to Harriman, radio message, 19 Aug 1944. FRUS, vol. 3, pp. 1381–2.

57. Ibid. n. 1. For other examples of American difficulty in securing Soviet military co-operation, see the memoirs of the Head of the US Military Mission to the Soviet Government. Gen. John R. Deane, *The Strange Alliance*. New York: The Viking Press, 1957, passim.

58. Roosevelt to Churchill, radio message, 19 Aug 1944. Ibid.

59. FRUS, 1944, Vol. 3, p. 1383.

60. Ibid. p. 1385.

61. Roosevelt to Churchill, radio message, 24 Aug 1944. Roosevelt Papers, Map Room Papers, Box No. 6.

62. Churchill to Roosevelt, radio message, 25 Aug 1944. Ibid.

63. Roosevelt to Churchill, radio message, 26 Aug 1944. Ibid.

64. Winston S. Churchill, *The Second World War: Triumph and Tragedy*. London: Cassell & Co. Ltd, vol. 6, 1954, p. 124.

65. Eden, op. cit., p. 549.

66. APUMST, File Interwencja, radio message from Washington, No. 7118, 2 Sept 1944, L. dz. 1113/44.

67. Orkan to Sobol (Government Delegate Jankowski), radio message L. dz. 5082/44, 4 Sept 1944, PISM, File Archiwum Krajowe.

68. AK, pp. 857–9.

69. PISM, Memorandum 'Air Support of Uprising', Supreme Commander's Staff, Operations Branch, L. dz. 1500, A.XII.23/5, 1 Mar 1944.

70. PISM, Inspectorat Lotnictwa, Wydzial Studiow Operacyjnych, A.XII.23/5, L. dz. 69/Stud./Op./tjn./44.

71. Kalinowski, op. cit., p. 279.

72. British Cabinet Papers, CAB 65/47; WM 115(44), 2. Minutes of the meeting 4 Sept 1944 at 12.30 p.m. Public Record Office.

73. Churchill to Roosevelt, radio message, 4 Sept 1944. Roosevelt Papers, Map Room Papers, Box 7.

74. Churchill to Stalin (copy to Roosevelt), radio message, 4 Sept 1944. Ibid.

75. Roosevelt to Churchill, radio message, 5 Sept 1944. Ibid.

76. Churchill, *Triumph and Tragedy*, p. 127.

77. FRUS, 1944, Vol. 3, p. 1396.

78. FRUS, *The Conference at Quebec* (second), 1944, no Vol., Publication No. 4400−1384, pp. 198−200 and 200 n. See also pp. 181, 185−90, 194, 198, 201−6, 296, 311−12, 368, 396−9, 404−7, 407 n., 491.

79. H. L. Hopkins Papers, Box 142, Book 10. Declassified 5 May 1972.

80. Ibid. Hopkins was determined to withhold Churchill's telegrams on the subject of Warsaw from Roosevelt's eyes; for evidence, see Spaatz Papers, Box 18, Manuscript Division, Library of Congress, Washington, DC, as cited by Richard C. Lukas, 'The Big Three and the Warsaw Uprising', *Military Affairs*, Oct 1975, pp. 132 and p. 133, n. 36.

81. Jan Ciechanowski, *Defeat in Victory*. Garden City, New York: Doubleday & Co., 1947, p. 232.

82. British Cabinet Papers, CAB 65/4 7; 123(44), 9. Minutes of the meeting 18 Sept 1944 at 5.30 p.m. Public Record Office.

83. Garlinski, *Politycy i Zolnierze* [*Politicians and Soldiers*], p. 211.

84. Ibid. p. 211.

85. Kazimierz Malinowski (Mirski),

'Pomoc z Powietrza dla Walczacej Warszawy' ['Air Assistance for Fighting Warsaw'], *Tygodnik Powszechny*, Cracow, No. 43, 10 Oct 1969.

86. US Air Force, Third Bombardment Division. Operational Narrative. Mission to Warsaw, 18 Sept 1944. Signed 'Partridge'. APUMST, File Zrzuty Powietrzne.

87. Jan J. Wieckowski (Drogoslaw), 2nd Lieutenant, executive officer of a company, Old Town, AK. Interview: Philadelphia, 29 Mar 1967.

88. Stanislaw Komornicki, *63 Dni* [Sixty-Three Days]. Warsaw: Ministerstwo Obrony Narodowej, 1965, p. 40.

89. APUMST, File Zrzuty Powietrzne, Bor's radio message L. dz. 8186/44, 11 Sept 1944.

90. Ibid. Bor's radio message No. 741/VV/111, 31 Aug 1944.

91. Ibid. Radio message Baza No. 11, L. dz. 1911/44, Sept 1944.

92. Garlinski, *Politycy i Zolnierze* [*Politicians and Soldiers*], pp. 252, 219−21; AK, pp. 789−800; compare with Kalinowski, op. cit., pp. 266−81.

93. Garlinski, op. cit., p. 215.

94. US Air Forces. USAF Historical Division. *The Army Air Forces in World War II*. Prepared under the Editorship of Wesley Frank Craven (and) James Lea Cate. Chicago: University of Chicago Press, 1948−66, vol. 3, pp. 316−17.

95. Ibid.

96. From Commanding General, US Strategic Forces in Europe, London, to US Army Air Forces, France; top secret and priority radio message, 3 Oct 1944. Declassified 1 Nov 1972. Roosevelt Papers, Map Room Papers, Box 31.

Chapter 8. The Battle for Old Town

1. Karol Jan Ziemski (Wachnowski), Colonel Deputy Commander of the Uprising of Warsaw, Deputy Commander of the Warsaw

Corps of AK, Commander of the Defence of Old Town. After the war he was promoted to the rank of brigadier-general. Conversation, London, 11 May 1965. Died in London, 1974.

2. Stanislaw Balszczak (Rog), Major, Commander of Rog Sector, Old Town, Commander of 36th Infantry Regiment, AK. Interview: Chicago, 21 May 1966.

3. Stanislaw Podlewski, *Przemarsz Przez Pieklo* [*Marching through Hell*]. Warsaw: Pax, 1957, p. 399.

4. Ibid. p. 341.

5. Ibid. p. 411.

6. Lucjan Fajer, *Zolnierze Starowki: Dziennik Bojowy Kpt. Orgnistego* [*Soldiers of Old Town: The War Diary of Captain Ognisty*]. Warsaw: Iskry, 1957, p. 160.

7. Stanczyk Boleslaw (Xen). 2nd Lieutenant. Executive officer of a company. The Polish Home Army AK. Interview: Chicago, 18 May 1966.

8. Zlotnicki Witold (Witold). 2nd Lieutenant. Company Commander. The Polish Home Army AK. Interview: London, 20 Mar 1965.

9. Kozlowski, interview.

10. Tuleja, interview.

11. Kwiatkowski Bohdan (Lewar). Major. Chief of Staff Sector Warszawa–Srodmiescie. The last officer for special assignments to General Okulicki (The last commander-in-chief of the Polish Home Army AK). Interview: Chicago, 21 May 1966.

12. Tronski, Bronislaw. *Tedy Przeszla Smierc: Zapiski z Powstania Warszawskiego* [*Death Passed through Here: Notes from the Warsaw Uprising*]. Warsaw: Czytelnik, 1957, p. 230.

13. Tuleja, interview.

14. Turkowska, Irena Danuta (Danka). Combat Nurse. The Polish Home Army AK. Interview: Hamilton, Canada, 27 Aug 1966.

15. Bronislaw Tronski, *Tedy Przeszla Smierc: Zapiski a Powstania Warszawskiego* [*Death Passed through Here: Notes from the Warsaw Uprising*], p. 130.

16. Felicjan Majorkiewicz, 'Ostatnie Dni Starowki' ['The Last Days of Old Town']. *Tygodnik Powszechny*, Cracow, 28 Aug 1960, passim.

17. Antoni Przygonski, 'Armii Ludowa w Powstaniu Warszawskim na Starym Miescie' ['The People's Army in the Warsaw Uprising in the Old Town'], *Wojskowy Przeglad Historyczny*, Warsaw, No. 3, 1965, pp. 96–138, passim.

18. Rostworowski (Tomasz), Major, chaplain to the Supreme AK HQ. Interview: Rome, 15 June 1967.

19. A copy in author's possession.

20. Majorkiewicz, op. cit., passim.

21. APUMST, File Stare Miasto.

22. Podlewski, op. cit., p. 413.

23. Fajer, op. cit., p. 182.

24. Podlewski, op. cit., p. 311.

25. Ibid. p. 553.

26. Ibid.

27. Ziemski, interview: London, 11 May 1965.

28. Jan J. Wieckowski (Drogoslaw), 2nd Lieutenant, executive officer of a company, Old Town, AK. Interview: Philadelphia, 29 Mar 1967.

29. Ibid.; see also Fajer, op. cit., p. 350; Majorkiewicz, op. cit., pp. 233–42.

30. The author relied on an excellent description of this incident by Podlewski, op. cit., pp. 499–505. This story has been verified by Tadeusz Borowski ('Ireneusz'), an eyewitness who participated as Second Lieutenant and platoon commander in this action. In a conversation with the author in Los Angeles on 21 Nov 1976, he confirmed the details of this operation.

31. Majorkiewicz, op. cit., p. 238.

32. For details see ibid. pp. 298–303.

33. Tadeusz Pogorski (Morwa), MD, Commandant of a field hospital in

Old Town. Interview: Cleveland, 27 Aug 1969.

34. Helena Balicka-Kozlowska, *Mur Mial Dwie Strony* [*The Wall Had Two Sides*]. Warsaw: Ministerstwo Obrony Narodowej, 1958, p. 171.

35. Podlewski, op. cit., p. 555.

36. Irena Kwiatowska-Komorowska (Baska), 2nd Lieutenant, adjutant, secretary and liaison co-ordinator to the Commander of Old Town and 2nd in Command of the Uprising of Warsaw, Col. K. Ziemski, AK. Interview: Toronto, 26 Aug 1966.

37. Ibid.

38. Bartelski, op. cit., p. 106.

39. Personal memoirs of Mr Leszek Pawlikowski, made available to the author in Apr 1964 by Mr Witold Zlotnicki, passim.

40. Prof. Zbigniew Pelczynski of Pembroke College, Oxford University, told the author of this experience on 18 Jan 1969.

41. Chalko, interview.

42. Podlewski, op. cit., p. 414.

43. Henryk Olczak (Turtle), Corporal, Old Town, AK. Interview: Toronto, 26 Aug 1966.

44. Karol Popiel, *Na Mogilach Przyjaciol* [*On the Graves of Friends*]. London: Odnowa, 1966, p. 81.

45. Fajer, op. cit., p. 371.

46. Their names: Jerzy Stawinski, Witold Zlotnicki, and Leszek Pawlikowski. Bartelski, op. cit., p. 246.

47. Ziemski (reporting his discussion with Bor), conversation, London, 6 Jan 1972; also interview, London, 11 May 1965.

48. Bundesarchiv – Militärarchiv: H-12-9/3 bis H-12-9/9. 'Kriegstagebuch der 9. Armee mit Anlagebänden, Kartensammlungen und diversen Einzelaktenstücken' ['Daily War Reports of the 9th Army with Supplements, Collections of Maps and Diverse Single Documents'], microfilm: Records of German Field Commands, Armies, T-312, Roll 343–349. The National Archives of the United States, Washington, DC, T-312, R-346, F-7920145, 28 Aug 1944; see also Hanns von Krannhals, *Der Warschauer Aufstand 1944* [*The Warsaw Uprising, 1944*] Frankfurt am Main: Bernard & Graefe Verlag fur Wehrwenen, 1964, pp. 368–87.

49. Ziemski, interview, London, 11 May 1965.

50. APUMST, radio message from Bor No. 754/VV/999, 3 Sept 1944.

51. See Karol Ziemski (Wachnowski), 'Walczaca Starowka: Wspomniene z Powstania W Warszawie' ['Fighting Starowka: Recollections from the Warsaw Uprising'], *SPK w Kanadzie*, No. 3, July 1964, pp. 7–9.

52. Leslaw M. Bartelski, *Powstanie Warszawskie* [*The Warsaw Uprising*]. Warsaw: Iskry, 1965, p. 137.

53. Jan Dobraczynski, *W Rozwalonym Domu* [*In a Demolished House*]. Warsaw: Pax, 1969, introduction, passim.

Chapter 9. *The City under Seige*

1. Kazimierz Baginski, 'Wspomnienia z Pierwszego Okresu Powstania' ['Memories from the First Part of the Uprising'], *Nowy Swiat*, 2 Aug 1950, p.4.

2. Telephone conversation with Mr Stefan Korbonski, 10 Sept 1972. Mr Korbonski has had a distinguished career in the Polish Underground Movement and therefore is a source of valuable information. He was a Member of the Inter-Party Political Committee (the highest Polish underground authority), Oct 1939–July 1941; the Head of the Command of

General Resistance, 1941–5; since the Uprising, the Secretary of the Interior of the Polish Government (Underground), 1 September 1944–28 June 1945; Acting Deputy Prime Minister and the Head of the Polish Government (Underground), Mar 1945–28 June 1945. His writings are indispensable for understanding of the structure and processes of the Polish Government in Underground. See his books, especially *Fighting Warsaw: The Story of the Polish Underground State 1939–1945*. London: George Allen & Unwin Ltd, 1956, 495 pp.; also numerous articles in *Kultura*, Paris, 1948–53; and also especially in *Orzel Bialy*, London, July–Aug 1969, pp. 13–19. Also Stefan Korbonski (Nowak, Zielinski), Secretary of the Interior of the Polish Government. Interview: Washington, DC, 1 Jan 1968.

3. Jerzy Braun, Member of the Council of National Unity, Warsaw. Interview: Philadelphia, 29 Jan 1966.

4. Ibid.

5. Kazimierz Baginski, Vice-President of the Council of National Unity, Warsaw, Director of the Department of Internal Affairs attached to the Delegate of the Polish Government-in-Exile in Warsaw. Interview: Phoenix, 17 and 18 Apr 1966.

6. Letter from Mr Kazimierz Baginski, 15 Jan 1966.

7. Ibid.

8. APUMST, RJN, radio message, L. dz. K. 4630/44.

9. Braun, interview.

10. Conversation with Mr Stefan Korbonski, Washington, DC, 23 May 1972.

11. Baginski, interview.

12. Ibid.

13. Stanislaw Mikolajczyk (Stem), Prime Minister, the Polish Government-in-Exile Interview: Princeton, 31 Mar 1957.

14. Karol Popiel, *Na Mogilach Przyjaciol* [*On the Graves of Friends*]. London: Odnowa, 1966, p. 57.

15. Konrad Sieniewicz, Cadet, commander of a barricade, Governmental Delegate for Region I, Warszawa – Powisle, AK. Interview: Rome, 14 May 1967.

16. Popiel, op. cit., pp. 80, 103, 41, passim; *contra* AK, p. 802.

17. Unverified but reported by several sources.

18. Janina Zorawska (Joanna), Lieutenant, combat messenger and commander of women's auxiliaries in Lesnik unit, AK. Interview: London, 26 Mar 1965.

19. Jan Nowak, Zdzislaw Jezioranski (Janek, Zych), Captain, the Liaison Officer of the Supreme HQ of the AK to England, chief editor of broadcasts in English by the Polish underground radio station Lightning. Interview: Munich, 25 May 1965.

20. APUMST, File Warszawa – Srodmiescie, Lieut. Zygmunt's report, p. 5.

21. Franciszek Dziubinski (Dolega), Corporal, AK. Interview: Chicago, 19 May 1966.

22. Ewa Maria Bukowska (Wawa), 2nd Lieutenant, Instructor of women's auxiliaries, AK. Interview: London, 26 Mar 1965.

23. Zorawska, interview.

24. Witold Zlotnicki (Witold), 2nd Lieutenant, Company Commander, AK. Interview: London, 20 Mar 1965.

25. Stanislaw Komornicki, *63 Dni* [*Sixty-three Days*]. Warsaw: Ministerstwo Obroy Narodowej, 1965. p. 44.

26. Bordon Maciejewski, 'Opowiesc o Powstanczych Listach' ['The Story of Insurgents' Letters'], *Krajowa Agencja Informacyjna*, No. 11/531, 1970, pp. 4–6.

27. Ibid.

28. Jozef i Maria Czapscy, *Dwuglos Wspomnien* [*Reminiscences in Two*

Voices]. London: Polska Fundacja Kulturalna, 1965, p. 129.

29. Irena Lukomska (Dziembowska), 2nd Lieutenant, commander of a women's auxiliary unit, AK. Interview: Chicago, 17 May 1966.

30. *Biuletyn Informacyjny*, 20 Aug 1944, p. 2.

31. APUMST, File Radio Station Lightning. Monitoring Service.

32. Halina Degorska (Iga), 2nd Lieutenant, messenger, Old Town, AK. Interview: Philadelphia, 23 Feb 1967.

33. Jan J. Wieckowski (Drogoslaw), 2nd Lieutenant, executive officer of a company, Old Town, AK. Interview: Philadelphia, 29 Mar 1967.

34. Boleslaw Stanczyk (Xen), 2nd Lieutenant, executive officer of a company, AK. Interview: Chicago, 18 May 1966.

35. Grazyna Zipser (Grazyna), combat messenger, AK. Interview: New York, 31 Mar 1968.

36. APUMST, File Warszawa – Srodmiescie, Jadwiga Wojtowska's testimony, p. 3.

37. *Pamietniki Zolnierzy Baonu Zoska: Powstanie Warszawkie* [*Diaries of Soldiers of Group Zoska: Warsaw Uprising*]. Warsaw: Nasza Ksiegarnia, 1957, p. 331.

38. Maria Bisping (Ola), Lieutenant, Internal Communication Section, Supreme HQ of AK. Interview: London, 26 Mar 1965.

39. Monter, Report No. 10, 7 Aug 1944.

40. Monter, Report No. 13, 10 Aug 1944.

41. Monter, Report No. 40a, 5 Sept 1944.

42. Monter, Report No. 40b, 5 Sept 1944.

43. Tadeusz Stawski, 'Wrzesniowy Kryzys Powstania Warszawskiego' ['The September Crisis of the Uprising of Warsaw'], *Kultura*, Paris, Instytut Literacki, No. 9, 1950, p. 124.

44. APUMST, radio message L. dz. K. 5166/44, No. 122.

45. Felicjan Majorkiewicz, *Dane Nam Bylo Przezyc* [*Our Fate Was to Survive*]. Warsaw, Instytut Wydawniczy, Pax, 1972, p. 328.

46. AK, p. 683.

47. Aleksander Skarzynski, *Polityczne Przyczyny Powstania Warszawskiego* [*Political Determinants of the Warsaw Uprising*]. Warsaw: Panstwowe Wydawnictwo Naukowe, 1965, pp. 405–6.

48. Tadeusz Dolega-Kamienski (Badacz), *Powstanie Warszawskie: Kwatermistrzostwo* [*The Warsaw Uprising: The Quartermaster*]. Typescript. The author was the Chief Quartermaster of the Uprising. Jozef Pilsudski Institute of America, New York, 35 pp. Cited as Dolega.

49. Ibid. p. 4.

50. Ibid.

51. Ibid. p. 6.

52. Ibid. p. 8.

53. Ibid. p. 4.

54. APUMST, File Warszawa-Srodmiescie, Celina Mikolajczyk's report.

55. APUMST, insurgents' radio Lightning, 8 Aug 1944.

56. Letter from Mr Konrad Sieniewicz dated 11 Nov 1966.

57. Henryk Grzymala-Rosiek, 2nd Lieutenant, AK. *Wspomnienia z Okresu Powstania w 1944 roku* [*Memoirs from the Time of the Uprising, 1944*]. Typescript in the possession of Col. M. Niedzielski, Chicago, p. 4.

58. Leslaw M. Bartelski. *Powstanie Warszawskie* [*The Uprising of Warsaw*]. 2nd ed. Warsaw: Iskry, 1967, p. 186.

59. Ibid. p. 231.

60. Maria Bninska (Siostra Maria), nurse, the Polish Red Cross, Warsaw. Interview: Delray, Florida, Feb 1970.

61. Wladyslaw Furka (Emil), Private, AK. Interview: New York, 1 Apr 1968.

62. Irene Kwiatkowska Komo-

rowska (Baska), 2nd Lieutenant, adjutant, secretary and liaison coordinator to the Commander of Old Town and to second-in-command of the Uprising of Warsaw, Col. K. Ziemski. Interview: Toronto, 26 Aug 1966.

63. APUMST, Bor's radio message, VI, L. dz. 8326/44. The message was actually dispatched on 13 Sept 1944.

64. APUMST, Bor's radio message, VI, L. dz. 8798/44, 21 Sept 1944.

65. Zofia, Kukla (Krystyna, Krystyna-Zofia), Corporal, combat messenger, nurse, cook, AK. Interview: London, 26 Mar 1965.

66. Ibid.

67. APUMST, File Warszawa-Srodmiescie, Celina Mikolajeczna's testimony, pp. 4–5.

68. Stanislaw Komornicki, *Na Barykadach Warszawy* [*On the Barricades of Warsaw*]. Warsaw: Wydawnictwo/ Ministerstwo Obrony Narokowej, 1964, p. 306.

69. Stanislaw Zadrozny, *Tu-Warszawa: Dzieje Radiostacji Powstanczej Blyskawica* [*Warsaw Calling: A History of the Uprising Radio Station Lightning*]. London: Nakladem Ksiegarni Orbis, 1964, p. 60.

70. Ibid. pp. 74–5.

71. Andrzej Pomian, *Wiersze i Piesni Powstania Warszawskiego* [*Songs and Poetry of the Uprising of Warsaw*]. London: Oficyna Poetow i Malarzy, 1952, passim.

72. Ibid., passim.

73. Dolega, op. cit., *passim.*; Skarzynski, op. cit., pp. 407–9; AK, p. 68.

74. Tuleja, interview.

75. Ibid.

76. Zbigniew Chalko (Cyganiewicz I), Cadet, Platoon Commander, AK. Interview: Chicago, 17 May 1966.

77. Tadeusz Pogorski (Morwa), MD, commandant of a field hospital in Old Town. Interview: Cleveland, 27 Aug 1969.

78. Dziubinski, interview.

79. Lukomska, interview.

80. Tuleja, interview.

81. Zadrozny, op. cit., pp. 80–1.

82. Maria Bninska (Siostra Maria), Interview.

83. We are referring to the famous painting of Madonna at Jasna Gora in Czestochowa.

84. Zadrozny, op. cit., p. 91.

85. Rev. Walerian Paczek (Giermen), Lieutenant-Colonel, Memorandum submitted to the author, 31 Dec 1966, p. 4.

86. Pawel Depta (Sokol), Private, AK. Interview: Harvard University, 7 May 1968.

87. Jozef Warszawski (Ojciec Pawel), Major, chaplain to Col. Radoslaw's unit, AK. Interview: 13 June 1967.

88. Paczek, op. cit., pp. 6–7.

89. Jadwiga Gac (Jadzia), Private, combat nurse and messenger, AK. Interview: Philadelphia, 7 May 1968.

90. Dolega, op. cit., section 'Problem of Water'.

91. See n. 17 above.

92. Stanislaw Podlewski, *Przemarsz Przez Pieklo* [*Marching through Hell*]. Warsaw: Pax, 1957, p. 411.

93. Bohdan Kwiatowski (Lewar), Major, Chief of Staff of Warszawa – Srodmiescie Sector, the last officer for special assignments to Gen. Okulicki (the last commander-in-chief of AK). Interview: Chicago, 21 May 1966.

94. Mikolajczyk Papers, File Depesze Maj 1943–Listopad 30, 1944, pos. 327, radio message L. dz. K5551/ 44.

95. Marian Glowacki (Peaceful), Lieutenant, 'Notes Bojowy' ['Combat Notes'], manuscript in Polish made available to the author. London, spring 1969.

Chapter 10. The Red Army at the Gates

1. APUMST, File Radio Station Lightning. Monitoring Service, 31 Aug 1944.

2. Ibid.

3. APUMST, passim. Content analysis of Bor's radio messages to his supervisors in London.

4. APUMST, Bor's radio message O.VI. L. dz. 8025/44, 18 Sept 1944.

5. APUMST, Bor's radio message L. dz. 8025/44, 6 Sept 1944.

6. Ibid.

7. APUMST, joint radio message, L. dz. 7991/44, 6 Sept 1944.

8. APUMST, Bor's radio message No. 886/VV/iii, 26 Sept 1944.

9. APUMST, Bor's radio message No. 849/XXX/555, 19 Sept 1944.

10. APUMST, Bor's radio message No. 885/VV/999, 29 Sept 1944.

11. Signed also by Bor and the Chairman of the Council of National Unity. APUMST, radio message L. dz. 7692/44, 31 Aug 1944.

12. Signed also by the Chairman of the Council of National Unity. APUMST, radio message L. dz. 7200/44, 23 Aug 1944.

13. APUMST, Bor's radio message L. dz. 8069/44, 7 Sept 1944.

14. Wincenty Iwanowski, 'Poczatek Wielkiej Ofenzywy Radzieckiej Podczas Drugiej Wojny Swiatowej' ['The Beginning of the Great Soviet Offensive during the Second World War'], Wojskowy Przeglad Historyczny, Warsaw, No. 2, 1966, p. 121.

15. B. H. Liddell Hart, ed., The Red Army. Gloucester, Massachusetts: Peter Smith, 1968 pp. 373–4.

16. Ibid. p. 122.

17. Gen. Jerzy Bordzilowski, 'Zolnierska Droga: Czesc XV' ['The Soldier's Journey: Part XV'], Wojskowy Przeglad Historyczny, Warsaw, No. 3, 1970, p. 160.

18. Adam Borkiewicz. Powstanie Warszawskie 1944: Zarys Dzialan Natury Wojskowej. [The Uprising of Warsaw: 1944: Military Aspects]. Warsaw: Instytut Wydawniczy, Pax, 1964, pp. 353–4, n. 116, 358.

19. Kazimierz Kaczmarek, Osmy Bydgoski [The Regiment Nr. 8 from Bydgoszcz]. Warszawa: Wydawnictwo Ministerstwa Obrony Narodowej, 1962, p. 108.

20. Mikolajczyk Papers, File Warszawa.

21. Kazimierz Iranek-Osmecki (Makary, Heller, Kazimierz Jarecki), Colonel, Chief of Section II (Intelligence), the Supreme HQ of AK. Interview: London, 13 May 1965; see also AK, pp. 865–6.

22. PISM, File Prezydium Rady Ministrow, radio message from Warsaw L. dz. 8781/44, 21 Sept 1944.

23. Gen. Heinz Guderian, Panzer Leader. New York: Ballantine Books. 4th American Printing, 1967, pp. 284–5.

24. Maj.-Gen. F. W. von Mellenthin, Panzer Battles: A Study of the Employment of Armour in the Second World War. New York: Ballantine Books, 1971, p. 347.

25. Hanns von Krannhals, Der Warschauer Aufstand 1944 [The Warsaw Uprising, 1944]. Frankfurt am Main, Bernard & Graefe Verlag für Wehrwesen, 1964, p. 195.

26. Ibid. pp. 162–9.

27. Ibid. p. 166.

28. Ibid. pp. 149–50.

29. K. Rokossovsky. A Soldier's Duty. Moscow: Progress Publishers, 1972, pp. 260–1.

30. Majorkiewicz, Felicjan. Dane Nam Bylo Przezyc [Our Fate Was to Survive]. Warsaw: Instytut Wydawniczy, Pax. 1972, p. 324.

31. Report of the Rear Services of the Red Army, 26 July 1944, concerning cars, supplies and foodstuffs for the Polish Committee of National Lib-

eration, allotted and dispatched. AMD USSR, Set 67, No. 12014, vol. 100, pp. 304–5. Point No. 4: ' . . . PKWN the Polish Committee to receive 150 food rations according to classification No. 5 and 10 rations according to classification No. 1 . . . for public relations purposes.' Among these allotments were 70 bottles of wine, 20 litres of vodka, thousands of cigarettes, etc. Zbigniewicz, *Wojskowy Przeglad Historyczny*, vol. 1, 1968, pp. 347–9.

32. See particularly the editorials and Wasilewska's writings and speeches in *Wolna Polska* printed in Moscow in Polish, Nos 1, 2, 6, 9, 11, and 20, 1943.

33. 'The Pole Must Fight', *Wolna Polska*, Moscow, No. 1, 1 Mar 1943.

34. Wiktor Grosz, ibid., No. 6, 13 April 1944.

35. Stanislaw Paprocki, 'Wyciagi z Podziemnej Prasy Kommunistycznej w Kraju, z Nasluchow Radiostacji 'Kosciuszki' i Zwiazku Patriotow Polskich, Oskarzajace A.K. o Biernosc i Wzywajace do Zbrojnych Wystapien (1943–1944)' ['Excerpts from the Underground Communist Press at Home, from Monitors of the 'Kosciuszko' Radio, and the Union of Polish Patriots, Accusing the Home Army of Passivity and Calling for Organized Army Action (1943–1944)'], APUMST, B II, No. 1968. This broadcast was actually transmitted in Polish from Moscow on 5 July 1944 at 8.15 p.m. and was registered by the BBC monitoring service.

36. Ibid., broadcast in Polish from Radio Moscow on 23 July 1944 at 8.15 p.m.

37. Ibid., broadcast in Polish from Radio Moscow on 1 April 1944 8.15 p.m.

38. Margules, *Boje 1 Armii WP w Obszarze Warszawy (Sierpien-Wrzesien 1944* [*The Battles of the First Polish Army in the Area of Warsaw*

(August–September 1944)], pp. 336–7.

39. Wojskowy Instytut Historyczny, Centralne Archiwum Wojskowe. *Organizacja i Dzialania Bojowe Ludowego Wojska Polskiego W Latach 1943–1945: Wybor Materialow Zrodlowych* [*Organization and Combat Activities of Polish People's Army, 1943–1945: Selected Materials*], pp. 522–3.

40. Tadeusz Rawski, Z. Stapor, and J. Zamorski, *Wojna Wyzwolencza Narodu Polskiego w Latach 1939–1945* [*The War of Liberation of the Polish Nation during the Years 1939–1945*]. Warsaw: Wydawnictwo Ministerstwa Obrony Narodowej, 1966, p. 501, n. 28. For organization of this force, see: Waclaw Jurgielewicz, *Organizacja Ludowego Wojska Polskiego : 22. VII. 1944–9. V. 1945* [*The Organization of the Polish People's Army: 22. VII. 1944–9. V. 1945*]. Warsaw: Wojskowy Instytut Historyczny, 1968, 459 pp.; Boleslaw, Dolata, 'O Naczelnych Wladzach i Instytucjach Ludowego Wojska Polskiego w Latach 1944–1945' ['Supreme Authorities and Institutions of the Polish People's Army, 1944–1945'], *Wojskowy Przeglad Historyczny*, Warsaw, No. 4, 1964, pp. 3–54. For a diagram depicting the organization of the Polish forces under Soviet command as of 1 July 1944, see Rawski *et al.*, op cit., enclosure No. 50.

41. CHPPR, Dziennik Ustaw RP [Statute-at-Large], No. 9, Article 4, Polish Government, Angers, 30 Apr 1940, p. 29. This document acquired through courtesy of the late Mr Pawel Jankowski, Chief of Chancery of President of Poland.

42. The Soldier's Oath, Tadeusz Kosciuszko's First Polish Infantry Division, Moscow, 8 July 1943. Polska Zjednoczona Partia Robotnicza. Komitet Centralny. Zaklad Historii Partii. *Publicystyka Zwiazku Patriotow Polskich 1943–1944: Wybor* [*The Politi-*

cal Journalism of the Union of Polish Patriots, 1943–1944: A Selection]. Warsaw: Ksiazka i Wiedza, 1967, pp. 405–6.

43. *The crucial directive* seems to be from Marshal Rokossovsky (signed by the Chief of Staff at the First Byelorussian Front, Col.-Gen. Malinin) to Gen. Berling. It orders Berling's forces to 'seize eastern [opposite insurgents'] shore of Vistula river . . . to . . . reconnoitre place for forcing the river in order to establish a bridgehead on the river's western [insurgents'] shore in the region of Warsaw.' AMD USSR, Set 233, No. 2307, Vol. 179. The directive was written in Russian and dated 15 Sept 1944. Cited in Jozef Margules, *Boje 1 Armii WP w Obszarze Warszawy (Sierpien-Wrzesien 1944 [The Battles of the First Polish Army in the Area of Warsaw (August–September 1944)*]. Warsaw: Wydawnictwo Ministerstwa Obrony Narodowej, 1967, p. 464.

Other orders to be studied are: The Order of the First Byelorussian Front, 13 Sept 1944, The Archives of the Ministry of Defence USSR, Set 402, No. 15370, Vol. 4, pp. 216–17; also orders 052/OP, 053/OP, 054/Op (Woloszyn, op. cit., p. 186, n. 90); handwritten order of the commander of 125th Infantry Corps, 13 Sept 1944, ibid. p. 187, n. 95. For a detailed description of the activities of the First Polish Army near Warsaw at that time, consult ibid. pp. 159–308.

Also Margules, op. cit., passim. See also Wojskowy Instytut Historyczny, IV/1, pp. 234–5; 252–3, and the Archives of the Ministry of Defence of the USSR, Set 296, No. 15758, Vol. II, pp. 212–13 as cited in Margules, op. cit., p. 72, n. 6. Margules also encloses selected documents of the First Polish Army, Armia Krajowa and of the Soviet Commanders, pp. 331–522.

44. Jerzy Bordzilowski, General, 'Zolnierska Droga: Czesc XIII'

['The Soldier's Journey: Part XIII'], *Wojskowy Przeglad Historyczny*, Warsaw, Vol. 15, No. 1, 1970, p. 132.

45. Ibid.

46. Ibid. p. 133. See also other Soviet sources: V. I. Klokov, *Bor'ba Narodov Slavianskikh Stran Protiv Fashistskikh Porabotitelei [Struggle of People of Slavic Countries against Fascist Oppressors*]. Kiev: Izd-vo AN Ukr. SSR, 1961, p. 307; F. G. Zuev, *Pol'skii Narod v Bor'be Protiv Fashizma [Polish Nation in Combat against Fascism*]. Moscow: Nauka, 1967, pp. 126–9.

47. Kaczmarek, *Osmy Bydgoski [The Regiment No. 8 from Bydgoszcz*], p. 110.

48. Leslaw M. Bartelski, *Powstanie Warszawskie [The Warsaw Uprising*]. Warsaw: Iskry, 1965, p. 208.

49. For details, consult works by Woloszyn and Margules cited in this chapter.

50. Margules, *Boje i Armii WP w Obszarze Warszawy (Sierpien–Wrzesien 1944). [The Battles of the First Polish Army in the Area of Warsaw (August–September 1944)*], p. 311.

51. Harriman to the President, radio message, 24 Sept 1944. Roosevelt Papers, Map Room, Box 31, 052 Polish–Russian Relations (1), Sec. 2.

52. Shtemenko, *Zeszyty Historyczne*, No. 200, 1971. p. 56.

53. Komunistyczna Partia Polski. Komitet Centralny. Zaklad Historii Partii. Antoni Przygonski, *Udzial PPR i AL w Powstaniu Warszawskim [Participation of PPR and AL in the Uprising of Warsaw*]. Warsaw: Ksiazka i Wiedza, 1970, pp. 181–3.

54. Broner Adam. Noncommissioned officer. Deputy platoon commander and political instructor, 8th Infantry Rgt, I Polish Army (under Soviet command). Interview: Princeton, 2 Aug 1972.

55. Letters from Gen. Zygmunt Berling to the author, 23 Oct 1969; and also 14 May 1969.

56. Kazimierz Malinowski 'Zrzuty Radzieckie i I Armii WP' ['Soviet and First Polish Army Air Supplies'], *Tygodnik Powszechny*, Cracow, 26 Oct 1969.

57. AMD USSR, Set 233, No. 2380, Vol. 22, pp. 159–61, as cited in Fryderyk Zbigniewicz, 'Pomoc Armii Radzieckiej dla Polski w Swietle Dokumentow z Lat 1944–1945' ['The Assistance of the Soviet Army to Poland in the Light of Documents, 1944–1945'], *Wojskowy Przeglad Historyczny*, Warsaw, No. 1, 1968, p. 347. See also *Velikaia Otechestvennaia Voina Sovetskogo Soiuza 1941–1945: Kratkaia Istoriia [The Great Patriotic War of the USSR, 1941–1945: A Short History]*. Moscow: Voennoe Izdatel'stvo Ministerstva Oborony SSSr, 1965, p. 383; M. I. Semiriaga, *Vtoraia Mirovaia Voina i Proletarskii Internatsionalizm [The Second World War and Internationalism of the Proletariat]*, pp. 177–8; Fryderyk Zbigniewicz, 'Pomoc Armii Radzieckiej dla Polski w Swietle Dokumentow z Lat 1944–1945' ['The Assistance of the Soviet Army to Poland in the Light of Documents, 1944–1945'] *Wojskowy-Przeglad Historyczny*, Warsaw, No. 1, 1968, pp. 341–7.

58. Kaczmarek, *Osmy Bydgoski [The Regiment No. 8 from Bydgoszcz]*. p. 103.

59. APUMST, O.VI., Bor to Commander-in-Chief, radio message L. dz. 8619/44, 17 Sept 1944.

60. Margules, op. cit., pp. 433–44.

61. Monter's Order No. 83, 13 Sept 1944. Ibid. pp. 436–8.

62. Stanislaw Weber (Surgeon, Popiel), Lieutenant-Colonel, Chief of Staff to the Commander of the Uprising of Warsaw, AK. Interview: London, 15 May 1965.

63. Handwritten memorandum by Lt-Col. Stanislaw Weber dated 22 July 2965, London, deposited at APUMST, archive entry No. 2233/2.

64. Monter Reports, No. 60, dated 16 Sept 1944. Jerzy Kirchmayer, *et al.*, 'Meldunki Sytuacyjne "Montera" z Powstania Warszawskiego' ['General Monter's Combat Reports of the Warsaw Uprising'], *Najnowsze Dzieje Polski: Materialy i Studia z Okresu II Wojny Swiatowej*, Warsaw, Vol. 3, 1959, p. 148. Cited as Monter Reports.

65. Kazimierz Iranek-Osmecki (Makary, Heller, Kazimierz, Jarecki), Colonel, Chief of Section II (Intelligence), the Supreme HQ of AK. Interview: London, 13 May 1965.

66. Bartelski, op. cit., pp. 211–12.

67. Ibid.

68. APUMST, Bor to the Commander-in-Chief, radio message dated 17 Sept 1944.

69. *Biuletyn Informacyjny*, No. 85, 17 Sept 1944, p. 1.

70. APUMST, Monter to Zywiciel, radio message No. 161/XXX/99. 21 Sept 1944.

71. Zygmunt Zaremba, *Wojna i Komspiracja [The War and the Underground]*. London: B. Swiderski, 1957, p. 261.

72. Verified by two sources: Tadeusz Zawadzki (Zenczykowski, Kania). Captain, Chief of Propaganda, Bureau of Information and Propaganda of the Supreme HQ of AK. Interview: Munich, 25 May 1965. Stanislaw Zadrozny (Pawlicz), 2nd Lieutenant, manager of the underground radio station Lightning, AK. Interview: Munich, 25 May 1965.

73. Harriman to Roosevelt, personal and secret, radio message 24 Sept 1944. Roosevelt Papers: Pres. Sec. File No. 53.

74. British Cabinet Papers, CAB 65/4 3; 127(44), 3. Minutes of the meeting 25 Sept 1944 at 5.30 p.m. Public Record Office.

75. Ibid.

76. House of Commons, 1944, Vol. 403, p. 219.

77. British Cabinet Papers, CAB

65/48; 130(44), 3. Minutes of the   Public Record Office.
meeting 2 Oct 1944 at 5.30 p.m.   78. Ibid.

Chapter 11. Capitulation

1. It was Mr Stanislaw Sopicki who urged consideration of cessation of fighting at that time. Minister of Reconstruction of Administration Karol Popiel presented Mr Sopicki's proposal to the Council of Ministers. Stanislaw Sopicki, 'Nie Musialo Trwac 63 Dni: Uwagi o Powstaniu Warszawskim' ['There Was No Need for Sixty-Three Days of Fighting: Some Comments about the Uprising of Warsaw']. *Wiadomosci*, London, 23 Oct 1949.

2. Felicijan Majorkiewicz, *Dane Nam Bylo Przezyc* [*Our Fate Was to Survive*]. Warsaw: Instytut Wydawniczy Pax, 1972, p. 247.

This rather inflexible stand of the AK command was particularly puzzling in view of the fact that a member of Bor's own staff, Col. Jan Rzepecki, submitted to him as early as 16 Aug 1944 a briefing on attitudes and morale among the soldiers of AK and the civilian population. In it he emphasized the fact that the majority of the people saw the solution to the predicament of the Uprising 'only in the collaboration of the Governmental Delegate and Bor-Komorowski with General Berling and the Polish Committee of National Liberation'. Cited in Felicjan Majorkiewicz, *Dane Nam Bylo Przezyc* [*Our Fate Was to Survive*]. Warsaw: Instytut Wydawniczy Pax, 1972, p. 325. Yet, in the last days of Sept, Gen. Okulicki was still considering extending the fight in Warsaw 'until the middle of October'. *Drogi Cichociemnych: Opowiadania Zebrane I Opracowane Przez Kolo Spadochroniarzy Armii Krajowej* ['*Silent-in-the-Dark': Reports Collected and Compiled by the Paratroopers of the Home Army*].

London: Nakladem Katolickiego Osrodka Wydawniczego Veritas, 1961, p. 227.

3. Kazimierz Baginski, Vice-President of the Council of National Unity, Warsaw; Director of Internal Affairs attached to the Delegate of the Polish Government-in-Exile in Warsaw. Interview: Phoenix, 17 and 18 Apr 1966.

4. Leslaw M. Bartelski, *Powstanie Warszawskie* [*The Warsaw Uprising*]. Warsaw: Iskry, 1965, p. 175.

5. Wojskowy Instytut Historyczny. *Wojna Wyzwolencza Narodu Polskiego w Latach 1939–1945* [*The War of Liberation of the Polish Nation 1939–1945*]. 2nd. ed.; Warsaw: Wydawnictwo Ministerstwa Obrony Narodowej, 1966, Vol. I, p. 598, n. 16.

6. Ibid.

7. Bartelski, op. cit., p. 176.

8. Adam Borkiewicz, *Powstanie Warszawskie 1944: Zarys Dzialan Natury Wojskowej* [*The Uprising of Warsaw: Military Aspects*]. Warsaw: Instytut Wydawniczy Pax, 1964, p. 561.

9. APUMST, Bor to the Commander-in-Chief in London, radio message L. dz. 9313/44, 29 Sept 1944.

10. APUMST, Bor to subordinate AK districts outside of Warsaw (code names: Muzeum, Jokla, Chodnik via Muzeum, Barka), radio message L. dz 9514/44, 1 Oct 1944.

11. Ibid.

12. Mieczyslaw Niedzielski (Zywiciel), Colonel, Commander of Zoliborz Sector, AK. Interview: Chicago, 18 May 1966; Stanislaw Podlewski, *Rapsodia Zoliborska* [*Zoliborz Rhapsody*]. Warsaw: Pax, 1957,

passim.

13. Kazimierz Szternal (Zryw), Deputy Commander of Mokotow.

14. Ibid.

15. Ibid.

16. Bundesarchiv-Militärarchiv: H-12-9/3 bis H-12-9/9. 'Kriegstagebuch der 9. Armee mit Anlagebänden, Kartensammlungen und diversen Einselaktenstücken' ['Daily War Reports of the 9th Army with Supplements, Collections of Maps and Divers Single Documents']. Microfilm: Records of German Field Commands, Armies, T-312, Rolls 343–9. The National Archives of the United States, Washington, DC; entry 4 Oct 1944, p. 528.

17. Borkiewicz, op. cit., p. 565.

18. For official German and Polish documents concerning capitulation see: Hanns von Krannhals, *Der Warschauer Aufstand 1944* [*The Warsaw Uprising, 1944*]. Frankfurt am Main: Bernard & Graefe Verlag fur Wehrwesen, 1964, 447 pp., Doc. Nos 48, 49, 50, 51, 58, 59, 60, 61; pp. 390–2; 402–8. Also 'Dokumenty do Kapitulacji Powstania Warszawskiego' ['Documents Concerning the capitulation of the Warsaw uprising'], *Najnowsze Dzieje Polski: Materialy i Studia z Okresu II Wojny Swiatowej*. Warsaw, Panstwowe Wydawnictwo Naukowe, Vol. 4, 1960, pp. 105–59.

19. *Biuletyn Informacyjny*, 3 Oct 1944, p. 1.

20. Borkiewicz, op. cit., p. 571.

21. Stanislaw Blaszczak (Rog), Major, Commander of the Rog Sector, Old Town, Commander of the 36th Infantry Regiment, AK Interview: Chicago, 21 May 1966.

22. Stefan Korbonski's radio speech to Poland via Radio Free Europe, 1 Aug 1967.

23. Ibid.; see also 'Odezwa Wydana Przez Rade Jednosci Narodowej i Krajowa Rade Ministrow po Katitulacji Warszawy' ['An Appeal Issued by the Council of National Unity and Home Council of Ministers after the Capitulation of Warsaw'], *Glos Polski*, Toronto, 20 Aug 1964, p. 14.

24. Jan Nowak, *Monitoring of Broadcasts from Lightning (AK) and Polish Radio (Delegate of the Polish Government in London Residing in Warsaw)*. Based on materials supplies by Mr S. Uszycki, Mr K. Bogacki and Mrs Bogacka. Polish Programme, Polish Section, BBC, 7 Oct 1951, 10.30 p.m. APUMST, File A, No. 587/3(1).

25. PISM, File Ministry of Foreign Affairs, No. 159, pp. 248–9.

26. Stanislaw Zadrozny, *Tu-Warszawa: Dzieje Radiostacji Powstanczej Blyskawica*. [*Warsaw Calling: A History of the Uprising Radio Station Lightning*]. London: Nakladem Ksiegarni Orbis, 1964, passim; also Stanislaw Zadrozny (Pawlicz), 2nd Lieutenant, manager of the underground radio station Lightning. AK. Interview: Munich, 25 May 1965.

27. Stanislaw Zadrozny. *Tu-Warszawa: Dzieje Radioslacji Powstanczej Blyskawica* [*Warsaw Calling: A History of the Uprising Radio Station Lightning*], p. 105.

28. Mikolajczyk Papers, File Warszawa, note for the Prime Minister.

29. Gert Buchheit, *Hitler der Feldherr: Die Zerstörung einer Legende* [*Hitler, the Commander-in-Chief: The Destruction of a Legend*]. Rastatt: Grote, 1958, pp. 469–70.

30. *Istoriia Velikoi Otechestvennoi Voiny Sovetskogo Soiuza 1941–1945* [*A History of the Great Patriotic War of the USSR, 1941–1945*]. Moscow: Voennoe Izdatel'stvo Ministerstva Oborony SSSR, Vol. 5, 1962, pp. 602–3.

31. Churchill to Roosevelt, radio message, 3 Oct 1944. Declassified 6 May 1972. Roosevelt Papers, Map Room Papers, Box 7.

32. Mikolajczyk Papers, File Rozmowy R.W.B. No. 156 to No. 290.

33. Roosevelt Papers. File 463, Box 1, Poland 1933–45.

34. Ibid.

35. Roosevelt Papers, Pres. Sec. File, Box 74, State Department, 1944.
36. Ibid.
37. Count Edward Raczynski, *In Allied London: The Wartime Diaries of the Polish Ambassador Count Edward Raczynski*. London: Weidenfeld & Nicolson, 1962, p. 246.
38. FRUS, 1944, Vol. 3, pp. 1442–3.
39. APUMST, Mikolajczyk to 'Homeland', radio message L. dz. 2335/44, 18 Aug 1944.
40. Stalin to Mikolajczyk, letter in Russian dated 16 Aug 1944. Mikolajczyk Papers, File Rozmowy R.W.B. No. 156, No. 209, ref. 196.
41. Gen. Izydor Modelski's typewritten note to the Soviet official 'Minister Volkov' in London dated 22 Aug 1944. A copy received through courtesy of the former Minister of the Polish Government-in-Exile, Mr Karol Popiel. Mr Popiel's letter to the author, 23 June 1965.
42. Ibid.
43. Ibid.
44. Boleslaw Biega (Sanocki), Secretary of the Council of National Unity and of Steering Committee of the Council, Warsaw. Interview: New York, 31 Mar 1968.
45. APUMST, Bor to the Commander-in-Chief and the Prime Minister, radio message No. 719/XXX/555, 29 Aug 1944.
46. Adam Ciolkosz. 'Nieznane Expose' ['Unknown Expose'], *Zeszyty Historyczne*, Paris, Instytut Literacki, No. 1, 1962, p. 13.
47. CHPPR, File Archiwum Krajowe M.S.Z. No. 50/212. Mikolajczyk to Government Delegate (Jankowski), radio message L. dz. 5037/44

31 Aug 1944.
48. Adam Ciolkosz, former Minister of Polish Parliament; Member of National Council of London; Polish political leader, writer, and commentator. Interview: London, 10 May 1969.
49. Edward Puacz, 'Powstanie Warszawskie w Protokolach PKWN' ['The Uprising of Warsaw in the Minutes of PKWN'], *Zeszyty Historyczne*, Paris, Instytut Literacki, No. 10, 1966, p. 183.
50. Ibid. p. 184.
51. Ibid. p. 188.
52. Georgi K. Zhukov. *The Memoirs of Marshal Zhukov*. New York: Delacorte Press, 1971, p. 583.
53. For pertinent radio messages and reports consult APUMST, File Soviet Attitude toward AK.
54. Zhukov, *The Memoirs of Marshal Zhukov*, p. 550.
55. Rokossovsky, *A Soldier's Duty*, p. 262.
56. Semiriaga, *Antifashitskie Narodnye Povstaniia* [*National Uprisings against Fascists*], p. 77.
57. Interview with Maj. Miszczak Franciszek (Bogucki), Chief of Intelligence Section of the Polish Home Army, AK. Interview: London, 13 May 1965; see also Jan Rzepecki, *Wojskowy Przeglad Historyczny*. No. 1, 1966, pp. 427–8.
58. See Table Nos 1 and 2.
59. Semiriaga, *Antifashitskie Narodnye Povstaniia* [*National Uprisings against Fascists*], p. 77–8.
60. Rokossovsky, *A Soldier's Duty*, passim.
61. FRUS, *The Conferences at Yalta and Malta*, 1945, pp. 589 91.

Appendix A

1. Adam Borkiewicz, *Powstanie Warszawskie 1944: Zarys Dzialan Natury Wojskowej* [*The Uprising of Warsaw: Military Aspects*], passim; Jerzy Kirchmayer, *Powstanie Warszawskie* [*The Warsaw Uprising*], passim; Hanns von Krannhals, *Der Warschauer Aufstand 1944* [*The Warsaw Uprising, 1944*], passim; AK, passim.

Appendix C

N.B. BIOGRAPHICAL DATA IS FOCUSED ON THE PERIOD OF THE
SECOND WORLD WAR

1. George Frost Kennan. Professor, the Institute for Advanced Study, Princeton, NJ, 1956– . US Foreign Service Officer, 1927–53; Minister-Counsellor, US Embassy, Moscow, 1944–6; Ambassador to the USSR, 1952 until retirement, 1953. Recalled to service by President Kennedy as Ambassador to Yugoslavia, 1961–3. Held many distinguished governmental and academic posts in his career: for details, consult standard biographical works.

2. J. K. Zawodny. A very Professor of International Relations, Claremont Graduate School and Pomona College.

3. Stanislaw Mikolajczyk. Prime Minister of the Polish Government-in-Exile, London, 1943–Nov 1944. Born 18 July 1901; died in Washington, DC, 13 Dec 1966.

4. William Averell Harriman. Chairman exec. com. Illinois Central Railroad, 1931–42; director, 1941–6. Many important posts with the US Government. US Ambassador to the USSR, 1943–6; to Great Britain, Apr–Oct 1946.

5. Jan Wszelaki. Polish foreign service officer. Minister-Counsellor of the Polish Embassy in Washington, DC, 1944–5 July 1945. Died in the USA after Second World War.

6. William C. Bullitt. US Ambassador to the Soviet Union, 1933–6.

7. Jan Ciechanowski. Polish foreign service officer. Polish Ambassador to the US Government, 1941–5 July 1945.

8. The Katyn Forest Massacre. Murder committed of about 4,400–4,800 Polish prisoners of war by the Soviet security forces in the spring–early summer 1940. Bodies of an additional 11,000 murdered have not yet been located owing to refusal of the Soviet Government to cooperate. In total, about 15,000 men were slaughtered, including 8,300–8,800 officers (among them 800 doctors of medicine).

9. Deportations of 1939–40. Some 1,200,000 civilians and 230,670 Polish soldiers were deported by Soviet authorities into the Soviet Union from the Polish territories seized in 1939.

10. Letter from Sir Archibald Clark Kerr, British Ambassador to the USSR, addressed to Tadeusz Romer, Minister for Foreign Affairs of the Polish Government. The letter was signed by Clark Kerr, dated Moscow, 2 Aug 1944 and delivered to Minister Romer in Moscow prior to Polish Prime Minister Mikolajczyk's discussions with Molotov and Stalin. A copy in Professor Zawodny's possession.

11. Sir Archibald John Clark Kerr. British Ambassador to the USSR, 1942–6. Born 1883; died 1951.

12. Polish forces-in-exile under the command of the Polish Government-in-Exile. About 200,000 Polish men and women in uniform serving within the British Forces. Major engagements: Battle of Britain, Norway, Tobruk, El Gazala, Monte Cassino, Piedimonte, Ankona, Falaise, Arnheim.

13. B. Bierut. Finished 'Lenin's International Communist School' in Moscow, 1930. Active in Poland, Bulgaria, Czechoslovakia and Austria. Assumed function of President of Poland as head of Communist-

294

organized National Council of Poland, 11 Sep 1944; assumed title of President of Poland on 19 Feb 1947. Born 8 Apr 1892; died in Moscow on 12 Mar 1956.

14. US Department of State, *Foreign Relations of the United States. 1944.* Washington, DC: US Government Printing Office, Vol. 3, 1965, pp. 1313–15.

15. Vyacheslav M. Molotov (real name Skryabin). Among other functions, USSR People's Commissar of Foreign Affairs, 30 May 1939 until 1949. Reappointed in this capacity again 1953–6.

16. Reference to Anglo-American attempts to secure Stalin's permission for the American planes to fly over Polish territory, drop supplies to the insurgents in Warsaw and land in the Soviet Union for refuelling.

17. Stefan Jedrychowski. Polish Communist writer. Member of the Soviet Government-sponsored Union of Polish Patriots; member of PKWN (Polish Committee of National Liberation) in Lublin, 1944; member of postwar Communist *élite* in Poland.

18. George F. Kennan. *Memoirs 1925–1950.* Boston: Little, Brown & Company, 1967, p. 211.

19. Loy Wesley Henderson. US Foreign Service Officer. Inspector diplomatic missions and consulate offices, 1942–3; counsellor of embassy and chargé d'affaires, Moscow and Kuibyshev, 1942. Posted to Iraq, 1943–5.

20. Elbridge Durbrow. US Foreign Service Officer. Assistant, Chief Division of Eastern European Affairs, 1944–6; counsellor of embassy, Moscow, 1946–8.

21. The statement of common principles for national policies signed by Roosevelt and Churchill on 14 Aug 1941. On 1 Jan 1942, twenty-six nations subscribed to and signed these principles. Articles one, two, three and four explicitly affirm that 'no territorial changes' will take place without the 'freely expressed wishes of the people concerned' and that the 'sovereign rights and self-government [be] restored to those who have been forcibly deprived of them'.

22. Earl of Avon, (Robert) Anthony Eden. Politician. British Secretary of State for Foreign Affairs, 1935–8; for Dominion Affairs, 1939–40; for War, 1940; for Foreign Affairs, 1940–5; leader of the House of Commons, 1942–5.

23. Harry Lloyd Hopkins. Friend of F. D. Roosevelt. Accompanied Roosevelt to the Casablanca, Cairo, Tehran, and Yalta Conferences and was his personal representative on special assignments to London and Moscow during the Second World War. Born 17 Aug 1890; died 29 Jan 1946.

24. Henry Morgenthau, Jr. Secretary of Treasury of the US Government, Jan 1934–July 1945. Born 11 May 1891; died 6 Feb 1967.

25. PKWN. Polski Commitet Wyzwolenia Narodowego (Polish Committee of National Liberation). Communist body organized under the auspices of the Soviet Government with its domicile in Lublin, 1944.

26. Nikolai A. Bulganin. Party and government official. Marshal of the Soviet Union. Hero of the Soviet Union. Member of the Military Council of the Western Front till 1943; Soviet Government representative to the Polish Committee of National Liberation, Lublin, July 1944; member, State Defence Committee, Nov 1944 USSR, First Deputy Minister of the Armed Forces, Mar 1946–Mar 1947.

27. Mikhail A. Suslov. During the Second World War, member of the Military Council, North Caucasian Front. Supervised mass deportations from Lithuania at the end of 1944.

28. Semen M. Budenny. Marshal of the Soviet Union. Hero of the Soviet Union. Appointed the First Deputy People's Commissar of Defence in

1940.

29. 'Who does in whom'.

30. Jozef Pilsudski. Great contributor to re-creation of independent Poland during the First World War. Commander-in-Chief of the Polish forces during Soviet–Polish War 1919–20. Marshal of Poland. Born 5 Dec 1867; died 12 May 1935.

31. German–Polish Non-Aggression Pact. Signed 26 Jan 1934 in Berlin. Ratified 24 Feb 1934, Warsaw. Duration: 10 years.

32. Kurt von Schuschnigg. Chancellor of Austria, 1934–Mar 1938. Imprisoned by government of Nazi Germany; liberated by American forces, 1945. Professor of Political Science, St Louis University, 1948– .

33. Herbert Feis, *Churchill, Roosevelt, Stalin: The War They Waged and the Peace They Sought*. Princeton: Princeton: Princeton University Press, 1967, pp. 378–9.

Bibliography

Primary Sources

PRIMARY SOURCES

I. Archives and Published Government Documents

1. Germany

Akten des Reichsfuhrers SS und Chef der deutschen Polizei [*Records of the Reichsfuhrer SS and Chief of the German Police*]. Washington, DC: The National Archives of the United States, Microfilm T–175.

Akten des Reichsministerium fur die deutschen Ostgebiete. [*Records of the Ministry for the*

German Occupied Eastern Territories], Washington, DC: The National Archives of the United States, Microfilm T−454.

Auswartiges Amt. *Akten zur deutschen a uswärtigen Politik 1918−1945. Aus dem Archiv des deutschen a uswartigen Amtes [Documents of German Foreign Policy 1918−1945. From the Archives of the German Foreign Office].* Serie D. Baden-Baden: Imprimerie Nationale, 1950.

Bundesarchiv − Militararchiv: h-12-9/3 bis H-12-9/9. 'Kriegstagebuch der 9. Armee mit Anlagebanden, Kartensammlungen und diversen Einzelakten-stucken' ['Daily War Reports of the 9th Army with Supplements, Collections of Maps, and Divers Single Documents]. Microfilm: Records of the German Field Commands: Armies. Washington, DC: The National Archives of the United States, Microfilm T−312, Rolls 343−9.

Bundesarchiv − Militararchiv. Smilo Frhr. von Luttwitz. Der Kampf der 9. Armee vom 21. September 1944 bis 20. Januar 1945. (1948) [The Battle of the 9th Army from the 21st September 1944 to the 20th January 1945]. H-o 8.10/6.

Hitler's Lagebesprechungen: Die Protokollfragmente seiner militarischen Konferenzen 1942−1945. Hrsg. von Helmut Heiber [*Hitler's Situation Reviews: Fragments of Records of His Military Conferences, 1942−1945.* Edited by Helmut Heiber]. Stuttgart: Deutsche Verlagsanstalt, 1962, 970 pp.

Kriegstagebuch des Oberkommandos der Wehrmacht. Eingeleitet und Erlautert von Helmuth Greiner und Percy Ernst Schramm [*War Diary of the Armed Forces Supreme Command.* Introduction and Commentary by Helmuth Greiner and Percy Ernst Schramm]. Frankfurt am Main: Bernard, [1961−5]. Vol. 4, 1 January 1944−22 May 1945.

Records of the German Field Commands: Rear Areas, etc. Washington, DC: The National Archives of the United States, Microfilm T−501.

United States Department of State. *Nazi − Soviet Relations 1939−1941. Documents from the Archives of the German Foreign Office.* Washington, DC: US Govern-ment Printing Office, 1948, Publication N. 3023, pp. 76−8.

Wehrmacht. Oberkommando. *Hitlers Weisungen fur Kriegsfuhrung 1939−1945. Dokumente des Oberkommandos der Wehrmacht.* Hrsg. von Walther Hubatsch [*Hitler's War Directives, 1939−1945. Documents of the Supreme Command of the Armed Forces.* Edited by Walther Hubatsch]. Frankfurt'am Main: Bernard and Graefe Verlag fur Wehrwesen, 1962, 330 pp.

Wehrmacht. Oberkommando. *Der Deutsche Wehrmachtsbericht 1939−1945: Ein Beitrag zur Untersuchung der Geistigen Kriegsfuehrung. Mit einer Dokumentation des Wehrmachtsberichtes vom 1.7.1944 bis zum 9.5.1945.* Von Erich Murawski [*The German Army's Communiqués, 1939−1945: A Contribution to the Examination of the Ideological Conduct of War. With Documentation of the Army's Communiqués from 1 July 1944 to 9 May 1945.* By Erich Murawski]. Boppard am Rhein: H.Boldt, 1962, 768 pp.

2. Great Britain

British Cabinet Papers. London: The Public Record Office, 1939−44.

Great Britain. *Documents Concerning German − Polish Relations and the Outbreak of Hostilities between Great Britain and Germany on September 2, 1939. Presented by the Secretary of State for Foreign Affairs to Parliament by Command of His Majesty.* London: His Majesty's Stationery Office, 1939, Misc. No. 9 (1939), Cmd. 6106, p. 36.

Parliamentary Debates: Commons, 1939–45.

Parliamentary Debates: Lords, 1939–45.

Public Record Office. *The Second World War: A Guide to Documents in the Public Record Office*. London: Her Majesty's Stationery Office, 1972, 303 pp.

3.   *Poland (Government-in-Exile)*

The Archives of the Polish Underground Movement (1939–1945) Study Trust. 'Materialy do Bibliografii Drukow Zwartych Wydanych Konspiracyjnie w Okresie Okupacji Niemieckiej (1939–1945)' ['Materials for the Bibliography of Underground Prints for the Years of German Occupation. *Armia Krajowa w Dokumentach, 1939–45*, Vols 3 –

'Dokumenty do Kapitulacji Powstania Warszawskiego' ['Documents Concerning the Capitulation of the Warsaw Uprising']. *Najnowsze, Dzieje Polski: Materialy i Studia z Okresu Wojny Swiatowej*. Warszawa: Panstwowe Wydawnictwo Naukowe, 1969. Tom IV, pp. 105–59.

Dziennik Ustaw RP, 1944 [Statutes at Large of the Polish Government, 1944]. No. 1, enclosure, 22 July 1944.

Poland. Komisja Historyczna Polskiego Sztabu Glownego w Londynie. *Polskie Sily Zbrojne W drugiej Wojnie Swiatowej. Armia Krajowa [Polish Armed Forces in the Second World War. The Home Army]*. London: Instytut Historyczny im. Gen. Sikorskiego, Vol. 3, 1950–1.

Poland. Ministerstwo Informacji. *Territory, Population, and Legal Status of the German and Soviet Occupations of Poland*. Angers, March 1940. 11 pp.

Poland. Ministerstwo Spraw Zagranicznych. *Stosunki Polsko-Sowieckie od Wrzesnia 1939 do Kwietnia 1943. Zbior Dokumentow. [Polish–Soviet Relations from September 1939 to April 1943. Collection of Documents]*. London: 1943, 317 pp. (Najscislej tajne–Top secret).

Poland. Polish Government-in-Exile. Council of Ministers. *Facts and Documents Concerning Polish Prisoners of War Captured by the USSR during the 1939 Campaign*. (Strictly confidential.) London: 1946, 454 pp.

Poland. Polish Government-in-Exile. Ministry of Foreign Affairs. *Stosunki Polsko–Sowieckie od Kwietnia 1943 do Wrzesnia 1946 [Polish–Soviet Relations from April 1943 to September 1946]*. Top Secret. Collection of Documents: 399 documents, telegrams, statements, etc. London: The Archives of the Polish Underground Movement (1939–1945) Study Trust, London. Deposit No. 11.

Poland. Polish Government-in-Exile. *Official Documents Concerning Polish–German and Polish–Soviet Relations 1933–1939*. London and Melbourne: Hutchinson & Co. Ltd, 1940, 222 pp.

Polska Sluzba Zagraniczna po l Wrzesnia 1939 [Polish Foreign Service after 1 September 1939]. Stowarzyszenie Pracownikow Polskiej Sluzby Zagranicznej w Londynie. Newtown: The Montgomeryshire Printing Co. Ltd, 1954, 180 pp.

Protocol of the Meeting of the Council of Ministers of the Polish Government-in-Exile, London, on 14 August 1944. No. 47. Sikorski Institute, London.

Protocols from Discussions at the J. Pilsudski Institute in London on the Subject of the Uprising of Warsaw, Fighting of AK and the Attitude of the Soviet Union. In Polish. Mimeographed. 1950. 4 Sets. File B II. London: The Archives of the Polish Underground Movement (1939–1945) Study Trust.

Sikorski Historical Institute. *Documents on Polish–Soviet Relations, 1939–1945*. London: Heinemann, Vol. 1, 1961, and Vol. 2, 1967.

Ustawa Konstytucyjna z dnia 23 Kwietnia 1935 r [*Constitution of the Republic of Poland from 23 April 1935*]. London: The Polish Government-in-Exile, 1967, 60 pp.

4. Poland (Polish People's Republic)

Documenta Occupationis Teutoniae.
Glowna Komisja Badan Zbrodni Niemieckich w Polsce. *Biuletyn Glownej Komisji Badan Zbrodni Niemieckich w Polsce*, I–X [*Bulletin of the Supreme Commission for Investigation of German Atrocities in Poland*, Vols. 1–10.] Warszawa: Wydawnictwo Glownej Komisji Badania Zbrodni Niemieckich w Polsce, 1946–58.

Glowna Komisja Badania Zbrodni Hitlerowskich w Polsce. *Zbrodnie Okupanta Hitlerowskiego na Ludnosci Cywilnej w Czasie Powstania Warszawskiego w 1944 Roku: w Dokumentach* [*Crimes of Hitler's Occupational Forces on the Civilian Population during the Warsaw Uprising 1944: Documents.*] Warszawa: Wydawnictwo Ministerstwa Obrony Narodowej, n.d., 443 pp.

Komunistyczna Partia Polski. Komitet Centralny. Zaklad Historii [Polish Communist Party. Central Committee. Historical Office]. Przygonski, Antoni. *Udzial PPR i AL w Powstaniu Warszawskim* [*Participation of PPR and AL in the Uprising of Warsaw*]. Warszawa: Ksiazka i Wiedza, 1970, 265 pp.

Ludnosc Cywilna w Powstaniu Warszawskim [*Civilian Population in the Warsaw Uprising*]. Red. Czeslaw Madajczyk. T. 1. Cz. 1–2. Oprac. M. Drozdowski, M. Maniakowna, T, Strzembosz; T. 2. Oprac. M. Getter, A. Janowski; T. 3. Oprac. W. Bartoszewski, L. Dobroszycki. Warszawa: II kw., 1973, 189 pp.

Polska Akademia Nauk. Wydzial Nauk Spolecznych. *2-ga Sesja Naukowa Poswiecona Wojnie Wyzwolenczej Narodu Polskiego 1939–1945* [*The Second Scientific Session Dedicated to the War for Independence of the Polish Nation, 1939–1945*]. Warszawa: Wydawnictwo Ministerstwa Obrony Narodowej, 1967, 1245 pp.

Polska Akademia Nauk. Zaklad Historii Stosunkow Polsko – Radzieckich. *Z Dziejow Stosunkow Polsko – Radzieckich: Studia i Materialy.* [*From the History of Polish – Soviet Relations: Studies and Materials*]. Vols 1–2. Warsaw: Ksiazka i Wiedza, 1965–6, 2 Vols.

Polska Zjednoczona Partia Robotnicza. Komitet Centralny. Zaklad Historii Partii. *Komunikaty Dowodztwa Glownego Gwardii Ludowej i Armii Ludowej. (Dokumenty)* [*Communiqués of the Supreme Command of the People's Guard and of the People's Army*]. Wyd. 2, opr. Ed. Markowa *et al.* Warszawa: Wydawnictwo Ministerstwa Obrony Narodowej, 1961, 351 pp.

Polska Zjednoczona Partia Robotnicza. Komitet Centralny. Zaklad Historii Partii. *Ksztaltowanie sie Podstaw Programowych Polskiej Partii Robotniczej w Latach 1942–1945: Wybor Materialow i Dokumentow* [*Polish United Workers' Party. Central Committee. Department of the Party's History. The Forming of the Fundamental Programme of the Polish Workers' Party during the Years 1942–1945: A Selection of Materials and Documents*]. Warsaw: Ksiazka i Wiedza, 1958, 590 pp.

Polska Zjednoczona Partia Robotnicza. Komitet Centralny. Zaklad Historii Partii. *Publicystyka Konspiracyjna PPR 1942–1945. Wybor artykulow.* Tom 3. 1944–1945 [*Underground Political Journalism of the Polish Workers' Party. A Selection of Articles.* Vol. 3. 1944–1945]. Warszawa: Ksiazka i Wiedza, 1967, 729 pp.

Polska Zjednoczona Partia Robotnicza. Komitet Centralny. Zaklad Historii

Partii. *Publicystyka Zwiazku patriotow Polskich 1943–1944. Wybor* [*The Political Journalism of the Union of Polish Patriots, 1943–1944. A Selection*]. Warszawa: Ksiazka i Wiedza, 1967, 445 pp.

Wojskowy Instytut Historyczny. Centralne Archiwum Wojskowe. *Organizacja i Dzialania Bojowe Ludowego Wojska Polskiego w Latach 1943–1945: Wybor Materialow Zrodlowych* [*Organization and Combat Activities of Polish People's Army, 1943–1945*]. Warszawa: Ministerstwo obrony Narodowej, Vol. 5, 1962.

Wojskowy Instytut Historyczny. *Wojna Wyzwolencza Narodu Polskiego w Latach 1939–1945* [*The War of Liberation of the Polish Nation, 1939–1945*]. Warszawa: Wydawnictwo Ministerstwa Obrony Narodowej, 1966. Vol. I, pp. 881. Vol. II, Maps and Tables, n.p.

Wojskowy Instytut Historyczny. Zaklad Historii Partii Przy KC PZPR. *Dowodztwo Glowne GL i AL. Zbior Dokumentow z Lat 1942–1944* [*Supreme Command of the GL and AL. Collection of Documents for the Years 1942–1944*]. Warszawa: Wydawnictwo MON, 1967, 425 pp.

5. *Soviet Union*

Adademiia Nauk SSSR. Institut Istorii. *SSSR v Period Velikoi Otechestvennoi Voiny (1941–1945gg): Ukazatel Dissertatsii i Avtoreferatov* [*The USSR during the Time of the Great Patriotic War (1941–1945): Guide to Dissertations and Reports*]. Moskva: 1961, 41 pp.

Akademii Nauk SSSR. Institut Istorii. *SSSR v Velikoi Otechestvennoi Voine 1941–1945: Kratkaia Khronika* [*The USSR in the Great Patriotic War, 1941–1945: A Short Chronicle*]. Moskva: Voennoe Izdatel'stvo Ministerstva Oborony SSSR, 1964, 866 pp.

Akademiia Nauk SSSr. Institut Slavianovedeniia. *Istoriia Pol'shi* [*A History of Poland*]. Dopolnitel'nyi tom. Moskva: Nauka, 1965, 582 pp.

Beitzell, Robert, ed. *Teheran, Yalta, Potsdam: The Soviet Protocols*. Hattiesburg, Mississippi: Academic International, 1970, 349 pp.

Instytut Marksizmu–Leninizmu. *Historia Wielkiej Wojny Narodowej Zwiazku Radzieckiego 1941–1945* [*History of the Great Patriotic War of the Soviet Union, 1941–1945*]. Warszawa: Wydawnictwo Ministerstwa Obrony Narodowej, 1965, Vol. 4, 871 pp.

Institut Marksizma–Leninizma. *Istoriia Velikoi Otechestvennoi Voiny Sovetskogo Soiuza* [*History of the Great Patriotic War of the USSR*]. 1960–5. 6 Vols.

Komisariat Ludowy Sprawiedliwosci ZSRR. *Sprawozdanie Sadowe w Sprawie Organizatorow, Kierownikow i Uczestnikow Polskiego Podziemia w Zapleczu Armii Czerwonej na Terytorium Polski, Litwy oraz Obwodow Zachodnich Bialorusi i Ukrainy* [*Minutes of the Court Proceedings Concerning the Organizers, Leaders, and Participants of the Polish Underground in the Rear of the Red Army on the Polish Territory, Lithuania, and the Western Areas of Bielorussia and the Ukraine*]. Moskva: Wydawnictwo Prawnicze Komisariatu Ludowego Sprawiedliwosci ZSRR, 1945, 319 pp.

Stalin, J. *Correspondence between the Chairman of the Council of Ministers of the USSR and the Presidents of the USA and the Prime Ministers of Great Britain during the Great Patriotic War of 1941–1945*. Moscow: Foreign language Publishing House, 1957, 2 Vols.

Stalin, J. *Perepiska Predsedatelia Soveta Ministrov SSSR s Prezidentami SShA i Prem'er Ministrami Velikobritanii vo Vremia Velikoi Otechestvennoi Voiny 1941–1945 gg* [*Correspondence between the Chairman of the Council of Ministers of the USSR, the*

Presidents of the United States, and the Prime Ministers of Great Britain during the Great Patriotic War of 1941–1945]. Moskva: Gosudarstvennoe Izdatel'stvo Politicheskoi Literatury, 1957, 2 Vols.

USSR. Spetsial'naya Komissiya po Ustanovleniiu i Rassledovaniiu Obstoyatel'stv Rasstrela Nemetsko-Fashistskimi Zakhvatchikami v Katynskom Lesu Voennoplennykh Pol'skikh Ofitserov [Special commission for ascertaining and investigating the circumstances of the shooting of Polish officer prisoners by the German-Fascist invaders in the Katyn Forest]. *Nota Sovetskogo Pravitel'stva Pravitel'stvu SShA; Soobshchenie Spetsial'noi Komissii [Note of the Soviet Government to the Government of the USA: Communication by the Special Commission]*. Moscow: Supplement to *Novoe Vremya*, No. 10, 1952, 20 pp.

Velikaia Otechestvennaia Voina Sovetskogo Soiuza 1941–1945. Kratkaia Istoriia [The Great Patriotic War of the Soviet Union, 1941–1945. A Short History]. Moskva: Voennoe Izdatel'stvo Ministerstva Oborony SSSR, 1965, 617 pp.

Vneshnaia Politika Sovetskogo Soiuza v Period Otechestvennoi Voiny: Dokumenty i Materialy [Foreign Policy of the Soviet Union during the Patriotic War: Documents and Materials]. Moskva: Gospolitizdat, 1944–7, Vols. 3.

Vorb'ev, F. D., i Kravtsov, V. M. *Velikaia Otechestvennaia Voina Sovetskogo Soiuza 1941–1945gg: Kratkii voenno-istoricheskii [The Great Patriotic War of the Soviet Union, 1941–1945: A Short Military-Historical Sketch]*. Moskva: Voennoe Izdatel'stvo Ministerstva Oborony SSSR, 1961, 455 pp.

Vtoraia Mirovaia Voina, 1939–1945gg. Voennoistoricheskii Ocherk [The Second World War, 1939–1945. A Military-Historical Outline]. Otv. Red. S. P. Platonov. Moskva: Voennoe Izdatel'stvo Ministerstva Oborony SSSR, 1958, 2 Vols.

6. United States

Cole, H. M. *The European Theater of Operations: The Lorraine Campaign.* Washington: Department of the Army, Historical Division, 1950, 657 pp.

General Staff. *General Marshall's Report: The Winning of the War in Europe and the Pacific Biennial Report of the Chief of Staff of the US Army July 1, 1943 to June 30, 1945 to the Secretary of War.* New York: Simon & Schuster, 1945, 123 pp.

Harriman, W. Averell. *Statement Regarding our Wartime Relations with the Soviet Union.* Washington, DC: US Committees on Armed Services and Foreign Relations of the Senate, 1951, 34 pp.

US Air Forces. *Operational Narrative.* 3rd Bombardment Division, Mission: Warsaw, 18 September 1944. London: The Archives of the Polish Underground Movement (1939–1945) Study Trust.

US Air Forces. *Bomber Report.* Headquarters VIII Fighter Command, Narrative of Operations, Intelligence Summary No. 283, Confidential, 18 September 1944. London: The Archives of the Polish Underground Movement (1939–1945) Study Trust.

US Air Forces. USAF Historical Division. *The Army Air Forces in World War II.* Prepared under the Editorship of Wesley Frank Craven and James Lea Cate. Chicago: University of Chicago Press, 1948–66, 7 Vols.

US Department of State. *American Foreign Policy 1950–1955: Basic Documents.* Vol. 2. Washington, DC: US Government Printing Office, 1957, 3222 pp.

US Department of State. *Foreign Relations of the United States, 1944.* Washington, DC: US Government Printing Office, Vol. 3, 1965, 1478 pp.

US Department of State. *Foreign Relations of the United States. Diplomatic*

Papers: The British Commonwealth, Eastern Europe, The Far East, 1943. Washington, DC: US Government Printing Office, 1963, Vol. 3, 1151 pp.

US Department of State. *Foreign Relations of the United States. Diplomatic Papers: The Conferences at Cairo and Tehran 1943.* Washington, DC: US Government Printing Office, 1961, 932 pp.

US Department of State. *Foreign Relations of the United States. The Conference of Berlin (Potsdam) 1945.* Washington, DC: US Government Printing Office, Vol. 1, 1960, 1088 pp.

US Department of State. *Foreign Relations of the United States. The Conference at Malta and Yalta 1945.* Washington, DC: US Government Printing Office, 1960, 1032 pp.

US Department of State. *Foreign Relations of the United States. The Conference at Quebec 1944.* Washington, DC: US Government Printing Office, Publication No. 4400–1384, 1972, 527 pp.

US House of Representatives. *Message of President Roosevelt to the Congress, August 21, 1941. Embodying Text of the Atlantic Charter.* 77th Congress, 1st Session, 1941. Washington, DC: Government Printing Office, 1941, Doc. No. 358.

US House of Representatives, 1939–45.

US National Archives. The Moscow Post File.

US Senate, 1939–45.

7. *International*

International Military Tribunal. Secretariat. *Trial of the Major War Criminals before the International Military Tribunal, Nuremburg, 14 November 1945–10 October 1946.* Nuremberg, Germany: 1947, 42 vols.

United Nations. Treaty Series. *Treaties and International Agreements Registered or Filed and Recorded with the Secretariat of the United Nations.* Geneva Convention Relative to the Treatment of Prisoners of War of August 12, 1949. Vol. 75, no. 972, 1950, pp. 135–285, 419–68.

II. *Unpublished Documents, Papers and Manuscripts*

Arciszewski, T. Prezes Rady Ministrow. *Broadcast to Insurgents in Warsaw*, 13 August 1944. File Prezydium Rady Ministrow, PRML, No. 26. Sikorski Institute, London.

Berhhard, Maria Ludwika, prof. dr. Handwritten report for the author. Princeton, 30 November 1971, 1 p.

Dolega-Kamienski, Tadeusz ('Badacz'). 'Powstanie Warszawskie: Kwater-mistrzostwo' ['The Warsaw Uprising: The Quartermaster']. Typescript. Jozef Pilsudski Institute of America, New York, 35 pp. The author was the Chief Quartermaster of the Uprising.

Golebiowski, Jan Gozdawa ('Dziryt'). ' "Koszta" w Akcji' [' "Koszta" in Action']. Typescript in Polish, 11 pp. In the possession of Professor J. K. Zawodny.

Glowacki, Marian, Lt ('Spokojny'). 'Notes Bojowy' ['Combat Notes']. Manuscript in Polish. Made available to the author. London, spring 1969, n.p.

Grzymala-Rosiek, 2nd Lt ('Henryk'). 'Wspomnienia z Okresu Powstania w 1944 roku' ['Memoirs from the Time of the Uprising, 1944']. Typescript in the possession of M. Niedzielski, Chicago, 16 pp.

Kopanski, Stanislaw, Gen. 'Concerning Radio Communication between the

Chief of Staff of the Polish Forces in Exile (Gen. Kopanski) in London, and the Supreme Commander of the Polish Forces (Gen. Sosnkowski) while on Inspection Tour of the Polish Forces in Italy.' Typewritten memo kindly given by Gen. Kopanski to the author on 17 May 1965. 2 pp.

Kopanski, Stanislaw, Gen. 'Uwagi gen. Kopanskiego do ksiazki W. Babinskiego' ['General Kopanski's Comments concerning W. Babinski's Book]. Typewritten notes made available through Gen. Kopanski's courtesy, n.d., 15 pp.

Kraczkiewicz, P., Lt-Col. 'Clandestine Production of Armaments and Sabotage Equipment' (chronological development; organizational table; technical drawings and specifications. Also attached notes concerning sabotage of the German war effort in occupied Poland during the Second World War). Typewritten pages in Polish, 68 pp. Given to this author by Lt-Col. Kraczkiewicz, who was the technical manager of the production of sabotage equipment (1940–4) for the Headquarters of the AK and from March 1944 until 1 August 1944 also the Deputy Chief for the Clandestine Production of Armaments of the AK. He also participated in policy formulation and operations with regard to sabotage units.

Mitkiewicz, Leon. 'Dossier: The Combined Chiefs of Staff'. Typescript (documents) in Polish made available by Col. Mitkiewicz to the author. Col. Mitkiewicz was Representative of the Polish Commander-in-Chief of the Polish Forces-in-Exile to the Combined Chiefs of Staff in Washington, DC, and Deputy Chief of Staff of the Polish Commander-in-Chief of the Polish Forces-in-Exile.

Mitkiewicz, Leon. 'Kulisy Powstania Warszawskiego' ['Informal Background of the Uprising of Warsaw']. Typescript in Polish made available by Col. Mitkiewicz to the author. New York, 1967. 84 pp.

Mitkiewicz, Leon. 'Na Obczyznie z Gen. Wladyslaw Sikorski, 1939–1945' ['In Exile with Gen. Wladyslaw Sikorski, 1939–1945']. Typescript in Polish made available by Col. Mitkiewicz to the author. New York, 1962, 930' pp.

Mitkiewicz, Leon. 'Ostatni Rozdzial (Moje Wspomnienia z Combined Chiefs of Staff 1943–1945) ['The Last Chapter: My Memories from Service with the Combined Chiefs of Staff']. Typescript in Polish made available by Col. Mitkiewicz to the author. New York, 1967, 394 pp.

Nowak, Jan. 'Monitoring of Broadcasts from Blyskawica (AK) and Polskie Radio' (Delegate of the Polish Government in London residing in Warsaw). Based on materials supplied by Mr S. Uszycki, and Mrs Bogacka. Polish Programme, Polish Section, BBC, 7 Oct 1951, 10.30 p.m. London: The Archives of the Polish Underground (1939–1945) Study Trust. File A, No. 587/3(1).

Paczek, Walerian, ks. mgr. pplk. ('Gierman'). 'Memorandum'. Made available to the author, 31 Dec 1966, 7 pp.

Paprocki, Stanislaw. 'Wyciagi z Podziemnej Prasy Komunistycznej w Kraju, z Nasluchow Radiostacji "Kosciuszki" i Zwiazku Patriotow Polskich, Oskarzajace AK o Biernosc i Wzywajace do Zbrojnych Wystapien (1943–1944)' ['Excerpts from the Underground Communist Press at Home, from Monitors of the "Kosciuszko" Radio, and the Union of Polish Patriots, Accusing the Home Army of Passivity and Calling for Organized Armed Action (1943–1944']. Maszynopis str. 311. London: The Archives of the Polish Underground Movement (1939–1945) Study Trust, B II–Nr., 1968.

Popiel, Karol. 'Sytuacja przed Powstaniem 1944 w Polsce w Oczach Czlonkow

Stronnictwa Pracy' ['The Situation before the Uprising 1944 in Poland as Seen by Members of the Polish Labour Party']. Memorandum made available to the author, spring 1965, 5 pp.

'Protocols from Discussions at the J. Pilsudski Institute in London on the Subject of the Uprising of Warsaw, Fighting of AK, and the Attitude of the Soviet Union'. In Polish. Mimeographed. 1950. 4 Sets. File B II. London: The Archives of the Polish Underground Movement (1939–1945) Study Trust.

Rayski, L. 'Royal Air Force Pilot's Flying Log Book of Air-Commodore L. Rayski', no. POZ. 68. (Original Log Book.)

Romer, T. 'Report of the Minister of Foreign Affairs of the Polish Government-in-Exile, T. Romer, Concerning the Diplomatic Activities in London with Regard to Assistance to Fighting Warsaw, 6 October 1944. File of the Polish Minister of Foreign Affairs, Position 172, pp. 262–79. Typescript in Polish. copy: The Archives of the Polish Underground Movement (1939–1945) Study Trust, London.

St Antony's College, Oxford University. 'Proceedings of a Conference on Britain and European Resistance 1939–1945 Organized by St Antony's College, Oxford'. 10–16 December 1962, mimeographed, n.p.

Sawicki, Lech, 'Kwas' ['Personal Account']. Copy of the typescript made available to the author. England: 1958, 12 pp.

Srebrzynski, Jozef. Deputy Commander of Communications of AK. Zagadnienie Lacznosci Krojowej i Zagranicznej w Okresie Konspiracji 1940–1944 ['The Problem of Communications in the Underground and with the Contacts Abroad during the Years of Conspiracy 1940–1944']. Typescript in Polish (133 pp.) including supplement 'Organizacja Lacznosci' (37 pp.) Original in the Polska Akademia Nauki, Warsaw. Copy: The Archives of the Polish Underground Movement (1939–1945) Study Trust, London.

Weber, Stanislaw, pplk. dypl., ps. ('Chirurg'). 'Sprawozdanie z wspolpracy Okregu Warszawskiego Armii Krajowej z Zydowska Organizacja Bojowa' ['Report on the Co-operation of the Warsaw Region of the Home Army with the Jewish Combat Organization']. Typescript. Studium Polski Podziemnej sygn. BI, 1608.

Zarzycki, Tadeusz. Relacja Dotyczaca Przebiegu Akcji Powstanczej Na Odcinku IV Rejonu I Obwodu: [Odcinka: Srodmiescie, Polnoc–Zachod] [Combat Report]. Copy of the typescript made available to the author. England: 1947, 26+2 pp.

III. Interviews

See Appendix E

IV. Published Diaries, Personal Memoirs and Eyewitness Accounts

1. Germany

Guderian, Heinz, Gen. *Panzer Leader*. New York: Ballantine Books, 4th American Printing, 1967, 490 pp.

Mellenthin, F. W. von., Maj. Gen. *Panzer Battles: A Study of the Employment of*

Armor in the Second World War. New York: Ballantine Books, 1971, 470 pp.

Strik-Strikfeldt, Wilfried. *Against Stalin and Hitler: 1941–1945.* New York: The John Day Company, 1973, 270 pp.

Warlimont, Walter. *Im Hauptquartier der deutschen Wehrmacht 1939–1945 [Inside the German Army Headquarters, 1939–1945].* Frankfurt am Main: Bernard & Graefe Verlag fuer Wehrwesen, 1962, 570 pp.

2. Great Britain

Churchill, Winston S. *The Second World War: The Hinge of Fate.* Boston: Houghton Mifflin Company, 1950, 1000 pp.

Churchill, Winston S. *The Second World War: Triumph and Tragedy.* London: Cassell & Co. Ltd, 1954, Vol. 6, 716 pp.

Eden, Anthony. *The Reckoning.* London: Cassell & Co. Ltd, 1965, 623 pp.

Moran, Lord (Sir Charles Wilson). *Churchill: Taken from the Diaries of Lord Moran: The Struggle for Survival 1940–1965.* Boston: Houghton Mifflin Company, 1966, 877 pp.

Slessor, John. *The Central Blue: The Autobiography.* New York: Frederick A. Praeger, 1957, 709 pp.

3. Poland (Government-in-Exile)

Bor-Komorowski, Tadeusz. *Armia Podziemna [The Secret Army].* 3rd edition. London: Nakladem Katolickiego Osrodka Wydawniczego Veritas, 1950, 399 pp.

—, *The Secret Army.* London: Victor Gollancz, 1951, 407 pp.

Chrusciel, Antoni (Monter). *Powstanie Warszawskie [The Warsaw Uprising].* London: n.p., 1948, 16 pp.

Ciechanowski, Jan. *Defeat in Victory.* Garden City, New York: Doubleday & Co., 1947, 397 pp.

Czapscy, Jozef i Maria. *Dwuglos Wspomnien [Reminiscences in Two Voices].* London: Polska Fundacja Kulturalna, 1965, 159 pp.

Drogi Cichociemnych: Opowiadania Zebrane I Opracowane Przez Kolo Spadochroniarzy Armii Krajowej ['Silent-in-the-Dark': Reports Collected and Compiled by the Paratroopers of the Home Army]. London: Nakladem Katolickiego Osrodka Wydawniczego 'Veritas', 1961, 346 pp.

Karski, Jan. *Story of a Secret State.* Boston: Houghton Mifflin Company, 1944, 391 pp.

Kopanski, Stanislaw. *Wspomnienia Wojenne 1939–1946 [War Memoirs, 1939–1946].* London: Nakladem Katolickiego Osrodka Wydawniczego 'Veritas', n.d., 394 pp.

Korbonski, Stefan. *Fighting Warsaw. The Story of the Polish Underground State 1939–1945.* London: George Allen & Unwin Ltd., 1956, 495 pp.

—, *W Imieniu Kremla [On Behalf of the Kremlin].* Paris: Instytut Literacki, 1956, 381 pp.

—, *W Imieniu Rzeczypospolitej [In the Name of the Polish Commonwealth].* London: Gryf Publications Ltd, 1964, 458 pp.

—, *Warsaw in Chains.* London: George Allen & Unwin Ltd, 1959, 319 pp.

—, *Warsaw in Exile.* New York: Frederick A. Praeger, 1966, 325 pp.

Mikolajczyk. Stanislaw. *The Pattern of Soviet Domination.* London: Samson Low, Marston & Co. Ltd, 1948, 353 pp.

Mitkiewicz, Leon. *W Najwyzszym Sztabie Zachodnich Aliantow 1943–1945* [*With the Combined Chiefs of Staff of the Western Allies, 1943–1945*]. London: Katolicki Osrodek Wydawniczy 'Veritas', 1971 294 pp.

Mitkiewicz, Leon. *Z Gen. Sikorskim na Obczyznie* [*In Exile with General Sikorski*]. Paris: Dokumenty. Instytut Literacki, 1968, 398 pp.

Nagorski, Zygmunt. *Wojna w Londynie: Wspomnienia 1939–1945* [*War in London: Memories, 1939–1945*]. Paris: Ksiegarnia Polska w Paryzu, 1966, 357 pp.

Pobog-Malinowski, Wladyslaw. *Najnowsza Historia Polityczna Polski 1864–1945.* Tom Trzeci. *Okres 1939–1945* [*The Latest Political History of Poland, 1864–1945.* Vol. 3. *1939–1945*]. London: n.p., 1960, 910 pp.

Popiel, Karol. *Na Mogilach Przyjaciol* [*On the Graves of Friends*]. London: Odnowa, 1966, 189 pp.

Raczynski, Count Edward. *In Allied London: The Wartime Diaries of the Polish Ambassador Count Edward Raczynski*. London: Weidenfeld & Nicolson, London, 1962, 381 pp.

Sosnkowski, Kazimierz. *Materialy Historyczne* [*Historical Materials*]. London: Gryf Publications Ltd, 1966, 688 pp.

Zadrozny, Stanislaw. *Tu – Warszawa: Dzieje Radiostacji Powstanczej 'Blyskawica'* [*Warsaw Calling: A History of the Uprising Radio Station 'Lightning'*]. London: Nakladem Ksiegarni Orbis, 1964, 112 pp.

Zagorski, Waclaw. *Wicher Wolnosci: Dziennik Powstanca* [*Wind of Freedom: Diary of an Insurgent*]. London: Nakladem Czytelnikow-przedplacicieli, staraniem SPK, Kolo Nr. 11, 1957, 391 pp.

Zaremba, Zygmunt. *Wojna i Konspiracja* [*The War and the Underground*]. London: B. Swiderski, 1957, 347 pp.

Zawodny, Janusz K. 'Raport Dowodcy Plutonu A. K. z Powstania Warszawskiego' ['The Battle Report of a Platoon Commander in the Uprising of Warsaw']. *Zeszyty Historyczne*. Paris: Institut Littéraire, No. 176, No. 16, pp. 176–90.

4. Poland (Polish People's Republic)

Bordzilowski, Jerzy, Gen. 'Zolnierska Droga': Czesc XIII ['The Soldier's Journey': Part XIII]. *Wojskowy Przeglad Historyczny*, Rok XV, no. 1. Warszawa: 1970, pp. 115–79.

Bordzilowski, Jerzy, Gen. 'Zolnierska Droga': Czesc XV ['The Soldier's Journey': Part XV]. *Wojskowy Przeglad Historyczny*, Rok XV, no. 3. Warszawa: 1970, pp. 148–84.

Fajer, Lucjan. *Zolnierze Starowki: Dziennik Bojowy Kpt. Ognistego* [*Soldiers of Starowka: The War Diary of Captain Ognisty*]. Warszawa: Iskry, 1957, 526 pp.

Kirchmayer, Jerzy, *et al.* 'Meldunki Sytuacyjne "Montera" z Powstania Warszawskiego' ['Monter's Combat Reports of the Warsaw Uprising']. *Najnowsze Dzieje Polski: Materialy i Studia z Okresu II Wojny Swiatowej.* Warszawa: Vol. 3, 1959, pp. 97–180.

Kliszko, Zenon. *Powstanie Warszawskie: Artykuly, Przemowienia, Wspomnienia, Dokumenty* [*The Warsaw Uprising: Articles, Speeches, Recollections, Documents*]. Warszawa: Ksiazka i Wiedza, 1967, 347 pp.

Majorkiewicz, Felicjan. *Dane Nam Bylo Przezyc* [*Our Fate Was to Survive*]. Warszawa: Instytut Wydawniczy, Pax, 1972, 382 pp.

Pamietniki Zolnierzy Baonu Zoska: Powstanie Warszawskie [*Diaries of Soldiers of the*

Group Zoska: Warsaw Uprising]. Warszawa: Nasza Ksiegarnia, 1957, 527 pp.
Sawicki, Jerzy. *Przed Polskim Prokuratorem: Dokumenty i Materialy [Before the Polish Prosecutor: Documents and Materials]*. Warszawa: Iskry, 1958, 345 pp.

5. *Soviet Union*

Chuikov, Vasili I. 'Konets Tret'ego Reikha' ['The End of the Third Reich']. *Oktiabr'*. *Moskva*, Year 40, no. 3−5, March−May 1964.
—, *The End of the Third Reich*. Introduction by Alistair Horne. Translated by Ruth Kisch. London: Macgibbon & Kee, 1967, 261 pp.
Djilas, Milovan. *Conversations with Stalin*. New York: Harcourt, Brace & World, Inc., 1962, 211 pp.
Konev, I. S. *Zapiski Komanduiushchego Frontom: 1943−1944 [Memoirs of the Front Commander, 1943−1944]*. Moskva: Nauka, 1972, 368 pp.
Poplavskii, s. g. *Tovarishchi v Bor'be [Comrades in Battle]*. Moskva: Voennoe izdatel'stvo Ministerstva Oborony SSSR, 1963, 260 pp.
Rokossovsky, K. *A Soldier's Duty*. Moscow: Progress Publishers, 1972, 340 pp.
Samsonov, A. M. *Osvobozhdenie Belorussii: 1944 [Liberation of Byelorussia, 1944]*. Moskva: Nauka, 1970, 772 pp.
Shtemenko, S., Gen. 'Na Drodze Do Zwyciestwa' ['On the Road to Victory']. *Zeszyty Historyczne*. Paris: Instytut Literacki, 1971, Vol. 200, pp. 36−63.
—, 'Pered Udarom w Belorussii' ['Before the Offensive in White Russia']. *Voenno-istoricheskii Zhurnal*. Moskva: no. 9, 1965, pp. 44−59.
Vysotskii, V. I. *et al. Gvardeiskaia Tankovaia [The Guard Tank Unit]*. Moskva: Voennoe Izdatel'stvo Ministerstva Oborony SSSR, 1963, 241 pp.
Zhukov, Georgi K. *Marshal Zhukov's Greatest Battles*. New York: Harper & Row, Publishers, 1969, 304 pp.
—, *The Memoirs of Marshal Zhukov*. New York: Delacorte Press, 1971, 703 pp.
—, 'O Powstaniu Warszawskim i Polsce' ['Concerning the Uprising of Warsaw and Poland']. *Zeszyty Historyczne*. Paris: Institut Literacki, 1969, Vol. 176, pp. 130−1.

6. *United States*

Bohlen, Charles E. *Witness to History 1929−1969*. New York: W. W. Norton & Company, Inc., 1973, 562 pp.
Deane, John R. *The Strange Alliance: The Story of Our Efforts at Wartime Cooperation with Russia*. New York: The Viking Press, 1947, 344 pp.
Harriman, Averell W., and Abel Ellie. *Special Envoy to Churchill and Stalin: 1941−1946*. New York: Random House, 9175, 595 pp.
Kennan, George F. *From Prague after Munich: Diplomatic Papers 1938−1940*. Princeton, New Jersey: Princeton University Press, 1968, 226 pp.
Kennan, George F. *Memoirs 1924−1950*. Boston: Little, Brown & Company, 1967, 583 pp.
Stettinius, Edward R. *Roosevelt and the Russians: The Yalta Conference*. Garden City, New York: Doubleday & Co. Inc., 1949, 367 pp.

SECONDARY SOURCES

V.   Books

Auderska, Halina and Zygmunt Ziolka, ed. *Akcja N* [*Action N*]. Warszawa: Czytelnik, 1972, 764 pp.

Babinski, Witold. *Przyczynki Historyczne od Okresu 1939–1945* [*Historical Supplements to the Period 1939–1945*]. London: B. Swiderski, 1967, 712 pp.

Balicka-Kozlowska, Helena. *Mur Mial Dwie Strony* [*The Wall Had Two Sides*]. Warszawa: Ministerstwo Obrony Narodowej, 1958, 188 pp.

Bartelski, Leslaw M. *Mokotow 1944* [*Mokotow 1944*]. Warszawa: Wydawnictwo Ministerstwa Obrony Narodowej, 1972, 708 pp.

—,*Powstanie Warszawskie* [*The Uprising of Warsaw*]. Warszawa: Iskry, 1965, 271 pp.

—,*Powstanie Warszawskie* [*The Uprising of Warsaw*]. 2nd ed. Warszawa: Iskry, 1967, 282 pp.

—,*W Kregu Bliskich: Szkice Do Portretow* [*In the Circle of Comrades: Sketches for Portraits*]. Krakow: Wydawnictwo Literackie, 1967, 209 pp.

Bartoszewski, Wladyslaw. *Erich von dem Bach*. Warszawa-Poznam: Wydawnictwo Zachodnie, 1961, 109 pp.

—, *Prawda o von dem Bachu* [*The Truth about von dem Bach*]. Warszawa-Poznan: Wydawnictwo Zachodnie, 1961, 144 pp.

Borkiewicz, Adam. *Powstanie Warszawskie 1944: Zarys Dzialan Natury Wojskowej* [*The Uprising of Warsaw: Military Aspects*]. Warszawa: Instytut Wydawniczy Pax, 1964, 610 pp.

Borwicz, Michael. 'Factors Influencing the Relations between the General Polish Underground and the Jewish Underground', in *Jewish Resistance during the Holocaust*. Jerusalem: Yad Vashem, n.d., pp. 343–52.

Broszat, Martin. *Nationalsozialistische Polenpolitik 1939–1945* [*National Socialist Policy towards Poles, 1939–1945*]. Frankfurtam Main: Fischer Bücherei, 1961, 228 pp.

Buchheit, Gert. *Hitler der Feldherr: Die Zerstorung einer Legende* [*Hitler, the Commander-in-Chief: The Destruction of a Legend*]. Rastatt: Grote, 1958, 560 pp.

Ciechanowski, Jan M. *Powstanie Warszawskie* [*Uprising of Warsaw*]. London: Odnowa, 1971, 399 pp.

Clark Alan. *Barbarossa: The Russian–German Conflict, 1941–45*. New York: Signet Book published by New American Library, 1966, 560 pp.

Czarski, Andrzej. *Najmlodsi Zolnierze Walczacej Warszawy* [*Fighting Warsaw's Youngest Soldiers*]. Warszawa: Pax, 1971, 403 pp.

Datner, Szymon, Gulkowski, Janusz and Leszczynski, Kazimierz. *Genocide 1903–1944*. Warszawa-Poznan: Wydawnictwo Zachodnie, 1953, 334 pp.

Dobraczynski, Jan. *W Rozwalonym Domu* [*In a Demolished House*]. Warszawa: Pax, 1969, 238 pp.

Dziekuje Wam Roadacy [*I Do Thank You My Countrymen*]. London: Polska Fundacja Kulturalna, 1973, 278 pp.

Gackenholz, Herman. 'Der Zusammenbruch der Heeresgruppe Mitte 1944' ['The Collapse of the Army Group Centre, 1944]. *Entscheidungsschlachten des Zweiten Weltkrieges*. Frankfurt am Main: Verlag für Wehrwesen Bernard & Graefe, 1960, pp. 445–78.

Garlinski, Jozef. *Miedzy Londynem i Warszawa* [*Between London and Warsaw*]. London: Gryf Publications Ltd, 1966, 160 pp.

Garlinski, Jozef. *Politycy i Zolnierze* [*Politicians and Soldiers*]. London: Polska Fundacja Kulturalna, 1968, 320 pp.

Gawenda, Jerzy August. *Legalizm Polski w Swietle Prawa Publicznego* [*Legal Continuity of the Polish State in the Light of Public Law*]. London: 1959, 127 pp.

Grechko, A. A. *Osvoboditelnaia Missiia Sovetskikh Vooruzhennykh Sil vo Vtoroi Mirovoi Voine* [*Liberation Mission of the Soviet Armed Forces in the Second World War*]. Moskva: Politizdat, 1971, 518 pp.

Gross, Feliks. *The Seizure of Political Power in a Century of Revolutions.* New York: Philosophical library, 1958, 398 pp.

Hart, B. H. Liddell, ed. *The Red Army.* Gloucester, Massachusetts: Peter Smith, 1968, 480 pp.

Kaczmarek, Kazimierz. *Osmy Bydgoski* [*The Regiment No. 8 from Bydgoszcz*]. Warszawa: Wydawnictwo Ministerstwa Obrony Narodowej, 1962, 444 pp.

Kalinowski, Franciszek. *Lotnictwo Polskie w Wielkiej Brytanii 1940–1945* [*The Polish Air Force in Great Britain, 1940–1945*] Paris: Instytut Literacki, 1969, 333 pp.

Kennan, George F. *American Diplomacy 1900–1950.* Chicago, Illinois: University of Chicago Press, 1952, 154 pp.

—, *On Dealing with the Communist World.* New York: Harper & Row, 1964, 57 pp.

—, *Realities of American Foreign Policy.* Princeton, New Jersey: Princeton University Press, 1954, 120 pp.

—, *Russia and the West under Lenin and Stalin.* Boston: Little, Brown & Company, 1961, 411 pp.

—, *Russia, the Atom, and the West.* New York: Harper & Brothers, n.d., 116 pp.

—, *Soviet Foreign Policy 1917–1951.* Princeton, New Jersey: D. Van Nostrand Company Inc., 1960, 192 pp.

Kirchmayer, Jerzy. *Powstanie Warszawskie* [*The Warsaw Uprising*]. Warszawa: Ksiazka i Wiedza, Czwarte Wydanie, 1964, 356 pp.

Klokov, V. I. *Bor'ba Narodov Slavianskikh Stran Protiv Fashistskikh Porabortitelei* [*Struggle of the people of the Slavic Countries against Fascist Oppressors*]. Kiev: Izdvo AN Ukr. SSR, 1961, 430 pp.

Komornicki, Stanislaw. *Na Barykadach Warszawy* [*On the Barricades of Warsaw*]. Warszawa: Wydawnictwo Ministerstwa Obrony Narodowej, 1964, 360 pp.

—, *Na Barykadach Warszawy* [*On the Barricades of Warsaw*] Warszawa: Wydawnictwo Ministerstwa Obrony Narodowej, 1967, Wyd. 3, 361 pp.

—, *63 Dni* [*Sixty-three Days*]. Warszawa: Wydawnictwo Ministerstwa Obrony Narodowej, 1965, 129 pp.

Kowalik, Jan. *'Kultura' 1947–1957: Bibliografia Zawartosci Tresci. Dzialalnosc Wydawnicza (1946–Maj 1959)* ['*Kultura' 1947–1957: Bibliography of the Contents. The Register of Publications (1946–May 1959)*] Paris: Instytut Literacki, 1959, 392 pp.

Krannhals, Hanns von. *Der Warschauer Aufstand 1944* [*The Warsaw Uprising 1944*]. Frankfurt am Main: Bernard & Graefe Verlag für Wehrwesen, 1964, 447 pp.

Kubalski, Tadeusz. *W Szeregach 'Baszty'* [*The Rank and File of 'Baszta'*]. Warszawa: Wydawnictwo Ministerstwa Obrony Narodowej, 1969, 376 pp.

Kuntiuba, Ivan Dmitrievich. *Sovetsko-Pol'skie Otnosheniia 1939–1945 gg* [*Soviet–Polish Relations, 1939–1945*]. Kiev: Izdatel'stvo Kievskogo Univer siteta, 1963, 206 pp.

Leszczynski, Kazimierz. *Heinz Reinefarth*. Warszawa-Poznan: Wydawnictwo Zachodnie, 1961, 98 pp.

Loewenheim, Francis, Langley, Harold D. and Jonas, Manfred. *Roosevelt and Churchill*. New York: Saturday Review Press and E. P. Dutton & Co., 1975, 805 pp.

Margules, Jozef. *Boje 1 Armii WP W Obszarze Warzawy. (Sierpien–Wrzesien 1944)* [*The Battles of the First Polish Army in the Area of Warsaw (August–September, 1944)*] Warszawa: Wydawnictwa Obrony Narodowej, 1967, 573 pp.

—, *Z Pomoca Powstancom Warszawskim* [*To the Assistance of Warsaw's Insurgents*]. Warszawa: Ksiazka i Wiedza, 1966, 84 pp.

Pobog-Malinowski, Wladyslaw. *Najnowsza Historia Polityczna Polski 1864–1945. Tom Trzeci. Okres 1939–1945* [*The Latest Political History of Poland, 1864–1945. Vol. 3. 1939–1945*] London: n.p., 1960, 910 pp.

Podlewski, Stanislaw. *Przemarsz Przez Pieklo* [*Marching through Hell*]. Warszawa: Pax, 1957, 719 pp.

Podlewski, Stanislaw. *Rapsodia Zoliborska* [*Zoliborz Rhapsody*]. Warszawa: Pax, 1957, 463 pp.

Polonsky, Antony. *The Great Powers and the Polish Question 1941–1945; A Documentary Study of Cold War Origins*. London School of Economics and Political Science, 1976, 282 pp.

Polska Zjednoczona Partia Robotnicza. Komitet Centralny. Zaklad Historii Partii. *Pol'skoe Rabochee Dvizhenie v Gody Voiny i Gitlerovski Okkupatsii* [*Polish Workers' Movement: During the War and Hitler's Occupation*]. Moskva: Izd-vo Polit. Lit-ry, 1968, 454 pp.

Pomian, Andrzej. *Wiersze i Piesni Powstania Warszawskiego* [*The Poems and Songs of the Warsaw Uprising*]. London: Oficyna Poetow i Malarzy, 1952, n.p.

Przygonski, Antoni. *Prasa Konspiracyjna PPR: Zarys, Katalog, Zyciorysy* (*The Underground Press of the Polish Workers' Party: Description, Catalog, Biographies*]. Warszaw: Ksiazka i Wiedza, 1966, 322 pp.

Przygonski, Antoni. *Udzial PPR i AL w Powstaniu Warszawskim* [*Participation of PPR and AL in the Uprising of Warsaw*]. Warszawa: Ksiazka i Wiedza, 1970, 265 pp.

Przygonski, Antoni. *Z Problematyki Powstania Warszawskiego* [*Among the Problems of the Warsaw Uprising*]. Warszawa: Wydawnictwo Ministerstwa Obrony Narodowej, 1964, 266 pp.

Rawski, Tadeusz, Stapor, Z. and Zamorski, J. *Wojna Wyzwolencza Narodu Polskiego w Latach 1939–1945* [*The War of Liberation of the Polish Nation during the Years 1939–1945*]. Warszawa: Wydawnictwo Ministerstwa Obrony Narodowej, 1966, 881 pp.

Roos, Hans. 'Polen in der Besatzungszeit' ['Poland during the Occupation']. *Osteuropa Handbuch Polen*. Köln: Boehlau Verlag, 1959, pp. 167–93.

Rozek, Edward J. *Allied Wartime Diplomacy: A Pattern In Poland*. New york: John Wiley & Sons Inc., 1958, 481 pp.

Sawicki, Jerzy. *Ludobojstwo: Od Pojecia do Konwencji 1933–1948* [*Genocide: From the Idea to the Convention, 1933–1948*]. Krakow: L. J. Jaroszewski, 1949, 224 pp.

Sawicki, Jerzy i Boleslaw Walawski. *Zbior Przepisow Specjalnych Przeciwko*

Zbrodniarzom Hitlerowskim i Zdrajcom Narodu z Komentarzem [*Collection of Special Regulations against the Hitler Criminals and the Traitors of the Nation, with Commentary*]. Warszawa: Czytelnik, 1945, 63 pp.

Semiriaga, M. I. *Antifashistskie Narodnye Povstaniia* [*National Uprisings against Fascists*]. Moskva: Nauka, 1965, 265 pp.

—, *Strany T Sentral' noi i I Ugo-Vostochnoi Evropy vo Vtoroi Mirovoi Voine* [*Countries of Central and South-East Europe in the Second World War*]. Moskva: Voenizdat, 1972, 302 pp.

—, *Vtoraia Mirovaia Voina i Proletarskii Internatsionalism* [*The Second World War and Internationalism of the Proletariat*]. Moskva: Voennoe Izdatel'stvo Ministerstva Oborony SSSR, 1962, 214 pp.

Serwanski, Edward *et al. Zbrodnia Niemiecka w Warszawie 1944: Zeznania-Zdjecia* [*German Atrocities in Warsaw, 1944: Testimony, Photographs*]. Poznan: Wydawnictwo Instytut Zachodniego, 1946, 246 pp.

Sherwood, Robert E. *Roosevelt and Hopkins: An Intimate History*. New York: Harper & Brothers, 1948, 979 pp.

Skarzynski, Aleksander. *Polityczne Przyczyny Powstania Warszawskiego* [*Political Determinants of the Warsaw Uprising*]. Warszawa: Panstwowe Wydawnictwo Naukowe, 1965, 431 pp.

Slusser, Robert, and Triska, Jan F. *A Calendar of Soviet Treaties 1917–1957*. Stanford: Stanford University Press, 1959, 530 pp.

Sosabowski, Stanislaw. *Najkrotsza Droga* [*By the Shortest Route*]. London: Komitet Wydawniczy Polskich Spadochroniarzy, 1957, 286 pp.

Tippelskirch, Kurt. *Geschichte des Zweiten Weltkrieges* [*A History of the Second World War*]. Bonn: Athenaeum Verlag, 1951, 731 pp.

Trevor-Roper, Hugh. *The Philby Affair: Espionage, Treason, and Secret Service*. London: William Kimber, 1968, 126 pp.

Tronski, Bronislaw. *Tedy Przeszla Smierc: Zapiski z Powstania Warszawkiego* [*Death Passed through Here: Notes from the Warsaw Uprising*]. Warszawa: Czytelnik, 1957, 355 pp.

Werth, Alexander. *Russia at War: 1941–1945*. New York: E. P. Dutton & Co. Inc., 1964, 1100 pp.

Woloszyn, Wlodzimierz. *Na Warszawskim Kierunku Operacyjnym: Dzialania l Frontu Bialoruskiego i l Armii Wp 18.VII-23.IX.1944 r* [*On the Operational Sector of Warsaw: Actions of the First Byelorussian Front and the First Polish Army, 18 July–23 September 1944*]. Warszawa: Wydawnictwo Ministerstwa Obrony Narodowej, 1964, 348 pp.

Zagorski, Waclaw. *Wicher Wolnosci: Dziennik Powstanca* [*Wind of Freedom: Diary of an Insurgent*]. London: Nakladem Czytelnikow-Przedplacicieli, staraniem SPK, Kolo Nr. 11, 1957, 391 pp.

Zambrzhitskii, V. A. *Germano-Sovetskaia Voina 1941–1945 gg* [*The German–Soviet War, 1941–1945*]. New York: Vselavianskoe izd-vo, 1967, 192 pp.

Zawodny, J. K. *Death in the Forest: The Story of the Katyn Forest Massacre*. Notre Dame: University of Notre Dame Press, 1962, 235 pp.

Zuev, F. G. *Pol'skii Narod Bor'be Protiv Fashizma* [*Polish Nation in Combat against Fascism*]. Moskva: Nauka, 1967, 134 pp.

VI. Journals

Babinski, Witold. 'General Kazimierz Sosnkowski'. *Zeszyty Historyczne*.

Paris: Instytut Literacki, 1970, No. 17, pp. 164–73.

—, 'List do Redakcji' [*Letter to the Editor*]. *Zeszyty Historyczne*. Paris: Instytut Literacki, 1969, No. 16, pp. 215–27.

—, 'Na Marginesie Wywiadu z Gen. Bor-Komorowskim' ['Some Comments Concerning an Interview with General Bor-Komorowski']. *Zeszyty Historyczne*. Paris: Instytut Literacki, 1967, No. 12, pp. 231–3.

—, 'Powstanie Warszawskie' ['The Warsaw Uprising'], *Zeszyty Historyczne*. Paris: Instytut Literacki, 1964, No. 6, pp. 45–63.

—, 'Refleksje Rocznicowe' [Reflections upon the Anniversary'] *Zeszyty Historyczne*. Paris: Instytut Literacki, 1965, Vol. 7, pp. 217–20.

Bordzilowski, Jerzy, Gen. 'Zolnierska Droga: Czesc XIII' ['The Soldier's Journey: Part XIII']. *Wojskowy Przeglad Historyczny*, Rok XV, No. 1. Warszawa: 1970, pp. 115–79; No. 3, pp. 148–84.

Bor-Komorowski, T. 'Sewer Warfare in the Warsaw Uprising.' *The Nineteenth Century and After*. Vol. 148, July 1950, pp. 24–31.

Ciolkosz, Adam. 'Nieznane Expose' [Expose]. *Zeszyty Historyczne*. Paris: Instytut Literacki, 1962, No. 1, pp. 9–25.

Dolata, Boleslaw. 'O Naczelnych Wladzach i Instytucjach Ludowego Wojska Polskiego w Latach 1944–1945' ['Supreme Authorities and Institutions of the Polish People's Army, 1944–1945']. *Wojskowy Przeglad Historyczny*, Rok. 9, No. 4. Warszawa: 1964, pp. 3–54.

Halicz, Emanuel. 'Doswiadczenia Powstania Styczniowego w Ujeciu Naczelnych Waladz Hitlerowskich' ['Experiences in the January Uprising as Interpreted by the Supreme German Authorities']. *Wojskowy Przeglad Historyczny*, Rok. 9, No. 3. Warszawa: 1965, pp. 356–68.

Iwanowski, Wincenty. 'Operacja Bialoruska Armii Radzieckiej 1944 R' ['Byelorussian Operations of the Soviet Army in 1944']. *Wojskowy Przeglad Historyczny*. Warszawa: 1969, No. 1, pp. 61–92.

—, 'Poczatek Wielkiej Ofenzywy Radzieckiej Podczas Drugiej Wojny Swiatowej' ['The Beginning of the Great Soviet Offensive during the Second World War']. *Wojskowy Przeglad Historyczny*, Rok. 11, No. 2. Warszawa: 1966, pp. 88–142.

Jurgielewicz, Waclaw. 'Organizacja Ludowego Wojska Polskiego: 22. VII. 1945–9. V. 1945' ['The Organisation of the Polish People's Army: 22 July 1944–9 May 1945']. Warszawa: Wojskowy Instytut Historyczny, 1968, 459 pp.

Kirchmayer, Jerzy. 'W Sprawie Decyzji Podjecia Walki w Warszawie: W Odpowiedzi na Artykul plk. Rzepeckiego' [The Decision to Undertake the Battle in Warsaw: An Answer to the Article of Colonel Rzepecki']. *Wojskowy Przeglad Historyczny*, Rok. 3, No. 3. Warszawa: 1958, pp. 358–83.

Kirkor, Stanislaw. 'Rozmowy Polsko-Sowieckie w 1944 Roku' ['Polish–Soviet Discussions in 1944']. *Zeszyty Historyczne*. Paris: Instytut Literacki, 1972, No. 22, pp. 41–64.

—, 'Urywek Wspomnien' ['Fragments of Memories']. *Zeszyty Historyczne*. Paris: Instytut Literacki, 1970, No. 18, pp. 99–108.

Korbonski, Andrzej. 'The Warsaw Uprising Revisited'. *Survey*, No. 76, Summer 1970, pp. 82–98.

Korbonski, Stefan. 'List do Redakcji' ['Letter to the Editor']. *Zeszyty Historyczne*. Paris: Instytut Literacki, 1969, No. 16, pp. 227–31.

—, 'List do Redakcji' [Letter to the Editor']. *Zeszyty Historyczne*. Paris: Instytut

'Literacki, 1971, No. 19, p. 223.

—, 'Powstanie Warszawskie w Oczach Komunistycznego Historyka' ['The Uprising of Warsaw Seen through the Eyes of a Communist Historian']. *Polemiki*. London: Polonia Book Fund, Zeszyt 3, Zima 1964–5, pp. 7–22.

Laskowski, Janusz. 'Radiostacja 'Swit'', Cz. I, i II ['The Radio Station "Swit"']. *Zeszyty Historyczne*. Paris: Instytut Literacki, 1966, No. 9, pp. 101–30; 1966, Vol. 10, pp. 203–23.

Lukas, Richard C. 'The Big Three and the Warsaw Uprising'. *Military Affairs*. October 1975, pp. 129–34.

Majorkiewicz, Felicjan. 'Kontakty z Wegrami w Czasie Powstania Warszawskiego' ['Contacts with Hungarians during the Warsaw Uprising']. *Wojskowy Prezeglad Historyczny*. Rok. 16, No. 1. Warszawa: 1971, pp. 406–10.

Malinowski, Kazimierz. 'Organizacja Lacznosci w Powstaniu Warszawskim' ['The Organization of Liaison Services during the Warsaw Uprising']. *Najnowsze Dzieje Polski: Materialy i Studia z Okresu II Wojny Swiatowej*. Warszawa: 1963, Vol. 7, pp. 39–56.

Mitkiewicz, Leon. 'Powstanie Warszawskie: Z mojego Notatnika w Washingtonie' ['The Warsaw Uprising: From My Diary in Washington']. *Zeszyty Historyczne*. Paris: Instytut Literacki, 1962, No. 1, pp. 95–156.

Nesteruk, Wanda. 'Sesja Popularno-Naukowa Powswiecona Udzialowi Kobiet Poskich w II Wojnie Swiatowej w Latach 1939–1945' ['The Conference on the Subject of the Participation of Polish Women in the Second World War, 1939–1945']. *Wojskowy Przeglad Historyczny*. Warszawa: 1971, No. 3, pp. 363–8.

Onacewicz, Wlodzimierz. 'Komentarze do Ksiazki Leona Mitkiewicza *Z Generalem Sikorskim*' ['Commentaries on Leon Mitkiewicz' Book *With General Sikorski*]. *Zeszyty Historyczne*. Paris: Instytut Literacki, 1970, No. 18, pp. 154–83.

Ortynskij, Lubomyr. 'Prawda o Ukrainskiej Dywizji' ['The Truth about the Ukrainian Division']. *Kultura*. Paris: Instytut Literacki, 1952, zeszyt 11, pp. 109–16.

Ploski, Stanislaw. 'Relacja von dem Bacha o Powstaniu Warszawskim' ['Report of von dem Bach on the Warsaw Uprising']. *Dzieje Najwsze.*, April–June 1947, Vol.1, No. 2, pp. 295–324.

Popkiewicz, S. 'List do Redakcji' ['Letter to the Editor']. *Zeszyty Historyczne*. Paris: Instytut Literacki, 1965, No. 7, pp. 211–15.

—, 'List do Redakcji' ['Letter to the Editor']. *Zeszyty Historyczne*. Paris: Instytut Literacki, 1966, Vol. 9, p. 235.

—, 'List do Redakcji' ['Letter to the Editor']. *Zeszyty Historyczne*. Paris: Instytut Literacki, 1969, Vol. 15, pp. 249–51.

—, 'Szczegoly Lacznosci Radiowej Miedzy Londynem i Warszawa' ['Details of Radio Communication between London and Warsaw']. *Zeszyty Historyczne*. Paris: Instytut Literacki, 1968, No. 13, pp. 215–20.

Prokopiuk, Nikolaj. plk w st. sp. 'Z Dzialalnosci Radzieckich Oddzialow Rozpoznawczo Dywersyjnych na Terenie Polski w Latach 1944–1945' ['Combat Activities of the Red Army Intelligence-Sabotage Units on Polish Territory, 1944–1945']. *Wojskowy Przeglad Historyczny*. Warszawa: January–March, 1968, No. 1, (45), pp. 235–65.

Przygonski, Antoni. 'Armia Ludowa w Dniu Wybuchu Powstania Warszawskiego i jej Walki na Woli od 1 do 7 Sierpnia 1944' [People's Army on the Day of the Warsaw Uprising: Its Battles at Wola from 1–7 August 1944']. *Najnowsze Dzieje Polski: Materially i Studia z Okresu li Wojny Swiatowej.* Warszawa: 1961, No. 5, pp. 51–102.

—, 'Armia Ludowa w Powstaniu Warszawskim na Starym Miescie' ['The People's Army in the Warsaw Uprising in the Old Town']. *Wojskowy Przeglad Historyczny*, Rok. 10, No. 3. Warszawa: 1965, pp. 96–138.

Puacz, Edward. 'Powstanie Warszawskie w Protokolach PKWN' ['The Uprising of Warsaw in the Minutes of PKWN']. *Zeszyty Historyczne.* Paris: Instytut Literacki, 1966, No. 10, pp. 175–92.

Rzepecki, Jan. 'List do Redackji' ['Letter to the Editor']. *Wojskowy Przeglad Historyczny.* Warszawa: 1966, No. 1, pp. 427–8.

—, 'W Sprawie Rozmow Miedzy Dowodztwem AK i PAL przed Wybuchem Powstania Warzawskiego' ['Concerning the Discussions between AK Headquarters and PAL before the Uprising of Warsaw']. *Wojskowy Przeglad Historyczny*, Rok. 11, No. 1. Warszawa: 1966, pp. 427–8.

Shankovskyi, L. 'Varshavske Povstannia i Ukraintsi u Svitli Dokumentiv' ['*Warsaw Uprising and Ukrainians in Documents*']. *Vyzvolnyi Shliakh.* London: 1967, No. 2(227), pp. 152–9.

Siemaszko, Z. S. 'Lacznosc i Polityka' [Communication and Politics']. *Zeszyty Historyczne.* Paris: Instytut Literacki, 1965, No. 8, pp. 187–207.

—, 'Lacznosc Radiowa Sztabu NW w Przede Dniu Powstania Warszawskiego' ['Radio Communication of the Commander-in-Chief's Staff on the Day Preceding the Beginning of the Warsaw Uprising']. *Zeszyty Historyczne.* Paris: Instytut Literacki, 1964, No. 6, 64–116.

—, 'List do Redakcji Dotyczacy Dr Rettingera'['Letter to the Editor Concerning Dr Rettinger']. *Kultura.* Paris: Instytut Literacki, No. 5, 1966, pp. 157–9.

—, 'List do Redakcji' ['Letter to the Editor']. *Zeszyty Historyczne.* Paris: Instytut Literacki, 1966, No. 9, pp. 236–8.

—, 'List do Redakcji' ['Letter to the Editor']. *Zeszyty Historyczne.* Paris: Instytut Literacki, 1969, Vol. 176, pp. 234–5.

—, 'Misja Kuriera Politycznego Mostwina' ['The Political Courier of Mostwin's Mission']. *Zeszyty Historyczne.* Paris: Instytut Literacki, 1973, No. 24, pp. 212–21.

—, 'Najwyzszy Czas Mowic Glosno' ['It's Time to Speak Aloud']. *Kultura.* Paris: Instytut Literacki, 1971, No. 1/280–2/281, pp. 198–205.

—, 'Powstanie Warszawskie: Kontakty z ZSRR i PKWN'] *Zeszyty Historyczne.* Paris: Instytut Literacki, 1919, No. 16, pp. 5–65.

—, 'Rettinger w Polsce w 1944' ['Rettinger in Poland, 1944']. *Zeszyty Historyczne*, Paris: Instytut Literacki, 1967, No. 12, pp. 56–115.

—, 'Rozmowy z Kapitanem Szabunia' ['*Conversations with Captain Szabuna*']. *Zeszyty Historyczne.* Paris: Instytut Literacki, 1973, No. 25, pp. 102–49.

Sobczak, Kazimierz. 'Kilka Uwag o Zamierzeniach Dowodztwa Radzieckiego w Rejonie Warszawy w Lecie 1944' ['Some Comments Concerning the Intentions of the Soviet Command in the Region of Warsaw in the Summer of 1944']. *Najnowsze Dzieje Polski.* Warszawa: 1967, Vol. 11, pp. 83–101.

Stawski, Taduesz. 'Wrzesniowy Kryzys Powstania Warszawskiego' ['The September Crisis of the Uprising of Warsaw']. *Kultura.* Paris: Instytut Literacki, 1950, No. 9, pp. 121–25.

Voznenko, V. 'Strategicheskow Nastuplenie Sovetskikh Vooruzhonykh Sil na

Tsentral'nom Uchastke Sovetsko-Germanskogo Fronta v liune – Avguste 1944 goda' ['Strategic Offensive of the Soviet Armed Forces in the Central Part of the Soviet–German Front in June and August, 1944']. *Voennoistoricheskii Zhurnal*. Moskva: 1960, No. 10 pp. 3–13.

Wankowiczowa, Zofia. 'Kombatantki (Powstanie Warszawskie) ['Women Combatants']. *Kultura*. Paris: Instytut Literacki, 1954, zeszyt 10, pp. 77–98.

Zbigniewicz, Fryderyk. 'Pomoc Armii Radzieckiej dia Polski w Swietle Dokumentow z Lai 1944–1945' ['The Assistance of the Soviet Army to Poland in the Light of Documents, 1944–1945]. *Woljskowy Przeglad Historyczny*. Warszawa: 1968, No. 1 (45), pp. 341–60.

VII. Newspapers and Magazines

Anders, W., General. 'Sprawa Powstania Warszawskiego' ['In the Matter of the Warsaw Uprising']. *Wiadomosci*, London, 3 October 1948, pp. 1–4.

Aurich, 'Peter. 'Der Verrat an der Weichsel' ['Betrayl on the Vistula']. *Deutsche Soldatenzeitung*, 2 July 1954, No. 21 p. 12.

Baginski, Kazimierz. 'Czy Mozna Bylo Uniknac Powstania Warszawskiego?' ['Could the Warsaw Uprising Have Been Avoided?']. *Dziennik Zwiazkowy*, 3 August 1960.

—, 'Nastroje Ludnosci w Powstaniu Warszawskim' ['Mood of the Population during the Warsaw Uprising']. *Robotnik Polski*, 3 August 1952, pp. 1–2.

—, 'W Rocznice Powstania' ['On the Anniversary of the Uprising']. Jutro Polski, 31 July 1949, n.p.

—, 'Wspomnienia z Pierwszego Okresu Powstania' ['Memories from the First Part of the Uprising']. *Nowy Swiat*, 2 August 1950, p. 4.

Biuletyn Informacyjny, 1944. (Survey.)

Czarnocka, Halina. 'Udzial Kobiet w Armii Krajowej' ['The Participation of Women in the Home Army']. *Biuletyn Informacyiny, Kolo AK*, London, December 1958–February 1959, No. 36, pp. 2–5.

Eyssen, J. L. van, Capt. 'Jak Lotnicy Afrykanscy Niesli Pomoc Warszawie' ['How South African Pilots Helped Warsaw']. *Orzel Bialy*, London. Part 1: 1 May 1958, No. 22, p. 2; Part 2, July 1958, No. 23, p. 2.

Garlinski, Jozef. 'Brytyjska Misja Wojskowa w Polsce 1944–1945' ['The British Military Missions in Poland, 1944–1945']. *Na Antenie (Wiadomosci)*, 28 February 1965, No. 987, p. 3.

—, 'Decyzja Podjecia Walki o Warszawe: Wywiad z Gen. Tadeuszem Borem-Komorowskim' ['The Decision to Begin the Struggle in Defence of Warsaw: Interview with General Taduesz Bor-Komorowski']. *Dziennik Polski i Dziennik Zolnierza*, London, 1 August 1964, Vol. 25, No. 21, p. 1.

—, 'Od Wrzesnia do Powstania' ['From September 1939 to the Uprising']. *Wiadomosci*, London, 1 March 1970, p. 2.

—, 'Powstanie Warszawskie' ['The Uprising of Warsaw']. *Wiadomosci*, London, 19 October 1969, p. 3.

—, 'Prasa Armii Krajowej' ['The Press of the Home Army']. *Biuletyn Informacyjny, Kolo AK*, London, October–December 1946, No. 3, pp. 2–3.

—, 'Z Perspektywy 24 Lat' ['From the Perspective of 24 Years']. *Wiadomosci*, London, 24 March 1968, p. 4.

Izvestia, 1944.

Klimowski, T. 'Powstanie Warszawskie J. Ciechanowskiego' ['J. Ciechanowski's

Warsaw Uprising]. *Biuletyn Informacyjny*, London, August 1972, No. 49, pp. 11–17.

Korbonski, Stefan. 'Co Moglo Zapobiec Powstaniu?' ['What Could Prevent the Uprising?']. *Dziennik Polski i Dziennik Zolnierza*, London, 4 August 1954, No. 184, p. 2.

—, 'Poles and Jews: A Common Bond'. *ACEN NEWS*, New York, November–December 1969, No. 143, pp. 6–20.

—, 'Polskie Panstwo Podziemne z Lat 1939–1945' ['The Polish Underground State, 1939–1945']. *Orzel Bialy*, London, July–August 1969, pp. 13–19.

Kumor, Emil. 'Powstancza Fabryka Granatow' ['Insurgents' Hand-grenade Factory']. *Kierunki*, Warsaw, 25 August 1957.

Kurier Codzienny, Warsaw, 1947. (Survey).

Maciejewski, Bogdan. 'Opowiese o Powstanczych Listach' ['The Story of the Insurgents' Letters']. *Krajowa Agencja Informacyjna*, 1970, No. 11/531, p. 46.

Majorkiewicz, Felicjan. 'Ostatnie Dni Starowki' ['The Last Days of Old Town']. *Tygodnik Powszechny*, Karkow, 28 August 1960. No. 35.

Malinowski, Kazimierz '('Mirski'). 'Pomoc z Powietrza dla Walczacej Warszawy' ['Air Assistance for Fighting Warsaw']. *Tygodnik Powszechny*, Krakow, 10 October 1969, No. 43.

Miklaszewicz, Julian. 'Gospodarka Pieniezna AK' ['Fiscal Management of the Home Army']. *Biuletyn Informacyjny Kolo AK*, London, February – March and April – May 2 and 3, pp. 4–5.

Le Monde, 1955. (Survey.)

'Odezwa Wydana Przez Rade Jednosci Narodowej i Krajowa Rade Ministrow po Kapitulacji Warszawy' ['An Appeal Issued by the Council of National Unity and Home Council of Ministers after the Capitulation of Warsaw']. *glos Polski*, Toronto, 20 August 1964, p. 14.

Olshansky, Boris. 'The Rokossovski Enigma: Ten Years After the Tragic Warsaw Uprising'. *The New Leader*, 27 September 1954, pp. 20–1.

Pelczynska, W. 'Rozglosnie Walczacej Warszaway' ['The Radio Stations of Fighting Warsaw']. *Tydzien Polski*, London, 5 December 19   p. 3.

Pluta-Czachowski, Kazimierz. 'Godzina "W" na Woli' [Hour "W" in Wola']. *Stolica*, 1969, No. 39, p. 6.

—, 'Na Posterunku Dowodzenia KG' [At the Command Post of the Supreme Headquarters of the AK']. *Za i Przeciew*, 1969, No. 38, pp. 14–16.

Pravada, 1944. (Survey.)

Slessor, Sir John. Letter to the Editor. *The Observer*, London, 16 August 1964.

Sopicki, Stanislaw. 'Nie Musialo trwac 63 Dni: Uwagi o Powstaniu Warszawskim' ['There Was No Need for 63 Days of Fighting: Some Comments about the Uprising of Warsaw']. *Wiadomosci*, London, 23 October 1949.

Szeleyko, Z. 'Meldunek z Kresow' ['Report from Eastern Poland']. *Biuletyn Informacyjny*, London, August 1972, No. 49, pp. 2–10.

Wejtko, Antoni. 'Lotnik Poludniowo-Afrykanski O Polsce' ['A South-African Pilot Talks about Poland']. *Wiadomasci*, London, 16 April 1961, No. 16, p. 1.

Wolna Polska, Moscow, 1943–4. (survey.)

Ziemski, Karol (Wachnowski). Walczaca Starowka: Wspomnienie Z Powstania W Warszawie' ['Fighting Starowka: Recollections from the Warsaw Uprising']. *SPK w Kanadzie*, July 1964, No. 3, pp. 7–9.

VIII. Ph.D. Dissertations

Ciechanowski, Jan M., 'The Political and Ideological Background of the Warsaw Rising, 1944'. University of London, Doctoral Dissertation, 1968.

Gallagher, Matthew Philip, 'Soviet Interpretations of the Second World War: The Official Line and Unofficial Views'. Harvard University, Doctoral Dissertation, 1959–60.

Jamgotch, Jr, Nish A., 'Eastern Europe as a Soviet Core Interest'. Claremont Graduate School, Doctoral Dissertation, 1963–4.

Katsaros, Thomas, 'Anglo-Soviet Relations During World War II with Special Reference to Europe'. New York University, Doctoral Dissertation, 1963–4.

May, Jr, Benjamin Mackall, 'Themes of Soviet War Propaganda 1941–1945'. Yale University, Doctoral Dissertation, 1957–8.

Misse, Jr, Benjamin Frederick, 'The Loss of Eastern Europe, 1938–1946'. University of Illinois, Doctoral Dissertation. 1964–5.

Rozek, Edward Jozef, 'Soviet–Polish Relations, 1939–1947: A Case Study of Soviet Foreign Policy'. Harvard University, Doctoral Dissertation, 1955–6.

Wojcik, Andrzej J., 'Attitudes of Certain Western public Communication Media toward the Polish Frontier Issues, 1939–1944'. Columbia University, Doctoral Dissertation, 1960–1.

IX. Miscellaneous

Pomian, Andrzej. *The Warsaw Rising: A Selection of Documents*. London: n.p., 1945, 95 pp. (First selection of the documents in the English language.)

—, *Powstanie Warszawskie: Krotki Wybor Dokumentow* [*The Uprising of Warsaw: Selected Documents*]. n.p., n.d. (First selection of the documents in the Polish language.)

Index

Abbots, 133

air raids, 22, 35, 47, 58, 60, 139

AK (Armia Krajowa): numbers, 15, 26, 80, 88–9, 93, 107, 137, 155, 210–11, 255; training, 16; nature of membership, 16; strategy, 16, 97; arms and ammunition, 17, 22, 26–32, 44, 46, 47, 93, 114, 122, 131, 133, 134, 141, 143, 146, 154, 163, 172, 173, 175, 184; defensive position, 17; tactical and material weakness, 17; loses initiative, 17; resources, 17, 25–38, 107; headquarters, 21, 26, 30, 35, 37, 40, 59, 61, 72, 97, 98, 102, 106, 109, 113, 114, 153, 155, 163, 164, 173, 177, 178, 185, 192, 201, 202, 205, 206, 214, 254; liaison with Russians, 21, 89, 90, 92, 179–80, 202–4, 204–5; intelligence, 21, 33, 40, 41, 44, 103, 104; field courts, 21; units outside Warsaw, 22, 43, 44, 61; units arrested by Russians, 22, 40, 43, 61, 70, 99, 175, 186; living conditions, 23; uniform, 23, 138; nationalities, 23–5; liberates Jews, 24; Wigry Battalion, 25; Engineers, 27; desertions, 29; money, 31–3, 44, 83, 93, 100–1, 134; food, 31, 49, 60, 131, 133, 138, 140, 154, 157–8, 159, 161–2, 163, 178, 189, 192, 194; communications, 33; 'Group North', 35, 142, 146, 167; power struggle with Communists, 39; printing presses, 44, 156; sabotage, 44, 97, 103, 104, 107; medical resources, 48–9, 63, 65–6, 131, 133, 139, 144, 164–5, 166, 168; blamed for Kaminski's death, 56; Giewont Company, 60; Koszta Company, 60; status, 61, 62, 112; executions, 62, 63–4; excesses, 64–5, 99, 140; 9th Division, 99; 27th Division, 99–100; main objectives, 103; diversionary activities, 103, 107; question of Allied aid, 102–5, 107, 109; 'group of criminals', 111; combat readiness, 118; illness, 139; Combat Group Pine, 141; dead and wounded, 141, 146, 147, 148, 149, 156, 165, 166, 168–9, 173, 210–11; 'Redhead', 144; 'Zophie', 144; Czata. 49, 144; evacuation, 145–9; Gozdawa Battalion, 147; Military Welfare Service, 155; postal service, 156–7; 'Protection of Human Beings', 157; chaplains, 167–8; water, 169–71, 173, 194; Military Service for Protection of the Uprising (WSOP), 169–70; electricity, 173; 'AK Warsaw Corps', 186; capitulation, 191–209, 214; German captivity, 193, 194; 'thoughtless adventure', 198; contacts with Germans, 206–7; territorial organisation, 252–3

AL (Armia Ludowa): Jews in, 24–5; 3rd Battalion, 24; numbers, 29, 138; arms, 29; relations with Russians, 39, 40; objective, 39–40; decision to fight with AK, 41, 61

Albania, 66

alcohol, 139, 148

Allies: air support, 30, 35, 37, 38, 44–